Lecture Notes of the Institute for Computer Sciences, Social Informatics and Telecommunications Engineering 401

More information about this series at http://www.springer.com/series/8197

Ivan Miguel Pires · Susanna Spinsante ·
Eftim Zdravevski · Petre Lameski (Eds.)

Smart Objects and Technologies for Social Good

7th EAI International Conference, GOODTECHS 2021
Virtual Event, September 15–17, 2021
Proceedings

 Springer

Editors
Ivan Miguel Pires 🆔
Instituto de Telecomunicações
Universidade da Beira Interior
Covilhã, Portugal

Eftim Zdravevski
Faculty of Computer Science and Engineering
Sts Cyril and Methodius University
Skopje, North Macedonia

Susanna Spinsante
Marche Polytechnic University
Ancona, Italy

Petre Lameski
Faculty of Computer Science and Engineering
Sts Cyril and Methodius University
Skopje, North Macedonia

ISSN 1867-8211 ISSN 1867-822X (electronic)
Lecture Notes of the Institute for Computer Sciences, Social Informatics
and Telecommunications Engineering
ISBN 978-3-030-91420-2 ISBN 978-3-030-91421-9 (eBook)
https://doi.org/10.1007/978-3-030-91421-9

This Springer imprint is published by the registered company Springer Nature Switzerland AG
The registered company address is: Gewerbestrasse 11, 6330 Cham, Switzerland

Preface

We are delighted to introduce the proceedings of the 7th edition of the European Alliance for Innovation (EAI) International Conference on Smart Objects and Technologies for Social Good (EAI GOODTECHS 2021) held on September 15–17, 2021. This conference has brought researchers, developers, and practitioners worldwide who are providing experiences with the design, implementation, deployment, operation, and evaluation of smart objects and technologies for social good. Social goods are products and services provided through private enterprises, government, or non-profit institutions and are related to healthcare, safety, sports, environment, democracy, computer science, and human rights. Ultimately, they will benefit people with special needs, including older adults, sport performance, and young people. The conference was organized by the Instituto de Telecomunicações, the leading institution of the General Chair, which provided active support for the organization of this conference.

As the whole world came to a stop due to the COVID-19 outbreak, this conference was not spared either EAI GOODTECHS 2021 was organized as an online conference for the second time in its history. As unfortunate as this situation is, it created an opportunity to provide access to the conference to a much broader audience in this virtual format.

In the 7th edition, the aim of the GOODTECHS conference remained to provide an opportunity for young researchers to present their work to a broader research community and facilitate multidisciplinary and regional collaboration. Despite the participation of scientists from the host country, a substantial number of participants from abroad attended the conference. Building on the success of the past six editions of this conference, this year the conference attracted 53 paper submissions, of which 24 were accepted as full papers, with an acceptance rate for full articles of 45%. The conference program spanned three days and included five keynote lectures attended by up to 50 attendees, which is among the highest attendance number in the history of the conference.

The technical program of EAI GOODTECHS 2021 consisted of 24 full papers in oral presentation sessions in all tracks. The conference tracks included: the main track, the workshop tracks, and the special session tracks. Thus, the conference tracks were: "Main Track", "WIP and Ph.D. track", "Sheldon COST Action CA16226: Solutions for Ageing Well at Home, in the Community and at Work", "International Workshop on Telehealth, patient empowerment, and education through technology", "IoT Healthcare Systems and Cyber Security", "Artificial Intelligence for Inclusiveness", "Cyber-Security and Integration on Social Good and Healthcare Services", and "Technologies for Quantifying Mobility and Health in Older Adults". Aside from the high-quality technical paper presentations, the technical program also featured five keynote speeches. The five keynote speeches were given by the Hugo Plácido da Silva (Instituto de Telecomunicações, Portugal, and Instituto Superior Técnico, University of Lisbon, Portugal); Andrzej Janusz (University of Warsaw, Poland); Miguel Tavares Coimbra (University of Oporto, Portugal); Miguel Pais Clemente (University of Oporto, Portugal); and Henrique Martins (Instituto Universitário de Lisboa, Portugal, and Universidade da Beira Interior, Portugal).

The coordination and organization of the steering chairs, Imrich Chlamtac and Bo Li were essential for the success of the conference. We sincerely appreciate their constant support and guidance. It was also a great pleasure to work with such an excellent Organizing Committee for their hard work while organizing and supporting the conference. In particular, the Technical Program Committee who completed the peer-review process for technical papers and helped to put together a high-quality technical program. We are also grateful to the conference manager, Viltare Plazner, for her support and all the authors who submitted their papers to the EAI GOODTECHS 2021 conference and workshops.

We strongly believe that the EAI GOODTECHS conference provides a good forum for all researchers, developers, and practitioners to discuss all science and technology aspects relevant to social goods. We also expect that the future EAI GOODTECHS conferences will be as successful and stimulating as this year's, indicated by the contributions presented in this volume.

September 2021

Ivan Miguel Pires
Susanna Spinsante
Eftim Zdravevski
Petre Lameski

Acknowledgements

This work is funded by FCT/MEC through national funds and, when applicable, co-funded by the FEDER-PT2020 partnership agreement under the project **UIDB/50008/2020**. This article is based upon work from COST Action IC1303-AAPELE—Architectures, Algorithms, and Protocols for Enhanced Living Environments and COST Action CA16226–SHELD-ON—Indoor living space improvement: Smart Habitat for the Elderly, supported by COST (European Cooperation in Science and Technology). COST is a funding agency for research and innovation networks. Our Actions help connect research initiatives across Europe and enable scientists to grow their ideas by sharing them with their peers. It boosts their research, career, and innovation. More information in www.cost.eu.

Organization

Steering Committee

Imrich Chlamtac   University of Trento, Italy

Organizing Committee

General Chair

Ivan Miguel Pires   Instituto de Telecomunicações, Universidade da Beira Interior, Portugal, and Universidade da Trás-os-Montes e Alto Douro, Portugal

General Co-chair

Nuno M. Garcia   Instituto de Telecomunicações, Universidade da Beira Interior, Portugal

Technical Program Committee Co-chairs

Eftim Zdravevski   Ss. Cyril and Methodius University of Skopje, North Macedonia
Ciprian Dobre   University Politehnica of Bucharest, Romania
Rossitza Goleva   New Bulgarian University, Bulgaria
Faisal Hussain   University of Engineering and Technology, Taxila, Pakistan

Sponsorship and Exhibit Chair

José Morgado   Instituto Politécnico de Viseu, Portugal

Local Chair

Susana Sargento   Universidade de Aveiro, Portugal

Workshops Chair

Petre Lameski   Ss. Cyril and Methodius University of Skopje, North Macedonia

Publicity and Social Media Chair

Gonçalo Marques   University of Coimbra, Portugal

Publications Chair

Susanna Spinsante   Marche Polytechnic University, Italy

Web Chair

Salome Oniani   Georgian Technical University, Georgia

Posters and PhD Track Chair

Sandeep Pirbhulal   Norwegian University of Science and Technology,
                                    Norway

Panels Chair

Valderi Leithardt   Instituto Politécnico de Portalegre, Portugal

Demos Chair

Ivan Chorbev   Ss. Cyril and Methodius University of Skopje, North
                                    Macedonia

Tutorials Chair

Vladimir Trajkovik   Ss. Cyril and Methodius University of Skopje, North
                                    Macedonia

Special Sessions Chairs

Maria João Cardoso   Instituto de Telecomunicações, Portugal
Hanna Denysyuk   Instituto de Telecomunicações, Portugal

Technical Program Committee

Abdul Hannan   University of Management and Technology, Taxila,
                                    Pakistan
Ake Arvidsson   Kristianstad University, Sweden
Ana Paula Silva   Instituto Politécnico de Castelo Branco, Portugal
Andrzej Janusz   University of Warsaw, Poland
Anna Sandak   University of Primorska, Slovenia
Arlindo Silva   Instituto Politécnico de Castelo Branco, Portugal

Birgitta Langhammer	Sunnaas Rehabilitation Hospital, Norway
Bruno Silva	Universidade da Beira Interior, Portugal
Carlos Albuquerque	Instituto Politécnico de Viseu, Portugal
Cem Ersoy	Boğaziçi University, Turkey
Constandinos Mavromoustakis	University of Nicosia, Cyprus
Daniel Hernandez	Universidad Pontificia de Salamanca, Spain
Daniel Marinho	Universidade da Beira Interior, Portugal
David Lamas	Tallinn University, Estonia
Diego Jiménez-Bravo	Universidad de Salamanca, Spain
Diogo Marques	Universidade da Beira Interior, Portugal
Dusan Kocur	Technical University of Kosice, Slovakia
Emmanuel Conchon	University of Limoges, France
Fernando Ribeiro	Instituto Politécnico de Castelo Branco, Portugal
Filipe Caldeira	Instituto Politécnico de Viseu, Portugal
Francico Melero	University of Granada, Spain
Francisco García Encinas	Universidad de Salamanca, Spain
Henrique Neiva	Universidade da Beira Interior, Portugal
Hugo Silva	Instituto de Telecomunicações, Portugal
Ivan Ganchev	University of Limerick, Ireland
Ivan Štajduhar	University of Rijeka, Croatia
Jake Kaner	Nottingham Trent University, UK
João Henriques	Instituto Politécnico de Viseu, Portugal
John Gialelis	University of Patras, Greece
Jonatan Lerga	University of Rijeka, Croatia
José Carlos Metrôlho	Instituto Politécnico de Castelo Branco, Portugal
José Lousado	Instituto Politécnico de Viseu, Portugal
Joshua Ellul	University of Malta, Malta
Juliana Sá	Centro Hospitalar e Universitário do Porto, Portugal
Kerli Mooses	University of Tartu, Estonia
Kuldar Taveter	University of Tartu, Estonia
Lambros Lambrinos	Cyprus University of Technology, Cyprus
Luis Augusto Silva	Universidad de Salamanca, Spain
Luis Rosa	University of Coimbra, Portugal
Madhusanka Liyanage	University College Dublin, Ireland
Manuel Noguera	University of Granada, Spain
Marcin Szczuka	University of Warsaw, Poland
María Vanessa Villasana	Centro Hospitalar do Baixo Vouga, Portugal
Mário Marques	Universidade da Beira Interior, Portugal
Michael Burnard	University of Primorska, Slovenia
Miguel Coimbra	University of Oporto, Portugal
Mónica Costa	Instituto Politécnico de Castelo Branco, Portugal
Natalia Diaz Rodriguez	University of Granada, Spain
Nuno Cruz Garcia	Universidade de Lisboa, Portugal
Paulo Novais	University of Minho, Portugal
Paulo Simões	University of Coimbra, Portugal
Piotr Lasek	Rzeszów University, Poland

Rafael Maestre	Institut de Bioenginyeria de Catalunya, Spain
Roberto Corizzo	American University, USA
Serge Autexier	German Research Centre for Artificial Intelligence (DFKI), Germany
Tiago Cruz	University of Coimbra, Portugal
Vasco Ponciano	Capgemini Engineering, Portugal
Vladimir Tomberg	Tallinn University, Estonia

Contents

Social Considerations of Technology

Technology and Ageing

Healthcare

Machine Learning

Balancing Activity Recognition and Privacy Preservation with a Multi-objective Evolutionary Algorithm

Angelica Poli[1], Angela M. Muñoz-Antón[2], Susanna Spinsante[1],
and Francisco Florez-Revuelta[3]([✉])

[1] Dipartimento di Ingegneria dell'Informazione, Università Politecnica delle Marche,
60131 Ancona, Italy
{a.poli,s.spinsante}@staff.univpm.it
[2] University of Alicante, 03690 Alicante, Spain
mma134@gcloud.ua.es
[3] Department of Computing Technology, University of Alicante,
03690 Alicante, Spain
francisco.florez@ua.es

Abstract. With the widespread of miniaturized inertial sensors embedded in wearable devices, an increasing number of individuals monitor their daily life activities through consumer electronic products. However, long-lasting data collection (e.g., from accelerometer) may expose the users to privacy violations, such as the leakage of personal details. To help mitigate these aspects, we propose an approach to conceal subject's personal attributes (i.e., gender) while maximizing the accuracy on both the monitoring and recognition of human activity. In particular, a Multi-Objective Evolutionary Algorithm (MOEA), namely the Non-dominated Sorting Genetic Algorithm II (NSGA-II), is applied to properly weight input features extracted from the raw accelerometer data acquired with a wrist-worn device (Empatica E4). Experiments were conducted on a large-scale and real life dataset, and validated by adopting the Random Forest algorithm with 10-fold cross validation. Findings demonstrate that the proposed method can highly limit gender recognition (from 89.37% using all the features to 64.38% after applying the MOEA algorithm) while only reducing the accuracy of activity recognition by 5.45% points (from 89.59% to 84.14%).

Keywords: Human Activity Recognition · Privacy preservation · Gender user identification · Wearable sensors · Multi-objective evolutionary algorithm

The support of the *More Years Better Lives JPI*, the Italian Ministero dell'Istruzione, Università e Ricerca (CUP: I36G17000380001) and the Spanish Agencia Estatal de Investigación (grant no: PCIN-2017-114), for this research activity carried out within the project PAAL - Privacy-Aware and Acceptable Lifelogging services for older and frail people, (JPI MYBL award number: PAAL_JTC2017) is gratefully acknowledged.

I. M. Pires et al. (Eds.): GOODTECHS 2021, LNICST 401, pp. 3–17, 2021.
https://doi.org/10.1007/978-3-030-91421-9_1

1   Introduction

Different sensors and sensing modalities can be adopted in *lifelogging* applications, which may expose the subject to risks associated with privacy violations, because of the pervasive and long-lasting collection of data [9,23,25]. Additionally, the potential threat to privacy is also determined by the subject's awareness about the undergoing collection of sensor data, while performing daily life activities. In fact, while the explicit user permission is typically requested, e.g. by mobile devices operating systems, to access and activate data collection from sensors such as cameras, microphones and positioning systems, which are generally perceived as information rich and intrusive of the user's privacy, other sensors such as accelerometers, gyroscopes and barometers are usually considered less dangerous in terms of privacy implications, if not taken into consideration at all [24]. Unfortunately, the vast majority of the accelerometers embedded in consumer wearables and smartphones are usually accessible to several third parties (manufacturers, service providers, developers of apps running on the hosting device), that are to be wisely considered as potentially untrusted if not malicious, especially because the user does not have any control on their capabilities to access the sensor data. As acceleration data collected from wearable devices is shown to enable the leakage of personal details [20,42], suitable approaches to privacy by design and by default in wearable devices, which are prescribed by privacy regulations such as the European GDPR [15], are needed [17].

1.1   Activity Recognition with Accelerometry

Human Activity Recognition (HAR) targets to automatically detect and predict human behaviors through motion data collection. Over the past years, both video- and sensors-based HAR have been explored in many application fields, such as ambient assisted living (AAL) [38], anomaly living patterns [16], fall detection [31], sport [47] and pandemic emergency like COVID-19 [19].

Generally, the development of a HAR system follows a specific sequence of steps, named Activity Recognition Chain (ARC), leading from collected raw data to activity recognition system performance. As detailed in [5], ARC consists of four consecutive steps that include the pre-processing, the segmentation, the feature extraction, and finally the selection of features and classifier training.

Within the context of sensor-based HAR, thanks to the quick spread of miniaturized inertial sensors (Inertial Measurement Units—IMUs) embedded in wearable electronic devices, motion-related raw data can be easily acquired from several consumer electronics products (e.g. smartwatches and smartphones), although their metrological properties are often unavailable [10]. Acceleration data are widely employed for HAR analysis [1,40]: such approaches offer an adequate, comfortable and affordable solution to directly measure the movement of the human body. Several studies focused on monitoring human activities have been reviewed in [13] and [39], where the accelerometer is used either alone or combined with other inertial sensors like gyroscopes and magnetometers.

Acceleration samples generated by the sensor capturing the current user's status may be continuously gathered from the wearable devices, processed and then used to classify the performed activities through the use of Machine Learning (ML) and Artificial Intelligence (AI) algorithms. Among others, some of the most commonly implemented classification algorithms include Naive Bayes (NB), Random Forest (RF), Decision Tree (DT), Support Vector Machine (SVM), k-Nearest Neighbor (kNN), Hidden Markov Model (HMM), Artificial Neural Network (ANN), Convolutional Neural Network (CNN) etc. [22,37]. However, different algorithms can be suitable for different scenarios of HAR, depending on the nature of the data collected [36] and also on the target item to classify (activity, gesture, pose, and so on). All of the mentioned algorithms exploit features computed on the acceleration data, either in the time or in the frequency domain; however, some of the features may capture not only the information strictly needed to classify the activity, but also personal details about the subject performing it. As a consequence, the risk is that the personal information is exposed with the HAR classification results.

1.2   Privacy Preservation

The very rapid growth in the adoption and popularity of wearable devices has nurtured the development of a huge amount of different applications exploiting not only the data collected by means of the on board sensors, but also the personal information each user may decide to provide, such as age, height, gender and weight.

For the latter, several mechanisms and approaches have been proposed in the literature, in order to guarantee anonymous sharing and avoidance of privacy disclosure [7,29,46]. However, the same personal information could be disclosed also without the explicit consensus of the user, by processing some of the motion-related data collected from wearable sensors, especially those generated by accelerometers. As explained in [43], for applications targeting HAR based on acceleration data, a potential privacy leakage exists about the user's identity, because it is possible to infer gait characteristics depending on a user's muscle growth, bone structure, height, and weight, from the sensed accelerometer data. Also, the authors show how feature selection and sampling rate adjustment have an impact on the accuracy of both activity and identity recognition, and they should be considered on the basis of their *mutual information* metric. Based on the above observations, motion data can be classified as a *quasi-identifier* [24], because it may allow the identification and tracking of a user. In fact, every individual has a distinctive way of walking, which is the reason why gait can be a key element of biometric techniques to authenticate and/or identify the user of a wearable device. Moreover, motion data can be drawn from wearables (such as smartbands) and mobile devices without the user's conscious participation or explicit permission, thus becoming a potential threat despite being generally thought to be harmless. Boutet et al. in their report [4] present a privacy-preserving tool to sanitize motion sensor data against unwanted sensitive inferences (thus improving privacy), while keeping an acceptable accuracy of the HAR (thus maintaining data utility). To do so, the tool builds several models to sanitize the motion data against the specified attribute (such as gender), by exploiting Generative Adversarial Networks (GANs). The generated sanitized data may result to be distorted with regards to the raw one, for the aim of the target application (HAR) so, based on a utility/privacy trade-off, several models may be necessary before finding the one that optimizes HAR performance loss, sensitive inference reduction, and data distortion. Authors present test results on available data collections, for which gender inference is reduced up to 41% while decreasing the HAR accuracy only by 3%.

While gait has been proved to enable a subject's identification from his/her motion data in the literature, in a previous paper we discussed the risk of exposure of personal information also when the collected acceleration data are not related to gait, but associated to different types of activities or gestures [34]. Taking all this into consideration, the main objective of this paper is to design a method to properly select features computed from the acceleration data acquired with a smart wristband while performing different activities, and used by supervised classification algorithms, so that HAR accuracy (i.e. the utility of the data) is not affected, while personal attributes (i.e. unnecessary private details in the processed data), such as gender, are concealed. A Multi-Objective Evolutionary Algorithm (MOEA) is applied to find appropriate weights for each feature, differently from the paper cited above which exploits GANs. The remainder of this paper is organized as follows. In Sect. 2 the initial method applied for HAR and gender recognition is presented. This Section also provides a description of the collected dataset, highlighting the features extracted from the accelerometer signal, which serve as input for the recognizing systems. In Sect. 3 a multi-objective evolutionary algorithm is described to find the relevance of each feature so that HAR accuracy percentage is maintained (or improved), while gender recognition is worsened to preserve the private information. Finally, Sect. 5 discusses the approach proposed in the paper and presents some future works.

2   Activity and Gender Recognition

2.1   The Dataset

This work employs the publicly available PAAL ADL Accelerometry dataset [32], a dataset acquired with a wearable multi-sensor device, the Empatica E4 [14], which provides raw activity motion data in real-life conditions.

To the aim of this work, among the signals collected by the sensors embedded in Empatica E4, only the acceleration has been extracted to monitor the users performing different activities of daily living. To promote the real-life acquisition procedure, subjects acted in their natural environment, with no instructions about how and for how long to perform each activity.

The dataset includes 24 different activities performed using real objects. Each activity was repeated between 3 and 5 times by 33 healthy subjects, characterized by a gender balance (19 females and 14 males), and a large age range (between 18 and 77 years, mean = 45.24 years and standard deviation = 18.24 years).

The list of activities is presented in Table 1. This dataset also includes information about the gender and age of each subject.

Table 1. List of activities performed by the subjects.

1. Drink water	7. Take off jacket	13. Sit down	19. Sneeze/cough
2. Eat meal	8. Put on jacket	14. Stand up	20. Blow nose
3. Open a bottle	9. Put on a shoe	15. Writing	21. Washing hands
4. Open a box	10. Take off a shoe	16. Phone call	22. Dusting
5. Brush teeth	11. Put on glasses	17. Type on a keyboard	23. Ironing
6. Brush hair	12. Take off glasses	18. Salute	24. Washing dishes

2.2 Signal Processing and Features Extraction

Each time series of acceleration samples A was filtered by applying a 4th order low-pass Butterworth filter (cut-off frequency: 15 Hz) for eliminating the high frequency noise and preserving the human activities and gestures [35]. In addition, a 3rd order median filter was applied to remove abnormal spikes. In order to infer the information contained in the human activity data, specific features were computed in both time- and frequency-domain, and then extracted, either from each spatial direction (A_x, A_y, A_z) and from the signal magnitude vector (SMV) of acceleration (defined as $SMV_i = \sqrt{A_{x,i}^2 + A_{y,i}^2 + A_{z,i}^2}$, where i is the index of the sample).

A successful technique for extracting features from accelerometer data is to divide the signals into windowed segments [28]. Therefore, we extract features from both raw data of the three axes and SMV, each segmented by fixed-size sliding windows of 5 s (i.e. 160 samples), with 20% (i.e. 1 s) of overlapping between two adjacent windows. Concerning the time domain analysis, features strictly related to the changes in the acceleration signal were evaluated. The frequency domain analysis was conducted by computing the magnitude of discrete Fast Fourier Transform (FFT) on the acceleration signals. The selected features were then extracted from the obtained signals. The list of 62 features used is presented in Table 2 [2,33].

2.3 Implementation

The overall implementation was made using the Python library Scikit-learn. Among the ML classifiers commonly selected to train and test the classification model, Random Forest (RF) was used thanks to its good performance reported in previous similar studies [18,44]. RF is designed to obtain accurate predictions by constructing multiple trees (named also estimators), where each tree is grown with a randomized subset of features. In this study, the whole set of features was used to build each tree of RF, measuring the quality of split with the information gain function. The number of trees was investigated by selecting different

Table 2. List of features extracted in time and frequency domain.

Domain	Features	Computation
Time	Mean	X, Y, Z axes, SMV
	Median	X, Y, Z axes, SMV
	Standard Deviation	X, Y, Z axes, SMV
	Maximum	X, Y, Z axes, SMV
	Minimum	X, Y, Z axes, SMV
	Range	X, Y, Z axes, SMV
	Axes Correlation	XY, YZ, ZX axes
	Signal Magnitude Area	SMV
	Coefficient of Variation	X, Y, Z axes, SMV
	Median Absolute Deviation	X, Y, Z axes, SMV
	Skewness	SMV
	Kurtosis	SMV
	Autocorrelation	SMV
	Percentiles (20th - 50th - 80th - 90th)	SMV
	Interquartile range	SMV
	No. of Peaks	SMV
	Peak - Peak Amplitude	SMV
	Energy	SMV
	Root Mean Square	SMV
Frequency	Spectral Entropy	SMV
	Spectral Energy	SMV
	Spectral Centroid	SMV
	Mean	X, Y, Z axes, SMV
	Standard Deviation	X, Y, Z axes, SMV
	Percentiles (25th - 50th - 75th)	SMV

numbers of estimators (from 10 to 170) to verify whether such parameter can improve the model accuracy for activity and gender recognition.

In order to train the model, the k-fold cross validation was implemented with $k = 10$. This means that the original dataset was randomly partitioned into k subsets: $k-1$ as training set, and the remaining as validation set. After k times, the average of the k performance measurements on the k validation sets gives the cross-validated performance.

2.4   Results

Generally, in the HAR context, supervised learning approaches are widely exploited by using labeled data as inputs for predicting the classification of unknown data through the ML algorithms. In this section, we present the results of the RF supervised approach used to investigate both the activity and gender recognition, separately.

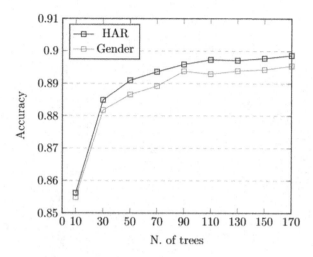

Fig. 1. Number of trees for RF classifier.

The experimental results are shown in Fig. 1, where the number of trees is associated to a value of accuracy percentage achieved by the RF algorithm. Contrary to what often may be thought, the results show that a large number of trees does not necessarily cause a better recognition performance for the RF algorithm. In fact, for both models, the percentages of improvement stabilize or slightly decrease as the number of trees increases, especially after a number of trees equal to 90. This means that the benefit in recognition performance from using more trees is lower than the cost in computation time for learning the additional trees. Therefore, at 90 estimators, the global accuracy percentage is 89.59% and 89.37% for human activity and gender recognition, respectively. Besides the accuracy, the performance of the activity and gender recognition was assessed using the confusion matrix, that summarizes the information about the actual and predicted classes, either correctly or wrongly classified. Figure 2 shows the results obtained for the RF algorithm to classify each activity. As it is clear, the highly misclassified activities are the following ones: open a box classified as open bottle, take off a shoe classified as put on a shoe, take off glasses classified as put on glasses, and stand up classified as sit down. On the other hand, Fig. 3 shows the performance obtained for the RF algorithm in distinguishing the gender of the participants. Male subjects were confused more than female ones, probably because there are more female users in the dataset.

3   Concealing Private Information with a Multi-objective Evolutionary Algorithm

The above results can be considered good for HAR. However, if the goal is to protect identity details of the users performing those activities, this set of features also gets good results for gender recognition. Then, the question is:

Confusion matrix (rows = Actual class, columns = Predicted class):

Actual class	drink water	eat meal	open bottle	open a box	brush teeth	brush hair	take off jacket	put on jacket	put on a shoe	take off a shoe	put on glasses	take off glasses	sit down	stand up	writing	phone call	type on a keyboard	salute	sneeze/cough	blow nose	washing hands	dusting	ironing	washing dishes
drink water	90	1											3	3	1			1	1	2				
eat meal	2	55	5	4							5	3	6	7		3			5	5				
open bottle	1	4	44	30					1	1	1	3	3	1		1			1	1	9			
open a box	1	1	24	57							1	2	1			1			1	1	9			
brush teeth					95	0	0	0	0	1						1					0	0	2	0
brush hair	0				1	90	1	2	2	0				0				0	0		0	1	2	0
take off jacket						1	84	9	1	1								2					1	
put on jacket						1	3	87	4	0					0							2	1	1
put on a shoe		0			0	1	0	0	85	3			0			0			1	1	1	4	3	
take off a shoe		1	3	1	1	0	1		14	51	0		4	2	0	0	0	1	3	3	2	3	4	3
put on glasses	5	3		1							70	11	1	3		6			1	1				
take off glasses	5	3	3	6						1	12	54	4	2		1			4	3	1			
sit down		0	2	1						1	0	1	72	16					1	1	1			1
stand up		4	2	1						2		1	18	69					1	1	1			
writing															98		1						0	
phone call		3		2			1	2			1	10	3	1	2	73		1	1					1
type on a keyboard												0				3	96		0	0			1	
salute						1	1	1			1	1	3			3		90						
sneeze/cough	3	6	6	8							2	8	5	5		6	1	6	41	3	1	1		
blow nose	3	4	4	5	1	1			1	1	1	1	2			1	1	1	4	67		1	1	2
washing hands		0							0	0	1	1				1	0				92	0	0	4
dusting				0	0	1	1	1	3	2			0					1		0	1	85	2	2
ironing			0	0					0	0	0		0	0				2	0	0		0	96	1
washing dishes				0	0	0			1	0									1	0		2	1	95

Fig. 2. Confusion matrix for HAR recognition.

Actual \ Predicted	male	female
male	79	21
female	4	96

Fig. 3. Confusion matrix for gender recognition.

Can the input features be transformed so that HAR remains good but gender (or any other private data) recognition accuracy decreases? This would lead to systems that perform well for HAR, maintaining the utility of the data, but, simultaneously, conceal private information. This work presents a mechanism to filter the input features in order to obtain this objective. We propose the use of a multi-objective evolutionary algorithm to find appropriate weights for each feature.

3.1 Evolutionary Feature Weighting

This is a similar objective to previous works on evolutionary feature subset selection or feature weighting. This is, trying to approximate the optimal degree of influence of individual features using a training set. However, the final goal of this work is to filter the signal captured by the wristband trying to maximize the

HAR accuracy while at the same time to minimize the recognition of personal characteristics of the subjects, e.g. gender or age.

In the case of evolutionary feature weighting, the approach is to consider an individual as a real vector where each gene represents the weight given to each feature. Two main models are presented in the literature to implement this [6, 45]: the filter model and the wrapper model. The former selects the features based on a priori decisions on feature relevance according to some measures (information, distance, dependence or consistency) [30], ignoring the learning algorithm underneath. In the latter, the feature selection algorithm exists as a wrapper around the learning algorithm; in the search of a feature subset, the learning algorithm itself is used as part of the evaluation function [21]. The main disadvantage of the wrapper approach is the time needed for the evaluation of each feature weight [26]. On the other hand, filter-based approaches, although faster, find worse solutions in general [6].

This paper follows the wrapper approach, trying to find appropriate weights for the features presented in Table 2 using RF as classifier.

3.2   Multi-objective Evolutionary Algorithms

In multi-objective optimization, the goal is to optimize simultaneously several objective functions. These different functions have conflicting objectives, i.e., optimizing one affects the others. Therefore, there is not a unique solution but a set of solutions. The set of solutions in which the different objective components cannot be simultaneously improved constitute a Pareto front. Each solution in the Pareto front represents a trade-off between the objectives. MOEAs [8] are heuristic algorithms to solve problems with multiple objective functions. The three goals of an MOEA are [41]: (1) to find a set of solutions as close as possible to the Pareto front (convergence); (2) to maintain a diverse population that contains dissimilar individuals to promote exploration and to avoid poor performance due to premature convergence (diversity); and (3) to obtain a set of solutions that spreads in a more uniform way over the Pareto front (coverage).

This work employs the Non-dominated Sorting Genetic Algorithm II (NSGA-II) [11] as wrapper algorithm. NSGA-II has the three following features: (1) it uses an elitist principle, i.e., the elites of a population are given the opportunity to be carried to the next generation; (2) it uses an explicit diversity preserving mechanism (Crowding distance); and (3) it emphasizes the non-dominated solutions. The algorithm will obtain a set of solutions, some of them optimizing one over the other objective and vice versa. From these set of solutions, a specific solution fulfilling particular conditions could be selected.

3.3   Characteristics of the Algorithm

An individual in the population (potential solution) is encoded as a real vector U whose elements $u_j, \forall j \in [1..62]$ represent the weight of a particular feature during the classification (62 being the number of features, see Table 2), i.e. each feature is multiplied by the appropriate weight before being input to the classifier.

The fitness functions to be optimized are:

$$f_1 = HAR \tag{1}$$

$$f_2 = \left| Gender\ Recognition - \frac{1}{2} \right| \tag{2}$$

The objective will be to maximize f_1 while minimizing f_2, i.e. maximizing HAR while taking gender recognition close to random. Therefore, for other private information, the second term in f_2 must be $\frac{1}{Number\ of\ categories}$.

4   Results

This work has employed the implementation of NSGA-II offered by pymoo [3], a multi-objective optimization framework in Python, using the following parameters, which have been selected experimentally:

– Size of the population: 50;
– New individuals (offsprings) created per generation: 10; and
– Number of generations without changes in the best individual to stop the algorithm: 100

Some other characteristics of the algorithm are:

– The individuals in the initial population are created with random real values between 0 and 1;
– Binary tournament is used to select the parents to generate a new offspring;
– Simulated Binary Crossover (SBX) [12] with default parameters is employed to create each individual;
– Each new individual is mutated by applying Polynomial Mutation [12] with default parameters; and
– Duplicates are eliminated after merging the parent and the offspring population. If there are duplicates with respect to the current population or in the offsprings itself they are removed and the mating process is repeated to fill up the offsprings until the desired number of unique offsprings is met.

The application of this algorithm obtains a set of solutions, some of them optimizing one over the other objective and vice versa (Fig. 4). From these set of solutions, this work selects the solution closer (using Euclidean distance) to perfect HAR (value equal to 1) and random gender recognition (value equal to 0.5). The accuracy results of this selected final solution (marked in green in the Figure) are 84.14% and 64.38%, for activity and gender recognition, respectively. Comparing with the results presented in Sect. 2.4 (in red in the Figure), in which all the features are equally considered, HAR accuracy has been reduced 5.45% points while gender recognition has worsened 24.99.

Figure 5 shows that results are similar to those shown in Fig. 2, although accuracy has been reduced for most of the classes. However, gender classification has been dramatically affected by applying the MOEA as almost all the inputs are now identified as being performed by a female user (Fig. 6).

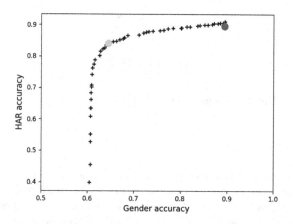

Fig. 4. Final set of solutions for a run of the MOEA algorithm. The best balanced solution is marked in green. The initial result in which all features are equally considered (presented in Sect. 2.4) is marked in red. For the sake of clarity, 0.5 has been added to f_2, which is then the gender accuracy. (Color figure online)

Predicted class

Actual class	drink water	eat meal	open bottle	open a box	brush teeth	brush hair	take off jacket	put on jacket	put on a shoe	take off a shoe	put on glasses	take off glasses	sit down	stand up	writing	phone call	type on a keyboard	salute	sneeze/cough	blow nose	washing hands	dusting	ironing	washing dishes
drink water	83	1	1								7	4	1	1	1	1			1				1	
eat meal	3	43	7	8					1	1	3	5	7	7	1	3		1	5	4			2	
open bottle	1	5	41	26					2	2	3	1	3	1	2			1	1	3	5	1		
open a box	1	1	27	50					1		2	1	3	3	1	1		1	1	2	3	1		
brush teeth					91		0	0	0						1	2					0	0	4	1
brush hair	0				3	79	0	2	2	0	0	0				0		0		0	0	1	7	3
take off jacket					0	1	74	18	1	0								1			0	1	0	1
put on jacket						1	1	84	2						1			0	0			3	1	5
put on a shoe					2	1	0	0	68	1	1	0	1			1					2	1	6	16
take off a shoe		1	5	0		7	1	1	9	16	0	3	3	9	1	1		2	2	0	5	1	11	21
put on glasses	6	3	1	1							63	12	2			8			3	1			1	
take off glasses	9	2	5	6							14	42	6	2	1	2	1		7	2			1	
sit down		2	2	3	1				1	2	1	2	65	16	1	2			1	2			1	1
stand up		5	1	1						1	1	1	13	70	1	2			1	2			1	1
writing															98		2							0
phone call	1	3		1		1	2		1		7	3	2	1		67		5		1	1	4	1	1
type on a keyboard																6	93						1	
salute		1		1	1	1	1				1	4	1			6		82					1	
sneeze/cough	2	3	5	5	1				1		10	5	5	6	3	1	1	8	36	3		1	3	
blow nose	1	2	6	4	3	1			1		1	1	1	2	1	6	1	6	1	48		1	12	5
washing hands	0		0				0	0	0		0	0	0			0					84	0	0	13
dusting					3	1	2	3	0	1						0		0			1	72	5	13
ironing					1				0	0			1	0				3	0	0	0	0	92	1
washing dishes					1				0	0								0			1	0	1	96

Fig. 5. Confusion matrix related to the HAR.

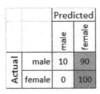

Fig. 6. Confusion matrix related to the gender.

5 Conclusion

In this work, the authors propose a method for privacy preservation in non gait-related human motion data collection. More precisely, an MOEA is applied on a dataset of 24 different activities of daily living performed in realistic conditions by 33 healthy subjects, and for which acceleration signals were collected from the medical grade wrist worn device Empatica E4.

In order to investigate how much private information (i.e. related to gender) is included in the set of features extracted from accelerometer data, the RF algorithm was firstly adopted for both the activity and gender recognition separately. Then, the NSGA-II was employed as a wrapper algorithm to find the appropriate weights for each feature so that HAR accuracy is maximized while simultaneously gender accuracy is minimized. In order to validate the MOEA with respect to the initial method, the classification accuracy along with the confusion matrices were investigated.

Initial results show a global accuracy percentage of 89.59% and 89.37% for human activity and gender recognition, respectively, by adopting the RF algorithm with a number of trees equal to 90. In particular, the confusion matrix for HAR suggests that some activities are highly misclassified because they are difficult to distinguish using only a single accelerometer worn on the wrist, as the movement of the device may be similar in some contrary activities (e.g. stand up and sit down). Also, the same activity performed with two different tools was harder to distinguish (e.g. open a box and open bottle). Regarding gender recognition, the results demonstrate that the user's gender can be easily detected from the wrist motion data. Finding the appropriate weights by using an MOEA allows to conceal the gender of the user while HAR is not considerably affected, resulting in a global accuracy of 84.14% and 64.38% for human activity and gender recognition, respectively. Additionally, Fig. 4 shows that the output of the multi-objective evolutionary algorithm is not a single set of weights (single solution) but a set of solutions constituting a Pareto front. Therefore, under some conditions instead of choosing the best balanced solution (as this work proposes) any other of the obtained solutions could be chosen, for instance in the case that, for a specific user, activity recognition needs to be prioritized over privacy protection. Getting back to the motivations of this study, implementing a concealing strategy on-board the sensor based on the selected condition on the Pareto front, could be seen as a way to implement what is envisaged as a privacy-by-design approach by the regulations.

In the future, this work will be extended to consider other private information which users would like to conceal, e.g. age. In that case, in which more than two objective functions were to be considered, the optimization will be carried out with a many-objective evolutionary algorithms [27]. Additionally, other set of features extracted from the accelerometer data will be explored. For instance, extracting deep features from the original data instead of using the handcrafted features presented in Table 2.

References

1. Balli, S., Sağbaş, E.A., Peker, M.: Human activity recognition from smart watch sensor data using a hybrid of principal component analysis and random forest algorithm. Meas. Control **52**(1–2), 37–45 (2019)
2. Bautista-Salinas, D., González, J., Méndez, I., Mozos, O.: Monitoring and prediction of mood in elderly people during daily life activities. In: 41st Annual International Conference of the IEEE Engineering in Medicine and Biology Society. IEEE Engineering in Medicine and Biology Society. Conference (EMBC), vol. 2019, pp. 6930–6934. IEEE (2019)
3. Blank, J., Deb, K.: Pymoo: multi-objective optimization in python. IEEE Access **8**, 89497–89509 (2020)
4. Boutet, A., Frindel, C., Gambs, S., Jourdan, T., Ngueveu, R.C.: DYSAN: dynamically sanitizing motion sensor data against sensitive inferences through adversarial networks. In: INRIA Informatics Mathematics, pp. 1–26. INRIA (2020)
5. Bulling, A., Blanke, U., Schiele, B.: A tutorial on human activity recognition using body-worn inertial sensors. ACM Comput. Surv. (CSUR) **46**(3), 1–33 (2014)
6. Cantú-Paz, E.: Feature subset selection, class separability, and genetic algorithms. In: Deb, K. (ed.) GECCO 2004. LNCS, vol. 3102, pp. 959–970. Springer, Heidelberg (2004). https://doi.org/10.1007/978-3-540-24854-5_96
7. Chen, C.M., Xiang, B., Wu, T.Y., Wang, K.H.: An anonymous mutual authenticated key agreement scheme for wearable sensors in wireless body area networks. Appl. Sci. (Switzerland) **8**(7) (2018). https://doi.org/10.3390/app8071074
8. Coello, C.A.C., Lamont, G.B., Van Veldhuizen, D.A., et al.: Evolutionary Algorithms for Solving Multi-objective Problems, vol. 5. Springer, Heidelberg (2007). https://doi.org/10.1007/978-0-387-36797-2
9. Connor, P., Ross, A.: Biometric recognition by gait: a survey of modalities and features. Comput. Vis. Image Underst. **167**, 1–27 (2018)
10. Cosoli, G., Spinsante, S., Scalise, L.: Wrist-worn and chest-strap wearable devices: systematic review on accuracy and metrological characteristics. Measurement **159**, 107789 (2020)
11. Deb, K., Pratap, A., Agarwal, S., Meyarivan, T.: A fast and elitist multiobjective genetic algorithm: NSGA-II. IEEE Trans. Evol. Comput. **6**(2), 182–197 (2002)
12. Deb, K., Sindhya, K., Okabe, T.: Self-adaptive simulated binary crossover for real-parameter optimization. In: Proceedings of the 9th Annual Conference on Genetic and Evolutionary Computation, GECCO 2007, pp. 1187–1194. Association for Computing Machinery, New York (2007)
13. Elbasiony, R., Gomaa, W.: A survey on human activity recognition based on temporal signals of portable inertial sensors. In: Hassanien, A.E., Azar, A.T., Gaber, T., Bhatnagar, R., F. Tolba, M. (eds.) AMLTA 2019. AISC, vol. 921, pp. 734–745. Springer, Cham (2020). https://doi.org/10.1007/978-3-030-14118-9_72

14. Empatica Inc.: Empatica E4. https://www.empatica.com/en-eu/research/e4/. Accessed 29 Apr 2021

15. European Commission: Regulation (EU) 2016/679 of the European Parliament and of the Council of 27 April 2016 on the protection of natural persons with regard to the processing of personal data and on the free movement of such data, and repealing Directive 95/46/EC (General Data Protection Regulation) (2016). https://eur-lex.europa.eu/. Accessed 26 July 2021

16. Fahad, L.G., Tahir, S.F.: Activity recognition and anomaly detection in smart homes. Neurocomputing **423**, 362–372 (2021)

17. Flórez-Revuelta, F., Mihailidis, A., Ziefle, M., Colonna, L., Spinsante, S.: Privacy-aware and acceptable lifelogging services for older and frail people: the PAAL project. In: 2018 IEEE 8th International Conference on Consumer Electronics - Berlin (ICCE-Berlin), pp. 1–4, September 2018

18. Gomaa, W.: Comparative analysis of different approaches to human activity recognition based on accelerometer signals. In: Hassanien, A.E., Darwish, A. (eds.) Machine Learning and Big Data Analytics Paradigms: Analysis, Applications and Challenges. SBD, vol. 77, pp. 303–322. Springer, Cham (2021). https://doi.org/10.1007/978-3-030-59338-4_16

19. Hoang, M.L., Carratù, M., Paciello, V., Pietrosanto, A.: Body temperature—indoor condition monitor and activity recognition by MEMS accelerometer based on IoT-alert system for people in quarantine due to COVID-19. Sensors **21**(7) (2021)

20. Jain, A., Kanhangad, V.: Gender classification in smartphones using gait information. Expert Syst. Appl. **93**, 257–266 (2018)

21. John, G.H., Kohavi, R., Pfleger, K.: Irrelevant features and the subset selection problem. In: Machine Learning Proceedings 1994, pp. 121–129. Elsevier (1994)

22. Kilic, S., Kaya, Y., Askerbeyli, I.: A new approach for human recognition through wearable sensor signals. Arab. J. Sci. Eng. **46**, 4175–4189 (2021)

23. Kim, J.W., Lim, J.H., Moon, S.M., Jang, B.: Collecting health lifelog data from smartwatch users in a privacy-preserving manner. IEEE Trans. Consum. Electron. **65**(3), 369–378 (2019). https://doi.org/10.1109/TCE.2019.2924466

24. Kröger, J.: Unexpected inferences from sensor data: a hidden privacy threat in the Internet of Things. In: Strous, L., Cerf, V.G. (eds.) IFIPIoT 2018. IAICT, vol. 548, pp. 147–159. Springer, Cham (2019). https://doi.org/10.1007/978-3-030-15651-0_13

25. Ksibi, A., Alluhaidan, A.S.D., Salhi, A., El-Rahman, S.A.: Overview of lifelogging: current challenges and advances. IEEE Access **9**, 62630–62641 (2021). https://doi.org/10.1109/ACCESS.2021.3073469

26. Lanzi, P.L.: Fast feature selection with genetic algorithms: a filter approach. In: Proceedings of 1997 IEEE International Conference on Evolutionary Computation (ICEC 1997), pp. 537–540. IEEE (1997)

27. Li, B., Li, J., Tang, K., Yao, X.: Many-objective evolutionary algorithms: a survey. ACM Comput. Surv. (CSUR) **48**(1), 1–35 (2015)

28. Li, J., Tian, L., Wang, H., An, Y., Wang, K., Yu, L.: Segmentation and recognition of basic and transitional activities for continuous physical human activity. IEEE Access **7**, 42565–42576 (2019)

29. Liu, F., Li, T.: A clustering k-anonymity privacy-preserving method for wearable IoT devices. Secur. Commun. Netw. **2018** (2018). https://doi.org/10.1155/2018/4945152

30. Liu, H., Motoda, H.: Feature Selection for Knowledge Discovery and Data Mining, vol. 454. Springer, Heidelberg (2012)

31. Montanini, L., Del Campo, A., Perla, D., Spinsante, S., Gambi, E.: A footwear-based methodology for fall detection. IEEE Sens. J. **18**(3), 1233–1242 (2017)
32. Muñoz-Anton, A.M., Poli, A., Spinsante, S., Florez-Revuelta, F.: PAAL ADL Accelerometry dataset (2021). https://doi.org/10.5281/zenodo.4750904
33. Poli, A., Scalise, L., Spinsante, S., Strazza, A.: ADLs monitoring by accelerometer-based wearable sensors: effect of measurement device and data uncertainty on classification accuracy. In: 2020 IEEE International Symposium on Medical Measurements and Applications (MeMeA), pp. 1–6. IEEE (2020)
34. Poli, A., Strazza, A., Cecchi, S., Spinsante, S.: Identification issues associated with the use of wearable accelerometers in lifelogging. In: Gao, Q., Zhou, J. (eds.) HCII 2020. LNCS, vol. 12207, pp. 338–351. Springer, Cham (2020). https://doi.org/10.1007/978-3-030-50252-2_26
35. Poli, A., Spinsante, S., Nugent, C., Cleland, I.: Improving the collection and understanding the quality of datasets for the aim of human activity recognition. In: Chen, F., García-Betances, R.I., Chen, L., Cabrera-Umpiérrez, M.F., Nugent, C. (eds.) Smart Assisted Living. CCN, pp. 147–165. Springer, Cham (2020). https://doi.org/10.1007/978-3-030-25590-9_7
36. Rafferty, J., Nugent, C.D., Liu, J., Chen, L.: From activity recognition to intention recognition for assisted living within smart homes. IEEE Trans. Hum.-Mach. Syst. **47**(3), 368–379 (2017)
37. Joy Rakesh, Y., Kavitha, R., Julian, J.: Human activity recognition using wearable sensors. In: Satapathy, S.C., Zhang, Y.-D., Bhateja, V., Majhi, R. (eds.) Intelligent Data Engineering and Analytics. AISC, vol. 1177, pp. 527–538. Springer, Singapore (2021). https://doi.org/10.1007/978-981-15-5679-1_51
38. Ranieri, C.M., MacLeod, S., Dragone, M., Vargas, P.A., Romero, R.A.F.: Activity recognition for ambient assisted living with videos, inertial units and ambient sensors. Sensors **21**(3) (2021)
39. Slim, S., Atia, A., Elfattah, M., Mostafa, M.S.M.: Survey on human activity recognition based on acceleration data. Intl. J. Adv. Comput. Sci. Appl **10**, 84–98 (2019)
40. Sousa Lima, W., Souto, E., El-Khatib, K., Jalali, R., Gama, J.: Human activity recognition using inertial sensors in a smartphone: an overview. Sensors **19**(14) (2019)
41. Trivedi, A., Srinivasan, D., Sanyal, K., Ghosh, A.: A survey of multiobjective evolutionary algorithms based on decomposition. IEEE Trans. Evol. Comput. **21**(3), 440–462 (2017)
42. Van hamme, T., Garofalo, G., Argones Rúa, E., Preuveneers, D., Joosen, W.: A systematic comparison of age and gender prediction on IMU sensor-based gait traces. Sensors **19**(13) (2019). https://doi.org/10.3390/s19132945. https://www.mdpi.com/1424-8220/19/13/2945
43. Xiao, F., et al.: An information-aware visualization for privacy-preserving accelerometer data sharing. HCIS **8**(1), 1–28 (2018). https://doi.org/10.1186/s13673-018-0137-6
44. Yacchirema, D.C., de Puga, J.S., Palau, C., Esteve, M.: Fall detection system for elderly people using IoT and ensemble machine learning algorithm. Pers. Ubiquit. Comput. **23**, 801–817 (2019)
45. Yusta, S.C.: Different metaheuristic strategies to solve the feature selection problem. Pattern Recogn. Lett. **30**(5), 525–534 (2009)
46. Zhang, Z., Wang, X., Uden, L., Zhang, P., Zhao, Y.: e-DMDAV: a new privacy preserving algorithm for wearable enterprise information systems. Enterp. Inf. Syst. **12**(4), 492–504 (2018)
47. Zhuang, Z., Xue, Y.: Sport-related human activity detection and recognition using a smartwatch. Sensors **19**(22), 5001 (2019)

Biometric Data Capture as a Way to Identify Lack of Physical Activity in Daily Life

Luís Marques[1], Luca Lopes[1], Miguel Ferreira[1], Joao Henriques[1,3,4(✉)],
Ivan Miguel Pires[1,2,3], Filipe Caldeira[1,4], and Cristina Wanzeller[1,4]

[1] Department of Computer Science, Polytechnic of Viseu, 3504-510 Viseu, Portugal
{estgv5989,estgv13082,estgv7447}@alunos.estgv.ipv.pt,
{joaohenriques,impires,caldeira,cwanzeller}@estgv.ipv.pt
[2] Instituto de Telecomunicações, Universidade da Beira Interior,
6200-001 Covilhã, Portugal
[3] Department of Informatics Engineering, University of Coimbra,
3030-290 Coimbra, Portugal
[4] CISeD—Research Centre in Digital Services, Polytechnic of Viseu,
3504-510 Viseu, Portugal

Abstract. Given the impact of the pandemic era, it is important the effects of physical activity on human beings, physically and mentally. The significant advance in the technology industry of biomedical sensors and mobile devices allowed the arrival of new health monitoring prototypes to improve people's lives. This work implements a data capture system, using an electrocardiogram (ECG) and accelerometer (ACC) type sensor to collect a large volume of data for further analysis to obtain metrics to assess the activity level during this pandemic phase. Using a BITalino device that allows us to collect a large amount of information from various sensors, we, therefore, chose to use it as a platform to capture data from the sensors mentioned above. In the first phase, we will capture the largest possible amount of data from the subject in the test phase. Then, the collected data will be sent to a web server, where it will be processed. Finally, in a third phase, the data will be presented in a more summarized and graphical way. In this way, we will analyze the impact of movement/inactivity on the test subjects' daily life with the referred sensors' biometric data.

Keywords: Biometric · Data capture · ECG · Accelerometer · BITalino

1 Introduction

Interest in biometrics has gained momentum in the last years, mostly due to the massive use of daily life devices like smartwatches, smartphones, and laptops [10,11]. From a technical perspective, biometrics can be classified into two

I. M. Pires et al. (Eds.): GOODTECHS 2021, LNICST 401, pp. 18–26, 2021.
https://doi.org/10.1007/978-3-030-91421-9_2

main groups depending on whether they use physiological or behavioral signals. Examples of physiological signals include fingerprints, iris, retina, heart, and brain signals, whereas voice, signature analysis, or keystroke dynamics are behavioral signals [8].

The research outcome in this area is that most gadgets, such as smartphones, tablets, wearables, and Implantable Medical Devices (IMDs), have been equipped with one or more embedded sensors to measure biometric parameters from the bearer. Besides having biometrics sensors, most (if not all) of these devices are enhanced with some wireless communication technology, e.g., Bluetooth, WiFi, or Radio Frequency(RF), allowing them to share data and to perform remote reconfiguration [6].

Nowadays, mobile devices have increased, and this trend will continue in the coming years. Due to their widespread integration with the users' lifestyles, mobile devices can support personal activities anywhere at any time. Also, these devices integrate numerous sensors that allow signal acquisition related to different aspects of medical or assisted living purposes in different environments [13].

Mobile devices integrate sensors and features that help healthcare professionals treat their patients with permanent connectivity. Mobile applications help collect data related to physical activity, human body images, and other aspects related to healthcare [13].

Although mobile devices integrate many sensors, over recent years, the Do-it-Yourself (DiY) community has been contributing to the development of low-cost, easy-to-use hardware platforms targeting biomedical engineering and equipped with multiple sensors useful for a wide range of applications [4]. One of these hardware platforms, explicitly designed to suit the needs of the physiological computing community, is BITalino device [14].

BITalino device a low-cost and highly versatile hardware framework designed to allow anyone, from students to professional app developers, to create projects and applications with physiological sensors [14].

Jupyter notebooks provide an environment where you can freely combine human-readable narrative with computer-readable code. This lesson describes how to install the Jupyter Notebook software, run and create Jupyter notebook files, and contexts where Jupyter notebooks can be particularly helpful [7].

In our daily life, we have continuous access to a plethora of sensors in our mobile devices. With the use of specialized sensors such as the ones provided by the BITalino platform, the information captured with these sensors can give us many data to analyze. In this study, we intend to correlate some of these sensors data in daily life to detect lack or not of physical activity.

This document is organized into five sections. In Sect. 2, we identify related work. Section 3, presents the method applied in study. Section 4, shows the obtained results. Finally, in Sect. 5 conclusions are drawn, followed by future work guidelines.

2   Related Work

This section's overall goal is to describe the related research areas and place the method's contributions in this context. This chapter surveys previous work in biometric data capture to identify a lack of physical activity in daily life. In general terms, the biometric data will be captured through a device called BITalino and its sensors, such as an ECG sensor to measure the heartbeat of the subject and accelerometer sensors to measure subject movement, respectively. The biometric data will be sent to a server, processed the signals, and finally, the information will be displayed graphically and resumed to be better visualized. This process aims to understand the lack of physical activity and the relation with this critical phase that we are trying to pass through.

A device and an ECG sensor will do this process, but first a little bit of history about it, this device was designed in Portugal and is one of the ten main European innovations in the Industrial & Enabling Tech category of the Innovations Radar Prize 2017 [3].

Nowadays, biometric data is a subject in vogue by the general public and not only by the people who work in medicine. Thus, portable devices such as smartwatches and smart fitness bands play a crucial role in evolving how it diagnoses several health disorders before they step into a high-risk medical field. It is significantly accessible to recording data. There is a tremendous interest in devices that can help people control or measure their physical condition or health and well-being. Furthermore, biometric data has become a critical topic of study for the global engineering community and, as a consequence, shows that biometric data is a topic of growing interest [9,12,14].

In this project, it will be captured biometric data from three or four subjects. For this purpose, a BITalino device will be used with the respective sensors to capture biometric data. This equipment will be described in the following topic to understand better this technology [15].

Currently, there is a need to create innovative hardware at a low cost. In this specific case, we are talking about BITalino devices. It is a versatile hardware structure designed with good raw material at a reduced price, allowing anyone to create projects and applications with physiological sensors. This device is probably the most well-established and recognized system for biomedical research and education. Although BITalino device has a variety of sensors and functionalities, we chose to use the sensor because, for the intended purpose, it is the most suitable sensor. This sensor analyzes four different activities: spine, seated, deep breathing, and recovery after exercise [1,2,5].

3   Experimental Work

At this stage, our project's first step was to obtain the data from a BITalino device from the two sensors used in this study, in this case, an ECG and accelerometer sensors. The procedure was to establish a connection between the BITalino device and an Android smartphone using the OpenSignals application to collect this data. OpenSignals, from the creators of the BITalino device, allow to capture data from the sensors and save it to a text file with the sensors' outcome results. After the capture is done, the same data text file is sent to an FTP server. The server folder, where the data files are received, is constantly monitored for new files. When a new file arrives, the server processes it and creates a new Jupyter Notebook file from a template and the received file data. These generated files can then be opened in Jupyter Server or Jupyter Lab, where we can visualize charts with the sensors' metrics. This process's architecture is demonstrated in the picture Fig. 1 presented below. Firstly, on the Android side, the OpenSignals app looks like the following pictures presented in Fig. 5. Secondly, on the server-side, the stack consisted of an File Transfer Protocol (FTP) server receiving the data collected from Android application to a folder (see Figs. 2 and 3), and the server monitoring these folders for processing the received data files. Finally, in Fig. 4, the Jupyter Lab server with a processed notebook is presented.

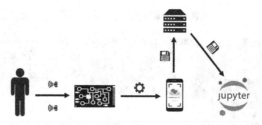

Fig. 1. Schema of the proposed system.

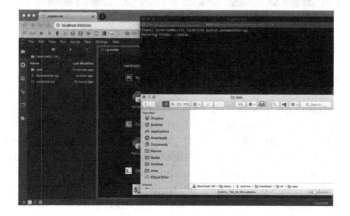

Fig. 2. Server Stack

Fig. 3. Server Stack 1

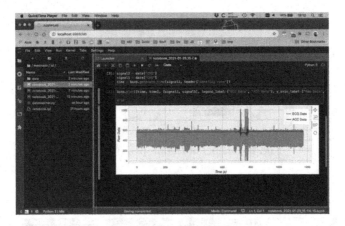

Fig. 4. Jupyter Notebook Processed Data

4   Preliminary Results

From the captured data collected from a single subject, the results obtained
from the sensors can be seen in the chart presented in Fig. 6 or 7. The result
data serves as an example for a small part of a day. The Fig. 6 represents a
portion of roughly 18 min and Fig. 7 represents a portion of roughly 2 h and
18 min. The data had to be collected in chunks due to the large volume of data
captured, making it much more difficult to handle in devices like mobile phones
and even transform it into a simple laptop computer.

As shown in both charts, the data collected induce us to a correlation between
spikes in ECG signal and spikes in the accelerometer signal, representing periods
of movement from the subject. Although the periods described in charts are not
from a full day from continuous measurements, we observed the same pattern of

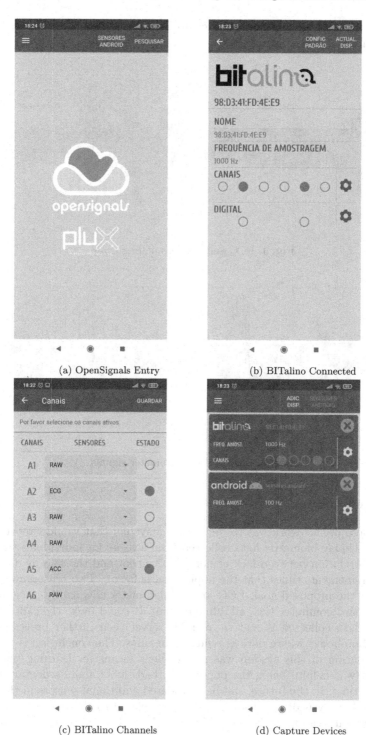

(a) OpenSignals Entry

(b) BITalino Connected

(c) BITalino Channels

(d) Capture Devices

Fig. 5. OpenSignals

motion, or lack of movement in this case of the subject, as we suspected from the beginning of this work.

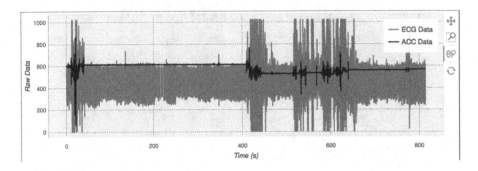

Fig. 6. ECC and accelerometer signals

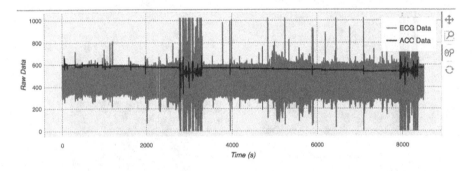

Fig. 7. ECC and accelerometer signals

5   Conclusion

The purpose of this work was to implement a system that would capture, process, and display biometric data collected from sensors for individuals to try to make a correlation between lack or not of movement and the sensors data, due to the confinements times that the population is facing. Two sensors were used to achieve the proposed goal, ECG and accelerometer adequately integrated in a single-board computer (i.e., BITalino device). It could make the capture, and then the data collected is sent to an FTP server then further processes to a Jupyter Notebooks where data is rendered in carts. The conclusion is that the implementation of this system was an excellent means for learning purposes. Finally, it was helpful being the population tends to be more sedentary in the pandemic time. In the future, can be considered additional sensors in the monitoring and analysis of metrics and indicators related to the well-being of individuals. Finally, can be explored machine learning algorithms on processing the data to get new insights.

Acknowledgements. This work is funded by FCT/MEC through national funds and, when applicable, co-funded by the FEDER-PT2020 partnership agreement under the project **UIDB/50008/2020**. (*Este trabalho é financiado pela FCT/MEC através de fundos nacionais e cofinanciado pelo FEDER, no âmbito do Acordo de Parceria PT2020 no âmbito do projeto UIDB/50008/2020*). This work is also funded by National Funds through the FCT - Foundation for Science and Technology, I.P., within the scope of the projects **UIDB/00742/2020** and **UIDB/05583/2020**. This article is based upon work from COST Action IC1303-AAPELE-Architectures, Algorithms, and Protocols for Enhanced Living Environments and COST Action CA16226-SHELD-ON-Indoor living space improvement: Smart Habitat for the Elderly, supported by COST (European Cooperation in Science and Technology). COST is a funding agency for research and innovation networks. Our Actions help connect research initiatives across Europe and enable scientists to grow their ideas by sharing them with their peers. It boosts their research, career, and innovation. More information in www.cost.eu. Furthermore, we would like to thank the Research Center in Digital Services (CISeD) and the Polytechnic of Viseu for their support.

References

1. Ahmed, N., Zhu, Y.: Early detection of atrial fibrillation based on ECG signals. Bioengineering **7**(1) (2020)
2. Alexandre, C.M.A.: Recolha e análise de bio-sinais em ambientes abertos. Master's thesis, Master's dissertation - Universidade da Beira Interior (2018)
3. Biosignals, P.W.: Bitalino, December 2020. https://bitalino.com/
4. da Silva, H.P., Fred, A., Martins, R.: Biosignals for everyone. IEEE Pervasive Comput. **13**(4), 64–71 (2014)
5. de Miranda Tavares, P.M.: Development of a smart sensor node based on BITalino. Master's thesis, Master's dissertation - University of Oporto (2016)
6. Denning, T., Borning, A., Friedman, B., Gill, B.T., Kohno, T., Maisel, W.H.: Patients, pacemakers, and implantable defibrillators: human values and security for wireless implantable medical devices. In: Proceedings of the SIGCHI Conference on Human Factors in Computing Systems, CHI 2010, pp. 917–926. Association for Computing Machinery, New York (2010)
7. Dombrowski, Q., Gniady, T., Kloster, D.: Introduction to Jupyter Notebooks. The Programming Historian (2019)
8. Eng, A., Wahsheh, L.A.: Look into my eyes: a survey of biometric security. In: 2013 10th International Conference on Information Technology: New Generations, pp. 422–427 (2013)
9. Guerreiro, J., Martins, R., Plácido da Silva, H., Lourenco, A., Fred, A.: BITalino: a multimodal platform for physiological computing. In: Proceedings of the 10th International Conference on Informatics in Control, Automation and Robotics, ICINCO 2013, vol. 1, July 2013
10. Hamidi, H.: An approach to develop the smart health using internet of things and authentication based on biometric technology. Futur. Gener. Comput. Syst. **91**, 434–449 (2019)
11. Kumar, S., Singh, S.K.: Monitoring of pet animal in smart cities using animal biometrics. Futur. Gener. Comput. Syst. **83**, 553–563 (2018)
12. Matias, I., et al.: Prediction of atrial fibrillation using artificial intelligence on electrocardiograms: a systematic review. Comput. Sci. Rev. **39**, 100334 (2021)

13. Pires, I., Marques, G., Garcia, N., Flórez-Revuelta, F., Ponciano, V., Oniani, S.: A research on the classification and applicability of the mobile health applications. J. Personalized Med. **10**, 11 (2020)

14. Plácido da Silva, H., Guerreiro, J., Lourenco, A., Fred, A., Martins, R.: BITalino: a novel hardware framework for physiological computing. In: Proceedings of the International Conference on Physiological Computing Systems, PhyCS 2014, January 2014

15. Ponciano, V., Pires, I.M., Ribeiro, F.R., Garcia, N.M.: Data acquisition of timed-up and go test with older adults: accelerometer, magnetometer, electrocardiography and electroencephalography sensors' data. Data Brief **32**, 106306 (2020)

Comparative Analysis of Process Mining Algorithms in Python

André Filipe Domingos Gomes[1], Ana Cristina Wanzeller Guedes de Lacerda[2], and Joana Rita da Silva Fialho[3(✉)]

[1] Polytechnic Institute of Viseu, Viseu, Portugal
estgv15362@alunos.estgv.ipv.pt
[2] Escola Superior Tecnologia e Gestão de Viseu, CISeD, Polytechnic Institute of Viseu, Viseu, Portugal
cwanzeller@estgv.ipv.pt
[3] Escola Superior Tecnologia e Gestão de Viseu, CI&DEI, Polytechnic Institute of Viseu, Viseu, Portugal
jfialho@estgv.ipv.pt

Abstract. In many sectors, there is a large amount of data collected and stored, which is not analyzed. The health area is a good example. This situation is not desirable, as the data can provide historical information or trends that may help to improve organizations performance in the future. Process mining allows the extraction of knowledge from data generated and stored in the information systems.

This work aims to contribute to the aforementioned knowledge extraction, comparing different algorithms in process mining techniques, using health care processes and data. The results showed that Inductive Miner and Heuristic Miner are the algorithms with better results. Considering the execution times, Petri Net is the type of model that takes longer, but it is the one that allows a better analysis.

Keywords: Big data in healthcare · PM4Py · Process mining · Process discovery · Conformance checking

1 Introduction

Health processes are complex and involve steps performed by people from various disciplines and sub-areas. This complexity makes this area interesting, but difficult to analyze and understand. These processes make use of information systems that record large volumes of data, but which are difficult to exploit.

Process mining intends to gain knowledge about a particular running process and allows to have an accurate model of its behavior. The purpose is to improve the implementation and evaluation of health care processes. Moreover, the model can help configuring any additional requirements not included in the system [1].

To evaluate the feasibility of some process mining algorithms, using health care processes, each one will be tested to understand its limitations and advantages. For this

I. M. Pires et al. (Eds.): GOODTECHS 2021, LNICST 401, pp. 27–43, 2021.
https://doi.org/10.1007/978-3-030-91421-9_3

purpose, the Process Mining for Python framework (PM4Py) [2] will be used, as it allows an algorithmic customization that other tools do not allow. Furthermore, it has a good variety of other features of interest.

Usually, the event logs used for analysis provide timestamps for the steps/activities that compose the process, as well as their description and other information. The dataset used was extracted from the MIMIC-III database [3].

Subsequently, specific scenarios with certain characteristics are created in order to test different situations that may expose limitations of the algorithms. In addition, the variants are analyzed [4]: select the variants with more occurrences and exclude specific cases that could generate noise in the process analysis. It is also interesting to filter the dataset, taking into account features that make sense in the set of logs. Finally, we intend to test techniques and tools to verify the conformance of the generated model.

It is also possible to calculate different statistics on the event logs of the dataset, as well as to create graphs that allow to understand various aspects of the dataset.

This document is organized into 6 sections. In Sect. 2, the main process discovery algorithms are presented. Section 3 analyzes PM4Py, justifying the choice of this tool. Section 4 explains the experimental scenarios. Section 5 shows the results. Finally, Sect. 6 presents conclusions about this work and future work.

2   Process Mining Algorithms

In the last decade, process mining has emerged as a new field of research that focuses on process analysis, using event data. Classic data mining techniques do not focus on business process models [5]. Thus, process mining focuses on processes, step by step, because the availability of event data and new techniques are increasing, allowing the discovery and the conformance verification of the processes [6].

Process models are used to analyze process execution through Business Process Management (BPM) systems. These process management tools are widely used to support operational process administration. However, they do not use event data [7].

The activities performed by people, machines, and software leave traces in the so called event logs [5]. Process mining techniques use these logs to discover, analyze and improve business processes [8].

Process mining is used to find patterns and understand the causes of certain process behaviors. On the other hand, process mining helps to understand how processes are being performed. For this purpose, specialized mining algorithms are applied to identify patterns from event data recorded in the information management systems [9].

There are several algorithms for process mining. The internal local relations between the activity data are modeled by the Heuristic Miner algorithm. This is the most widely used algorithm, mainly due to its ability to deal with noisy[1] and incomplete data, common in the health area. Global or external relationships between activities are modeled by Genetic Miner algorithms [10] and Fuzzy Miner [11].

Alfa Miner algorithm examines the event log for specific patterns. This algorithm works, simultaneously, a set of sequences of events, following a certain activities order

---

[1] Noise is the result of data quality problems, such as registration errors, which infrequently manifest themselves in the behavior of the process [13].

in the event log, and shows the result in a Petri Net[2] project diagram. For example, if activity X is followed by Y, but Y is never followed by X, then it is assumed that there is a causal dependency between X and Y. However, Alpha Miner is unable to highlight the bottlenecks of the process [12].

Most business process mining tools use Directly-Follows Graph (DFGs) as a first approach of exploring event data. To deal with complexity, DFGs are simplified by removing nodes and edges based on frequency restrictions. This simplicity can make these DFGs misleading, as they can be misinterpreted, leading to different conclusions. In addition, bottleneck information can be misleading, especially after simplifying the model. This can lead to all kinds of interpretation problems, due to "invisible gaps" in the model [15].

Heuristic algorithms use the order or sequence of activities and the events frequency. They find the frequent and infrequent paths in the process. In this sense, they are more robust relatively to the process frequencies [16]. Heuristic Miner is very similar to Alpha algorithm, because it deals with similar problems. Furthermore, it catches more real problems. The Heuristic Miner uses logical XOR and AND connectors of dependency relationships. The result of this miner is a heuristic network that helps to visualize the process and predict the flow [12].

Inductive Miner is used widely in different areas, with very promising results. This algorithm has an improvement over the Alpha and Heuristics Miners, as it explore easily an event log. It ensures solidity, as it is able to deal with infrequent behaviors and large event logs. The basic concept of Inductive Miner is to detect a pattern in the logs and then search for that pattern until a base case is found [17].

Table 1 shows the algorithms comparison, according to their characteristics and limitations [18].

3   Process Mining for Python (PM4Py)

Process Mining for Python framework (PM4Py) [2] is a process mining software, easily extensible. It allows conducting large scale experiments easily, and also algorithmic customization. In addition, it is possible to integrate large-scale applications, through a new process mining library. Other libraries can be integrated, such as pandas, numpy, scipy and scikit-learn [20].

The main advantages of the PM4Py library are:

- Allows algorithmic development and customization more easily, when compared to existing tools like ProM [21], RapidProM [21], Disco [22] or Celonis [23];
- Enables easy integration of process mining algorithms with algorithms from other areas of data science, implemented in several state-of-the-art Python packages.
- PM4Py provides support for different types of event data structures, namely event logs, where each line is a list of events. Events are structured as key-value maps;

---

[2] A Petri net has two types of elements, positions and transitions. A position can contain one or more tokens. A transition is enabled if all inputs (positions connected to itself) contain, at least, one token [14].

Table 1. Comparison of Process Mining algorithms.

	Alpha Miner	Directly-Follows Graph	Heuristic Miner	Inductive Miner
Description	First mining approach that allows discovering a Workflow network from event logs.	Used as a first approach to exploit event data but can be misleading.	Generates a process model based on different frequency metrics.	It is an improvement over Alpha Miner and Heuristic Miner.
Output	Workflow network.	Directly-Follows Graph (DFG[a]).	Heuristic/casual network.	It can generate several types of models.
Challenges	Noise; Data incomplete; Loop involving one or two stages; Choose not free.	Activities that have a flexible order lead to Spaghetti[b] DFGs with loops	Split and join rules are only considered locally, which results in networks that are not solid.	Generates a solid model from a recursive pattern search.
Result	Extensions can face some challenges.	Performance information can be misleading; Interpretation problems due to gaps in the model.	Can mine long outbuildings successfully; Sometimes it generates many dependencies.	Generates a model that guarantees solidity.
Event logs	Does not deal with incomplete data or noise.	Does not handle long processes, due to its frequency limit.	Possibly, it can handle with incomplete data.	Handles with infrequent behavior and large event logs.

[a] Directly Follows are graphs where nodes represent events/activities in the log. Directed links between nodes exist if there is at least one trace in the log where the originating event/activity is followed by the target event/activity. On the top of these targeted links, metrics, such as frequency (counting the number of times the source event/activity is followed by the target event/activity) and performance (the average time between the two events/activities), are represented [15].

[b] For processes that are not well structured and have many different behaviors, existing process mining techniques generate highly complex models that are often difficult to understand; these models are called spaghetti models, or spaghetti [19].

- Provides conversion features to transform event data objects from one format to another. Also, PM4Py supports the use of Pandas data frames, which are efficient in case of using larger event data. Other objects currently supported by PM4Py include heuristic networks, Petri networks, process trees[3] and transition systems[4].

PM4Py provides several main process mining techniques, including:

- Process discovery, based on Alpha Miner algorithms [24], Directly-Follows Graph [15], Heuristic Miner [16] and Inductive Miner [17];
- Conformance verification, through token-based alignment and reproduction [25];
- Measurement of suitability, precision, generalization, and simplicity of process models [26];

---

[3] Process tree is a tree-structured process model, where leaf nodes represent activities, and non-leaf nodes represent control flow operators [28].

[4] Transitional system is used to describe the potential behavior of discrete systems. It consists of states and transitions between states [29].

- Filtering based on time interval, case performance, input and output events, variants, attributes, and paths;
- Case management: statistics on variants and cases;
- Graphs: duration of the case, events by time, distribution of numeric attribute values;
- Social Network Analysis [27]: work handover, joint work, subcontracting and networks of related activities.

PM4Py also provides Python visualization libraries, such as:

- GraphViz: representation of direct sequence graphs, Petri Nets, transition systems, process trees;
- NetworkX: static representation of social networks;
- Pyvis: dynamic web-based social network representation.

4 Data and Experimental Scenario

For the experimental scenarios, data was selected and processed, from the MIMIC-III database. Then, data was converted into the necessary format for the process discovery algorithms of PM4Py application. Finally, for a better analysis of the algorithms, certain test scenarios were defined in order to expose them to different challenges.

4.1 Data Processing

The table schema of the MIMIC-III database (demo version) was analyzed to find the desired information for the test dataset. A subset of tables was selected satisfying the proposed requirements, Fig. 1.

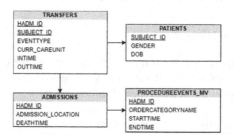

Fig. 1. Scheme of test data.

Analyzing the scheme, the main table is TRANSFERS. It contains the physical locations of patients during hospitalization. The main attributes of this table are: the care unit (CURR_CAREUNIT), if it is a specialty; the entry date and time (INTIME) and the exit date and time (OUTTIME); the type of event (EVENTTYPE) which can be one of three: *admit,* for procedures performed in the patient's admission/evaluation phase; *transef* for the patient's transfer/stay phases and *discharge* for the patient's discharge phases.

Note that, when there is no specialty, the acronym GCU was inserted, translated into General Care Unit. The description of the remaining acronyms of the specialized care units are presented in the Table 2.

Table 2. Description of care units (Adapted from https://mimic.physionet.org/mimictables/transf ers/).

Care unit	Description
CCU	Coronary care unit
CSRU	Cardiac surgery recovery unit
MICU	Medical intensive care unit
NICU	Neonatal intensive care unit
NWARD	Neonatal ward
SICU	Surgical intensive care unit
TSICU	Trauma/surgical intensive care unit

The SUBJECT_ID attribute connects to the PATIENTS table, which has information about the patients, namely the attributes gender (GENDER) and date of birth (DOB).

Subsequently, HADM_ID attribute is used to access the ADMISSIONS table that contains information about the patient's admission. Using this table, it is possible to collect information about the type/place of admission (ADMISSION_LOCATION) and date of discharge (DISCHTIME) or death (DEATHTIME). It also allows accessing to the PROCEDUREEVENTS_MV table to obtain data related to the events performed in each admission.

The PROCEDUREEVENTS_MV table includes the name of the process (ORDER-CATEGORYNAME) and the date and time of start (STARTTIME) and end (ENDTIME) of the process. Notice that, at this stage, the processes are synchronized with the physical locations, by the respective start/entry and end/exit dates.

4.2 Preparation of the Dataset

From the excel data importation, the respective treatment was made to obtain the dataset format required for the application of the PM4Py process discovery algorithms.

The required format consists in 3 types of information:

- Case ID - a unique identifier for each process;
- Event - a step in the process, any activity that is part of the process;
- Timestamp - date and time for a given event.

The HADM_ID was used as a case identifier, because it is unique. For each stage of the process, the type of event (admission, transfer, or discharge), the care unit (an identifying acronym) and the name of the process performed were added. For the timestamp of the stage, the start date of the process was used or, in cases where a process was not identified, the date of entry into the care unit.

Moreover, other information was used, such as the type of admission, the type of exit (death or discharge), the patient's date of birth, the gender, and the day of the week on which the event has occurred. In the end, possible duplications were removed from the synchronization of processes with physical locations. Notice that, to use the algorithms in this dataset, the dataset was converted into log format, ordered by timestamp, getting a total of 1163 logs.

4.3   Test Scenarios for the Algorithms

Through the algorithm's analysis and comparison, it was verified that loops between steps and duplications may arise. Thus, admissions were selected to allow testing all these scenarios in isolation.

In an initial scenario, simple admissions were chosen, where none of the cases described above were verified. This scenario, Fig. 2, has, as main objective, a first interaction to test algorithms and their models.

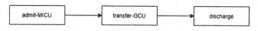

Fig. 2. Simple scenario.

Next, a scenario with duplicate steps, Fig. 3, was selected: there is a step that occurs repeatedly.

Fig. 3. Scenario with duplicate steps.

In the last scenario, the algorithms were exposed to loops between steps. Figure 4 shows a loop occurrence between 2 steps.

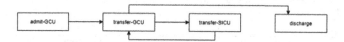

Fig. 4. Scenario with loops between stages.

5   Results

In this section, the results of the tests are presented. The models generated for each tested scenario, execution times, analysis of the log set variants, log set, log set statistics and conformance verification are presented and analyzed.

5.1   Models Analysis for Each Test Scenario

Table 3 presents the models results from the test scenarios. Alpha Miner is unable to create a valid Petri Net model, because it isolates duplicate steps. This result was predictable because this algorithm, admittedly, does not support duplicate steps, neither

Table 3. Models for each test scenario.

Algorithm	Scenario	Result	Models
Alpha Miner	Simple	Valid	
	With duplicate steps	Invalid	
	With loops between 2 steps	Invalid	
Directly-Follows Graph	Simple	Valid	
	With duplicate steps	Valid	
	With loops between 2 steps	Valid	
	For all logs	Invalid	[Spaghetti models]
Heuristic Miner	Simple	Valid	
	With duplicate steps	Valid	
	With loops between 2 steps	Valid	
	For all logs	Valid	[Spaghetti models]
Inductive Miner	Simple	Valid	
	With duplicate steps	Valid	
	With loops between 2 steps	Valid	
	For all logs	Valid	[Spaghetti models]

loops of length one or two [18]. For loops between 2 steps, it generates an invalid Petri Net model, isolating one of the loop steps.

For all logs, Directly-Follows Graph generated a log too large, a spaghetti model. Despite generating this DFG model, it is not a valid one, as the admissions are broken. This result can be justified due the fact that the DFGs are simplified, removing nodes and connections based on frequency limits [15]. However, for other scenarios, the DFG model performance can be considered good.

Heuristic Miner allows the presentation of the frequency of the stages and connections, but it does not mark the most frequent stages and connections [16], which is a disadvantage relatively to Petri Net. This algorithm is compatible with duplicate steps and loop challenges. When the algorithm was converted to Petri Net, the model showed hidden transactions. For a larger number of logs the resulting model is difficult to analyze, as it has created spaghetti models.

Considering all logs, Inductive Miner seems to generate a smaller model, with fewer steps and connections. An explanation of this result may be the improvement that this algorithm has in the search for splits/patterns in the logs. Moreover, it uses many hidden transactions to overcome loops in parts of the model [26].

5.2 Execution Times

Table 4 shows the average of the execution times, in seconds, of the Heuristic Miner and Inductive Miner algorithms for the entire set of logs. These algorithms were able to present a valid model. Notice that each algorithm and model were tested 5 times, under the same conditions, and the average time was calculated after removing the maximum and minimum times. The execution times correspond to the execution of the algorithms, because all logs were already loaded into memory.

Table 4. Execution times for the entire set of logs.

Heuristic Miner	Heuristics Net	Petri Net	Inductive Miner	Process Tree	Petri Net
	4.655	83,254		14,967	34,700

5.3 Variant Analysis

The analysis of variants is extremely important, as it considers the number of occurrences of the variants. This analysis allows to remove the least relevant variants. A variant is a set of cases that share the same perspective of control flow, therefore, a set of cases that share the same events/activities, in the same order [4].

Inductive Miner algorithm was used in this analysis. The results are in Table 5 and contain the description of the variant, the number of occurrences and the respective percentage. Table 6 presents the models generated for different frequencies of variants. The remaining variants have a lower number of occurrences and were discharged. If they were considered, all logs were included, which could turn the analysis impossible and inefficient.

Table 5. Variants.

	Variant	Number of occurrences	Percentage
0	admit-MICU, transfer-GCU, discharge	10	7.75%
1	admit-MICU, discharge	5	3.88%
2	admit-TSICU, discharge	4	3.10%
3	admit-MICU, transfer-GCU, transfer-GCU, discharge	3	2.33%
4	admit-MICU-Peripheral Lines, transfer-GCU, discharge	2	1.55%
5	admit-GCU, transfer-SICU, transfer-GCU, transfer-GCU, transfer-GCU, discharge	2	1.55%
6	admit-GCU, transfer-GCU, transfer-SICU, transfer-GCU, discharge	2	1.55%
7	admit-GCU, transfer-GCU, transfer-GCU, transfer-MICU, transfer-GCU, discharge	2	1.55%
8	admit-GCU, transfer-GCU, transfer-GCU, transfer-MICU, discharge	2	1.55%
9	admit-CCU, transfer-GCU, transfer-GCU, discharge	2	1.55%
10... 104	...	1	0.78%

Table 6. Models of different frequencies of variants.

Number of occurrences	Number of Variants	Model
10 or more	1	
5 or more	2	
4 or more	3	
3 or more	4	
2 or more	10	

5.4 Filtering Event Data

In this section, filtrations were tested, Table 7, in the most frequent variants, in order to analyze the process in a different detail. Inductive Miner algorithm was used with the result in a Petri Net model.

5.5 Log Set Statistics

In PM4Py, it is possible to calculate different statistics on the event logs. At Table 8 two statistics can be analyzed using the dataset: average case duration and case dispersion ratio. This last is the average distance between the completion of two consecutive cases in the log.

It is also possible to create graphics, Table 9, to understand various aspects of the dataset used in the model, such as, for example, the distribution of a numeric attribute, the distribution of the case duration, or the distribution of events over time.

Table 7. Filtering models.

Filtering	Value	Model
Timeframe	"2161-09-19 17:54:42"; "2163-11-21 19:01:00"	
Start activity	"admit-TSICU"; "admit-MICU-Peripheral Lines"	
Attributes values	Type of admission: "TRANSFER FROM SKILLED NUR"	

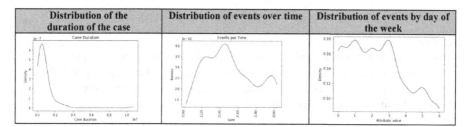

Table 8. Statistics results to dataset.

Statistics	
Average duration of cases	Average distance
571283.0	93077625.03

Table 9. Event distribution graphs.

Distribution of the duration of the case	Distribution of events over time	Distribution of events by day of the week

5.6 Conformance Verification for Test Logs

Conformance verification is a technique to compare the predicted/expected model of the process with the real model of the process, that is, the set of real event logs for that process. The objective is to verify if the logs are in accordance with the model and vice versa [30]. In PM4Py, two fundamental techniques can be implemented: token-based reproduction and alignments [26].

For this analysis, Inductive Miner algorithm was used with the result in a Petri Net model. Variants with one occurrence were removed. Furthermore, when necessary, a set of two logs was used, where one of them belongs to the predictive model and the other does not.

Token-Based Repetition

The token-based replay corresponds to a Petri Net tracking model, starting from the initial location, to find out which transitions are performed and in which locations there are remaining or missing tokens for the tested log instance. A log conforms to the model if, during its execution, transitions can be triggered without the need to insert any missing tokens [31].

For the model and the set of logs tested, the result is represented in Fig. 5. In the first log, it is clear that the model was unable to satisfy it. The attribute *trace_is_fit* is False, because, in the attribute *transitions_with_problems*, there was a transition in which the path was unable to follow. Hence, 9 produced tokens were consumed and 1 token was missing. Since it managed to satisfy a large part of the route, *trace_fitness* ends up being close to 1, being approximately 0.889.

For the second log, *trace_is_fit* is True. Thus, the model satisfied all the transitions of the log, having consumed all tokens produced, 10, and with no remaining or missing tokens.

trace_is_fit	trace_fitness	activated_transitions	reached_marking	enabled_transitions_in_marking	transitions_with_problems	missing_tokens	consumed_tokens	remaining_tokens	produced_tokens
False	0.8888888888 888888	[admit-GCU, tauSplit_2, transfer-MICU, transfer-MICU, transfer-GCU, tauJoin_3, discharge]	['p_11:1', 'sink:1']	set()	[transfer-MICU]	1	9	1	9
True	1.0	[admit-MICU, tauSplit_2, transfer-GCU, transfer-MICU, skip_6, transfer-GCU, tauJoin_3, discharge]	['sink:1']	set()	[]	0	10	0	10

Fig. 5. Conformance results using token-based repetition.

Alignments

Alignment-based reproduction aims to find one of the best alignments between the log and the model. For each log, the output of an alignment is a list of pairs where the first element is a log event and the second element is a model transition. For each pair, the following classification can be provided [32]:

- Synchronization movement: the classification of the event corresponds to the name of the transition; in this case, the log and the model advance in the same way during the replay;
- Move in the record: pairs where the second element is». This symbol in the second element corresponds to a repetition movement in the log that is not similar in the model. This type of movement is inappropriate and there is a deviation between the log and the model;
- Move in the model: pairs where the first element is». This situation corresponds to a repetition movement in the model that is not similar in the log. For movements in the model, we can make the following distinction:

  - Movements in the model involving hidden transitions: in this case, even if it is not a synchronized movement, the movement is adequate;
  - Movements in the model that do not involve hidden transitions: in this case, the movement is inappropriate and means a deviation between the log and the model.

Each log conformance check is associated with a dictionary, containing, among others, the following information:

- Alignment: contains the alignment (synchronization movements, movements in the register, movements in the model);
- Cost: contains the cost of the alignment according to the cost function provided, which can be customized;
- Fitness: is equal to 1 if the log is perfectly adequate.

For the model and the set of logs tested, the first log had a fitness close to 1, that is, there is an adaptation to the model close to 1 (but lower than 1), indicating that it was not able to complete the entire process path from the model. On the other hand, in the second log, the process was able to finalize the log path, Fig. 6.

alignment	cost	queued_states	visited_states	closed_set_length	num_visited_markings	exact_heu_calculations	fitness
[('admit-GCU', 'admit-GCU'), ('transfer-MICU', '>>'), ('>>', None), ('transfer-MICU', 'transfer-MICU'), ('transfer-GCU', 'transfer-GCU'), ('>>', None), ('discharge', 'discharge')]	10000	20	10	7	8	3	0.8571428571428572
[('admit-MICU', 'admit-MICU'), ('>>', None), ('transfer-GCU', 'transfer-GCU'), ('transfer-MICU', 'transfer-MICU'), ('>>', None), ('transfer-GCU', 'transfer-GCU'), ('>>', None), ('discharge', 'discharge')]	0	21	10.	8	8	1	1.0

Fig. 6. Results of alignments.

Overall Assessment of the Model by the Set of Test Logs

In PM4Py, it is possible to obtain different information on the comparison between the behavior contained in the test logs and the behavior contained in the model, to verify if and how they correspond. There are four different dimensions of conformance in Process Mining: the measurement of the adequacy of the replay, the measurement of precision, the measurement of generalization and the measurement of simplicity.

The calculation of the adequacy of the replay aims to calculate how much of the behavior in the log is admitted by the process model. Two methods are proposed to calculate the adequacy of replay: replay and alignments, both based on token, previously used for isolated logs.

For precision or accuracy, the set of transitions in the process model is compared with the set of activities logs that follow the model [26]. For that, unvisited branches are counted. Unvisited branches are decisions that are possible in the model and not in the event log. If not, the accuracy is perfect. This analysis can also be obtained from the two methods mentioned in the previous subsection, where token-based reproduction is faster, but based on heuristics. Therefore, the result may not be accurate [31]. Alignments are accurate, work on any type of network, but can be slow [32].

Generalization is the third dimension to analyze how the log and the process model coincide. Basically, a model is general if the elements of the model are visited often enough during a reproduction operation.

Finally, simplicity is the fourth dimension for analyzing a process model. In this case, simplicity is defined considering only the Petri Net model. This metric considers the number of incoming and outgoing connections that each transition has [33]. For all these metrics, the resulting value varies between 0 and 1.

Figure 7 describes those evaluations, showing that, according to the calculation of the adequacy of the replay, the adaptation of the set of logs tested to the model was high, but not complete. Precision, on the other hand, proved to be quite low, for both approaches. The using of hidden transactions and the fact of one of the logs had not completed the path can explain this result. The set of logs tested has many repeated steps, leading to a low generalization. Besides, it was considered a few steps in the model. As the model has hidden transactions and loops, simplicity is low, since there are situations of join or split in steps.

Replay Fitness		Precision		Generalization	Simplicity
Token-based Replay	Alignments	Token-based Replay	Alignments		
0.944444444444444	0.9285714285714286	0.34615384615384615	0.34615384615384615	0.12314136557579325	0.5789473684210527

Fig. 7. Results of the evaluation of the Log-Model.

6 Conclusion

From the results with the experience scenarios, Alpha Miner was not able to deal with duplicated steps and loops between two steps. Directly-Follows Graph achieved that, but in turn, for a larger set of logs, the generated model was invalid, not being able to represent cases with more than 5 steps.

For the other algorithms, they were really able to deal with challenges and larger volumes of logs. Inductive Miner was the algorithm that better handled with duplicated steps and loops between 2 steps. It uses hidden steps more recurrently, mainly in loop parts.

Considering the models tested, the Process Trees are the most difficult to analyze due to their syntax. The Petri Net models proved to be more efficient and structured. Based on the execution times, Petri Net is the type of model that takes longer to run for a larger volume of logs but allows a better analysis.

For large amounts of data, the Petri Net model of Inductive Miner was the one that had the longest execution time, but it was also the one that had the best result. Due to the improvement that this algorithm has, the model, in general, is more organized and easier to analyze [26].

Table 10 summarizes the results achieved where the comparison parameters are presented in order of priority. If an algorithm has limitations to challenges, it is no longer analyzed in the next parameters. Thus, the most suitable algorithm is the Inductive Miner.

Table 10. Summary of the conclusions.

Algorithm	Limitations on challenges	Petri Net model simplicity	Runtime
Alpha Miner	-		
Directly-Follows Graph	-		
Heuristic Miner	+	-	-
Inductive Miner	+	+	+

For future work it is intended to expand these experiences to different areas and types of dataset. Another important aspect would be the execution of these same tests in other existing tools, as they may have different implementations of algorithms and functionalities.

Acknowledgements. This work is funded by National Funds through the FCT - Foundation for Science and Technology, I.P., within the scope of the project Ref UIDB/05583/2020. Furthermore, we would like to thank the Research Centre in Digital Services (CISeD), the Polytechnic of Viseu for their support.

This work is also funded by National Funds through the FCT - Foundation for Science and Technology, I.P., within the scope of the project Refª UIDB/05507/2020. Furthermore we would like to thank the Centre for Studies in Education and Innovation (CI&DEI) and the Polytechnic of Viseu for their support.

References

1. Hendricks, R.: Process mining of incoming patients with sepsis. Online J. Public Health Inform. **11**(2) (2019). https://doi.org/10.5210/ojphi.v11i2.10151
2. Fraunhofer Institute for Applied Information Technology: Process Mining for Python (PM4Py). Process Mining for Python (PM4Py) (2021). https://pypi.org/project/pm4py/
3. Kurniati, A.P., Hall, G., Hogg, D., Johnson, O.: Process mining in oncology using the MIMIC-III dataset. In: Journal of Physics: Conference Series, vol. 971, no. 1 (2018). https://doi.org/10.1088/1742-6596/971/1/012008
4. Bolt, A., van der Aalst, W.M.P., de Leoni, M.: Finding process variants in event logs. In: Panetto, H., et al. (eds.) OTM 2017. LNCS, vol. 10573, pp. 45–52. Springer, Cham (2017). https://doi.org/10.1007/978-3-319-69462-7_4
5. Van Der Aalst, W.: Process mining: overview and opportunities. ACM Trans. Manag. Inf. Syst. **3**(2), 1–17 (2012). https://doi.org/10.1145/2229156.2229157
6. Mans, R.S., Van Der Aalst, W.M.P., Vanwersch, R.J.B.: Process Mining in the Healthcare (2015)
7. Pegoraro, M., Uysal, M.S., van der Aalst, W.M.P.: Discovering process models from uncertain event data. In: Di Francescomarino, C., Dijkman, R., Zdun, U. (eds.) BPM 2019. LNBIP, vol. 362, pp. 238–249. Springer, Cham (2019). https://doi.org/10.1007/978-3-030-37453-2_20
8. Batista, E., Solanas, A.: Process mining in healthcare: a systematic review. In: 2018 9th International Conference on Information, Intelligence, Systems and Applications, IISA 2018, pp. 1–6 (2019). https://doi.org/10.1109/IISA.2018.8633608
9. Rojas, E., Cifuentes, A., Burattin, A., Munoz-Gama, J., Sepúlveda, M., Capurro, D.: Performance analysis of emergency room episodes through process mining. Int. J. Environ. Res. Public Health **16**(7) (2019). https://doi.org/10.3390/ijerph16071274
10. Shinde, S.A., Rajeswari, P.R.: Intelligent health risk prediction systems using machine learning: a review. Int. J. Eng. Technol. (UAE) **7**(3), 1019–1023 (2018). https://doi.org/10.14419/ijet.v7i3.12654
11. Wang, L., Du, Y., Qi, L.: Efficient deviation detection between a process model and event logs. IEEE/CAA J. Automatica Sinica **6**(6), 1352–1364 (2019). https://doi.org/10.1109/JAS.2019.1911750
12. Sundari, M.S., Nayak, R.K.: Process mining in healthcare systems: a critical review and its future. Int. J. Emerg. Trends Eng. Res. **8**(9), 5197–5208 (2020). https://doi.org/10.30534/ijeter/2020/50892020

13. Conforti, R., La Rosa, M., ter Hofstede, A.H.M.: Noise Filtering of Process Execution Logs based on Outliers Detection. Institute for Future Environments, School of Information Systems; Science & Engineering Faculty, pp. 1–16 (2015)
14. de Petri, R.: Rede de Petri. Wikipédia, a enciclopédia livre (2019). https://pt.wikipedia.org/w/index.php?title=Rede_de_Petri&oldid=55172483
15. Van Der Aalst, W.M.P.: A practitioner's guide to process mining: limitations of the directly-follows graph. Procedia Comput. Sci. **164**, 321–328 (2019). https://doi.org/10.1016/j.procs.2019.12.189
16. Weijters, A.J.M.M., van der Aalst, W.M.P., de Medeiros, A.K.A.: Process Mining with the Heuristics Miner Algorithm. Beta Working Papers (2006)
17. Bogarín, A., Cerezo, R., Romero, C.: Discovering learning processes using inductive miner: a case study with learning management systems (LMSs). Psicothema **30**(3), 322–329 (2018). https://doi.org/10.7334/psicothema2018.116
18. Breitmayer, M.: Applying Process Mining Algorithms in the Context of Data Collection Scenarios (2018)
19. Veiga, G.M., Ferreira, D.R.: Understanding spaghetti models with sequence clustering for ProM. In: Rinderle-Ma, S., Sadiq, S., Leymann, F. (eds.) BPM 2009. LNBIP, vol. 43, pp. 92–103. Springer, Heidelberg (2010). https://doi.org/10.1007/978-3-642-12186-9_10
20. Berti, A., Van Zelst, S.J., Van Der Aalst, W.M.P., Gesellschaf, F.: Process mining for python (PM4py): bridging the gap between process-and data science. In: CEUR Workshop Proceedings, vol. 2374, pp. 13–16 (2019)
21. van Dongen, B.F., de Medeiros, A.K.A., Verbeek, H.M.W., Weijters, A.J.M.M., van der Aalst, W.M.P.: The ProM framework: a new era in process mining tool support. In: Ciardo, G., Darondeau, P. (eds.) ICATPN 2005. LNCS, vol. 3536, pp. 444–454. Springer, Heidelberg (2005). https://doi.org/10.1007/11494744_25
22. Lohmann, N.M.: Discover Your Processes Disc. Proceedings, September (2012)
23. Badakhshan, P., Geyer-Klingeberg, J., El-Halaby, M., Lutzeyer, T., Affonseca, G.V.L.: Celonis process repository: a bridge between business process management and process mining. In: CEUR Workshop Proceedings, vol. 2673, pp. 67–71 (2020)
24. Van Der Aalst, W., Weijters, T., Maruster, L.: Workflow mining: discovering process models from event logs. IEEE Trans. Knowl. Data Eng. **16**(9), 1128–1142 (2004). https://doi.org/10.1109/TKDE.2004.47
25. Adriansyah, A., Sidorova, N., Van Dongen, B.F.: Cost-based fitness in conformance checking. In: Proceedings - International Conference on Application of Concurrency to System Design, ACSD 2011, pp. 57–66 (2011). https://doi.org/10.1109/ACSD.2011.19
26. Pohl, T.: An Inductive Miner Implementation for the PM4PY Framework, pp. 1–66 (2019)
27. van der Aalst, W.M.P., Song, M.: Mining social networks: uncovering interaction patterns in business processes. In: Desel, J., Pernici, B., Weske, M. (eds.) BPM 2004. LNCS, vol. 3080, pp. 244–260. Springer, Heidelberg (2004). https://doi.org/10.1007/978-3-540-25970-1_16
28. Arriagada-Benítez, M., Sepúlveda, M., Munoz-Gama, J., Buijs, J.C.A.M.: Strategies to automatically derive a process model from a configurable process model based on event data. Appl. Sci. (Switzerland) **7**(10) (2017). https://doi.org/10.3390/app7101023
29. See, E.: Transition System on, pp. 1–17 (2005)
30. Munoz-Gama, J., Carmona, J.: Enhancing precision in process conformance: stability, confidence, and severity. In: IEEE SSCI 2011: Symposium Series on Computational Intelligence - CIDM 2011: 2011 IEEE Symposium on Computational Intelligence and Data Mining, pp. 184–191 (2011). https://doi.org/10.1109/CIDM.2011.5949451
31. Berti, A., van der Aalst, W.M.P.: A novel token-based replay technique to speed up conformance checking and process enhancement. In: Koutny, M., Kordon, F., Pomello, L. (eds.) Transactions on Petri Nets and Other Models of Concurrency XV. LNCS, vol. 12530, pp. 1–26. Springer, Heidelberg (2021). https://doi.org/10.1007/978-3-662-63079-2_1

32. Bloemen, V., Van Zelst, S., Van Der Aalst, W.: Aligning Observed and Modeled Behavior by Maximizing Synchronous Moves and Using Milestones (2019)
33. Buijs, J.C.A.M., Van Dongen, B.F., Van Der Aalst, W.M.P.: Quality dimensions in process discovery: the importance of fitness, precision, generalization, and simplicity. Int. J. Coop. Inf. Syst. **23**(1), 1–39 (2014). https://doi.org/10.1142/S0218843014400012

COVID-19 Next Day Trend Forecast

Marcelo Costa[1], Margarida Rodrigues[1], Pedro Baptista[1],
João Henriques[1,3,4(✉)], Ivan Miguel Pires[1,2,4], Cristina Wanzeller[1,4],
and Filipe Caldeira[1,4]

[1] Department of Computer Science, Polytechnic of Viseu, 3504-510 Viseu, Portugal
{estgv16800,estgv16061,estgv17058}@alunos.estgv.ipv.pt,
{joaohenriques,impires,cwanzeller,caldeira}@estgv.ipv.pt
[2] Instituto de Telecomunicações, Universidade da Beira Interior,
6200-001 Covilhã, Portugal
[3] Department of Informatics Engineering, University of Coimbra,
3030-290 Coimbra, Portugal
[4] CISeD—Research Centre in Digital Services, Polytechnic of Viseu,
3504-510 Viseu, Portugal

Abstract. Historically, weather conditions are depicted as an essential factor to be considered in predicting variation infections due to respiratory diseases, including influenza and Severe Acute Respiratory Syndrome SARS-CoV-2, best known as COVID-19. Predicting the number of cases will contribute to plan human and non-human resources in hospital facilities, including beds, ventilators, and support policy decisions on sanitary population warnings, and help to provision the demand for COVID-19 tests. In this work, an integrated framework predicts the number of cases for the upcoming days by considering the COVID-19 cases and temperature records supported by a kNN algorithm.

Keywords: KNN · COVID-19 cases · Temperature

1 Introduction

In 2003, in Guangdong, the outbreak of Severe Acute Respiratory Syndrome (SARS) gradually disappeared with the arrival of warm weather. Temperature and its variations may have affected the SARS outbreak [14]. Few studies report that COVID-19 was related to meteorological factors, which decreased with increasing temperature. On 28 November, Portugal recorded more than 280.000 COVID-19 cases [4]. After the peak in the first wave on 17 April, the curve began to decrease. According to experts, one of the main factors was lockdown [3,5]. By this time of the year, the season in Portugal is Spring, which means the average temperature is around 11 °C and 20 °C. An analysis of the number of COVID-19 cases and the places manifested more intensively was carried out. The conclusion was that a very close relationship between the new cases and the climate could be established. The data analysis revealed that SARS-Cov2

I. M. Pires et al. (Eds.): GOODTECHS 2021, LNICST 401, pp. 44–50, 2021.
https://doi.org/10.1007/978-3-030-91421-9_4

increases virulence with temperatures between 6 °C and 11 °C and the presence of lower humidity levels in the air [2]. According to DGS, Portugal is in the second wave of COVID-19. Portugal is also facing the flu season, with the aggravating factor that the amount of flu vaccines available was manifestly insufficient [8,12]. National Health System includes 21,000 beds as the total capacity, while 17,700 are allocated to COVID-19 assistance [11]. The number of COVID-19 cases growth put pressure on hospitals. On 4 November, Portugal realized 444 hospitalized patients by COVID-19 in the Intensive Care Unit (ICU), which is 90% of the capacity of the ICU [6]. In 2016 the ICU occupation average was above 75% [10], considering this behavior is stable across the years. Another question raises how prevent ICU rupture if these numbers get back to previous years standard value. Given the lack of evidence, it is essential to understand the weather conditions impact on COVID-19 transmission. In this case, the relationship between weather conditions and several COVID-19 cases exists. It will be possible help to manage human resources and keep up with the demand for beds material resources (beds, ventilators, etc.) in hospital facilities and help sanitary populations' warnings decisions.

The remainder of this work is organized as follows. Section 2 presents the related work. Section 3 presents the architecture. Section 4 supporting our approach to assess data quality. In Sect. 5 we present the final product preview. Finally, in Sect. 6 conclusions are drawn, followed by future work guidelines.

2   Related Work

As in a common sense, weather conditions are an essential factor that impacts the number of infections due to respiratory diseases, such as Severe Acute Respiratory Syndrome (SARS) and influenza, also known as "the flu". Studies presented after the outbreak of SARS concluded the disease gradually disappeared with the arrival of warm weather. Temperature and its variations may have affected the SARS outbreak [14]. An exciting study relates the number of COVID-19 deaths in Wuhan with the temperature and humidity. The conclusions reached by this study were that the daily mortality of COVID-19 is positively correlated with DTR (diurnal temperature range) but negatively with absolute humidity. This study suggests the temperature variation and humidity may also be important factors affecting the COVID-19 mortality [9]. Another study pursues the relationship between ambient temperature and daily COVID-19 confirmed cases in 122 Chinese cities. The results indicate that mean temperature linearly relates with the number of COVID-19 cases when the temperature is below 3 °C. Notwithstanding, no evidence supporting such and relationship, especially a decreasing number of COVID-19 cases when the weather gets warmer [15].

3   Architecture

The following elements were identified to obtain prediction results: the sensors (DH11) and the board (Raspberry Pi 3), the API, the database, and the trained prediction model. Each of these is represented on Image 1.

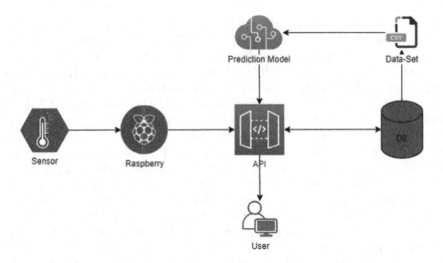

Fig. 1. Solution architecture

Each raspberry pi and the respective DH11 sensor are installed in the area where the user wants to obtain the prediction. It's a requisite to ensure the COVID-19 number of new cases are available for the selected geographic area. Temperature data is stored through API calls on the database server. This persistent data is used for temperature mean calculation and provided when needed to the predictive model. The following variables were selected to train the model:

- Health sub-region;
- The municipalities average maximum temperature in the health sub-region for the respective date;
- The municipalities average maximum temperature in the health sub-region between day n and n − 7 days;
- Comparing the average of the number of new cases of COVID-19 in the health sub-region counties between days n and n − 7 and the number of new cases of n.

The target consists of predicting whether the number of new cases of n + 1 is higher or lower than the number of new cases of n (n = current day).

4   Experiment

The experiment involved a Raspberry PI (version 3) with a DH11 attached. The central server, deployed as a Virtual Machine, consists of 2 cores operating at 3 GHz with 4 GB of RAM, running the API and the predictive Model. The MongoDB Atlas service provided the database support. APIs providing the municipality temperature data [7] and COVID-19 cases [13] were collected with a Python application. This application aggregates municipalities by health sub-region and averages their maximum temperature. After collecting temperature data, we accessed the COVID-19 API and extracted the number of cases corresponding to each health sub-region. The application produces a CSV file and includes the following features: date, health sub-region of the North, number of cases in the North, health sub-region of the "Centro", number of cases in the "Centro", health sub-region of "Lisboa and Vale do Tejo", number of cases in "Lisboa and Vale do Tejo", health sub-region of "Alentejo", number of cases in "Alentejo", health sub-region of "Algarve", number of cases in the "Algarve". Subsequently, another Python program was developed that creates our dataset CSV file including the following features:

– Health sub-region;
– Daily municipalities average maximum temperature for health sub-region;
– Municipalities average maximum temperature for sub-region between n and n − 7 (days);
– Average number of new cases of COVID-19 in the municipalities of the health sub-region between n and n − 7 (days);
– Number of new cases from n.

Our approach is to predict whether the tomorrow's number of new cases (day n + 1) by considering the number of new cases occurred today (day n). A training dataset will be considered as input to the predictive model. With all mounting and setup done, we collected the previous temperature and COVID-19 data to train our model. It's possible to keep "feeding" our dataset through this API and test different predictive models' inputs. A visual explanation is available on Image 2.

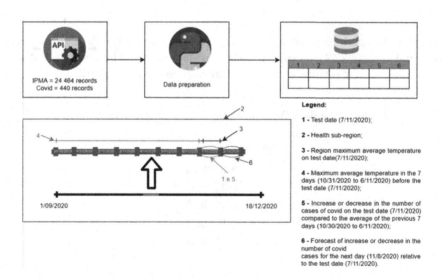

Fig. 2. Dataset diagram

5   Results

Our previous analysis supported selecting the kNN as the first algorithm for our predictive model, which makes predictions using the training dataset directly. Predictions were made for a new instance (x) by searching through the entire training set for the K most similar instances (the neighbors) and summarizing the output variable for those K instances. For regression, this might be the mean output variable. In classification, this might be the mode (or most common) class value [1]. The distance was used to determine the most similar K instances in the training dataset to a new input. For real-valued input variables, the most popular distance measure is Euclidean distance. After tuning the K value, we conclude that 3 corresponds to the value providing the higher accuracy while the chosen metric was Minkowski. The Table 1 shows the accuracy values obtained with kNN for different day intervals and 15% and 30% test size.

Table 1. kNN accuracy scores (k = 3)

Days	15%	30%
6	0.49	0.55
7	0.66	0.58
8	0.54	0.44
9	0.45	0.47
10	0.59	0.50

Further research and testing allowed us to explore the Random Forest algorithm and achieve 72.4% accuracy with 41 n_estimators. This result will define the response of our predictive model setup as presented in Table 2.

Table 2. Random Forest accuracy scores (n_estimators = 41)

Days	15%	30%
6	0.45	0.54
7	0.72	0.61
8	0.56	0.52
9	0.45	0.52
10	0.53	0.47

6   Conclusion

Predictive analytic tools give users deep, real-time insights into an almost endless array of business activities. These tools can be used to predict different behaviors and patterns, including the demand for COVID-19 tests, basing predictions on an analysis of data collected over some time. According to the achieved result, the presented model is achieved 72% accuracy in predicting the number of COVID-19 cases for the next day. For this result, we considered as main variables the temperature and evolution of the last 7 days of the number of COVID-19 cases. This model may be implemented under any circumstances considering temperature collection is ensured, and the number of new cases of COVID-19 in the area concerned is known. Following the implementation of the proposed architecture, it is possible to set up a complete system without substantial investment. It was also essential to state the importance of "days interval" in the model. As the first symptoms appear after the 4 days, knowing that, between the COVID-19 test schedule and the result's registration. Next, the patients wait 2 or 3 days. The results obtained are consistent with the sources consulted. On the seventh day, we established the relationship capable of generating the most satisfactory results regarding the prediction.

It will become essential to consider a more extended period of days as the forecasting weather conditions are pretty precise. Moreover, given the low achieved model accuracy suggests exploring new features, such as the humidity, day of the week, or wind speed.

Acknowledgements. This work is funded by FCT/MEC through national funds and, when applicable, co-funded by the FEDER-PT2020 partnership agreement under the project **UIDB/50008/2020**. (*Este trabalho é financiado pela FCT/MEC através de fundos nacionais e cofinanciado pelo FEDER, no âmbito do Acordo de Parceria PT2020 no âmbito do projeto UIDB/50008/2020*). This work is also funded by National Funds through the FCT - Foundation for Science and Technology, I.P., within the scope of the projects **UIDB/00742/2020** and **UIDB/05583/2020**. This article is based upon work from COST Action IC1303-AAPELE—Architectures, Algorithms, and Protocols for Enhanced Living Environments and COST Action CA16226-SHELD-ON-Indoor living space improvement: Smart Habitat for the Elderly, supported by COST (European Cooperation in Science and Technology). COST is a funding agency for research and innovation networks. Our Actions help connect research initiatives across Europe and enable scientists to grow their ideas by sharing them with their peers. It boosts their research, career, and innovation. More information in www.cost.eu. Furthermore, we would like to thank the Research Center in Digital Services (CISeD) and the Polytechnic of Viseu for their support.

References

1. Brownlee, J.: K-nearest neighbors for machine learning, August 2020. https://books.google.pt/books?hl=pt-PT&lr=&id=n-oDwAAQBAJ&oi=fnd& pg=PP1&dq=J.+Brownlee.+K-nearest+neighbors+for+machine+learning& ots=3kfEYbkCsc&sig=eyhGIdPfBSIrFXEo_avVbkfbywk&redir_esc=y# v=onepage&q&f=false

2. Carvalho, P.: Coronavírus: relação "estreita" com o clima aponta para verão mais calmo em portugal, March 2020. https://www.publico.pt/2020/03/13/ciencia/noticia/coronavirus-relacao-estreita-clima-aponta-verao-calmo-portugal-1907601

3. Claudino, H.M.: Sete gráficos para compreender as diferenças entre a primeira e a segunda vaga, November 2020. https://tvi24.iol.pt/geral/29-11-2020/sete-graficos-para-compreender-as-diferencas-entre-a-primeira-e-a-segunda-vaga

4. DGS: Covid-19 - página inicial, November 2020. https://covid19.min-saude.pt/

5. e Pinto, J.V.: Podemos estar a sair do "pico" da segunda vaga, mas "não é altura para descansar", November 2020. https://www.publico.pt/2020/11/27/sociedade/noticia/covid19-incidencia-abranda-portugal-nao-altura-descansar-1940973

6. Inácio, A.M.: Internamentos não atingem estimativas, mas uci só têm vagas quando alguém morre ou tem alta, November 2020. https://www.dn.pt/edicao-do-dia/04-nov-2020/internamentos-nao-atingem-estimativas-mas-uci-so-tem-vagas-quando-alguem-morre-ou-tem-alta-12994838.html

7. IPMA: Temperature API, December 2020. https://api.ipma.pt/

8. Lopes, M.J.: A procura deve aumentar, mas "não vai haver falta de vacinas" da gripe para quem as deve tomar, October 2020. https://www.publico.pt/2020/10/19/sociedade/noticia/procura-aumentar-nao-vai-haver-falta-vacinas-gripe-tomar-1935801

9. Ma, Y.: Effects of temperature variation and humidity on the death of Covid-19 in Wuhan, China, July 2020. https://www.sciencedirect.com/science/article/abs/pii/S0048969720317393

10. SNS: Avaliação da situação nacional das unidades de cuidados intensivos (2016). https://www.sns.gov.pt/wp-content/uploads/2016/05/Avalia%C3%A7%C3%A3o-nacional-da-situa%C3%A7%C3%A3o-das-unidades-de-cuidados-intensivos.pdf

11. SNS: Sns conta com um total de 17.700 camas para assistência à pandemia, October 2020. https://www.sns.gov.pt/noticias/2020/10/23/covid-19-capacidade-instalada/

12. Sol: Falta de vacinas da gripe preocupa farmacêuticos, October 2020. https://sol.sapo.pt/artigo/712179/falta-de-vacinas-da-gripe-preocupa-farmac-uticos

13. VOST: Covid-19 API, December 2020. https://covid19-api.vost.pt/

14. Wallis, P.: Disease metaphors in new epidemics: the UK media framing of the 2003 SARS epidemic, June 2005. https://www.sciencedirect.com/science/article/abs/pii/S0277953604005891?via%3Dihub

15. Xie, J.: Association between ambient temperature and Covid-19 infection in 122 cities from China, July 2020. https://reader.elsevier.com/reader/sd/pii/S0048969720317149

Anomaly Detection in Cellular IoT
with Machine Learning

Bernardo Santos[1]([✉]), Imran Qayyrm Khan[1], Bruno Dzogovic[1], Boning Feng[1],
Van Thuan Do[1,2], Niels Jacot[2], and Thanh Van Do[1,3]

[1] Oslo Metropolitan Univeristy, Pilestredet 35, 0167 Oslo, Norway
{bersan,bruno.dzogovic,boning.feng}@oslomet.no
[2] Wolffia AS, Haugerudvn. 40, 0673 Oslo, Norway
{vt.do,n.jacot}@wolffia.net
[3] Telenor ASA, Snarøyveien 30, 1331 Fornebu, Norway
thanh-van.do@telenor.com

Abstract. The number of Internet of Things (IoT) devices used in eldercare are
increasing day by day and bringing big security challenges especially for health
care organizations, IoT service providers and most seriously for the elderly users.
Attackers launch many attacks using compromised IoT devices such as Distributed
Denial of Services (DDoS), among others. To detect and prevent these types of
attacks on IoT devices connected to the cellular network, it is essential to have
a proper overview of the existing threats and vulnerabilities. The main objective
of this work is to present and compare different machine learning algorithms for
anomaly detection in the cellular IoT scenario. Five supervised machine learning
algorithms, namely KNN, Naïve Bayes, Decision Tree and Logistic Regression are
used and evaluated by their performance. We see that, for both normal (using a local
test dataset) and attack traffic (CICDDoS2019 (**CICDDoS2019 Dataset:** https://
www.unb.ca/cic/datasets/ddos-2019.html.)) datasets, the accuracy and precision
of the models are in average above 90%.

Keywords: Machine learning · Anomaly detection · Mobile network security ·
IoT security · Cross layer security

1 Introduction

Internet of Things (IoT) is described as a *"network to connect anything with the Internet based on stipulated protocols through information sensing equipments to conduct
information exchange and communications in order to achieve smart recognitions,
positioning, tracing, monitoring, and administration."* [1].

IoT is nowadays an outlet to provide applications and services such as smart healthcare, control energy, process monitoring, environmental observation and fleet management [2, 3] to companies in the industry or to end consumers at their own homes.
As per 2020 forecasts in [4], 50 billion internet of things including cardiac monitors,

© ICST Institute for Computer Sciences, Social Informatics and Telecommunications Engineering 2021
Published by Springer Nature Switzerland AG 2021. All Rights Reserved
I. M. Pires et al. (Eds.): GOODTECHS 2021, LNICST 401, pp. 51–64, 2021.
https://doi.org/10.1007/978-3-030-91421-9_5

thermostats, smart phones, surveillance cameras, kitchen applications, cars, television everything will be connected via Internet.

Ericsson forecast report (C-IoT connections by segment and technology) states that *"The Massive IoT technologies NB-IoT and Cat-M1 continue to be rolled out around the world, but at a slightly slower pace in 2020 than previously forecasted due to the impact of COVID-19. 2G and 3G connectivity still enables the majority of IoT applications, but during 2019, the number of Massive IoT connections increased by a factor of 3, reaching close to 100 million connections at the end of the year."* [5]. As shown in Fig. 1, Ericsson has predicted that some 29 billion IoT gadgets will be usable by 2025 [6].

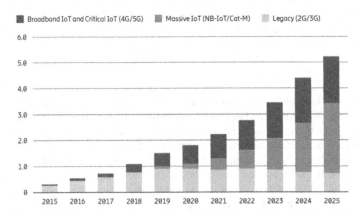

Fig. 1. Cellular IoT connections by segment and technology (billion) [6]

Due to the COVID-19 pandemic, cyber criminals gave us massive challenges specially in the health field. Due to this health crisis, they took advantage to develop their attacks on healthcare, hospitals, medical research centres and on international health public organizations. Because of this, the International Committee of Red Cross (ICRC) and other members have published a letter to various governments to do more on security and safety on these medical organizations from cyber-attacks [7].

There has been a huge interest and investment into bringing IoT capabilities to elderly care to provide senior citizens a more pleasant and lasting experience in the comfort of their own homes, even after going through some sort of incident, avoiding the need to move them to a senior home and providing the autonomy they are still accustomed to. This can be possible by deploying devices that would monitor (unobtrusively) not only the environment that the elderly person is living in, but also the elderly itself by measuring periodically its vital signs and provide immediate actions when an emergency happens (e.g., fall). As an example, the Body Sensor Network (BSN) innovation is a breakthrough that makes it possible for a physician to collect data from patients to additionally screen them via extremely compulsive devices that use lightweight protocol f or transmission of data such as CoAP [8].

The protection and security of these devices' sensors is extremely important because they hold the patient's critical data. Any unauthorized entry, leakage and capture of these devices can cause serious harm to patients. The information segment can be tampered due to manipulation in packets that can be dangerous and life critical [8, 9]. If an intruder inflicts DoS on devices that change the value of the patient's high heartbeat, the device will not be triggered, and this will cause real problems and, in some cases, death.

IoT DDoS attacks were a main dominant attack in 2017, in line with the Arbor Security report [7], and 65% of the attacks carried out in 2016 were in majority DDoS attacks. The Mirai DDoS attack [10] was triggered by the contamination of defective IoT devices, being one of the biggest attacks ever to this segment. Consequently, DDoS attacks should be detected and mitigated. Transmission Control Protocol (TCP), User Datagram Protocol (UDP), and DNS flooding are the most common attacks on DDoS. Protection measurements are challenging to enforce due to memory limitations, power and the heterogeneous nature of IoT devices.

To provide a way to mitigate these issues, the work presented in this paper aims at analysing different machine learning techniques that can help in detecting or even predicting an exploit targeting IoT devices connected to cellular networks. The hypothesis is as follows: If we can obtain information from the control and data plane in a cellular network, coming from IoT devices, we can use machine learning and anomaly detection algorithms in these data to see if it allows us to detect or even predict an upcoming attack.

The paper is organized as follows: In Sect. 2, we discuss about what kind of technologies and concepts are needed for this work. In Sect. 3, we showcase the planned steps that are important to consider given the problem statement. In Sect. 4, we present the outcome given on what was implemented and in Sect. 5, some take home messages are provided as to what to do with the scenarios described in this work. Finally, in Sect. 6, we make a summary by highlighting the obtained results and provide guidelines for purposes of further developing this research topic.

2 Background and Related Work

2.1 Cellular Networks

Currently there are 16 billion cellular customers from 2G to 4G and it is gradually increasing [11] to the 5G generation, with approximately 50 billion including IoT devices. 5G comes as a breakthrough for digital voice and data capacity but also for special features like IoT (Internet of Things) and AR (Augmented Reality), VR (Virtual Reality). Anything from smart cars to city grids, using different protocols such as the CISCO CCN and the MQTT protocols. Packet switching technology is used in 5G network. The latency in 5G network is only 1 ms [12].

2.2 IoT (Internet of Things)

As described in [13], IoT has a lot of security threats and challenges. According to the researchers, we need to understand the new features of IoT regarding security threats in IoT device. We define some security threats of IoT that cause attack in IoT devices as follows:

1. **Ubiquitous:** It is involved in our daily life and use all our resources. Individuals do not have an idea of the security of devices and still use them, and manufacturers

provide very little safety advice or recommendations given that the device collects sensitive data. The unsafe default configuration of these devices is one of the latest and common attacks' triggers.

2. **Diversity:** IoT has several devices that are involved in use cases and applications. IoT tracks different cloud networks through distinctive security elements and conventions. Differences in device capabilities and requirements make it difficult to create a global defence mechanism. To deploy DDoS attacks, attackers exploit these distinct qualities. The Intrusion Detection Systems (IDS), and Intrusion Prevention Systems (IPS) can provide help in preventing intrusion attacks.

3. **Privacy:** A few sensors jointly gather important any sensitive information, and it can be an easy task for a hacker to obtain it. An example of such event is described in [14], regarding a smart home activity arrangement by a home network traffic.

4. **Unattended:** Some IoT devices are special purpose devices, such as Implantable Medical Devices (IMDs). These types of devices have been operating in an unprecedented physical world for a long time without human mediation. It is extremely difficult to apply security computing and monitor if these devices are remotely hacked. In [15] authors proposed a lightweight, stable execution environment for these types of devices.

5. **Mobile:** Several IoT devices are portable and switch from network to network. As an example, a smart vehicle that collects street data when driving from one place to another. If the attacker injects the code by mobile devices, the device configuration or activity is changed. However, the change of device configuration is very difficult special when the network portability is configured on a device.

2.3 DDoS

DDoS stands for 'Distributed Denial-of-Service' and it is a kind of DoS (Denial-of-Service) where the intruder performs a attack through several locations from different sources simultaneously. DoS attacks are most driven by directing or shutting down a specific resource, and one method of operation is to exploit a system deficiency and cause failure of processing or saturation of system resources.

The authors in [16] claim that battery, computation, memory and radio transmission capability are limited in IoT devices. In this way, it is not easy to enforce security actions that involve a massive communication stack and more computing resources. Authors also suggest the usage of machine learning techniques, that is important for finding the vulnerability and security threats in IoTs.

The authors in [17] proposed a DDoS machine learning detection system that would include one pre-trained module to detect suspicious activities inside virtual machines and another online learning module to revise the pre-trained module. The structure is tested against TCP SYN, ICMP, DNS reflection and SSH brute-force attacks on nine separate machine learning algorithms and described as machine learning highlights. The finding result is the 93% accuracy by using the supervised approach in machine learning algorithm such as Naïve Bayes, SVM and Decision Tree.

Pattern discovery can be an instrument that identifies attacks by recognizing the signature of known attacks. Pattern position systems are often used as a virus detection system. Snort detecting the attack by using the attack signature is one of the good detecting systems proposed in [18]. In sum, Payload Inspection and Machine Learning-based behaviour detection are the two feasible approaches for DDoS detection.

2.4 Machine Learning

Several machine learning techniques have been used to detect DDoS attacks. Each approach is distinguishing between the distinctive DDoS attacks and different results that are based on the data properties of the algorithm. A one-of-a-kind solution with a range of features to recognize all kinds of DDoS attacks is still not available. Due to massive amount of network data, it is difficult to recognize if the generated data is done by legitimate users or from real-time attack. Peter et al. [19] tests show that the Long Short-Term Memory Recurrent Neural Network (LSTM RNN) deep learning approach gives impressive results for detecting a DDoS attack in a network. The choice of supervised or unsupervised machine learning algorithms depends on specific parameters, such as the volume and structure of information and the form of DDoS. Five supervised machine learning approaches for detecting DDoS attack in IoT are briefly described below:

1. **K-Nearest Neighbours:** KNN [20] could be an effective and robust classification algorithm. KNN is known as an 'Instance-based Learner', which implies that the memorization of algorithm relies on continuous training experiences. KNN is a paradigm of machine learning that build on labelled dataset of the sampling data (x, y) and predicts the relationship between x and y. The main purpose is to learn the function $h : x \rightarrow y$ to predict the undetectable understanding of the target x, $h(x)$.
2. **Decision Tree:** The Decision Tree [21] is a well-known machine learning algorithm used to classify unknown data from trained data. A decision tree may be either a binary or non-binary tree that includes a root, internal and leaf node. All perceptions are placed in the root node, and each of the inner nodes holds the testing of features.
3. **Support Vector Machines (SVM):** In machine learning, support vector machines [22] are administered learning models with related learning calculations that dissect information utilized for characterization and relapse investigation. Given a lot of preparing precedents, each set apart as having a place with either of two classes, a SVM preparing calculation constructs a model that doles out new guides to one classification or the other, making it a non-probabilistic double direct classifier.
4. **Naïve Bayes Classifier:** Based on the Bayes Hypothesis, the Naïve Bayes can be a simple probabilistic classifier that is useful to large datasets [23]. When the features within the datasets are independent of each other, the Naïve Bayes model is easy to build, being a classifier that provides a speedy performance.
5. **Logistic Regression:** This model [24] is a broadly utilized statistical model that, in its fundamental shape, utilizes a logistic calculation to display a binary dependent variable. In regression analysis, logistic regression is assessing the parameters of a strategic model.

3 Approach

The aim of this work is to detect DDoS attacks through machine learning in cellular network via the packets generated by IoT devices. Here, we elaborate about the basis of

our proposed solution and describe the steps taken to be able to experiment and validate
our hypothesis.

3.1 Design Phase

Our proposed method captures packets from Serving Gateway (SGW) and performs
packet inspection to recognize malicious packets by extracting the features that can
indicate a DDoS attack. After that, machine learning classification algorithms can seg-
regate between normal and abnormal packets. If the packet is classified as normal traffic,
it will be forward through the network and reaches the IoT application server. If it is
considered abnormal and further verified as an attack, the device's info is forwarded to
the Identity Management System (IDMS), which is the responsible for the temporary
or permanent block of devices meaning that a device will not be able to connect to the
network. For further explanation on how the proposed model detects DDoS attacks, we
need to describe how the packets travel from IoT devices to IoT application servers.
In a core 4G cellular network generally, the user packet transfers from the eNodeB
to the SGW. The packets are then forwarded from SGW towards the Packet Gateway
(PGW) which afterwards forwards these packets towards the application server. In this
packet, the eNodeB attaches another IP packet that has a GTP header, which will provide
information elements that can help us foresee if an attack is imminent (Fig. 2).

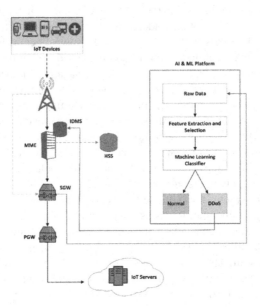

Fig. 2. Proposed method for anomaly detection

3.2 Implementation and Experimental Phase

We use different tools and packages for generating normal and DDoS traffic and analyse patterns by using machine learning technology. The tools and packages that we are using are described below:

3.2.1 Data Collection

1. **Wireshark**[1]**:** is an open-sourced and free packet analyser software that is used for analysis, network troubleshooting, communication and software protocol development. Wireshark is using the Qt widget toolkit that is implemented in the interface by using *pcap* to capture the packets. We use Wireshark in our work for capturing packets that coming from IoT devices.

Normal Dataset: For generating normal traffic, in our Secure 5G4IoT lab[2] in OsloMet, we had mobile devices (e.g., smartphones and raspberry Pi with IoT boards) connected through Wi-Fi to a mobile gateway. This gateway has a programmable SIM card that allows to connect to our test cellular network using consumer available hardware and open-source software.

DDoS Dataset: For DDoS traffic we use the CICDDoS2019[3] dataset, due to access and time restraints given the COVID-19 pandemic, available for machine learning research. This dataset is based on simulation and dated between 2016 to 2019. For this study we select this dataset as it provides a comprehensive analysis or various type of DDoS attacks.

3.2.2 Feature Extraction

To distinguish between DDoS and normal IoT traffic, we need to indicate the packet features that are selected for machine learning classification. Protocol type, port, source and destination IP and packet length have been used for recognizing most DDoS attacks. We have chosen the characteristics below to differentiate between ordinary traffic and DDoS [25, 26].

1. **Packet Size:** Under a timestamp, DDoS disperses a large number of packets, and these packets are smaller compared to an ordinary packet. Rohan et al. [26] maintain that the DDoS bundle is less than 100 bytes, while the normal operating bundle is between 100 and 1200 bytes. However, for the TCP SYN attack, the DDoS packet estimate is set at 58, 60 and 174 bytes.
2. **Packet Time Interval:** The interval between parcels in a DDoS attack is close to zero [26].
3. **Packet Size Variance:** For the most part, parcels of assault activity have the same estimate, while regular traffic has different packet measurements [26].

---

[1] **Wireshark:** www.wireshark.com.

[2] **Secure 5G4IoT Lab:** https://5g4iot.vlab.cs.hioa.no/.

[3] **CICDDoS2019 Dataset:** https://www.unb.ca/cic/datasets/ddos-2019.html.

4. **Protocol Type:** Two protocols (TCP and UDP) have been used for attack operations, allowing us to focus on them for our work.
5. **Destination IP:** IoT devices communicate with many expected target numbers and seldom modify their target IP over time. This highlight can also display a DDoS attacks. Inside a short timestamp, a single gadget interaction with a range of specific targets shows an attack [26].

3.2.3   Data Processing

When dealing with data pre-processing, some techniques need to be considered:

1. **Missing Values:** It is very difficult to handle the missing values in machine learning because it could create an incorrect prediction for any model. The null values and respective entries are then removed.
2. **Transformation:** The arrangement of the data collected might not be appropriate for modelling. As illustrated by the CRISP-DM method [27], in such cases, the type of data should be changed in such a way that the information can be integrated into the models at that point. Here, a few data features have been converted to numeric or float type.
3. **Labelling:** Our dataset represents the two types of classes: first packets with length below 100 packets size are represented with 1 (meaning an anomaly) and other length of packets are represented with 0 (normal traffic). Second type of data, if a packet has a length between 50 to 70 and 160 to 180 it is then represented with 1, and if the packet does not fit those intervals, it is represented with 0.
4. **Dataset Splitting:** Datasets are divided into two subsets; training and testing. The split data is divided in 70/30 ratio. The *train_test_split* helper method is used from scikit-learn library for splitting of data. With this approach, training data is divided into two parts, training and validation. The training set is used to train the model in start, then validation set is used to estimate the performance of data.

To help with this process, the following tools can be used:

1. **Python[4]:** It is a general purpose, high level open-source programming language. Ease of learning, efficient code and easy communication are some of the features of Python, many researchers use this programming language in this field. We use this language for machine learning experiment.
2. **Scikit-Learn[5]:** As open-source machine learning tool for Python programming language. It is a simple tool for data analysis and data mining. Scikit-learn consists of different algorithms for implementation for supervised and unsupervised learning.

---

[4] **Python:** www.python.org.
[5] **Scikit-Learn:** www.scikit-learn.org.

3.2.4 Evaluation

Evaluation is a very crucial part for understanding the performance of a chosen model. This part defines the performance of the models. Below are described the various metrics used in this study.

1. **Accuracy:** It is one way to describe your model performance by the count of correct and incorrect classifier elements. These correct and incorrect values are represented in the values of accuracy, which determines the performance of classifier.
2. **Precision:** For assessing the performance of learning model accuracy is not enough. The accuracy gives an idea that the model is trained correctly, but it does not give the detailed information of the specific application. For that reason, we use the other performance measurements, such as precision, which is the rate of correctly classified true positive or true negative.
3. **Recall:** Recall is measuring how many actual positive values are measured or recalled.

4   Results

Experiments were carried out to verify the performance and accuracy of the classifier for various combinations and sizes of data. Our DDoS detection test was based on TCP SYN attack due to time constraints. We use two different threshold scenarios in both datasets: First, we set the threshold of packets below 100 bytes. Second threshold is set between 50 and 70 or between 160 and 180 bytes.

4.1   First Threshold - Packet Length Below 100 Bytes

4.1.1   Normal Scenario

Table 1 shows how accurate they performed with normal traffic. SVM performed well in this experiment as it gives no anomaly, however rest of the algorithms show possible anomalies.

Table 1. Performance metrics: first threshold – normal scenario

Classifier name	Accuracy (%)	Precision (%)	Recall (%)
K-NN	83.70	86.72	83.70
SVM	82.55	86.15	82.55
Naïve-Bayes	75.51	82.70	75.51
Decision Tree	83.70	86.72	83.70
Logistic Regression	82.55	86.15	82.55

4.1.2 DDoS Scenario

Table 2 shows how accurate they performed with DDoS traffic. The SVM shows no anomaly in this experiment, but other classifiers show anomalies. Naïve Bayes performs well to detect the anomaly but with lower accuracy.

Table 2. Performance metrics: first threshold – DDoS scenario

Classifier name	Accuracy (%)	Precision (%)	Recall (%)
K-NN	98.21	97.54	98.21
SVM	98.19	96.42	98.19
Naïve-Bayes	97.98	97.07	97.98
Decision Tree	98.21	97.57	98.21
Logistic Regression	98.18	97.22	98.18

4.2 Second Threshold – Packet Length Between 50 and 70 Bytes and Between 160 and 180 Bytes

4.2.1 Normal Scenario

Table 3 shows how accurate they performed with normal traffic. The KNN performed well in this experiment. In the normal dataset SVM, decision tree and logistic regression give no anomaly, but KNN and Naïve Bayes classifiers show possible anomalies.

Table 3. Performance metrics: second threshold – normal scenario

Classifier name	Accuracy (%)	Precision (%)	Recall (%)
K-NN	84.52	80.85	84.52
SVM	84.25	70.98	84.25
Naïve-Bayes	82.61	78.82	82.61
Decision Tree	84.51	80.70	84.51
Logistic Regression	84.22	78.33	84.22

4.2.2 DDoS Scenario

Table 4 shows how accurate they performed with DDoS traffic. In this dataset K-NN and SVM show good results with this threshold.

Table 4. Performance metrics: second threshold – DDoS scenario

Classifier name	Accuracy (%)	Precision (%)	Recall (%)
K-NN	99.19	98.85	99.19
SVM	99.19	98.39	99.19
Naïve-Bayes	98.92	98.69	98.92
Decision Tree	99.20	98.90	99.20
Logistic Regression	99.18	98.77	99.18

5 Discussion

This study was conducted to analyse the action, performance and utilization of the machine learning algorithms in the context of intrusion detection system. Researchers and industry are working to find out good solutions in the field of machine learning and artificial intelligence for intrusion detection and prevention. However, different business partners and researchers often find it difficult to obtain excellent quality datasets to test and evaluate their machine learning models for detection of threats. This problem is the main motivation of this study, and basis for research questions. To ensure that the experiment is carried out in an appropriate manner, all classifiers were chosen based on literature review. The results were evaluated using a set of performance metrics, including precision, accuracy and recall.

5.1 First Threshold

In 1st threshold, the KNN performance metrics are fair. It achieved 83.70% accuracy with precision of 86.72%. When trained with the CICDDoS2019 dataset, KNN shows much better precision and accuracy scores averaging 98%. SVM gives 98.19% result, but it does not find any anomaly in this dataset. Naïve Bayes gives 97.98%, logistic regression gives 98.18% and decision tree gives 98.21% accuracy. Overall, for this threshold, KNN is the best classifier.

5.2 Second Threshold

If we talk about the second threshold in the CICDDoS2019 dataset, KNN also gives the good precision and accuracy scores averaging 99%. SVM gives 99.19% accuracy. Naïve Bayes gives 98.92%, logistic regression 99.18% and decision tree gives 99.20%. In this threshold, KNN also turns out to be the classifier that performs the best.

5.3 Evaluation

Throughout this work we were able to conclude that some classifiers are more sensitive hence producing results that were not the expected ones. A reason for these discrepancies is most likely due to the thresholds chosen. An establishment of more robust thresholds that are more adequate to our studied scenario is needed to provide more reliable results. Nevertheless, we were able to detect the attack given by the supervised and labelled dataset even the with differences in performance depending on the classifier. In a real-life context and given the early stage of the implementation, the result data would have been sent to the corresponding security expert team in a telecom operator for further validation.

6 Conclusion

This work was set to look into the issues of IoT protection from the point of view of the Cellular Network in terms of the security challenges. Recognizing attacks within the cellular network is not the same as recognizing attacks in an IP network. For instance, a sudden increase in the acceptance of packets in a single node from the number of distinctive MME nodes in the case of IoT could suggest an attack, as IoT devices do not transmit packets in a very high frequency.

This work presents an overview of how other researchers discuss the issue of discovery of intrusion detection with the use of machine learning. This has provided a much better understanding that how different algorithms work and can help understand how to mitigate the propagation of DDoS attacks. In addition, it also provides an understanding of which algorithms are commonly used to deal with problems in this area.

Normal and DDoS datasets have been used and with five classification methods, such as KNN, Decision Tree, and Naïve Bayes, SVM and logistic regression, we analysed their performance as to detect possible attacks. The focus was on TCP attacks, as this protocol is commonly used to launch an attack, and due to time constraints, we just focus on the SYN attack.

Our primary focus not only for this work but also in our research is to provide ways to develop and provide a secure environment towards device-driven solutions that could enhance the quality of life of an elderly person at their own homes, but the proposal herein presented can be applicable to other verticals in which IoT can be a beneficial added factor.

The point was to identify DDoS attacks within the context of the cellular network in this proposed work, and the aim was to propose an arrangement that could lead to a specific use in the future. Subsequently, the strategy recommends a full-scale DDoS detection technique within the cellular network, and offline data has been used for training and testing of the model. We would like to recommend that this methodology be tested in a true research setting for future work. In addition, this strategy focused only on the TCP SYN flood. To secure IoT devices and services in the future, we would like to incorporate all potential DDoS attacks. We hope that this study starts as a basis to create a helping tool for telecom operators that could be used in the future to detect DDoS and other types of attacks in a more automated fashion.

Acknowledgement. This paper is a result of the H2020 Concordia project (https://www.concordia-h2020.eu) which has received funding from the EU H2020 programme under grant agreement No 830927. The CONCORDIA consortium includes 23 partners from industry and other organizations such as Telenor, Telefonica, Telecom Italia, Ericsson, Siemens, Airbus, etc. and 23 partners from academia such as CODE, university of Twente, OsloMet, etc.

References

1. Patel, K.K., Patel, S.M., et al.: Internet of things-IOT: definition, characteristics, architecture, enabling technologies, application & future challenges. Int. J. Eng. Sci. Comput. **6**(5), 6122–6131 (2016)
2. Chen, S., et al.: A vision of IoT: applications, challenges, and opportunities with china perspective. IEEE Internet Things J. **1**(4), 349–359 (2014)
3. Lee, I., Lee, K.: The Internet of Things (IoT): applications, investments, and challenges for enterprises. Bus. Horizons **58**(4), 431–440 (2015)
4. Rawat, P., Singh, K.D., Bonnin, J.M.: Cognitive radio for M2M and Internet of Things: a survey. Comput. Commun. **94**, 1–29 (2016)
5. Ericsson: IoT connections outlook. https://www.ericsson.com/en/mobility-report/reports/june-2020/iot-connectionsoutlook
6. Jejdling, F. (Ericsson): Ericsson Mobility Report. https://www.ericsson.com/en/mobility-report/reports
7. Stackpole, B.: Symantec Security Summary, June 2020. COVID-19 attacks continue and new threats on the rise. https://symantec-enterprise-blogs.security.com/blogs/featurestories/symantec-security-summary-june-2020
8. Khoi, N.M., et al.: IReHMo: an efficient IoT-based remote health monitoring system for smart regions. In: 2015 17th International Conference on E-health Networking, Application and Services (Health-Com), pp. 563–568. IEEE (2015)
9. Gope, P., Hwang, T.: BSN-care: a secure IoT-based modern healthcare system using body sensor network. IEEE Sens. J. **16**(5), 1368–1376 (2015)
10. Heer, T., et al.: Security challenges in the IP-based Internet of Things. Wirel. Pers. Commun. **61**, 527–542 (2011)
11. Van der Elzen, I., van Heugten, J.: Techniques for detecting compromised IoT devices. University of Amsterdam (2017)
12. Saqlain, J.: IoT and 5G: history evolution and its architecture their compatibility and future (2018)
13. Zhou, W., et al.: The effect of IoT new features on security and privacy: new threats, existing solutions, and challenges yet to be solved. IEEE Internet Things J. **6**(2), 1606–1616 (2018)
14. Copos, B., et al.: Is anybody home? Inferring activity from smart home network traffic. In: 2016 IEEE Security and Privacy Workshops (SPW), pp. 245–251. IEEE (2016)
15. Noorman, J., et al.: Sancus: low-cost trustworthy extensible networked devices with a zero-software trusted computing base. In: 22nd fUSENIXg Security Symposium (fUSENIXg Security 2013), pp. 479–498 (2013)
16. Xiao, L., et al.: IoT security techniques based on machine learning: how do IoT devices use AI to enhance security? IEEE Signal Process. Mag. **35**(5), 41–49 (2018)
17. He, Z., Zhang, T., Lee, R.B.: Machine learning based DDoS attack detection from source side in cloud. In: 2017 IEEE 4th International Conference on Cyber Security and Cloud Computing (CSCloud), pp. 114–120. IEEE (2017)
18. Bakker, J.: Intelligent traffic classification for detecting DDoS attacks using SDN/OpenFlow (2017)
19. Bediako, P.K.: Long short-term memory recurrent neural network for detecting DDoS flooding attacks within TensorFlow implementation framework (2017)
20. Adeniyi, D.A., Wei, Z., Yongquan, Y.: Automated web usage data mining and recommendation system using K-Nearest Neighbor (KNN) classification method. Appl. Comput. Inform. **12**(1), 90–108 (2016)
21. Tian, F., et al.: Research on flight phase division based on decision tree classifier. In: 2017 2nd IEEE International Conference on Computational Intelligence and Applications (ICCIA), pp. 372–375. IEEE (2017)

22. Cortes, C., Vapnik, V.: Support-vector networks. Mach. Learn. **20**(3), 273–297 (1995)
23. Patil, T.R., Sherekar, S.S.: Performance analysis of Naive Bayes and J48 classification algorithm for data classification. J. Comput. Sci. Appl. **6**(2), 256–261 (2013)
24. Wikipedia: Logistic regression. https://en.wikipedia.org/wiki/Logistic_regression
25. Oo, T.T., Phyu, T.: Analysis of DDoS detection system based on anomaly detection system. In: International Conference on Advances in Engineering and Technology (ICAET 2014), Singapore (2014)
26. Doshi, R., Apthorpe, N., Feamster, N.: Machine learning DDoS detection for consumer internet of things devices. In: 2018 IEEE Security and Privacy Workshops (SPW), pp. 29–35. IEEE (2018)
27. Cross-industry standard process for data mining. https://en.wikipedia.org/wiki/Cross-industry_standard_process_for_data_mining

Internet of Things

A Smart IoT System for Water Monitoring and Analysis

João Miguel Santos[1,2](✉) [iD], Raúl Carvalho[1] [iD], João Carlos Martins[1] [iD],
João Filipe Santos[1] [iD], Patrícia Palma[3,4] [iD], Dalmiro Maia[6] [iD],
João Paulo Barraca[2,5] [iD], Diogo Gomes[2,5] [iD], Miguel Bergano[2,7] [iD],
Domingos Barbosa[2] [iD], and José Jasnau Caeiro[1] [iD]

[1] Dep. de Engenharia, Instituto Politécnico de Beja, Beja, Portugal
{joao.santos,joao.martins,joaof.santos,j.caeiro}@ipbeja.pt,
756@stu.ipbeja.pt
[2] Instituto de Telecomunicações, Aveiro, Portugal
{jpbarraca,dgomes,jbergano,dbarbosa}@av.it.pt
[3] Dep. Technologias e Ciências Aplicadas, Instituto Politécnico de Beja,
Beja, Portugal
ppalma@ipbeja.pt
[4] ICT, Instituto de Ciências da Terra, Universidade de Évora, Évora, Portugal
[5] Universidade de Aveiro, Aveiro, Portugal
[6] Faculdade de Ciências da Universidade do Porto, Porto, Portugal
dmaia@fc.up.pt
[7] Escola Superior de Tecnologia e Gestão de Águeda da Universidade de Aveiro,
Águeda, Portugal

Abstract. A general architecture for collection and processing of water resources data, in terms of quality and quantity, is presented and discussed. The proposed architecture includes the sensing of physical and chemical water parameters, data communications, and high levels of information processing, namely machine learning. The architecture adopts an Internet of Things perspective and resulted from a survey of the most commonly measured water quality parameters, processing and data acquisition computing modules, and communications hardware and software protocols. It integrates state of the art technologies in the fields of long distance communications, software containers and blockchain technologies. Geographical information is associated with the sensor data. The top layer joins data analysis and machine learning of all the gathered information. Visualization of the raw data and of the results

The authors would like to thank the support from the European Union under the auspices of the Alentejo2020, Portugal2020, FEDER program with the reference ALT20-03-0145-FEDER-039494, to the Project ENGAGE SKA, Infrastructure (ENGAGE SKA), with reference POCI-01-0145-FEDER-022217, financed by Programa Operacional Competitividade e Internacionalização (COMPETE 2020), FEDER, and by the Fundação para a Ciência e Tecnologia, I.P., Portugal (FCT). This work was also funded by FCT and Ministério da Ciência, Tecnologia e Ensino Superior (MCTES) through national funds and when applicable co-funded EU funds under the project UIDB/50008/2020-UIDP/50008/2020.

I. M. Pires et al. (Eds.): GOODTECHS 2021, LNICST 401, pp. 67–79, 2021.
https://doi.org/10.1007/978-3-030-91421-9_6

of the data analysis and machine learning procedures is also part of the system. The integration of weather and remote sensing data, and offline biochemical information is presented in this architecture. The architecture is supported on common commercial of the shelf components and open source software.

Keywords: Internet of Things · Sensing · System architectures · Water resources · Water quality

1 Introduction

Advances in one area of science are eventually accompanied by new possibilities and advances in related or, sometimes, not so related technological areas. On the other way, advances in several fields can motivate and boost the progress in a particular area. As an example, radio astronomy, which moved from a single very large antenna to farms of small simple standalone antennas, disposed as an array, was made possible by the advances in the capability of computers to synchronize and process large amounts of data and fast communications links. This architecture is common to many applications, namely the deployment of sensor nodes to monitor environmental parameters scattered along a region or territory.

The Engage-SKA project[1] aims to make the bridge between radio-astronomy and social good by enabling the transfer of technology to other domains like smart agriculture, environment and water monitoring.

The paper presents a system for monitoring water surface quality and quantity by deploying several monitoring stations along a vast area. It will collect and centralize data in the cloud. The information will be subject to data analysis and machine learning procedures with the addition of data from other sources, namely remote sensing. Water has been considered to be among the main social resources [4], being unlike any other because it is an essential component of all forms of life. Its scarcity and value have always marked the need for its public administration and regulation. Not only the quantity but also an adequate quality is essential for the well-being and health of populations. Therefore, a careful monitoring of water quality and the judicious management of water quantity is a major concern in all countries, particularly in southern Europe, where water is becoming a precious and scarce resource. The need to monitor the water resources is becoming even more relevant in industrialized countries due to pollution and contamination and to the increasing demand of this resource, aggravated by climate change [7]. Smart environmental monitoring, in which smart water monitoring can be included, catalyzes progress in the capabilities of data collection, communication, data analysis and early warning [5].

Recent technological advances in sensors, microcontrollers and communication's technologies, with a significant drop on the energy consumption and cost,

---

[1] Enable Green E-Sciences for the Square Kilometer Array (Engage SKA), https:// engageska-portugal.pt/.

led to the Internet of Things (IoT). For the continuous monitoring of water quality and quantity with the aim to improve efficiency in the use of water resources, IoT based systems may be adopted [11,16,20,21]. Following the study of a set of state of the art papers describing water monitoring systems, the design of the architecture of a smart surface water monitoring system is presented with the corresponding hardware and software infrastructure. The system is designed to employ cutting edge processing platforms, sensors, communications infrastructures and protocols, and cloud based software to provide a complete water quality and quantity monitoring architecture.

The state of the art of smart water monitoring using an IoT approach is the topic of Sect. 2. It presents the results of a survey on published work on this type of systems during the last few years. The latter survey substantiates Sect. 3. It starts with a layer based description of a general system for smart water monitoring and presents a general architecture of a water quality and quantity data collection and analysis IoT based system. The paper concludes with a summary of the main aspects of this work, its relevance for water as a social good and some perspectives for future research in Sect. 4.

2   Smart Water Monitoring

There is not a single method that covers all water monitoring situations and for each case the best method should be investigated to monitor water resources in that particular case [23]. However, there are a couple of architectures that can be applied to a broad range of situations [1,5,8].

Surface water monitoring implies the acquisition of data at a set of different locations along the water surface, at different depths and at regular time intervals [2,6]. The data can be used to establish the water's quality and quantity and, associated with a pattern recognition system and information from other sources, provides the possibility to preview future problems, for example in terms of biological or chemical contamination. It may also provide hints about climate change consequences.

The IoT is playing a major role in monitoring water quality and quantity in real time. An IoT system comprises both the monitoring of a single *thing* or the interconnection of millions of *things*, with the ability to deliver complex services and applications [13].

Among the reasons for the rapid increase on the quantity of IoT systems is the availability of low-cost, energy efficient and powerful hardware for sensing, acquiring, processing and transmitting data to the cloud. Ubiquitous equipment in these systems are microcontroller units (MCUs), cost-effective devices that meet the real-time needs faced by IoT applications with the lower-power constraints of this kind of systems, including data-acquisition (DAQ) and communication capabilities [3]. Also, single board computers (SBC) have become increasingly present in IoT systems. These devices, capable of running a full operating system, increase the capabilities of local nodes, namely by boosting the processing power and data storage [10].

From published reviews on the subject [5, 14, 18] three main subsystems stand out in a smart water monitoring system: the data collection subsystem, at the device layer; the data transmission subsystem, at the network layer; the data management, including data storage and high level processing, subsystem, at the service support, application support and application layers [9].

The data collection system includes the sensors and the DAQ and pre-processing hardware (mainly built with MCUs and SBCs). The data transmission subsystem includes the transmission hardware and communication protocols. Finally, the data management subsystem includes the data storage, the data visualization and analysis components.

A survey over published work presenting this kind of systems was carried out to collect the most common options and their evolution within these three subsystems. A synthesis of the survey results for the sensed parameters is presented in Table 1. The DAQ and pre-processing hardware is shown in Table 2 and Table 3 refers to data communications.

Table 1. Physical and chemical parameters commonly measured in recently proposed smart water quality systems built within an IoT approach: potential of hydrogen (pH), temperature (T), turbidity (TU), electrical conductivity (EC), dissolved oxygen (DO), water level (W_L), water flow (W_{Fl}), oxidation and reduction potential (ORP), nitrates (NO_3^-), ammonia (NH_3), carbon dioxide (CO_2), nitrites (NO_2^-), total dissolved solids (TDS), ammonium (NH_4^+), sulfates (SO_4^{2-}), carbon monoxide (CO), phosphates (PO_4^{3-}), water depth (W_d), water pressure (W_p), salinity (S). [15–18]

Sensed parameters	# IoT Syst.	Freq.
pH	41	55%
T	40	54%
TU	26	35%
EC	19	26%
DO	18	24%
W_L	10	14%
W_{Fl}	7	9%
ORP	6	8%
NO_3^-	4	5%
NH_3	3	4%
CO_2	3	4%
NO_2^-	2	3%
TDS	2	3%
NH_4^+	1	1%
CO	1	1%
PO_4^{3-}	1	1%
W_d	1	1%
W_p	1	1%
S	1	1%

The most commonly measured physical and chemical water parameters are those that can be obtained from common commercial off the shelf (COTS) sensors: potential of hydrogen (pH), temperature (T), turbidity (TU), electrical conductivity (EC), dissolved oxygen (DO), water level (W_L), water flow (W_{Fl}), oxidation and reduction potential (ORP). The total dissolved solids (TDS) parameter has a very low occurrence but this may be related to the fact that it is usually obtained from the EC value. The same is true for salinity (S), a parameter often present in water quality monitoring systems within aquaculture. Less common measured water parameters are those obtained with more specific sensors, namely ion-selective electrodes: nitrates (NO_3^-), ammonia (NH_3), carbon dioxide (CO_2), nitrites (NO_2^-), ammonium (NH_4^+), sulfates (SO_4^{2-}), carbon monoxide (CO) and phosphates (PO_4^{3-}). Also water depth (W_d) and water pressure (W_p), parameters that are correlated, have a very low occurrence, though they can be measured with commonly used COTS sensors.

Table 2. Devices used for sensor control, DAQ and data pre-processing in recently proposed smart water quality systems built within an IoT approach: Microcontrolers (MCU), Single Board Computers (SBC) and Field Programmable Gate Arrays (FPGA). Though most of the MCUs are used in the form of development boards, the specific chip is listed. [17,18]

Config.	Line	MCU Model	SBC model	FPGA model	# IoT Syst.	Freq.
MCU	ATmega	ATmega8			1	47%
		ATmega16			1	
		ATmega128			1	
		ATmega328			7	
		ATmega2560			3	
		ATmega1281			3	
	ARM32	ESP8266			1	23%
		ESP32			1	
		STM32F767			1	
		STM32F103			1	
		LPC1768			1	
		LPC2138			2	
		LPC2148			1	
SBC	Galileo		GalileoGen2		1	3%
	RPi		RPi B+		1	
			RPi 3		2	
MCU+SBC	ATmega+RPi	ATmega2560	RPi 3		1	6%
		ATmega1281	RPi 3		1	
	ARM32+RPi	Kinetis K66	RPi Zero		1	
FPGA				CycloneV	1	9%
				AlteraNiosII	1	
				PSoC 5LP	1	

MCUs used in these systems usually control the sensors and the data acquisition. Sometimes they also preprocess the data, and send it to the transmission subsystem. They are generally used in the form of development boards. Some of these devices and/or development boards also feature wireless communication capabilities. Most of the systems are made with 8 bits AVR MCUs from the ATmega line. The ATmega328 series, which is the basis of the Arduino development board is the most used. More recent systems include more powerful 32 bits ARM Cortex-M MCUs from several lines, used in the form of development boards. Low-cost and low-energy MCUs from the SMT32 line and from the ESP 8266/32 line, featuring wireless communications capabilities, are used in the most recent systems.

SBCs usually appear in two configurations: either replacing the MCUs for sensors control and DAQ, or working as data aggregators and/or communication gateways. In this latter configuration they receive data from MCU/SBC based sensor nodes, process it and sent the result to a remote server. The majority of these SBCs belong to the Raspberry Pi set of microcomputer boards.

A very small part of the systems use Field Programmable Gate Arrays (FPGA) or a combination of MCU and FPGA for DAQ and pre-processing. It is a solution that gives the possibility of system reconfiguration, but it typically comes at a higher implementation cost.

Table 3. Communication technologies used in recently proposed smart water quality systems built within an IoT approach: technology and range/classification. Local Area Network (LAN), Wide Area Network (WAN), Low Power (LP). [15,17,18]

Technology		# IoT Syst.	Freq.
ZigBee	Short-range/LPLAN	21	43%
WiFi	Short-range/LAN	13	27%
Cellular Networks	Long-range/WAN	14	29%
Ethernet	Short-range/LAN	12	24%
LoRa	Long-range/LPWAN	4	8%
Others	–	4	8%
IEEE 802.15.4	Short-range/LPLAN	3	6%

Communication technologies used in these systems generally include short and long range classes. Some systems use only one class, others include both of them, depending on their configuration: single station, local or remote systems, or multiple sensing nodes (sensor network) systems. All cases may include wired, wireless or both types of communication.

Wired communications are mostly over Ethernet, though there are a few cases of other types such as RS232, RS485, and SDI-12.

Most systems are based on a wireless sensor network, with low-power ZigBee (and other variants of IEEE 802.15.4) being predominant for short-range communications. LoRa technology, despite having a very small expression in the set of systems analyzed, is increasingly popular within the IoT community. It is chosen, in particular, for water monitoring systems, because of its long range and low power features.

We excluded from this description the communication at sensor components and DAQ hardware level, with different protocols like UART, I^{2}C or SPI.

3 IoT System Architecture for Water Monitoring

The subject of this section is the presentation and description of a general IoT based system architecture for water monitoring. The layer based diagram is discussed in Subsect. 3.1 and it shows how the data starts to be collected at the lowest levels and flows through the system up to the point where it is presented to the users. The system architecture is presented and discussed in Subsect. 3.2. It uses the results of the state of the art analysis and incorporates several diverse data input sources. Namely data collected from sensors, remote sensing and asynchronous file based inputs.

3.1 IoT Based Architectures

An IoT system's architecture may be represented using different types of diagrams [19]. A widely adopted IoT reference architecture organized on layers, where each layer groups modules offering a cohesive set of services, is the one defined by the International Telecommunication Union (ITU). It consists of four layers: devices; network; service support and application support [9].

A layer based diagram for the proposed architecture of a general IoT surface water monitoring system is represented in Fig. 1. At the lowest level, the

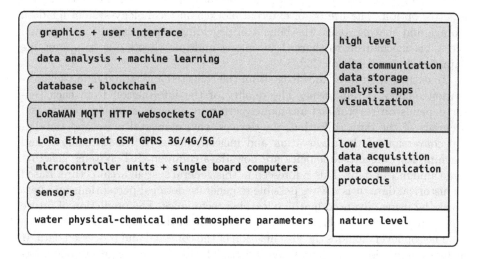

Fig. 1. A layer diagram of a general IoT water data collection system: each layer encompasses modules that offer a cohesive set of services.

nature level, we have the sources of data: surface water and the atmosphere. The parameters information is collected at the device layer, which comprises sensors, MCUs and SBCs. Sensors are at the lower level of the IOT water data collection system. They are responsible for sensing the physical and chemical parameters from the surface water and from the surrounding atmosphere, and convert them to electrical signals. At the next level, MCUs and SBCs acquire these signals, in digital or analog form, and convert them to an adequate digital format, ready to be sent through data communication hardware, to the network layer.

The network layer comprises the communication technologies and data transmission protocols. It is responsible for receiving the data from the data collection subsystem and transport it to other smart *things*, network devices and servers.

The choice of communication technologies is defined by the existing conditions at the data collection site, in particular the geographical conditions, the communications infrastructure and the power sources. As depicted in the diagram, it can be the long-range, low-energy LoRa transmission hardware or other communication technologies: GSM, GPSRS, 3G, 4G, 5G. It may even be the combination of more than one of these technologies. Data exchange protocols are responsible for communications with the service support and the application support layer. The diagram represents a series of application protocols like LoRaWAN, MQTT, HTTP, WebSockets and COAP, commonly used in IoT systems.

The service and the application support layer, represents services that enable IoT applications and services. This level comprises the treatment, analysis and storage of the collected data. The data must be stored and used intelligently for smart monitoring and actuation. In the field of database technology, there are two primary types of databases to store data: relational databases and non-relational databases. There are numerous commercial and open-source options for each form. In certain instances, having different kinds for different tasks is a better option. The use of an external blockchain technology system for data storage and sharing, offers the benefit of providing a safe, easy-to-manage and accessible mechanism to share data among multiple clients due to immutable data and decentralization [22].

To extract high-level knowledge from the collected and stored data the information quality is important. The quality of the information from each sensor depends on several factors, namely errors in measurements, precision and accuracy of the data collection, the devices' environmental noise and the digital conversion of the observation and measurements [12]. Data analysis and machine learning methodologies are nowadays common. IoT systems generate large amounts of data. This is foreseen in this general system architecture. Based on historical data, it is always possible to generate detailed perceptions into past events by using advanced machine learning techniques. The prediction of future events, namely due to climate change, is present in the architecture.

The top level includes the visualization of the collected and processed data. It includes predictions and action suggestions. The integration of geographic information system (GIS) and the usage of remote sensing tools and data provides a rich integration of information from *in-situ* with that from satellite sources.

3.2   A General Architecture for Smart Water Monitoring and Analysis

The proposed general architecture of a water quality and quantity data collection and analysis system is represented in Fig. 2. This may be divided into, *grosso modo*, the following types of data processing subsystems: data collection, data transmission and data management, which includes storage and high level processing.

The data collection subsystems are: the *water quality module*; the *water quantity module*; the *evaporation module*; the *weather station module*; the *manual data sources* input and the *GIS system*. The *water quality module* includes the acquisition of the most common physical and chemical water quality parameters, as shown in Table 1, namely: total dissolved solids (TDS); dissolved oxygen (DO); turbidity (TU); water temperature (T_W); oxidation and reduction potential (ORP); potential of hydrogen (pH); electrical conductivity (EC). The water pressure (W_p) is included to indicate at what depth the parameters are measured. The MCU, already incorporating the SMBus/I^{2}C protocol, collects data from some of the sensors, namely: pH; T; ORP; DO and EC. The remaining parameters are converted to the digital form using analog to digital converters (ADC) with I^{2}C output. The *water quantity module* acquires the data relative to water flow (W_{Fl}) and water level (W_L), either in digital form or in analogue form with proper ADC circuits. The *weather station module* collects air temperature, air humidity, precipitation, wind velocity and direction, luminosity and UV radiation data. The *evaporation module*, collects the water level variation in a class-A evaporation pan and refills the pan with water when necessary. The *manual data sources* subsystem allows the incorporation of non-periodic bio-chemical data, resulting from water samples analyzed in the laboratory, in the *DBMS data storage*. The *data analysis system* uses this data for more complex machine learning procedures.

There are two types of data communications present in the system. The first type is short distance wireless communication between local system's components. An example is the weather station. The sensors are placed some meters away from the microcomputer unit. The sensors data is captured and decoded with a software defined radio package installed at the microcomputer and afterwards sent to the LoRaWAN gateway. The second type is a long distance wireless communication based on the LoRa hardware and LoRaWAN software protocol architecture. The water quantity, water quality and weather station modules are each considered and registered as devices in the LoRaWAN network/application server. The data sent by these modules is therefore ciphered and uniquely identified in the system. The data is sent through a LoRa gateway registered at the LoRaWAN application server. The LoRa gateway receives the information from the devices that can be placed at distances ranging from some tens of meters to some kilometers away. The LoRa transmission frequency is in the 868MHz band. The LoRa gateway forwards the data through the 3G/4G network using an MQTT broker to publish the data and exchange control data with the LoRaWAN network/application server.

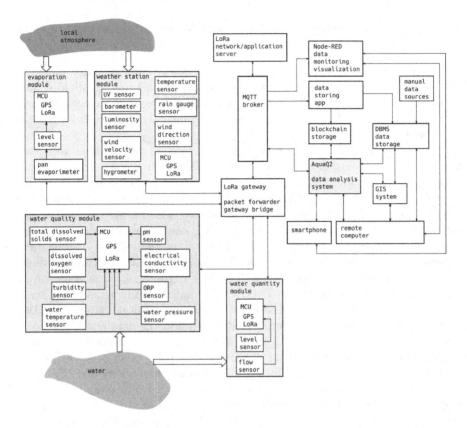

Fig. 2. The architecture of a water quality and quantity system based on the most common elements of an IoT approach.

The servers are launched using a Docker container based infrastructure. Namely the *LoRa network/application* server; the *Node-RED data monitoring and visualization* subsystem; the *data storing app*; the *blockchain storage*; the *DBMS data storage* and the *data analysis* system. The Docker container services are run in a Linux system.

The *Node-RED data monitoring and visualization* system provides a real time view of the status of the sensors using the Node-RED dashboard user interface.

The data storing app subscribes the *MQTT broker* for all the topics from the sensors and stores the information using the *DBMS data storage* server. The latter is a traditional relational model based server with geographical data representation extensions.

The *GIS system* uses the data from the sensors and geographical information data, like maps and remote sensing information, to enhance the data analysis capabilities. A non corruptible data image is maintained using *blockchain storage*. Critical data is kept by this subsystem.

The most complex subsystem in the architecture is the *data analysis system*. A large set of tasks are assigned to this system centralized around a Python based web framework. The system takes the data made available by the *DBMS data storage* server and using machine learning methods, provided by common Python packages, provides high level analysis to the users. This system also incorporates geographical data analysis with a Python based API for the *GIS system*.

4 Conclusions

Water resources have always had primacy among social goods, particularly with regard to water quantity and quality. With the accelerated pace of climate changes, its judicious use becomes more and more pressing and it is crucial to have immediate access to data that reliably characterizes it in order to better manage such a precious resource. The IoT revolution has made possible the collection of vast amounts of data from the physical world, in particular from the environment. IoT-based water and resource quality sensing systems using commercial off-the-shelf (COTS) components provide a fast and scalable way to deploy real-time in *situ* monitoring and data collection solutions. From the analysis of systems that comply with these characteristics a general IoT based architecture is proposed that generalizes the applicability to water resources, not only with a comprehensive set of water quality parameters, but also with water quantity data from in *situ* continuous monitoring. The architecture goes further, adding to the data collected continuously also in *situ* data from other sources: manually collected; remote sensing originated and from GIS, and a modern data analysis system.

The use of modern pattern recognition systems, machine learning and artificial intelligence software, together with techniques to guarantee the reliability of the information, will provide a dynamic, easy-to-follow, insight into the evolution of water quality and water quantity and the consequences of climate change and other human-related activities, such as pollution sources. The concrete implementation of cost-effective devices under the framework of this general architecture is underway in order to build a complete prototype of the proposed Smart IoT System for Water Monitoring and Analysis. Future work includes the testing of the prototype on location to begin the initial deployment of the whole system.

References

1. Andres, L., Boateng, K., Borja-Vega, C., Thomas, E.: A review of in-situ and remote sensing technologies to monitor water and sanitation interventions. Water **10**(6), 756 (2018). https://doi.org/10.3390/w10060756
2. Chapman, D.V., World Health Organization, UNESCO U.N.E.Programme: Water Quality Assessments: A Guide to the Use of Biota, Sediments and Water in Environmental Monitoring, 2nd edn. E & FN Spon, London (1996)

3. Cheour, R., Khriji, S., Abid, M., Kanoun, O.: Microcontrollers for IoT: optimizations, computing paradigms, and future directions. In: 2020 IEEE 6th World Forum on Internet of Things, WF-IoT 2020 - Symposium Proceedings, pp. 1–7 (2020). https://doi.org/10.1109/WF-IoT48130.2020.9221219
4. Day, D.: Water as a social good. Aust. J. Environ. Manag. **3**(1), 26–41 (1996). https://doi.org/10.1080/14486563.1996.10648341
5. Dong, J., Wang, G., Yan, H., Xu, J., Zhang, X.: A survey of smart water quality monitoring system. Environ. Sci. Pollut. Res. **22**(7), 4893–4906 (2015). https://doi.org/10.1007/s11356-014-4026-x
6. EPA (ed.): Parameters of Water Quality: Interpretation and Standards. Environmental Protection Agency, Ireland (2001)
7. Gaaloul, N., Eslamian, S., Katlane, R.: Impacts of climate change and water resources management in the Southern Mediterranean countries. Water Prod. J. **1**(1), 51–72 (2020). https://doi.org/10.22034/wpj.2020.119476
8. Huang, C., Chen, Y., Zhang, S., Wu, J.: Detecting, extracting, and monitoring surface water from space using optical sensors: a review. Rev. Geophys. **56**(2), 333–360 (2018). https://doi.org/10.1029/2018RG000598
9. Telecommunication Standardization Sector of ITU: ITU-T Recommendation Y.4000/Y.2060 : Global Information Infrastructure, Internet Protocol Aspects and Next-Generation Networks, Next Generation Networks-Frameworks and Functional Architecture Models, Overview of the Internet of Things. ITU (2012). https://www.itu.int/rec/T-REC-Y.2060-201206-I
10. Johnston, S.J., Apetroaie-Cristea, M., Scott, M., Cox, S.J.: Applicability of commodity, low cost, single board computers for Internet of Things devices. In: 2016 IEEE 3rd World Forum on Internet of Things (WF-IoT), pp. 141–146 (2016). https://doi.org/10.1109/WF-IoT.2016.7845414
11. Li, D., Liu, S. (eds.): Water Quality Monitoring and Management. Elsevier, Amsterdam (2019)
12. Mahdavinejad, M.S., Rezvan, M., Barekatain, M., Adibi, P., Barnaghi, P., Sheth, A.P.: Machine learning for internet of things data analysis: a survey. Digit. Commun. Netw. **4**(3), 161–175 (2018). https://doi.org/10.1016/j.dcan.2017.10.002
13. Minerva, R., Biru, A., Rotondi, D.: Towards a definition of the internet of things (IoT). Technical report. IEEE (2015)
14. Olatinwo, S.O., Joubert, T.H.: Enabling communication networks for water quality monitoring applications: a survey. IEEE Access **7**, 100332–100362 (2019). https://doi.org/10.1109/ACCESS.2019.2904945
15. Olatinwo, S.O., Joubert, T.H.: Energy efficient solutions in wireless sensor systems for water quality monitoring: a review. IEEE Sens. J. **19**(5), 1596–1625 (2019). https://doi.org/10.1109/JSEN.2018.2882424
16. Park, J., Kim, K.T., Lee, W.H.: Recent advances in information and communications technology (ICT) and sensor technology for monitoring water quality. Water **12**(2), 510 (2020). https://doi.org/10.3390/w12020510
17. Pule, M., Yahya, A., Chuma, J.: Wireless sensor networks: a survey on monitoring water quality. J. Appl. Res. Technol. **15**(6), 562–570 (2017). https://doi.org/10.1016/j.jart.2017.07.004
18. Santos, J.M., Caeiro, J.J., Martins, J.C., Santos, F., Palma, P.: Physical and chemical water quality parameters sensing IoT systems for improving water productivity. Water Prod. J. **1**(2), 33–46 (2020)
19. Serpanos, D., Wolf, M.: Internet-of-Things (IoT) Systems: Architectures, Algorithms, Methodologies. Springer, Heidelberg (2018). https://doi.org/10.1007/978-3-319-69715-4

20. Tiyasha, Tung, T.M., Yaseen, Z.M.: A survey on river water quality modelling using artificial intelligence models: 2000–2020. J. Hydrol. **585**, 124670 (2020). https://doi.org/10.1016/j.jhydrol.2020.124670
21. Topp, S.N., Pavelsky, T.M., Jensen, D., Simard, M., Ross, M.R.V.: Research trends in the use of remote sensing for inland water quality science: moving towards multidisciplinary applications. Water **12**(1), 169 (2020). https://doi.org/10.3390/w12010169
22. Tseng, L., Yao, X., Otoum, S., Aloqaily, M., Jararweh, Y.: Blockchain-based database in an IoT environment: challenges, opportunities, and analysis. Clust. Comput. **23**(3), 2151–2165 (2020). https://doi.org/10.1007/s10586-020-03138-7
23. World Meteorological Organization (ed.): Planning of Water-Quality Monitoring Systems. No. 3 in Technical Report Series, World Meteorological Organization (2013)

Decentralising the Internet of Medical Things with Distributed Ledger Technologies and Off-Chain Storages: A Proof of Concept

Gioele Bigini[1]([✉]) [iD], Valerio Freschi[1] [iD], Alessandro Bogliolo[1,2] [iD],
and Emanuele Lattanzi[1] [iD]

[1] Department of Pure and Applied Sciences, University of Urbino,
Piazza della Repubblica 13, 61029 Urbino, Italy
`g.bigini@campus.uniurb.it`
[2] DIGIT srl, Corso Garibaldi 66-68, 61029 Urbino, Italy

Abstract. The privacy issue limits the Internet of Medical Things. Medical information would enhance new medical studies, formulate new treatments, and deliver new digital health technologies. Solving the sharing issue will have a triple impact: handling sensitive information easily, contributing to international medical advancements, and enabling personalised care. A possible solution could be to decentralise the notion of privacy, distributing it directly to users. Solutions enabling this vision are closely linked to Distributed Ledger Technologies. This technology would allow privacy-compliant solutions in contexts where privacy is the first need through its characteristics of immutability and transparency. This work lays the foundations for a system that can provide adequate security in terms of privacy, allowing the sharing of information between participants. We introduce an Internet of Medical Things application use case called "Balance", networks of trusted peers to manage sensitive data access called "Halo", and eventually leverage Smart Contracts to safeguard third party rights over data. This architecture should enable the theoretical vision of privacy-based healthcare solutions running in a decentralised manner.

Keywords: Decentralised Health Data Management · Internet of Medical Things · Distributed Ledger Technology · Distributed Storage System

1 Introduction

The Internet of Medical Things (IoMT) devices generate a considerable amount of valuable data of inestimable value. However, sharing sensitive information

This research was funded by Regione Marche with DDPF n. 1189 and by the Department of Pure and Applied Sciences, University of Urbino.

I. M. Pires et al. (Eds.): GOODTECHS 2021, LNICST 401, pp. 80–90, 2021.
https://doi.org/10.1007/978-3-030-91421-9_7

between devices is limited by privacy regulations with good intentions but definitely impacting innovation. Solving the sharing problem could significantly impact the health of an individual.

Distributed Ledger Technology (DLT) is a promising technology to solve the sharing issue in IoMT. With the term DLT, we often refer to the technology that allows the transfer of digital assets in a distributed network. In a DLT, every transaction is transparent and visible to all the participants that secure immutability. A specific derivative of DLT is the Blockchain, a well-defined DLT implementation where the ledger consists of a chain of blocks linked together by hashes. The first known implementation is Bitcoin [15]. One of the most significant technology trends during the last ten years is to think of it as general-purpose, i.e. to use it to transfer data or to use it to track digital and real-world items. In this sense, immutable ledgers could enable data ownership, linking a digital asset to an individual. An example of DLT is the IOTA Tangle [19] that is a scalable DLT whose goal is to establish a solution for the IoT by using a Distributed Acyclic Graph (DAG) ledger. A proper feature of IOTA is the ability of being feeless, allowing free transactions. Examples of general-purpose Blockchains are Ethereum and Cardano. Ethereum 2.0 [2] is a Proof of Stake (PoS) protocol that represents the solution for the scalability of the Ethereum blockchain. A similar approach comes from Cardano that is a blockchain platform based on a peer-reviewed PoS protocol called Ouroboros [8].

Several DLTs integrate Smart Contracts that are a set of promises and protocols specified in digital form within which the parties perform on these promises [25]. One of the most interesting facts about Smart Contracts is the possibility to involve them in data sharing. Several general-purpose Blockchain platforms as the most famous Ethereum, Cardano, and IOTA implement Smart Contracts. A platform that is basing his workflow on Smart Contracts is Filecoin [6], a distributed network based on the Blockchain where miners are elected based on the amount of storage in their possession, allowing both the circulation of cryptocurrency in the network and the usage of storages made available by the miners. In fact, Filecoin is a platform designed to grant easy access to decentralised storage, such as the InterPlanetary File System (IPFS).

The biggest concerns that justify the deepening of DLTs for data sharing and decentralisation (potentially Big Data decentralisation) are scalability, since DLTs are not the best for storing extensive data due to their architecture, and compatibility with standards, as the Fast Healthcare Interoperability Resources (FHIR) [1] used to share health data in the healthcare industry. For the scalability issue, it could be convenient to couple DLT with the Distributed File System (DFS), a file system that allows the storage of files and resources in storage devices distributed on the network's nodes. An example of DFS is the previously cited IPFS, a peer to peer distributed file system where peer nodes do not have to trust each other to store and access data on the IPFS network, which makes it similar to the features offered by DLTs (as it supports decentralisation) but with a throughput higher when dealing with large chunks of data, which are stored with the cryptographic hash of their content. Moving to standards instead, DLTs are promising on boosting their adoption. The FHIR standard defines how healthcare information can be exchanged abstracting from how data is stored. So, it allows healthcare information to be more accessible but, it does not consider the possibility of healthcare systems decentralisation.

While both the DFS and DLT could be private and restricted to a consortium of participants, the choice of using them this way goes against decentralisation. To fix the problem, the usage of cryptography could be essential. The idea is to encrypt to the point that only those who have the credentials can read the files and so, the creator (or the authoritative holders).

In this work, we try to give a possible solution based on DLTs and off-chain storages to decentralise the IoMT and enable a secure data sharing mechanism across the IoMT network. We will show how this solution could work beside an IoMT smartphone application called "Balance", based on the work of E. Lattanzi et al. [11]. The work is structured as follows: Sect. 1, the introduction; Sect. 2, the case study; Sect. 3, the proposed solution; Sect. 4, the discussion and conclusions.

1.1 Related Works

There are many works available on decentralised data management, focusing attention on the sensitivity of health data and, therefore, on attempting to produce a shift to the decentralised paradigm. Most of them use multiple technologies, including decentralised storages such as IPFS, DLTs technologies as Blockchain or DAG, and sometimes cryptography. The key idea for each work is to connect patients and any health organisations and enable users to own data created. One of the most significant research in the field [17] uses the Ethereum network to save data through links saved on the Blockchain assisted by Smart Contracts. Moreover, the paper introduces the usage of mobile devices, i.e. the smartphones. Another interesting approach [13], in addition to IPFS and Smart Contracts, attempts to introduce a reputation system to encrypt and share data. An incremental solution to the latter [5] introduces an economic incentive for those who disseminate their health data since these effectively contribute to a piece of greater knowledge for personalised medicine. Similar idea on the usage of IPFS and Smart Contracts also belongs to other researchers [14,24], with some exception [10,23] which respectively uses IPFS, Blockchain and cloud technologies. On the other hand, others have focused mainly on monitoring practices, such as teleconsultation [9] or specific tracking-related problems such as organ transplantation [21] or more general health data [16]. Other works than look to the effective compliance of these systems with the healthcare sector [18], or the possibility of providing an identity to the participants anticipating a Health Digital Identity System. Finally, more complex works [7,26] use multiple blockchains intending to give different roles to the different players involved and separate systems for data management.

Other few solutions are based on the IOTA Tangle, addressing different issues. The first identified issue focus on the fact that patients and healthcare organisations must communicate and therefore be interoperable [22]. The research tries to understand the actual current standards used in health institutions to provide an approach that can be integrated with these standards already used in hospitals, including the Fast Healthcare Interoperability Resources (FHIR). In the paper, they try to use the Tangle with the already existing standards and, therefore, save the data produced by patients in the EHR systems of health institutions. The attempt is undoubtedly interesting and demonstrates the possibility of using these standards with DLT technologies. Other researchers instead focuses on studying the scalability of the blockchain in healthcare institutions [4]. That is, they try to understand if the available DLTs technologies are suitable for use in the presence of large volumes of transactions. Cardano in the paper is the best performer of technologies with the least need to use sidechains in order to speed up transactions. Similar works for data sharing have been investigated [12]. The idea is based on the Tangle and data owners interact with it through mobile devices. The Tangle is used for saving data but we think that it is also not recommended for privacy reasons, since the ledger is basically immutable. Authors of [3] focused on COVID-19 pandemic monitoring operations. The paper attempts to focus on emergency and response issues. The idea is to use the Tangle as a data layer used by local authorities and the US government locally for emergency management. It is unclear how the user can be the data owner since his interaction does not occur with the ledger but with institution-owned databases that potentially replicate data.

1.2   Contribution of This Paper

In the future, the possibility for individuals to manage their sensitive information could lead to the creation of billions of everlasting clinical histories useful to enhance new medical studies, formulate new treatments, and deliver new digital health technologies. Decentralisation could be inevitable, eclipsing central authorities as store of sensitive information, being replaced by individuals responsibility. This work propose an idea on how to decentralise the IoMT by presenting a case study with the aim of enabling data ownership, and sharing. Participants avoid revealing data locations on distributed storages and manage their data through decentralised private networks called Halo. In our solution, we propose the use of off-chain storages, DLTs, Smart Contracts, mobile devices, and the introduction of the Halo: networks of participants who secure and manage data against remote stakeholders. This will guarantee no direct access to data locations and that remote users would always be tracked and forced to accept sharing conditions.

2   The Case Study

Balance is a IoMT smartphone application that records the human postural stability indices of an individual through the sensors integrated within the smartphone. It aims to produce a stabilometric analysis by referencing the biomechanical model of the single inverse pendulum and the available traditional healthcare technology in the field [11]. The stabilometric analysis allows evaluating the patient's stability in the upright position by studying the dynamics of the center of gravity projection on a plane parallel to the ground. The smartphone application carry out the analysis with this scope, since the human sensory system can be considered at rest (except for the plantar skin receptors), and so, the body instability is reconducted to endogenous factors. During a static test, the patient is stationary and standing on a measurement surface with his eyes open or closed, without the presence of any external perturbation. The body moves due to the combination of internal correction forces, drawing the deformation they produce on the underlying plane. The point of force application is called the center of pressure (COP) since it is the center of the distribution of pressure on the surface of the foot.

2.1   Architecture

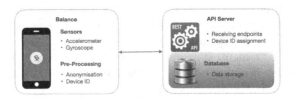

Fig. 1. Balance architecture

Balance architecture consists of a mobile application and a backend that resides in a centralised location (Fig. 1). The smartphone application performs all the pre-processing onboard the smartphone in order to comply with privacy regulations. The data is sent to the backend in a completely anonymous way. A unique ID generated by the backend and not associated with the user or his device is sent to the user to always refer to his data correctly.

2.2   Measurement Protocol

In traditional systems, the subject is placed at the center of a force platform for postural acquisition to perform the required test. In the case study, the Romberg test that is a test in which the patient performs the analysis with both eyes open or closed, allowing to understand the influence of the visual system on posture.

Through Balance, the repeatable test is performed through the smartphone in a few seconds. The test can be carried out with open or closed eyes by choosing the appropriate mode on the home screen. While performing a test, the user keeps a straight posture and holds the smartphone with two hands in a vertical position at the navel level, guided to maintain the correct position. The actual sensor measurement takes about 30 s. For the analysis to be meaningful, the test must be repeated periodically. In this way, it is possible to compare the past indices with the most recent ones and monitor the evolution of postural stability.

2.3   Data Collected

The static analysis generates two main insights: the statokinesigram (SKG), or sway-path, represents the displacement of the COP in the X,Y plane and allows for the extraction of global parameters and structural parameters; the former relates to the sway-pattern while the latter focus on trajectories applicable to extracting data from them. The Stabilogram, shows the change in COP over time expressed as a vector in two dimensions: Antero-Posterior (AP) and Medio-Lateral (ML).

The user is also asked for some personal information: age, gender, weight, any postural problems, the presence of postural problems in the family, the use of medicines that can interfere with posture, any other trauma, visual defects, and hearing defects. Potentially, it will be possible to extend and use them for several reasons that go from performing medical studies to personalised medicine.

3   The Proposed Solution

3.1   DLTs Comparison

It is worthwhile to evaluate several DLTs candidates for a decentralised data management solution. In this section we analyse Ethereum 2.0, Cardano, Filecoin and, IOTA 2.0 which results are shown in Table 1.

Based on the comparison, Cardano is going to provide the most appreciable result in terms of long-term objectives, promising the best results both from the Governance and the tps. A good compromise represents IOTA 2.0, which would allow greater freedom regarding the reduction of the cost of transactions. A little in the shadows is Ethereum 2.0, which does not seem to promise a high number of tps as the other implementations, even if it is good to highlight how it represents a consolidated Blockchain and it has the best development ecosystem worldwide. Finally, Filecoin represents an ad-hoc solution to be adopted for specific needs.

Table 1. DLTs Comparison *Highly Speculative

Category	Ethereum 2.0	Cardano	Filecoin	IOTA 2.0
DLT	Blockchain	Blockchain	Blockchain	DAG
General Purpose	Yes	Yes	No	Yes
Consensus	PoW/PoS	PoS	PoW	No/FPC
Smart Contracts	Yes	Yes	Yes	Yes
Dynamic Governance	No	Yes	No	No
Feeless	No	No	No	Yes
Transactions Per Second	15/*100k	250/*1m	Not Known	200/*300k

Ethereum 2.0. The biggest problems Ethereum 1.0 is suffering are higher transaction fees and low tps. The upgrade to the second version is to overcome both the problems, by replacing the Proof Of Work protocol with a PoS protocol. On the side of Governance, Ethereum is not so dynamic. Users, miners and developers can submit proposals but, on Github. The biggest obstacle to this is finding support for that proposal that needs to reach the Core developers through several channels like social media, conferences, articles. Once the proposal attracts interest could be taken into consideration. In the future, It is expected that Ethereum 2.0 could bring more than 100 thousand tps increasing the actual stage of about 15 tps.

Cardano. Thanks to Ouroboros, Cardano is one of the most scalable blockchains in the crypto-space with 250 tps on average, basing its success on its community of stake pools, actively contributing to the security of the network. Moreover, It has a dynamic governance system based on democratic voting on upgrade proposals that ensures the platform and its community can continuously fund and decide upon platform and ecosystem improvements. In the future, the system will implement a second layer solution under research called Hydra that is going to bring the tps to more than 1 million, a great achievement for the overall crypto-space.

IOTA 2.0. Unlike the first version of IOTA, where a centralised entity called coordinator was validating the transactions milestones (a checkpoint in the Tangle that was validating all the backward transactions), IOTA 2.0 will operate decentralised by introducing several features summed up in the Coordicide paper [20], designed to be modular and to ensure long-term success. Note that the second version is going to implement a Fast Probabilistic Consensus (FPC). IOTA governance is centralised but the development team is open to conversations. Several components have been developed between IOTA and community members. By the way, they do not have a voting system in this sense, but at least it is all transparent. Industry players help guide the development of the system. In the future, the Tangle is expected to bring more than 300 thousands tps.

Filecoin. Filecoin is a Blockchain with the specific aim to give permanence to data in a decentralised environment. Even if It is actually not seen as general-purpose, in addition to allow transactions, the Filecoin ledger implements Smart Contracts, and it implements a proprietary Virtual Machine (Filecoin VM) that offers control mechanisms that regulate the operation and acquisition of decentralised storage requested by the users. We could think of Filecoin as the first attempt to exploit Blockchain technology to achieve persistence of stored data on decentralised storages through paid agreements exactly as happening with the cloud technology. The system rewards participants as a mean of incentive for all who are willing to provide data storage.

3.2   Architectural View

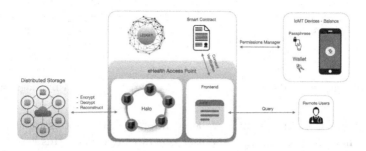

Fig. 2. System architecture

The IoMT comprises mobile devices, i.e. smartphones, devices, wearables. The need for these devices is the ability to perform operations that involve sensitive information. In the following sections, we try to give a view of the components and the architecture to achieve this result.

Components. The components of the architecture must reflect all the needs foreseen in the IoMT. A reference to the architecture is in Fig. 2 and includes:

- The IoMT Device is the location where the user's data are generated and the private keys, used for signing data, are stored. Safety issues relating to the device used are neglected. Through the Wallet, it is possible to access the Ledger and manage digital assets.
- The Ledger gives the user a potential anonymised criterion of being uniquely identified in the network.
- Smart Contracts are used to grant access to remote users using Non-Fungible Tokens (NFTs).
- Remote users represent all those interested parties in accessing sensitive information. They can be professionals, general users and healthcare organisations. The interaction happens through the web interface.
- The proposed Halo is a private network, similar to a oracle network, of explicitly trusted nodes which is involved in encrypting, decrypting, and reconstructing user's off-chain data, guaranteeing availability. Their role is of redundancy and data security.
- The Distributed Storage is where the data of the user are saved. Decentralised technologies, such as IPFS, are public storages, transparent and publicly accessible. For this reason, the data on the storage are sharded and anonymised, and the private network needs to reconstruct the data properly.

Workflow. Storing data from the IoMT devices should follow the steps shown in Fig. 3:

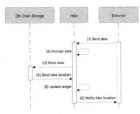

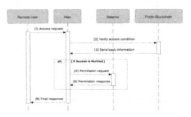

Fig. 3. Data store diagram   **Fig. 4.** Data sharing diagram

1. The system is composed of a wallet containing the cryptographic keys for signing new data. Every time the user generates new data, this is sent to the Halo.
2. Once data are successfully stored, the links to the decentralised storage could be sent to the DLT and saved as transactions or kept private into the smartphone, creating a recovery-proof mechanism.
3. The Halo eventually ensure data pinning to the store files on decentralised storage and privacy-compliant operations before storing.

Sharing information with remote users should follow the process in Fig. 4:

1. A remote user asks for health data by accessing the frontend and accepting conditions.
2. The Halo verifies the access on the public blockchain, ideally with the help of Smart Contracts, and then forwards the request to the data owner device, who is required to give consent.
3. If consent is given, the network processes the data and sends the final response to the user; otherwise, it will just notify the rejection.

4   Discussion and Conclusions

By using the proposed architecture, the health data are created and maintained by the owners. All remote users are subject to predefined rules, and Smart Contract constitutes a transparent way of managing permissions. Cryptography constitutes an essential tool and it will need advancements in the future. In fact, it is not a sufficient deterrent for keeping data secure with the advent of quantum computing, even if coupled with sharding and masking techniques constitutes a solution. It should be noted that this approach causes a decrease in performance by forcing rebuilding before the use. The usage of a two-layer solutions guarantees both transparency and logging, while the usage of Distributed Storages could allow for data relocation since data stored are persistent but not permanent.

In this work, we proposed a solution to decentralise the IoMT, enabling data sharing. Our solution is blockchain agnostic and demonstrates the role of DLT technology as an enabler for sharing sensitive data. The overall architecture could constitute a personal sensitive data portal with which healthcare systems can be interfaced directly to individuals. Smart Contracts can be essential in establishing agreements between the owner and remote users, highlighting the need for a Decentralised Digital Identity. As future work, we plan to develop the implementation of this solution by using DLTs technologies and IoMT applications to demonstrate the potentiality of the system in solving the sharing problem scenario without relying on any intermediary.

References

1. Bender, D., Sartipi, K.: HL7 FHIR: an agile and restful approach to healthcare information exchange. In: Proceedings of the 26th IEEE International Symposium on Computer-Based Medical Systems, pp. 326–331 (2013). https://doi.org/10.1109/CBMS.2013.6627810
2. Buterin, V., Griffith, V.: Casper the friendly finality gadget. arXiv preprint arXiv:1710.09437 (2017)
3. Cisneros, B., Ye, J., Park, C.H., Kim, Y.: CoviReader: using IOTA and QR code technology to control epidemic diseases across the us. In: 2021 IEEE 11th Annual Computing and Communication Workshop and Conference (CCWC), pp. 0610–0618. IEEE (2021). https://doi.org/10.1109/CCWC51732.2021.9376093
4. Donawa, A., Orukari, I., Baker, C.E.: Scaling blockchains to support electronic health records for hospital systems. In: 2019 IEEE 10th Annual Ubiquitous Computing, Electronics & Mobile Communication Conference (UEMCON), pp. 0550–0556. IEEE (2019). https://doi.org/10.1109/UEMCON47517.2019.8993101
5. Fernández-Caramés, T.M., Froiz-Míguez, I., Blanco-Novoa, O., Fraga-Lamas, P.: Enabling the internet of mobile crowdsourcing health things: a mobile fog computing, blockchain and IoT based continuous glucose monitoring system for diabetes mellitus research and care. Sensors **19**(15), 3319 (2019). https://doi.org/10.3390/s19153319
6. Filecoin: Filecoin - a decentralized storage network designed to store humanity's most important information (2017). https://filecoin.io
7. Jiang, S., Cao, J., Wu, H., Yang, Y., Ma, M., He, J.: BlocHIE: a blockchain-based platform for healthcare information exchange. In: 2018 IEEE International Conference on Smart Computing (Smartcomp), pp. 49–56. IEEE (2018). https://doi.org/10.1109/SMARTCOMP.2018.00073
8. Kiayias, A., Russell, A., David, B., Oliynykov, R.: Ouroboros: a provably secure proof-of-stake blockchain protocol. In: Katz, J., Shacham, H. (eds.) CRYPTO 2017. LNCS, vol. 10401, pp. 357–388. Springer, Cham (2017). https://doi.org/10.1007/978-3-319-63688-7_12
9. Kordestani, H., Barkaoui, K., Zahran, W.: HapiChain: a blockchain-based framework for patient-centric telemedicine. In: 2020 IEEE 8th International Conference on Serious Games and Applications for Health (SeGAH), pp. 1–6. IEEE (2020). https://doi.org/10.1109/SeGAH49190.2020.9201726
10. Kumar, R., Marchang, N., Tripathi, R.: Distributed off-chain storage of patient diagnostic reports in healthcare system using IPFS and blockchain. In: 2020 International Conference on COMmunication Systems & NETworkS (COMSNETS), pp. 1–5. IEEE (2020). https://doi.org/10.1109/COMSNETS48256.2020.9027313
11. Lattanzi, E., Freschi, V., Delpriori, S., Klopfenstein, L.C., Bogliolo, A.: Standing balance assessment by measurement of body center of gravity using smartphones. IEEE Access **8**, 96438–96448 (2020). https://doi.org/10.1109/ACCESS.2020.2996251

12. Lücking, M., Manke, R., Schinle, M., Kohout, L., Nickel, S., Stork, W.: Decentralized patient-centric data management for sharing IoT data streams. In: 2020 International Conference on Omni-layer Intelligent Systems (COINS), pp. 1–6. IEEE (2020). https://doi.org/10.1109/COINS49042.2020.9191653

13. Madine, M.M., et al.: Blockchain for giving patients control over their medical records. IEEE Access **8**, 193102–193115 (2020). https://doi.org/10.1109/ACCESS.2020.3032553

14. Marangappanavar, R.K., Kiran, M.: Inter-planetary file system enabled blockchain solution for securing healthcare records. In: 2020 Third ISEA Conference on Security and Privacy (ISEA-ISAP), pp. 171–178. IEEE (2020). https://doi.org/10.1109/ISEA-ISAP49340.2020.235016

15. Nakamoto, S.: Re: Bitcoin p2p e-cash paper. The Cryptography Mailing List (2008)

16. Nascimento Jr, J.R., Nunes, J.B., Falcão, E.L., Sampaio, L., Brito, A.: On the tracking of sensitive data and confidential executions. In: Proceedings of the 14th ACM International Conference on Distributed and Event-based Systems, pp. 51–60 (2020). https://doi.org/10.1145/3401025.3404097

17. Nguyen, D.C., Pathirana, P.N., Ding, M., Seneviratne, A.: Blockchain for secure EHRs sharing of mobile cloud based e-health systems. IEEE Access **7**, 66792–66806 (2019). https://doi.org/10.1109/ACCESS.2019.2917555

18. Omar, I.A., Jayaraman, R., Salah, K., Simsekler, M.C.E., Yaqoob, I., Ellahham, S.: Ensuring protocol compliance and data transparency in clinical trials using blockchain smart contracts. BMC Med. Res. Methodol. **20**(1), 1–17 (2020). https://doi.org/10.1186/s12874-020-01109-5

19. Popov, S.: The tangle. White Paper **1**, 3 (2018)

20. Popov, S., et al.: The coordicide, pp. 1–30 (2020). Accessed Jan

21. Ranjan, P., Srivastava, S., Gupta, V., Tapaswi, S., Kumar, N.: Decentralised and distributed system for organ/tissue donation and transplantation. In: 2019 IEEE Conference on Information and Communication Technology, pp. 1–6. IEEE (2019). https://doi.org/10.1109/CICT48419.2019.9066225

22. Saweros, E., Song, Y.T.: Connecting personal health records together with EHR using tangle. In: 2019 20th IEEE/ACIS International Conference on Software Engineering, Artificial Intelligence, Networking and Parallel/Distributed Computing (SNPD), pp. 547–554. IEEE (2019). https://doi.org/10.1109/SNPD.2019.8935646

23. Seliem, M., Elgazzar, K.: BioMT: blockchain for the internet of medical things. In: 2019 IEEE International Black Sea Conference on Communications and Networking (BlackSeaCom), pp. 1–4. IEEE (2019). https://doi.org/10.1109/BlackSeaCom.2019.8812784

24. Sultana, M., Hossain, A., Laila, F., Taher, K.A., Islam, M.N.: Towards developing a secure medical image sharing system based on zero trust principles and blockchain technology. BMC Med. Inform. Decis. Mak. **20**(1), 1–10 (2020). https://doi.org/10.1186/s12911-020-01275-y

25. Szabo, N.: Formalizing and securing relationships on public networks. First Monday (1997). https://doi.org/10.5210/fm.v2i9.548

26. Xu, J., et al.: Healthchain: a blockchain-based privacy preserving scheme for large-scale health data. IEEE Internet Things J. **6**(5), 8770–8781 (2019). https://doi.org/10.1109/JIOT.2019.2923525

Towards a Monitoring Framework for Users of Retirement Houses with Mobile Sensing

Fernando Terroso-Saenz⬤, Alberto Albaladejo, Antonio Llanes⬤,
Navjot Sidhu⬤, and Andrés Muñoz(✉)⬤

Universidad Católica de Murcia (UCAM), Campus de los Jerónimos, Guadalupe,
30107 Murcia, Spain
amunoz@ucam.edu

Abstract. The population of Western countries has notoriously aged during the last decades, thus increasing the number of people living in retirement houses. This causes that, in certain circumstances, the staff of these residences can not properly take care of all the users due to several situations. For that reason, the usage of solutions based on Information and Communications Technologies (ICT) to support such staff has arisen over the last years. In this context, the present work introduces a new Smart Assistance solution for retirement houses. Based on a mobile-sensing paradigm, the proposed framework is able to collect several health and physical parameters of the users and visualize them in a central multi-platform dashboard. Furthermore, the system allows detecting certain abnormal or dangerous situations related to the residence's users and send alarms to the staff providing also proactive functionalities. Our proposal is illustrated through a case of use for a patient in an early stage of the Alzheimer's disease and a tendency to be sedentary.

Keywords: Mobile application · Elderly patients · Retirement house · Smart habitat · Smart Assistance

1 Introduction

In the last three years, sales of wearable devices have grown by 50% and the number of smartwatches is expected to reach one billion by 2022[1]. Wristbands and smartwatches now include a palette of sensors able to collect information about the users and their health parameters. This information is valuable because it can be used to develop beneficial solutions within the health sector. More in detail, some advanced devices might include heart-rate, triaxial-acceleration, geomagnetic and air pressure sensors along with GPS antennas and Bluetooth connection, among other features. As it has been widely studied in the literature,

---

[1] https://www.statista.com/statistics/487291/global-connected-wearable-devices/.

© ICST Institute for Computer Sciences, Social Informatics and Telecommunications Engineering 2021
Published by Springer Nature Switzerland AG 2021. All Rights Reserved
I. M. Pires et al. (Eds.): GOODTECHS 2021, LNICST 401, pp. 91–104, 2021.
https://doi.org/10.1007/978-3-030-91421-9_8

this type of sensorization is able to capture a rich amount of contextual features of an end-user [7].

At the same time, the population of Western countries has been ageing steadily for the last decades. As a matter of fact, the rate of the population aged above 65 years will increase 49% between 2019 and 2050 [11]. In the particular case of Spain, 14.27% of the Spanish population was over 70 years old in 2019, which is equivalent to a total of 6,761,510 million people[2]. Furthermore, there are 5,417 retirement houses in Spain with a total of 372,985 available places [1].

In this context, it is sometimes very difficult for the staff working in these houses to effectively control and take care of all the residents and patients at the same time. This may cause some potentially-dangerous situations for such patients. For example, a mentally-ill patient might leave the residence's premises without any type of supervision causing him/her to be totally disoriented outdoors. This calls for the development of new and innovative solutions based on Information and Communication Technologies (ICT) to support such staff in the management of the residences and provide a more personal attention to their users.

The present work proposes a *Smart Assistance* service for retirement houses. By means of a client-server architecture, the solution is able to proactively collect relevant information about the physical activity and health parameters of the users of a residence (hereby users) through a set of smart bracelets. Moreover, the service is also able to identify certain events in such collected parameters that might reflect some abnormal or dangerous situations related to any of the users. In that case, the solution is also able to notify to the residence's staff. Lastly, the solution also includes a dashboard to allow the staff to visualise all the data collected from the users.

The rest of the paper is structured as follows. Section 2 provides an overview about current mobile-sensing solutions for elderly people. Next, Sect. 3 describes the architecture of the proposed application in detail. Section 4 puts forward a preliminary use case whereas Sect. 5 states the final conclusions and future lines of research derived from this work.

2   Related Work

Nowadays, it is possible to find in the literature many different solutions to support assisted-living centers. To start with, the robotics field has played an important role to develop solutions for elders. For example, a telescopic manipulator for elder-care facilities is stated in [9]. The device is used to, for example, help elder people to taking objects from high shelves. For its evaluation, a corntoss game was developed showing quite promising results. Other robotic arms have been used and tested with elderly people in other works, such as in [8], where authors develop a robotic arm with which they can also pick up objects from shelves as part of a game, and the level of acceptance by the elderly is very

[2] https://www.ine.es/jaxiT3/Datos.htm?t=31304#!tabs-tabla.

high. A further step is made in [2], where a full-body robot controller is developed to assist frail patients. This is an ambitious project in which a humanoid robot can even be responsible for initiating the assistance process in front of a person, establishing the first contacts with him or her.

A study that could complement any of the aforementioned ones is found elsewhere [10], in which the focus of the study is the feeling of confidence that the elderly have about this type of new technology that can replace human assistance. Through the study in different residences in Canada, with more than 150 users, the following relevant conclusions are reached: elderly people are not against an autonomous home care system, especially if they meet a series of conditions such as ease of use; people can develop a feeling of belonging to the systems; and the feeling of confidence can be higher if these systems can share feelings of socialization. Exploring this type of feelings of confidence towards these new robotic social assistance systems is also the focus of the work of Iglesias et al. [6]. They develop the idea of a long-term implementation in retirement houses, as well as evaluating the trust in it and its acceptance. This work is based on the assistance in simple and repetitive tasks by the robotic systems, in order to make the robot a facilitator of social feelings in a second term.

In [5] robotic assisting systems are tested with a segment of the population that has been growing in recent years, namely the elderly who suffer from some form of senile dementia. In the study, daily routines are recorded and analyzed, which helps the elderly to maintain their daily independence. The use of devices related to the Internet of Things makes these studies possible, which are closely related to our proposal.

Most of the approaches based on mobile sensing to provide health-care services for elderly people focus on detecting the physical activity and other kinematic-related features of the patient. Thus, the work of Hu et al. [4] studies a smart health system based on cell phones and wearable devices. The authors focus on the study of certain event-condition-action (ECA) rules, and how it would be possible to generate these rules from the study of the data generated and acquired from the different devices. Likewise, the work in [3] fuses data from a smart band and a smart phone so as to identify human activities. The key innovation of this work is that the target activities to be detected are not individual but family-related ones like *watching TV* or *talking*.

All the works previously mentioned study the monitoring of the health of the elderly from different perspectives by using different methods, such as robotics, sensors, wearable devices, mobile devices, etc. By combining all these methodologies and devices together, we can understand what the Smart Home for the Elders (SHfE) would be, with the processing of data from all these types of devices with the aim of caring for the health of our elderly. This vision is provided by a pilot project in [12].

3   Smart Assistance Service

Figure 1 depicts the general architecture of the proposed system that must be *instantiated* separately in each retirement house. As it can be seen, the solution has been split into two different modules. The *client application* is devoted to collect health, activity and location data of each user of a residence. The *administrative module* (AM) provides a dashboard to the staff of the residence to control the activity and health status of each of its members. Both modules are explained next.

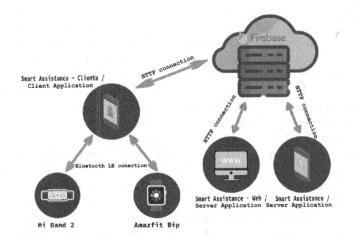

Fig. 1. Global architecture of the proposed system.

3.1   Client Application

The first module is in charge of collecting different features of each elder user of a residence. This is done by means of a set of smart bands and a mobile application running an Android *Smart Assistance-Client* application. Concerning the smart bands, our solution is compatible with two different models, the *Xiaomi Mi Band 2*[3] and the *Xiaomi Amazfit Bip*[4] (see Fig. 1). These two models have been selected because they are affordable devices, their energy consumption is limited and both of them have Bluetooth Low-Energy (LE) connectivity.

Each user must wear one of these two bands in his/her wrist and carry a mobile-phone with the mobile application in his pocket. The band is connected to the user's smart-phone via Bluetooth LE. It is worth mentioning that to carry out the synchronization between a user's smart band and his/her phone, it is necessary to enter a code generated automatically when the user is registered in the system by the administrators. Thus, we avoid potential intruders in the system.

Once the synchronization is done, the client application continuously collects data from different sensors of the smart band and the mobile-phone itself. Next,

---

[3] https://www.mi.com/global/miband2/.

[4] https://www.amazfit.com/en/bip.html.

it stores all the collected data in a central Firebase[5] datastore by means of a Rest-API connection. In particular, the application collects in real time the following parameters of the user directly from both the smart band and the smart phone:

– walking steps during the current day,
– distance covered during the current day,
– current dynamic state,
– calories consumed during the current day,
– heart beats per minute,
– current GPS location every two minutes.

By means of the first two parameters, the systems is able to control the physical activity of each user in terms of mobility. This information is completed with the current dynamic state of the user. This third item is inferred from the smart-band data and can take six different values, namely *walking*, *running*, *lying*, *quiet*, *sit* and *unknown*. Hence, it is possible to know the current state of the patient and his/her recent physical activity. As it will be explained in Sect. 3.2, all this information is instrumental so as to trigger alerts for the residence staff related with abnormal or dangerous behaviours of the users.

Finally, Fig. 2 shows the graphical user interface (GUI) of this application. Due to the fact that the data collection is done automatically, the GUI is limited to inform whether the aforementioned synchronization between the mobile phone and the smart band has been successfully performed.

3.2   Management Application

The key goal of this module is to provide a tool to the medical and administrative staff of the residence to control and monitor all their users. To do so, a mobile and web-based application have been developed. Both of them are fed with the data from the users' application described in the previous section that is stored in the central back-end repository (see Fig. 1).

To start with, both versions include a dashboard as initial view showing some general statistics of the residence premises and their users as depicted in Fig. 3. This view allows the staff to easily have a complete overview of the residence state at each moment. Then, the application has five key management features which are described next.

Register a New User of the Residence in the System. The administrative staff of the residence can easily register new users by means of the mobile and the web application (see Fig. 4). Each time a new user is registered, a unique code is generated for him/her that must be inserted during the synchronization of the smart band and the mobile phone as described in Sect. 3.1.

---

[5] https://firebase.google.com/.

Fig. 2. Graphic user interface of the *Smart Assistance-Client* application. The view informs that one *Amazfit Bit Watch* has been successfully connected to the mobile application.

Listing All the Users of the Residence Under Monitoring. Both applications provide a list of all the users who are using the client application as shown in Fig. 5. Hence, by means of this view, the staff can quickly review some health parameters of each user along with the battery level of their mobile-phones.

Furthermore, it is possible to visualize some of these parameters for a particular user with more detail. In particular, historic data related to the user's walking steps, daily covered distance, heart rate and consumed calories can be displayed. Figure 6 shows this view of the management application.

Remote Configuration and Sending Notifications to the Users' Devices. One of the instrumental features of the administrative part of the system is that it allows the management staff to perform certain actions on the user's devices.

On the one hand, the staff can remotely activate or deactivate the GPS sensor from a user's mobile device (see Fig. 7a). This way, it is possible to stop or start the location tracking of a user. The rationale behind this feature is because tracking is a rather energy-consuming task that might drain the battery of a users' mobile-phones quite quickly. For that reason, the staff should perform such a monitoring task only at certain hours of the day during which, for example, a user might move freely around the residence's premises.

On the other hand, it also possible to send alarms to the users. In that sense, an alarm just makes the user's smart band to vibrate. The rationale of this action

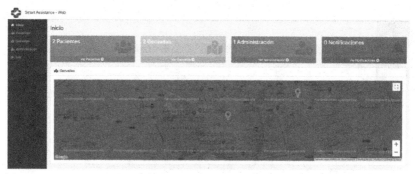

(a) View in the web application. In this case, the panel shows the location of two different premises of the residence.

(b) View in the mobile application.

Fig. 3. Initial dashboard of the management application showing some global statistics of the residence premises, user and staff. In particular, both panels inform that the residence has 2 patients and 1 person as staff.

is to provoke some type of stimulation on the patient to alert him/her about a dangerous or undesirable situation.

Generation of Health Reports. The continuous and proactive monitoring of the health state of each user is one of the paramount features of the proposed system. For that reason, the management application controls some of the health parameters captured by the mobile side and triggers a set of alerts when some

(a) View in the web application.

(b) View in the mobile application.

Fig. 4. Registration panel for new users in the system.

risky situations are detected. In particular, the system can generate two different alerts per user:

– Low heart-rate alarm. This alert is triggered when the heart rate of a user is below 50 beats per minute. This alarm relies on the heart-rate captured by the smart wrist of each patient and the goal is to generate early reports about certain dangerous situations with respect to the heart state of a user.
– Low activity-level alarm. This alert is generated when the client application of a user reports that his/her dynamic state has been *quiet* or *sit* for more than 2 h (see Sect. 3.1). The idea is to detect situations where a user might be without any physical activity during too much time. This way, the medical staff of the residence would be able to take certain actions to encourage the movement of the users avoiding sedentary behaviours. In that sense, Fig. 7b shows an example of some alerts generated in the mobile version of the application.

(a) View in the web application showing two different patients.

(b) View in the mobile application showing three different patients.

Fig. 5. List of all the users of a residence with the mobile app.

Definition of Geo-Fences. Most retirement houses allow users to leave their premises to, for example, go for a walk or to certain appointments. However, some users of these residences should not go out due to several reasons given their physical or mental health.

To control the fact that some users do not leave the residence without being supervised by the staff, the proposed system allows the generation of geo-fences, that is, geographical areas defining the spatial extension within which the users of the residence can roam without problems. Given these fences, whenever a user leaves any of them, the system automatically generates an alarm. This is possible because, as stated in Sect. 3.1, the client side of the system is able to periodically collect the current location of a residence user by means of the GPS sensor in the mobile phone.

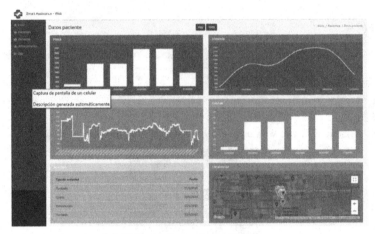

(a) View in the web application.

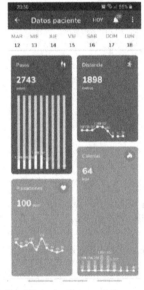

(b) View in the mobile application.

Fig. 6. Health data of a patient in the management application.

Figure 8 shows the interface of the application to generate such geo-fences. In the current version, it is required to define the geographical center of the fence as a pair of latitude-longitude coordinates and a radius in kilometers. As a result, it is possible to generate fences with circular shapes. Once a fence is created, the system performs a spatial-join operation between the fence's spatial area and each new GPS location generated by a user to detect whether he/she remains

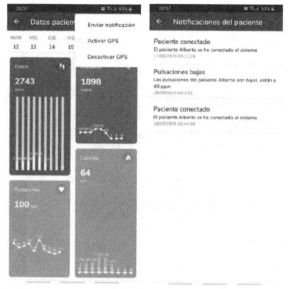

(a) Pop-up menu with the different actions available for the residence staff, send notification, activate and deactivate the GPS sensor.

(b) View with the notifications generated by a user. In particular, three different ones are listed, two informing that the user has connected to the system (*paciente conectado*) and other one reporting a very low heart rate (*pulsaciones bajas*).

Fig. 7. View panels related to the delivery and visualization of the notifications to the users.

inside the fence or not. If not, the system generates a new alarm informing about this event.

4   Applicability of the Proposal

As an illustrative example of the applicability of our proposal, we could consider a retirement house with an elder user who has early-stage Alzheimer's and a tendency to be sedentary.

To begin with, when this patient gets up in the morning, the client module would detect this situation by reporting a change in the patient's dynamic state from *lying* to *sit* or *walking* along with a slight increment in his heart rate. Hence, a member of the staff could go to the user's room to help him/her to get dress and have breakfast.

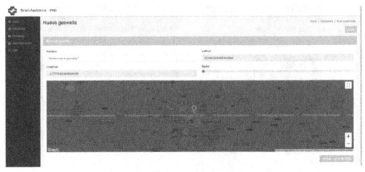

(a) View in the web application.

(b) View in the mobile application.

Fig. 8. View to generate the geo-fences with circular shape.

After having breakfast, the staff activates the GPS tracking of the patient's mobile phone so as to control that he/she does not leave the premises, defined by a geo-fence, without supervision. Furthermore, the staff also controls that the user does not remain seated for a long time and goes for a walk regularly. This can be done as the application also reports the patient's daily covered distance.

Once the patient has had lunch, the staff allows him/her to rest a bit and deactivates the GPS tracking of the phone to save battery. One hour latter, the staff detects that the user keeps sleeping and sends him/her an alert that makes the smart band to vibrate. Like in the morning, the staff can see through the dashboard of the management module whether the user has woken up or not.

Finally, in the evening the staff can prepare a dinner menu based on the total consumed calories of the user collected by the client module and displayed in the management web or mobile dashboard.

All in all, it can be seen that the described functionality of the system supports the staff at the retirement houses to control and provide a better service to their users at different moments of a regular day.

5   Conclusion and Future Work

Information and Communication Technology (ICT) solutions are a key enabler in the creation of smart habitats and applications for the elderly and their carers. In particular, this work focuses on the development of a monitoring framework for retirement houses aimed at helping the carers in their daily tasks. This framework allows for a more personalized monitoring of the residents by controlling not only their health parameters such as walking steps, daily covered distance, heart rate and consumed calories, but also their location in the residence and therefore detecting unauthorized walkaways. The framework is based on a client-server architecture, in which the client module consists of a low-cost smart band and smart phone for collecting the aforementioned data, whereas the server module is developed both as a web and an app services that enable the carers to efficiently monitor all the residents through five management features, including the remote configuration of users' devices and the notification of potential dangerous situations by means of alerts. A case of use for a patient in an early stage of the Alzheimer's disease and a tendency to be sedentary is shown to illustrate the functionality of the proposed framework.

We are currently working on extending the creation of geo-fence areas to different shapes other than circular to enable the definition of customized spatial extensions. Another future line of research is the combination of the current data from the mobile sensors in our framework with data obtained from fixed sensors embedded in the furniture of the retirement houses (e.g., beds, lights, doors, etc.) to augment the information available about the patients' behaviours. Moreover, machine learning methods will be applied to this data fusion to evaluate the possibility of predicting potential patient health risks.

Acknowledgments. This publication is based upon work from the Fundación Séneca del Centro de Coordinación de la Investigación de la Región de Murcia under Project 20813/PI/18 and from the Sheldon COST Action CA16226 Indoor Living Space Improvement: Smart Habitat for the Elderly, supported by COST (European Cooperation in Science and Technology). COST is a funding agency for research and innovation networks. Our Actions help connect research initiatives across Europe and enable scientists to grow their ideas by sharing them with their peers. This boosts their research, career and innovation. www.cost.eu

References

1. Abellan-Garcia, A., Aceituno-Nieto, M., Ramiro-Fariñas, D.: estadísticas sobre residencias: distribución de centros y plazas residenciales por provincia. datos de abril de 2019. Informes Envejecimiento en red 24 (2019)
2. Bolotnikova, A., Courtois, S., Kheddar, A.: Autonomous initiation of human physical assistance by a humanoid. In: 2020 29th IEEE International Conference on Robot and Human Interactive Communication (RO-MAN), pp. 857–862 (2020). https://doi.org/10.1109/RO-MAN47096.2020.9223519
3. Gu, F., Niu, J., He, Z., Jin, X., Rodrigues, J.J.P.C.: SmartBuddy: an integrated mobile sensing and detecting system for family activities. In: GLOBECOM 2017–2017 IEEE Global Communications Conference, pp. 1–7 (2017). https://doi.org/10.1109/GLOCOM.2017.8254140
4. Hu, S., Huang, M., Feng, W., Zhang, Y.: A smart health service model for elders based on ECA-S rules. In: 2017 IEEE 15th International Conference on Software Engineering Research, Management and Applications (SERA), pp. 93–97 (2017). https://doi.org/10.1109/SERA.2017.7965712
5. Hung, L.-P., Chen, C.-L., Sung, C.-T., Ho, C.-L.: Orientation training system for elders with dementia using internet of things. In: Lin, Y.-B., Deng, D.-J., You, I., Lin, C.-C. (eds.) IoTaaS 2017. LNICST, vol. 246, pp. 19–26. Springer, Cham (2018). https://doi.org/10.1007/978-3-030-00410-1_3
6. Iglesias, A., et al.: Towards long term acceptance of socially assistive robots in retirement houses: use case definition. In: 2020 IEEE International Conference on Autonomous Robot Systems and Competitions (ICARSC), pp. 134–139 (2020). https://doi.org/10.1109/ICARSC49921.2020.9096080
7. Laport-López, F., Serrano, E., Bajo, J., Campbell, A.T.: A review of mobile sensing systems, applications, and opportunities. Knowl. Inf. Syst. **62**(1), 145–174 (2019). https://doi.org/10.1007/s10115-019-01346-1
8. Minvielle, L., Audiffren, J.: NurseNet: monitoring elderly levels of activity with a piezoelectric floor. Sensors **19**(18) (2019). https://doi.org/10.3390/s19183851, https://www.mdpi.com/1424-8220/19/18/3851
9. Mucchiani, C., Torres, W.O., Edgar, D., Johnson, M.J., Cacchione, P.Z., Yim, M.: Development and deployment of a mobile manipulator for assisting and entertaining elders living in supportive apartment living facilities. In: 2018 27th IEEE International Symposium on Robot and Human Interactive Communication (RO-MAN), pp. 121–128 (2018). https://doi.org/10.1109/ROMAN.2018.8525826
10. Shareef, M.A., Kumar, V., Dwivedi, Y.K., Kumar, U., Akram, M.S., Raman, R.: A new health care system enabled by machine intelligence: elderly people's trust or losing self control. Technol. Forecast. Soc. Change **162**, 120334 (2021). https://doi.org/10.1016/j.techfore.2020.120334, https://www.sciencedirect.com/science/article/pii/S0040162520311604
11. United Nations, Department of Economic and Social Affairs: Population division (2019). World population ageing 2019: Highlights. Technical report, United Nations (2019)
12. Yu, J., An, N., Hassan, T., Kong, Q.: A pilot study on a smart home for elders based on continuous in-home unobtrusive monitoring technology. HERD: Health Environ. Res. Des. J. **12**(3), 206–219 (2019). https://doi.org/10.1177/1937586719826059, pMID: 30722699

Temporal Authorization Graphs: Pros, Cons and Limits

Riste Stojanov[1]([✉]), Ognen Popovski[2], Milos Jovanovik[1,3], Eftim Zdravevski[1], Petre Lameski[1], and Dimitar Trajanov[1]

[1] Faculty of Computer Science and Engineering, Ss. Cyril and Methodius University in Skopje, Skopje, Macedonia
{riste.stojanov,milos.jovanovik,eftim.zdravevski,
petre.lameski,dimitar.trajanov}@finki.ukim.mk
[2] Netcetera, Skopje, Macedonia
[3] OpenLink Software, Burlington, UK

Abstract. As more private data is entering the web, defining authorization about its access is crucial for privacy protection. This paper proposes a policy language that leverages SPARQL expressiveness and popularity for flexible access control management and enforces the protection using temporal graphs. The temporal graphs are created during the authentication phase and are cached for further usage. They enable design-time policy testing and debugging, which is necessary for correctness guarantee.

The security never comes with convenience, and this paper examines the environments in which the temporal graphs are suitable. Based on the evaluation results, an approximated function is defined for suitability determination based on the expected temporal graph size.

Keywords: Authorization · Temporal authorization graphs · Policy language · Semantic access control

1 Introduction

The expansion of the information technologies have produced vast amount of data that are stored in various systems and represent almost every aspect of our professional and private life. The authorization systems are the guardian of these data and regulate its access only to the granted requesters. The distributed environments in which the data is stored introduce many challenges for the authorization systems. The authorization is usually declared with policies that are enforced by an access control module implementation. The standards for policy definition, such as XACML [9], depend on the underlaying data model, and the policies are usually separately for each of the sub-systems. The separate authorization definition is mainly due to the lack of integration in multi-domain scenarios. There are multiple solutions for authentication in distributed environments, such as single-sign-on services [2], WebID [19,23] and OAuth [11], and there are frameworks that enable their integration and combination [18].

© ICST Institute for Computer Sciences, Social Informatics and Telecommunications Engineering 2021
Published by Springer Nature Switzerland AG 2021. All Rights Reserved
I. M. Pires et al. (Eds.): GOODTECHS 2021, LNICST 401, pp. 105–120, 2021.
https://doi.org/10.1007/978-3-030-91421-9_9

The semantic web [3] initiatives have provided solutions for the problems of different data representation in the various systems and have defined standards for bridging this gap. The linked data initiative [4] provides linking the same concepts with different representations from the various systems. However, even though these technologies solve most of the integration issues among various systems, there is no clear authorization solution that stands out and will bring them closer to the enterprise and personal applications.

The environment analyzed in this paper can be described through Definition 1 and Definition 2, using a data centric approach for authorization. The intent $\mathbb{I}$ is used to describe the set of facts presented by the requester or its agent application. It contains all the information necessary for the system to decide whether it will be further processed or not. It usually provides some evidence [14] about the requester, its environment and the intended action. It is also a common practice to include the software agent parameters as evidence, since it submits the intent on behalf of the requester. The system presented in this paper is not responsible for intent construction $\mathbb{I}$ and only provides interface for accepting it. However, it observes each intent change in order to determine the available resources for that state.

Definition 1. *Protecting data* ($\mathbb{D}$) *is a set of statements and resources that the authorization system should protect.*

Definition 2. *Intent* ($\mathbb{I}$) *is a set of statements and resources that define the requester intent together with its environment.*

The authorization systems usually operate in order to enforce a given set of client requirements. The clients define these requirements in a natural language and should be modeled in a suitable way for the system. An example requirement that an authorization system should model and enforce is shown in Requirement 1. It relates to both the data $\mathbb{D}$ and the intent $\mathbb{I}$, using the relations among them. The requirements are designed around the assumption that there is an implicit intent present. A most general abstraction can be that the requirement define a permission or prohibition of a certain interaction with a subset of the data for a given intent. It also may be observed as a set of rules that constrain an interaction using the connections among the intent and the data.

Requirement 1. *The professors can manage their active courses' grades from their faculty's network.*

This particular requirement permits a managing interaction with a grades, which courses are connected with some professor. Which particular grades are modeled with this requirement will be known when the intent will be present. Only the intents that contain a requester, an agent address and a manage action are applicable for this requirement. When suitable intent is present, the requirement can be materialized and the corresponding grades can be determined.

The requirements are represented as policies in the authorization systems, and the policy language and formalism defines its flexibility, understandability and maintainability. The flexibility describes the ability to transform the natural language requirements into the policies. If some requirement can not be modeled as a policy, than the system is not flexible enough for that kind of requirements. The time required for the administrators to learn and practice the policy language is referred to as understandability. The maintainability of the authorization system correlates to the human effort required to configure and maintain it. The transformation of the natural language requirements into policies, and their correctness assurance occupies most of the maintenance effort.

In order to rank better in respect with these features, the policy language should be based on well adopted and widely spread technologies and standards. It should be as close as possible with the natural language expressiveness, enabling flexibility to define multiple complex relations among the data and the intent. For better maintainability, the policy language should provide close one-to-one requirement to policy transformation, and ability to test it for correctness and consistency.

2   Related Work

The authorization policies are the formalized requirements that are enforced during the authorization.

The enforcement process is usually implemented differently in each system, but there are three main enforcement patterns that may be detected: **Resource** protection is the most commonly used pattern, where the system controls the access to each of the resources based on the authorization policies. This pattern is most widely used due to its simplicity [18]. However, the downside of this pattern is that it is coarse grained. Another pattern that is being used is with **creating authorized data set** for each user, implemented by constructing a graph that composed only of the permitted data [6,8,16,20,21]. The trade-off of the implementation simplicity of this pattern is the extra time required for graph construction per user login [13,16]. **Query Rewriting** enforcement is the most complex pattern that can be used [20,22]. It adds authorization constructs to each query that is executed in the system, such that only the permitted resources can be obtained. This pattern uses complex query rewriting algorithms that must be extensively tested for correctness [13].

Generalized policy format is described in [13] as:

$$< Subject, Resource, AccessRight > \tag{1}$$

The $Subject$[1] defines for **whom** the policy will be used i.e. the agent or the user that is interacting with the system. The $Resource$ defines **what** is protected by the policy, and the $Access\ Right$ defines whether certain action is **allowed or denied** by the policy. In other words, the **access right** defines whether

---

[1] In this paper we will use the term requester instead of subject, since it beater describes the actor that is interacting with the system.

the policy *permits* or *denies* interaction with the **resource** on behalf of the **requester** in a given context (referred to as condition expressiveness in [14]).

The semantic authorization systems correctness is poorly analyzed in most of the literature, with exception of [13], where the query rewriting is tested for correctness against a temporal graph containing only the permitted resources. However, the possible errors in the policy design and definition processes are not considered in this paper. We have addressed this issue in our previous work [20].

For simpler policy definition, many system allow both permit and deny policies. However, in this case conflicts may arise [5,7,14]. There are various ways to solve the conflicts, such as: default behavior [1,7,20], meta-policies [12], priorities [15,20], and detection and prevention [16,20,24].

The formalization in (1) is not sufficient, since it does not encounter contextual evidences and the relation between the requester description with the under-laying data. The access control models, on the other hand, are focused on separate elements from this policy format and none of them model the complete authorization environment. Additionally, only few systems enable flexibility for connecting the request's attributes with the protected data.

Policies have an essential role in data science applications to mitigate privacy and ethical concerns. For example, during feature engineering processes and when evaluating information value and feature importance of different data [26], also needs to consider whether that data is suitable to be used for that particular application in the first place. Therefore, different applications, such as in churn prediction, may be affected by the various policies in place [25]. Likewise, the computational requirements may affect the scalability of the whole cloud-based solution [10].

3   Policy Format

Definition 3 provides a formalization of the requirements described previously. The activation function α is responsible for testing and applying the intent's data that is implicitly assumed in the requirement. It is executed whenever the intent is changed and filters out the policies that are not suitable for the current state. It also replaces the implicit variables with concrete values form the intent for the suitable policies. The function φ filters the data that is protected by the policy, and ϵ defines whether that data is allowed or denied.

Definition 3. Policy *is a tuple of* $\langle \alpha, \varphi, \epsilon, \rho \rangle$ *that defines the condition* $\alpha(\mathbb{I} \cup \mathbb{D})$ *that an intent* $\mathbb{I}$ *should satisfy in relation to the protected data* $\mathbb{D}$, *so that interaction* $\epsilon \in \{allow, deny\}$ *will be enforced with the result data* $\mathbb{R} = \varphi(\mathbb{I} \cup \mathbb{D})$. *The element* ρ *is a priority that is used for conflict resolution,* α *stands for policy activation condition and* φ *represents a partial data filtering function.*

3.1   Policy Combination

The policy combination is important for two main reasons: (1) breaking down a complex authorization into simpler rules and (2) conflict resolution. Definition 4 gives a formal definition of a conflict.

Definition 4. *Two policies $P_1 = \langle \alpha_1, \varphi_1, \epsilon_1, \rho_1 \rangle$ and $P_1 = \langle \alpha_2, \varphi_2, \epsilon_2, \rho_2 \rangle$ are in conflict if:*

- $\epsilon_1 \neq \epsilon_2$,
- *there exist intent for which they are both active,*
- $\Phi_\cap \neq \emptyset$,

where $\Phi_\cap = \Phi_1 \cap \Phi_2$ and $\Phi_i = \varphi_i(\mathbb{D} \cup \mathbb{I}), i \in [1,2]$.

The policy combination is discussed in [7,17], and it suggests that the policies[2] should be combined with $\bigcup \varphi^+ \setminus \bigcup \varphi^-$. Even though this method provides policy combination, it is not flexible for conflict resolution, since the deny policies are always at a higher priority. The most common conflict resolution approaches include: (1) meta-policies, (2) priority, and (3) harmonization. The harmonization approach (3) requires disjoint policies that should be provided by the administrator of the system. In (1) rules for conflict resolutions are defined, which are with higher priority than the other policies, and this makes it a special case of (2).

The priority approach (2) is the most flexible, since it is similar to the way people solve the conflicts when they occur. It is much to define which rule is more important. This is leveraged with the ρ parameter in Definition 3. The Definition 5 defines an operator for combining an ordered set of policies.

Definition 5. *Policy result combination is a non-commutative operator $\odot$ such that:*

$$\langle \epsilon_1, \varphi_1 \rangle \odot \langle \epsilon_2, \varphi_2 \rangle = \begin{cases} \langle \epsilon_1, \varphi_1 \cup \varphi_2 \rangle, \epsilon_1 = \epsilon_2 \\ \langle \epsilon_1, \varphi_1 \setminus \varphi_2 \rangle, \epsilon_1 \neq \epsilon_2 \end{cases}$$

The operator $\odot$ is able to produce different output for different policy priority assignments. For example, if there are policies that allow the data Φ_1, Φ_2, and deny the Φ_3 part of the data, so that $\Phi_\cap = \Phi_1 \cap \Phi_2 \cap \Phi_3$ and $\Phi_\cap \neq \emptyset$. If the policies are activated for same intent , then they are in conflict and one of their 6 possible orderings can be chosen. Here are three example orderings together with the protected data results:

$$\rho_1 < \rho_2 < \rho_3 \Rightarrow \langle \epsilon_+, (\Phi_1 \cup \Phi_2) \setminus \Phi_3 \rangle$$
$$\rho_1 < \rho_3 < \rho_2 \Rightarrow \langle \epsilon_+, (\Phi_1 \setminus \Phi_3) \cup \Phi_2 \rangle$$
$$\rho_3 < \rho_2 < \rho_1 \Rightarrow \langle \epsilon_-, (\Phi_3 \setminus \Phi_2) \setminus \Phi_1 \rangle$$

3.2 Policy Language

The policy language defines the level of flexibility, understandability and maintainability. In this paper, the policies are defined in RDF format that enables actual representation of the policy elements described in Definition 3. The RDF

---

[2] In this description the partial data filter function φ has superscript $+$ or $-$ if it is part of a policy with enforcement method ϵ_+ and ϵ_-, correspondingly.

and SPARQL are combined together in order to bridge the understandability gap, and provide better flexibility and maintainability. Even though SPARQL can be difficult to learn, it is chosen for representation of the activation function (in the policy ontology it is p:intent_binding) and the partial result filtering function (p:protected_data) in order to provide flexibility for requirement modeling. Since the data is stored in semantic format, its query language SPARQL provides greater flexibility for data selection using various patterns. This policy format also enables easier requirement transformation into policies, with approximately one policy per requirement, which improves the system maintainability.

Example 1 shows the policy representation for the requirement Requirement 1. It is with low priority of 1. The prefix p:[3] is a lightweight policy ontology that describes the policy language of the system, while int:[4] is a basic ontology that define the most common intent classes and properties. Example 1 shows the classes int:$Requester$ and int:$Agent$ which are used to define who the requester is and its agent definition, in this case containing the requesting IP address. This way the policy language can model the requirement that are context dependent, using these queries and the dynamic nature of the intent.

Example 1. _p a p:Policy;
```
  p:intent_binding 'select ?s ?a ?n where {
    ?s a int:Requester. ?a a acl:Read.
    ?ag a int:Agent. ?ag int:address ?ip. ?ip int:network ?n}';
  p:protected_data 'construct { ?g ?p ?o } where {
    ?g a univ:Grade. ?g univ:for_course ?c.
    ?c univ:has_professor ?s. ?s univ:works_at ?f.
    ?f univ:has_network ?n. ?g ?p ?o}';
  p:enforce 'allow';
  p:priority 1.0^^xsd:double.
```

4   Enforcement Architecture

The system presented in this paper relies on the policies defined in the format and language presented in Sect. 3.2. The enforcement process always starts with a requester's intent. The requester can choose to provide multiple pieces of evidence in the intent, among which can be its identity, additional attributes about him/her, the environment in which it operates, the action he/she intends to invoke, and some additional action parameters. The intent is represented as a separate semantic graph. The data contained in this graph is not controlled by the authorization system presented here. It only provides interface for intent provisioning.

The authorization system intercepts the intent and builds a temporal graph that corresponds to the data available for that intent. This process is illustrated

---

[3] http://github.com/ristes/univ-datasets/ont/policy.owl.
[4] http://github.com/ristes/univ-datasets/ont/intent.owl.

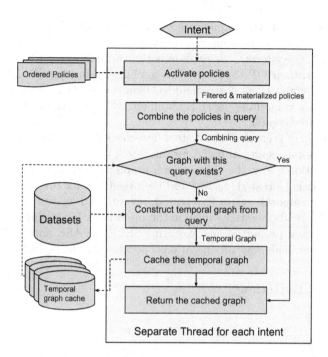

Fig. 1. Temporal graph maintenance

in Fig. 1. It is invoked every time the intent is changed. In this temporal graph creation, only the policies for protecting read operations are considered.

As Fig. 1 shows, the intent is used for policy activation. This process activates the policies using the query provided in the property *p:intent_binding*, which is defined in the policy language. This query is executed against the intent graph (from now on referred to as $\mathbb{I}$), and the resulting variable bindings are used to rewrite the *p:protected_data* query. The rewriting process replaces the variables that are mentioned in the both queries. If the *p:intent_binding* query does not return results, the policy is filtered out as inadequate.

The active policies with rewritten partial data filtering query are then combined using the $\odot$ operator described in Sect. 3.1. The only change made in the implementation is that if the lowest priority policy is denying access, a new implicit allow policy for all data is inserted with even lower priority, in order to obtain a temporal graph which always holds the permitted data. The policy combination is implemented using the Jena library[5]. As described in Sect. 3.2, each of these queries are in the form *construct T where OP*, where T is the triple pattern that describes which data will be select in the temporal graph, and OP defines the condition that should be meet by these triples. The system presented

---

[5] http://jena.apache.org.

here, first rewrites all these queries so that all of them has $T=?s\ ?p\ ?o$[6]. If the triple from some of these queries contains a term[7] then the OP is extended with *FILTER (?var=term)*, where *?var* is the variable used at that position in the triple. Next, their OP conditions are combined using the SPARQL *UNION* and *MINUS* operators that correspond to $\cup$ and $\setminus$ operations from Definition 5. After this step, a combining query is obtained, which has the form *construct ?s ?p ?o where CombinedOP*.

Once this query is created, the system first check if it is different from the version from the previous intent. If the current intent does not change the temporal graph construction query, the old temporal graph is returned, and otherwise the temporal graph is recreated, cached and then returned for further usage.

Once the temporal graph is created, every read operation is executed against it. The read operations include the operations for fetching resources or triples, listing their properties and executing SELECT, ASK and CONSTRUCT SPARQL queries. This way, all operations operate over the permitted data only.

4.1 Conflict Detection

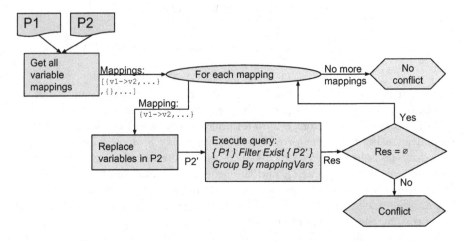

Fig. 2. Conflict detection

Definition 4 defines when two policies are in conflict. The temporal graph implementation enables conflicts to be detected automatically, with execution of the partial data selection queries of each pair of policies with different enforcement method. This is illustrated in Fig. 2, where at the beginning all variables from the policies' activation queries are mapped (all mappings are generated). Then,

---

[6] The variable names ?s, ?p and ?o are chosen for convenience, while in the implementation their names are randomly generated.

[7] The term unifies the IRI and literal elements.

for each mapping the variables in P2 are rewritten, and the partial data queries are combined together with FILTER EXIST operation. Group by element is added for all mapped variable in order to find a results that are returned for that particular variable combination. When this query returns results, a conflict is detected. This way the administrator can be alerted about the conflict, and can solve them using the policy priorities.

5 Evaluation

As it was previously described, the main overhead that is imposed by this authorization enforcement system is the temporal graph management described in Fig. 1. The policy activation and combination steps are carried out completely in memory, while the graph construction is carried out by the underlaying storage engine, which may uses multiple I/O operations with the disk. Because of this, the main focus in the evaluation was to determine the factors and their influence to the graph creation time.

Multiple datasets were generated and stored using the Jena TDB semantic storage. The dataset generators and evaluation code is based on the Jena API and can be easily extended for other storage engines. Multiple queries with different features were generated, and each of them was executed 40 times, 20 of witch were warm-up.

24 datasets were generated for the evaluation process. The data was generated following university ontology[8]. The dataset size can be expressed with this formula: $|DS_i| = |DS_{i-1}| + |generateGrades(100 * (i\%6 + 1) * 10^{i/6}, i)|$ where $i \in [1..24]$ and DS_0 contains only one faculty, one study program and 4 technical staff users. The generateGrades function takes an argument which defines the number of grades that should be generated as a first argument, and the identifier for the course for which this grades will be generated as a second argument. It first generates the course, and then each grade is assigned to that course and to a newly generated student resource.

The fixed number of grades for each course is leveraged for query construction, so that it is possible to determine the query processing time correlation with the dataset size and the number of returned results. The template of these query is shown in Example 2. Another variant to determine the time is evaluated by just adding *FILTER (?v > 6)*. The *<courseIri>* part is different in each evaluation query, and this enables obtaining different number of results.

Example 2. CONSTRUCT { ?g ?p ?o } WHERE {
  ?g univ:for_course <courseIri>. ?g univ:grade_value ?v. ?g ?p ?o
}

Since the temporal graph is created with a query composed of multiple SPARQL UNION and MINUS elements, few query variants were made to explore

---

[8] http://github.com/ristes/univ-datasets/ont/univ.owl.

the dependency from the number of these constructs. These queries are combining the WHERE part shown in Example 2 for a different *courseIri* replacements. All the queries used for evaluation, together with the results are available in the generator project repository[9].

5.1   Evaluation Results

In Fig. 3 part of the query results are shown. Each line represents the dependency of the query processing time from the number of obtained results for some of the generated datasets. All of the queries tested here are composed of a basic graph pattern without filters. It shows that for this type of queries, the processing time depends only from the number of selected results, and not from the dataset size. The queries with the filter appended to them also does not depend on the dataset size, but they took more time to return the same number of results.

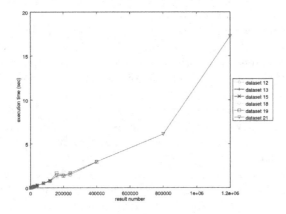

Fig. 3. Temporal graph maintenance

The execution of the queries containing union and minus clauses revealed that the union operation queries does not depend on the dataset size and the number of union expressions, but only on the selected results. On the other hand, the MINUS operation increases the time for query processing depending on the total returned plus the total removed results (the one selected in the minus clauses).

In terms of performance, the enforcement approach with temporal authorization graphs is inferior when executed once for every intended action [7,13,16]. This is why this paper investigates the graph construction performances in order to defines the limits in which this approach is suitable.

The suitability limits are calculated using the following approximate expectations as inputs:

---

[9] http://github.com/ristes/univ-datasets.

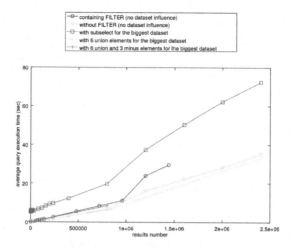

Fig. 4. Different query types comparison

- $|\varphi(p)|$: Average expected protected triples
- *icr*: Expected intent change rate (changes/minute)

The results presented here show the correlations between the processing time and the query types, resulting data size and the dataset size. Since in the most of the cases the dataset size does not have significant impact, the expected processing time function $f(|\varphi(p)|)$ is interpolated from the presented results, averaged for all query types. The average is added since it is expected that multiple policies of various types will be activated, and the average best fits this diversity. An important note is that the function f does not calculate the actual execution time, but it is intended to find the approximate expected processing time based on the expected query results.

The Fig. 4 shows the time required for a different types of queries based on the results they select. This figure shows that the queries containing *FILTER* or *MINUS* expressions are slightly slower than the other one. The reason for this is because the TDB engine has to process all suitable results that match the triple patterns, and then filters out part of those results, leading that these variants of queries require more processing time per result. Our analysis shows that the performance in general depend on the number of processed triples, not on the returned one. This way of observation shows that it is enough to execute all basic graph patterns from all policies combined with union, and for this particular engine (Jena TDB) the results will depend on the number of returned results.

During the experiments all the resulting Jena models were serialized as bytes, and they gave an average of 80 bytes per stored triple. Even though this value depends on the type of the data being stored in the dataset, it can be used to estimate the required memory for temporal graph storing through the system.

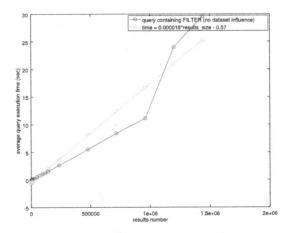

Fig. 5. Linear approximation function

The linear approximation function f shown in (2) can be used to give fast expectation about the query execution time, where $results\_size$ represents the number of expected results from all policy basic graph pattern combined. Even though this approximation gives lower values for result sizes above 1 M triples, as Fig. 5 shows, the time for this amount of data is more that 10 s which in our opinion exceeds the reasonable limits for login time, and thus the approximation function is no further fitted.

$$f : time = 1.8 * 10^{-5} * results\_size - 0.57 \tag{2}$$

6   Discussion

The policy language presented in this paper provides flexibility for capturing most of the client requirements. The policy combination is designed to follow the requirement process, since it is easier to order the policies by their priority. The *Intent* enables using all available evidences as a semantic statements and their incorporation within the policies. The policies enable combination of the intent's data with the protecting data in the activation and filtering phases, which matches the flexibility in the natural language used in the requirements. This way the policy language can model the requirement that are context dependent, using these queries and the dynamic nature of the intent. The activation query, and its results combination with the partial data filtering enables flexible selection of the requesters for which the policy should be applied. This is even more flexible than the ABAC authentication systems, since more than just property values can be selected. The policy language defined in this paper can select the relevant requester using its contextual evidences, its properties and its connections with the rest of the data, which provides great flexibility in the requirement transformation process. The protection granularity enables protection of resources, triples, quads and graphs., actions and aggregate operations.

This range of protection elements makes this policy language unique, especially in terms of the aggregate operations, which often are requested as exceptions of the standard rules. Such example that infers the average grade for each student in the dataset is shown in Example 3. This policy allows access to the student's average grade for all professors, with a high priority that is likely to be added to the temporal graph.

Example 3. _p1 a p:Policy;
```
  p:intent_binding 'select ?r ?a where {
   ?r a int:Requester. ?a a acl:Read
  }';
  p:partial_data 'construct { ?st univ:has_average ?avg }
  where {
   ?r a univ:User. ?c univ:has_professor ?r.
   { select (avg(?v) as ?avg) ?st
    where {
     ?g univ:for_student ?st. ?g univ:grade_value ?v
    } group by ?st
   } }';
  p:enforce 'allow';
  p:priority 150.0^^xsd:double.
```

The policy language is chosen to be close to the natural language, and using tools like sentence dependency graph can lower the ambiguity in the process of policy design. The use of a SPARQL for policy activation and partial data selection provides a number of policies close to that of the separate requirement scenarios. The popularity of the technologies used in the policy language will lower the time required to learn it, and the large number of resources will make the policy format more understandable.

The temporal graph can be used in the policy design phase for testing. The administrator can use simulated intents to test the correctness of the policies. This provides early policy inconsistency detection. Also, when the temporal graph is used, there is no way of inferring some data with multiple query probes. For instance, if the authorization system forbids the grades of the students, but allows querying data with filter by the grade value, the grades of the students may be induced with multiple query executions. This can not be done when temporal graphs are used.

6.1 Use Case

In order to demonstrate how the results form this paper can be used in real life scenario. Lets assume that a faculty has 100 professors that can see only the grades for the courses they have lectured. For simplicity, let every course have 100 students. In worst case scenario, if all the professors are employed for 30 years, and in every semester they have held 3 courses, their temporal graph will contain in total 30 years * 2 semesters/year * 3 courses/semester * 100 students/course * 1 grade/student * 4 statements/grade = 72000 statements for the grades, which gives something less that 7.2 MB for the grades. Even though many students overlap over the courses, lets assume that all the students are different and this gives as additional 10 MB, or roughly around 20 MB per professor temporal graph. This graph will contain in total around 200000 statements.

Given the approximation formula (2), the expected time for each professor temporal graph creation will be $1.8 * 10^{-5} * 2 * 10^5 - 0.57 = 3.03$ seconds approximately in worst case. Since the grades are not frequently changed and the professor environment does not influence to the permitted data for the professor, there wont be many temporal graph re-creations, which makes the caching time acceptable, especially given the implicit security provided by the temporal graph that contains only the permitted data.

The memory requirement for the system will be 2 GB of RAM, if all of the professors are using the system in parallel only for the temporal graphs, which now days is the memory that the mobile phones have.

However, the temporal graphs are not always suitable. One such case can be a scenario that contains temporal policies, which will induce many re-creation of the temporal graphs, so no matter how small they are, there will be a lot of overhead.

7 Conclusion

The temporal authorization graphs by their nature provide convenience with the implicit security they provide. Additionally, it is easy to test the policies in the design phase using this approach, leading to higher correctness of the authorization system. Even though their creation may introduce significant performance deterioration, the caching mechanism proposed in this paper overcomes this issue, when there are no frequent changes in the system.

The policy formalism and language presented in this paper enable flexible requirement to policy transformation. The use of the SPARQL in the policy language helps in this process, by allowing selection of arbitrary peaces of data, and following the natural language of the requirements. This way the maintenance of the system is improved, because each requirement is represented with one or few policies, while the temporal graph simplifies their testing.

Finally, this paper shows that there are use cases for which the temporal authorization graphs introduce benefits, and the approximated formula (2) provides a tool that simplifies this process for the Jena TDB storage. During the evaluation process few datasets were created, together with evaluation scenarios, which can be used to fit this formula for other semantic data storage engines.

References

1. Abel, F., De Coi, J.L., Henze, N., Koesling, A.W., Krause, D., Olmedilla, D.: Enabling advanced and context-dependent access control in RDF stores. In: Aberer, K., et al. (eds.) The Semantic Web, ASWC/ISWC -2007. LNCS, vol. 4825, pp. 1–14. Springer, Heidelberg (2007). https://doi.org/10.1007/978-3-540-76298-0_1

2. Armando, A., Carbone, R., Compagna, L., Cuellar, J., Tobarra. L.: Formal analysis of saml 2.0 web browser single sign-on: breaking the saml-based single sign-on for google apps. In: Proceedings of the 6th ACM Workshop on Formal Methods in Security Engineering, pp 1–10. ACM (2008)
3. Berners-Lee, T., Hendler, J., Lassila, O., et al.: The semantic web. Sci. Am. **284**(5), 28–37 (2001)
4. Bizer, C., Heath, T., Berners-Lee. T.: Linked data-the story so far. In: Semantic Services, Interoperability and Web Applications: Emerging Concepts, pp. 205–227 (2009)
5. Costabello, L., Villata, S., Rodriguez Rocha, O., Gandon, F.: Access control for HTTP operations on linked data. In: Cimiano, P., Corcho, O., Presutti, V., Hollink, L., Rudolph, S. (eds.) The Semantic Web: Semantics and Big Data, ESWC 2013. LNCS, vol. 7882, pp. 185–199. Springer, Heidelberg (2013). https://doi.org/10.1007/978-3-642-38288-8_13
6. Dietzold, S., Auer, S.: Access control on RDF triple stores from a semantic wiki perspective. In: ESWC Workshop on Scripting for the Semantic Web. Citeseer (2006)
7. Flouris, G., Fundulaki, I., Michou, M., Antoniou, G.: Controlling access to RDF graphs. In: Berre, A.J., Gómez-Pérez, A., Tutschku, Kurt, Fensel, D. (eds.) Future Internet - FIS 2010, FIS 2010. LNCS, vol. 6369, pp. 107–117. Springer, Heidelberg (2010). https://doi.org/10.1007/978-3-642-15877-3_12
8. Franzoni, S., Mazzoleni, P., Valtolina, S., Bertino, E.: Towards a fine-grained access control model and mechanisms for semantic databases. In: IEEE International Conference on Web Services (ICWS 2007), pp. 993–1000. IEEE (2007)
9. Godik, S., Anderson, A., Parducci, B., Humenn, P., Vajjhala. S.: Oasis extensible access control 2 markup language (xacml) 3. Technical report, OASIS (2002)
10. Grzegorowski, M., Zdravevski, E., Janusz, A., Lameski, P., Apanowicz, C., Slezak, D.: Cost optimization for big data workloads based on dynamic scheduling and cluster-size tuning. Big Data Res. **25**, 100203 (2021)
11. Hardt, D.: The OAuth 2.0 authorization framework (2012)
12. Kagal, L., Finin, T., Joshi, A.: A policy language for a pervasive computing environment. In: Policies for Distributed Systems and Networks, 2003. Proceedings. POLICY 2003. IEEE 4th International Workshop on, pp. 63–74. IEEE (2003)
13. Kirrane, S.: Linked data with access control. Ph.D. Thesis (2015)
14. Kirrane, S., Mileo, A., Decker, S.: Access control and the resource description framework: a survey. Seman. Web **8**(2), 311–352 (2017)
15. Kolovski, V., Hendler, J., Parsia, B.: Analyzing web access control policies. In: Proceedings of the 16th international conference on World Wide Web, pp. 677–686. ACM (2007)
16. Muhleisen, H., Kost, M., Freytag, J.-C.: SWRL-based access policies for linked data. Procs of SPOT, **80** (2010)
17. Oulmakhzoune, S., Cuppens-Boulahia, N., Cuppens, F., Morucci, S.: fQuery: SPARQL query rewriting to enforce data confidentiality. In: Foresti, S., Jajodia, S. (eds.) Data and Applications Security and Privacy XXIV, DBSec 2010. LNCS, vol. 6166, pp. 146–161. Springer, Heidelberg (2010). https://doi.org/10.1007/978-3-642-13739-6_10
18. Scarioni, C.: Pro Spring Security. Apress, New York City (2013)
19. Sporny, M., Inkster, T., Story, H., Harbulot, B., Bachmann-Gmür, R.: Webid 1.0: Web identification and discovery. Editor's draft, W3C (2011)
20. Stojanov, R., Gramatikov, S., Mishkovski, I., Trajanov, D.: Linked data authorization platform. IEEE Access **6**, 1189–1213 (2017)

21. Stojanov, R., Gramatikov, S., Popovski, O., Trajanov, D.: Semantic-driven secured data access in distributed IoT systems. In: 2018 26th Telecommunications Forum (TELFOR), pp. 420–425. IEEE (2018)
22. Stojanov, R., Jovanovik, M.: Authorization proxy for SPARQL endpoints. In: Trajanov, D., Bakeva, V. (eds.) ICT Innovations 2017. CCIS, vol. 778, pp. 205–218. Springer, Cham (2017). https://doi.org/10.1007/978-3-319-67597-8_20
23. Story, H., Harbulot, B., Jacobi, I., Jones, M.: FOAF+ SSl: restful authentication for the social web. In: Proceedings of the First Workshop on Trust and Privacy on the Social and Semantic Web (SPOT2009) (2009)
24. Toninelli, A., Montanari, R., Kagal, L., Lassila, O.: Proteus: a semantic context-aware adaptive policy model. In: Eighth IEEE International Workshop on Policies for Distributed Systems and Networks (POLICY'07), pp. 129–140. IEEE (2007)
25. Zdravevski, E., Lameski, P., Apanowicz, C., Ślęzak, D.: From big data to business analytics: the case study of churn prediction. Appl. Soft Comput. **90**, 106164 (2020)
26. Zdravevski, E., Lameski, P., Kulakov, A., Filiposka, S., Trajanov, D., Jakimovski, B.: Parallel computation of information gain using Hadoop and MapReduce. In: 2015 Federated Conference on Computer Science and Information Systems (Fed-CSIS), pp. 181–192 (2015)

Advanced 5G Network Slicing Isolation Using Enhanced VPN+ for Healthcare Verticals

Bruno Dzogovic[1(✉)], Tariq Mahmood[2], Bernardo Santos[1], Boning Feng[1],
Van Thuan Do[3,1], Niels Jacot[3], and Thanh Van Do[4,1]

[1] Oslo Metropolitan Univeristy, Pilestredet 35, 0167 Oslo, Norway
{bruno.dzogovic,bersan,boning.feng}@oslomet.no
[2] University of Oslo, Gaustadalléen 23B, 0373 Oslo, Norway
tariqmah@ifi.uio.no
[3] Wolffia AS, Haugerudvn. 40, 0673 Oslo, Norway
{vt.do,n.jacot}@wolffia.net
[4] Telenor ASA., Snarøyveien 30, 1331 Fornebu, Norway
thanh-van.do@telenor.com

Abstract. Alongside enabling connectivity for people and societies, the fifth-Generation networks (5G) aimed towards establishing an all-inclusive ecosystem for Internet of Things to sustain variety of industrial verticals such as e-health, smart home, smart city, etc. With the successful implementation of 5G infrastructure, it is understood that the traditional security approaches incorporated in the previous 4th generation networks (4G) may not suffice to protect users and industries from adversaries that develop more advanced attack vectors. This is mostly attributed the vulnerabilities imposed by softwareization (Softwareization of networks, clouds, and internet of things https://onlinelibrary.wiley.com/doi/pdf/10.1002/nem.1967.) and virtualization of the network which compromise the isolation and protection of the 5G network slices essential for the support of IoT verticals. In this work, we propose an innovative approach to enhance the isolation of network slices by employing the Enhanced Virtual Private Network+ (VPN+) technology. Furthermore, we demonstrate the impact of an encrypted communication at the transport backhaul network in 5G scenario in terms of defensive success against virtualization layer attacks in the cloud.

Keywords: 5G · Enhanced VPN+ · Network slicing · IoT security · OpenStack

1 Introduction

Many service providers rely on open infrastructures and the open-source model to provide 5G services and connectivity for customers [1]. However, there are many limitations to consider, including cybersecurity-related ramifications and risks that make the 5G network slicing not sufficiently secure, i.e., for the digital elderly care solution we proposed at the secure 5G4IoT lab [2]. 5G is known to inherit most of the proven security practices from the 4G Long-Term Evolution (LTE), but as the network and infrastructure become

© ICST Institute for Computer Sciences, Social Informatics and Telecommunications Engineering 2021
Published by Springer Nature Switzerland AG 2021. All Rights Reserved
I. M. Pires et al. (Eds.): GOODTECHS 2021, LNICST 401, pp. 121–135, 2021.
https://doi.org/10.1007/978-3-030-91421-9_10

softwareized and deployed in public clouds to support the additional industry verticals (like smart infrastructure, smart homes, Internet of Things, automated transportation etc.), these may be insufficient to secure mission-critical applications and even the average user [3]. To handle issues that emerge because of isolation insufficiency between tenants in the provider's infrastructure, the 3rd Generation Partnership Project (3GPP) introduces the concept of network slicing that aims towards segregation of network resources into logical segments, to provide diverse Quality of Service (QoS) and Quality of Experience (QoE) for the end users or industry verticals. Most vulnerabilities from the cloud can shift into the 5G infrastructure, and these are characterized within a Common Vulnerabilities and Exposure list of records within the MITRE project, initiated by MIT university [4]. Network slicing by itself is not sufficient to provide satisfactory levels of isolation and therefore additional methods are needed to avoid certain vulnerabilities. Some of those involve:

- policy-based networking,
- traffic engineering and autonomous smart dynamic routing,
- hardware-level isolation (if applicable),
- anomaly detection as part of Intrusion Detection/Prevention systems (IDS/IPS)
- other techniques that involve fine-grained dynamic and automated threat intelligence.

This research work investigates the virtualization plane of the communication between the 5G and 4G core networks and the radio frontend; namely, what is sufficient to provide an isolation between network slices in the backhaul of a Network Function Virtualization (NFV)-enabled cloud. To deliver network slicing, currently there is no standardized consensus about the methodology and which approach is to be used, as virtualization of network functions can be achieved in various ways. This suggests that it is required to be stringent in terms of security and isolation. To achieve that, we experiment with the enhanced VPN framework [5] in a cloud environment, while using an open-source methodology to deliver security augmentation of the 5G infrastructure.

The paper begins with an introduction to the background topics and technologies and their role in healthcare. Subsequently, we proceed with elucidating details about the 5G infrastructure as well as the concept of network slicing and its isolation. To finalize, the methodology of implementation is described followed by an evaluation that is comprised of performance assessment and demonstrates the network slices isolation. As a conclusion, we cover the lessons learned and provide details about future possibilities for researching topics related to this question.

2   Background and Related Work

2.1   5G in Healthcare

To retain the confidentiality of information between a healthcare provider and patients, there must be an end-to-end secure communication. Various healthcare management systems rely on the assumption that the healthcare providers should ensure the safety and reliability of patient information. However, it has been shown that in majority of incidents involving threats to healthcare systems like the THIS (Total Hospital Information System), are vastly attributed to human error [6]. Despite efforts of governments to establish protection standards and regulation about EHRs (Electronic Health Records) information, nonetheless they are greatly targeted by cyber-criminals because of flaws in personal and organizational management [7]. One of the key areas of our society that benefits significantly from 5G is exactly the healthcare. Amalgamating together the Internet of Things (IoT), big data and Machine Learning/Artificial Intelligence (AI/ML), 5G brings the smart infrastructure aspect to the healthcare verticals. This indicates that there will be a high requirement for automation of handling patient data, as well as real-time monitoring practices of patients that are outside of the hospital premises (i.e., in their own homes). Consequently, the probability of human errors will increase, allowing for additional cyber threats to emerge and put at risk the private information of patients [8].

2.2   5G Reference Architecture

The general architecture of the 4G and 5G networks established at the Oslo Metropolitan University are following the 3GPP, European Telecommunication Standards Institute (ETSI) and the International Telecommunications Union (ITU) specifications, designated in the corresponding technical specification TS 23.501 (v15.8.0) [9]. As described in Fig. 1, the virtualized functions of the 4G and 5G Core Networks are deployed in the OpenStack cloud [10], provisioned within containerized environment using the Docker containerization technology [11]. Containers enable a lightweight immutable infrastructure and when paired with orchestrators such as Kubernetes, resilience, self-healing, and certain level of autonomy [12]. The 4G and 5G infrastructure is achieved by instantiating the vNFs of the Core Networks in containers forming a virtual 4G EPC core (vEPC) and a 5G Core (5GC), tightly integrated within a default Docker runtime environment as a base for controlled experimental conditions.

Containers communicate in a mesh network structure, which is a simple and efficient approach but also a security liability as they share the same kernel of the operating system and thus the networking stack. Therein the requirement for more rigorous isolation and securing the communication between the containerized Core Networks and the virtualized Radio Access Network (vRAN) [13]. As indicated in Fig. 1, the mobile network is deployed according to the Radio Access Network model, where the User-Plane (UP) is separated from the Control-Plane (CP) into different functions, i.e., UPF (User Plane Function) and a C-function group that contains the AMF (Access and Mobility Function) and the other 5GC virtual functions, forming a container cluster. The Next-Generation 5G Radio Access Network communicates with the Control Plane via the UPF and this is referred to as "functional split" to achieve more refined control over the radio frontend, for the sake of optimal resource utilization planning [14].

The split of functionalities for the vRAN is regulated according to 3GPP specification TR 38.801 [15] and relates to the decisions of the operator that deploys the infrastructure including the hardware requirements, topology of the transport network, logical organization etc. (see Fig. 2).

To realize a 4G LTE vEPC, we utilize the OpenAirInterface core network and Remote Radio Unit (RRU) [16], while maintaining a Centralized Unit/Distributed Unit (CU/DU)

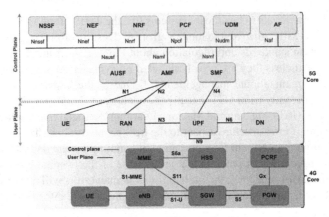

Fig. 1. 4G and 5G Core Networks architecture. 5G decouples the user and control-plane functions unlike the 4G core [14]

split on option 7 according to 3GPP [17]. The 5G next generation RAN and core functions are deployed using the Open5GS core network [18].

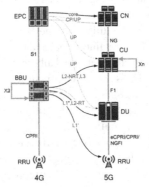

Fig. 2. 4G and 5G functional splits for the transport network. One of many ways 5G moves computationally intensive tasks away from the radio frontend into the cloud and splits the functionality into Centralized and Distributed units.

2.3 Container Virtualization

Containers can deploy various software in a lightweight and immutable manner. Therefore, the Software-Defined Networking (SDN) and slicing controllers, software modems for the evolved Node-B/next-generation Node-B (eNB/gNB) radio frontend for 4G/5G correspondingly, as well as network functions of the 5GC/EPC are provisioned within container environments; that is particularly suitable for Multi-Access Edge and Fog computing scenarios (MEC). The cloud requires support for NFV and a possibility to deliver virtual network functions on-demand or automatically. For that purpose, we utilize the

Tacker module from OpenStack that follows the TOSCA model for NFV. The fundamental advantage of this approach is the possibility to perform service function chaining (SFC), which enables integration of service functions with the SDN controller (O-RAN and OpenDaylight). The traffic is then managed through a VNFFG (VNF Forwarding Graph). The SFC consists of an ordered list of VNFs for traffic to traverse, while the classifier decides which traffic should go through them [19].

The Container Networking Functions are managed and automated with Kubernetes and by using the Tacker module in OpenStack and is not the focus of this current work [20]. Another important module that allows segregation of network resources into virtual and subsequent physical network functions, is the SR-IOV (Single-Input/Output Virtualization) developed by Intel. A rather older approach, the SR-IOV maps and assigns virtual network functions to physical functions [21]. In OpenStack, the SR-IOV runs as an agent on the compute/controller nodes as an element of the Neutron OvS (Open vSwitch) networking component. The agent provides connectivity of instances to the corresponding network infrastructure for VMs via the Intel's VT-d virtualization (that also needs to be supported at a hardware level) [22].

There are various security concerns from running containers in an open infrastructure. Containers suffer of inherent lack of visibility. Most of the underlying infrastructure vulnerabilities that translate into containers are overlooked and this renders many deployments substantially insecure. By using insecure images that do not undergo strict vulnerability analysis practices, an accepting policy can have detrimental consequences to the security of the infrastructure. Containers share the kernel of the host's operating system and cross-talk between namespaces of processes and threads can become a problem.

2.4 Enhanced VPN (VPN+) as Part of the SDN Controller

The 4G/5G infrastructure follows a flat network model, which transports traffic of different types such as the communication between eNBs/gNBs, MME/AMF (Mobility Management Entity/Access and Mobility Function) and cross-handover traffic on the X2-U and X2-C interfaces between the base stations, etc. Furthermore, in 4G the flat IP architecture distributed Radio Network Controller (RNC) functions with eNBs, MME, S-GW and were directly connected to the core network [23]. This led to challenges to provide a secure traffic in the mobile backhaul networks [24].

The enhanced VPN+ facilitates a hard isolation, or specifically an overall separation of underlying network between different network slices with different traffic flows [25]. To resolve this, we refer to the ACTN (Abstraction and Control of Traffic Engineered Networks) framework [25] provided in the realization of a transport network slice, where a vertical industry customers assign the input of their requirements (see Fig. 3). Presumably, the UHD slice is given with MTNC ID = 1, the slice for phone access as MTNC ID = 2, Massive IoT slice with MTNC ID = 3 and URLLC slice MTNC ID = 4. These ID numbers will be appended in TPM (CNC controller) and communicated with the MDSC.

Since the SDN-C has an abstraction of traffic-engineered network topology, it will assign the path to these slices. This same SDN-C has the logical abstraction of the topology in case the vertical industry does not want hard isolation and can build a

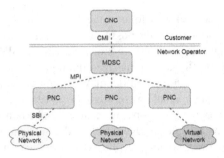

Fig. 3. ACTN architecture components. The network operator controls the infrastructure based on the CNC requests the customers initiate [25]

tunnel based on MPLS or VxLAN VPN. Nevertheless, since we focus on hard isolation, the vertical industry can choose their private tunnel between the two endpoints, which enables for a complete protection of their data without concerns about the interference of other slices' traffic and whether it shall consume the available network resources. In case of a vertical industry requiring an instance of a slice, they can distinguish the slice with a concept of "differentiator", that is an insertion of an additional parameter of MTNC sub-differentiator i.e., MTNC ID 1.1 (where this case represents another instance of slice MTNC 1).

2.5 Network Slicing

Network slicing (or *netslicing*) is defined as a method for delivering customized virtual networks, segmented into logical divisions and according to the requirements of the end users or industry verticals in terms of performance and quality of service. That subdivision is a product of multitude of conditions for connectivity to specific 5G Public Land Mobile Networks (PLMN). 5G defines three major use-cases of connectivity: Ultra Reliable Low-Latency Communication (URLLC), enhanced Mobile Broadband (eMBB) and Machine-to-Machine communications (M2M), also referred to as MIoT (Massive IoT) [26]. The 5G Infrastructure Public Private Partnership Project (5GPPP) has proposed network slicing architecture comprising of four layers, such as infrastructure layer, orchestration layer, business function layer and network function layer (see Fig. 4) [29].

A rather complex set of structures and methods, network slicing enriches service continuity through advanced roaming across networks. A slicing controller administers a virtual network segment that runs on physical infrastructure (cloud), with traffic that traverses multiple local or national PLMN networks. Another way is to allow the host network to create an optimized virtual network that reproduces the one presented by a roaming device's home network [30, 31]. While service function chaining is an excellent paradigm and can deliver great Quality of Experience for the end users, there are numerous security aspects to ponder, mainly when international traffic roaming considered.

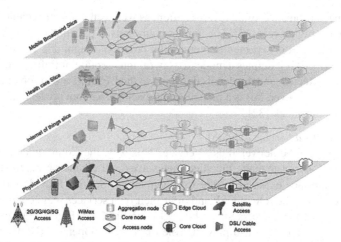

Fig. 4. A 4-layer network slicing architecture. Each slice represents an industry vertical or service chain. Network slicing begins from radio resource scheduling and up to application layer control (courtesy of 5GPPP) [29]

2.6 Isolation of Network Slices

Network slicing can be studied as a 4-phase process, or explicitly:

- Preparation,
- Commissioning,
- Operation and
- Decommissioning.

Considerable amount of focus on network slicing can be attributed to the management and orchestration layer in 5G, which tightly integrates within SDN controllers [26]. However, many security aspects are still deficient and there is no clear indication of isolation of network slices beyond the said policy enforcement and network segregation on lower layers. The major efforts on securing a 5G network is done on the core-network side, where each virtualized network function is secured with corresponding cryptographic procedures and keys (i.e., gNB Access Stratum keys vs. 5GC Non-Access Stratum keys). This continues with the introduction of similar practices to 4G for utilization of cryptographic algorithms in the user-plane and control-plane traffic, as well as the NAS signaling and RRC signaling separately. These security principles are exceptionally important during state transitions and mobility of User Equipment (UE) [30].

Security Threats in 5G and IoT
Various applications of 5G have different requirements in terms of performance, quality of service and security. An example of related work is the healthcare and ensuring a safe ecosystem for providers to reach the patients in a secure manner. Furthermore, availability of this network slice is of paramount importance because a smart healthcare infrastructure shall provide emergency services uninterruptedly [2]. Meanwhile,

the patients need protection of their information, as well as the doctor-patient confidentiality ensured at high levels [14]. The immense amounts of data that shall flow through the adjacent 5G slices is expected to increase by orders of magnitude compared to the 4G networks [13]. 3GPP defines a model for lawful interception of traffic, provided that an adversary is detected, and the details delivered to the LEMF (Law Enforcement Monitoring Facility). However, this is a proactive approach and cannot prevent the adversary from finalizing the attack [32].

Network Slicing as a Service (NSaaS)
Network slicing can be delivered as a service. This way, the Communication Service Customers (CSCs) can manage the slice themselves and decide on parameters via a management interface exposed by the Communication Service Providers (CSPs). In turn, a CSC can play the role of CSP and offer their own services (e.g., communication services) on top of the network slice obtained from the CSP (Fig. 5). For example, a network slice customer can also play the role of Network Operator (NOP) and could build their own network containing the slice(s) obtained from the CSP as a "building block". In this model, both CSP offering NSaaS and CSC consuming NSaaS have the knowledge of the existence of network slices [26].

Network Slicing as NOP Internals
In the "network slices as NOP internals" model, network slices are not part of the NOP service offered and hence are not visible to customers. However, the NOP, to provide support to communication services, may decide to deploy network slices, e.g., for internal network optimization purposes. This model allows CSC to use the network as the end user or optionally allows CSC to monitor the service status (as an assurance of the SLA associated with the internally offered network slice) [26].

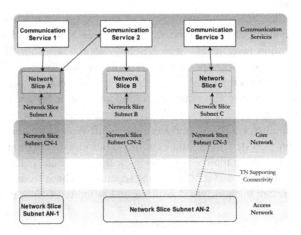

Fig. 5. A variety of communication services provided by multiple network slices. Each slice can be separated at the transport layer and its subnets restricted communication, unless required otherwise [26]

3 Methodology and Implementation

To experiment with enhanced VPN isolation of network slices beyond the hard isolation and using the hardware-level segmentation and virtual network functions, we designed a testbed that is comprised of a communication between the 4G/5G radio frontend and the core network. The core functions are provisioned in the OpenStack cloud and Edge hosting a portion of the vRAN (see Fig. 6).

An enhanced VPN+ framework is utilized to establish an encrypted communication between the Centralized Units in the vRAN and the vEPC/5GC core networks in the transport backhaul network. This communication is based on fiber networking on Layer-1, offering a 10 Gbps end-to-end communication bandwidth. For provisioning and maintaining persistent deployment, as well as minimize experimental error, we rely on the immutable infrastructure concept that is delivered by container virtualization and automation tools such as Ansible and Kubernetes. These tools offer seamless automation of the SDN controllers (O-RAN), which serve as network slicing function controllers for orchestrating the three slices represented in Fig. 6 [27].

Within the OpenStack cloud, service layers are defined for provisioning the corresponding vNFs of each slice, allowing traffic to be routed through the Neutron Open vSwitch DPDK networking module [28]. Kubernetes orchestrates the core network infrastructure and ensures immutability and stability in cases when the entire infrastructure needs to be automatically re-deployed due to escalating problems. As described previously, we establish a tunnel between the two endpoints in the cloud, which are the Core Network (5GC) and the Centralized Unit (Baseband Unit). For securing the tunnel, AES-256 encryption is used and its impact on the performance measured. The tunnel should be able to accommodate the virtual functions instantiated by the SDN controller. The Docker containers can communicate with the Neutron service in OpenStack using the Kuryr plugin. To allow this, we set the proper ID of the user and VM instance running the 4G and 5G Core Networks. The container performs authentication through the Kuryr plugin via the OpenStack's Keystone service for handling the authentication procedures of users accessing the core networks in the cloud (CSPs).

3.1 Implementation Stage

Core Network

Conclusively, an enhanced VPN+ deployment is manufactured between the two SR-IOV endpoints in the Docker containers, allowing for encrypted communication without a MPLS-BGP encapsulation. This will provide a clear understanding on the impact of CPU-accelerated encryption using the AES-256 algorithm, and its influence on the performance of the backhaul 4G/5G transport network. As SR-IOV can achieve a hardware-level isolation between endpoints using VLAN segmentation and mapping virtual functions (see Fig. 7), this may prove to be insufficient in a multitenant environment, because additional containers and services can then access the 5G core, which should be isolated. One method for maintaining isolation is by policy enforcement, guiding traffic to the 5GC core from only sources that should access it (i.e., a Centralized Unit or multiple Centralized Units). For operators who desire an additional layer of isolation, despite the underlying policy, a VPN instances are established between the SR-IOV endpoints.

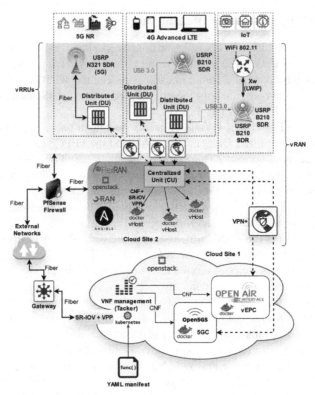

Fig. 6. 4G and 5G hybrid infrastructure at the Secure 5G4IoT Lab within the Oslo Metropolitan University. Each network slice in this case is controlled by a single CU and distinct DUs. In this case, one slice per generation of network (4G and 5G are regarded as different slices)

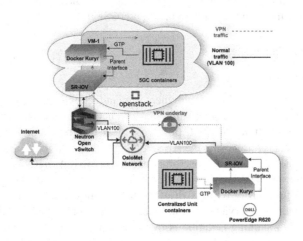

Fig. 7. VLAN segmentation using SR-IOV and VPN instance in the transport network between the Centralized Unit containers and the 5G Core Network in the cloud

3.2 Evaluation

The evaluation stage is comprised of two phases and an initial assumption that an adversary is attempting to demultiplex the transport network stream between the 5G core network containers and the Centralized Unit containers. The attacker hijacks an insecure Docker container running in the same namespace and attempts a Man in the Middle attack, capturing the entire communication and decoupling the control plane Non-Access Stratum (NAS) signaling as well as Packet Data Convergence Protocol (PDCP) packets to obtain information from the UE.

The second stage of the evaluation is the establishment of a VPN+ transport network between the 5GC and the Centralized Unit. In this situation, the adversary shall not be able to decapsulate the traffic due to the inability to decipher an AES-256 encrypted tunnel. This will indicate that in case of virtualization vulnerability exploitation, an adversary will encounter a rather challenging obstacle that will prevent personal information of healthcare patients to be exposed.

4 Results

The total number of captured packets in both scenarios is 1000. By utilizing logistic regression, we measure the classifiers of the attack vectors for attempting a reconnaissance activity on the 5G transport network and capture PDCP information from devices. One such example is the 802.15.4 LR-WPAN IoT device (see Fig. 8), where the traffic can be obtained and the frames from the packet read successfully. Based on the success of the decapsulation outcome, we can predict the difference between the attempts in cases of plain communication, compared to the one that is transmitted through the VPN+ and where the TLS handshake is detected but the content of the communication cannot be viewed without decrypting the traffic with TLS certificates and the private key (sample Wireshark capture in Fig. 9).

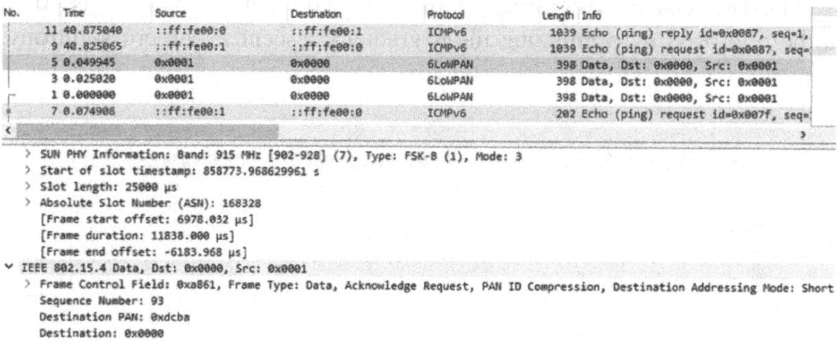

Fig. 8. In case without any encryption, the attacker can target vulnerable devices such as IoT that work on less secure protocols such as 802.15.4 LR-WPAN

The classifiers are defined via a sigmoid function that maps between actions, which allow the attacker to read the communication, compared to actions in which the attacker

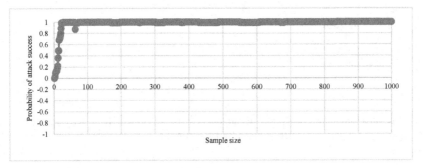

Fig. 9. With the VPN instantiated at the transport network, the attacker can only view the TLS handshake between the cloud core network and the CU

cannot read the communication considering the sample size of 1000 packets. The outcome variable is binary (true or false) and the predictive values are the number of protocols that are encapsulated within PDCP that can be compromised during an attack. The sigmoid function will serve as activation function for the logistic regression and is defined as:

$$f(x) = \frac{1}{1 + e^{-x}} \tag{1}$$

We define a cross-entropy cost function due to the lack of positive second derivative for square error and avoid local optima:

$$J(\theta) = -\frac{1}{m} \sum_{i=1}^{m} [y^{(i)} \cdot \log(h_\theta(x^{(i)}) + (1 - y^{(i)}) \cdot \log(1 - h_\theta(x^{(i)}))] \tag{2}$$

Where: m is the number of examples, $x^{(i)}$ is the feature vector for the ith example, $y^{(i)}$ is the value for the ith example and θ is the parameters vector.

The results are evident according to the tests that the attacker has a probability of 0.98452 to read the communication from the 1000 packet sample size, including decapsulating the PDCP headers (which is 98% of the entire communication) when there is no VPN tunneling, compared to -0.99442 probability in the other case (Fig. 10 and Fig. 11). The relative error deviation in the logistic regression model is ~0.02 and this can be improved by optimizing the θ gradient descent in the cross-entropy cost function.

Fig. 10. Logistic regression analysis on the likelihood an attacker will obtain information from the end devices connected in to the 5G core without VPN+ tunneling

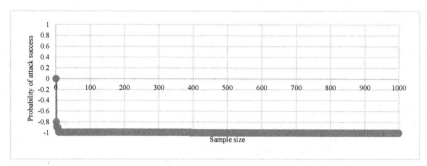

Fig. 11. Logistic regression analysis on the probability an attacker will obtain information from the transport network that is tunneled, and AES-256 encryption enabled

5 Discussion

The logistic regression analysis in this research demonstrates feasibility of an attacker to achieve Man in the Middle attack on a transport network in 5G, compared to when an enhanced VPN+ tunneling is initialized. This use-case however does not consider additional factors that can prove beneficial for the attacker, or supplementary security mechanisms that can influence end-to-end security.

The utilization of enhanced VPN approach for strengthening the isolation of network slices is not sufficient to protect against DDoS/Flooding attacks. This is because the latter requires more stringent mechanism for traffic steering incorporated within the SDN controller, which needs to react based on an input from a threat intelligence system for prevention of flooding attacks. One method to allow for more granular control is the introduction of SR-MPLS (Segment Routing) for IPv6 to enforce dynamic policy shifts in case of flooding and DDoS cyber-attacks.

6 Conclusion

Conclusively to the experimentation, we have demonstrated the successful implementation of an enhanced VPN+ transport network between the Centralized Unit of a 5G C-RAN and the Core Network in the TN. Despite the lack of performance evaluation of the approach, the combination of hardware offloading, isolation using distinct PFs (Physical Functions) and VFs (Virtual Functions) as well as policy enforcement, provides substantial security level that most enterprises deploying 5G will consider. Nevertheless, in some instances where the expense of network performance is not an issue, VPNs may prove a viable possibility to harden the isolation between 5G network slices (i.e., critical infrastructure). For IoT slices that do not require high bandwidth and low latency, the enhanced VPN can introduce great security benefits.

Acknowledgement. This paper is a result of the H2020 Concordia project (https://www.concordia-h2020.eu) which has received funding from the EU H2020 programme under grant agreement No 830927. The CONCORDIA consortium includes 23 partners from industry and other organizations such as Telenor, Telefonica, Telecom Italia, Ericsson, Siemens, Airbus, etc. and 23 partners from academia such as CODE, university of Twente, OsloMet, etc.

References

1. OpenStack Foundation: Over 60 Global Organizations Join in Establishing 'Open Infrastructure Foundation' to Build the Next Decade of Infrastructure for AI, 5G, Edge. https://www.openstack.org/news/view/463/over-60-global-organizations-join-in-establishing-open-infrastructure-foundation-to-build-the-next-decade-of-infrastructure-for-ai-5g-edge. Accessed 22 Dec 2020
2. Feng, B., et al.: Secure 5G network slicing for elderly care. In: Awan, I., Younas, M., Ünal, P., Aleksy, M. (eds.) MobiWIS 2019. LNCS, vol. 11673, pp. 202–213. Springer, Cham (2019). https://doi.org/10.1007/978-3-030-27192-3_16
3. Ahmad, I., Kumar, T., et al.: Overview of 5G security challenges and solutions. IEEE Commun. Stand. Mag. **2**(1), 36–43 (2018). https://doi.org/10.1109/MCOMSTD.2018.1700063
4. MITRE project: Common Vulnerabilities and Exposures (2021). https://cve.mitre.org/
5. IETF TEAS Working Group: A framework for enhanced virtual private networks (VPN+) service (2020). https://tools.ietf.org/html/draft-ietf-teas-enhanced-vpn-06
6. Narayana Samy, G., Ahmad, R., Ismail, Z.: Security threats categories in healthcare information systems. Health Inf. J. **16**, 201–209 (2010). https://doi.org/10.1177/1460458210377468
7. McDermott, D.S., Kamerer, J.L., Birk, A.T.: Electronic health records - a literature review of cyber threats and security measures. Int. J. Cyber Res. Educ. (IJCRE) **1**, 42–49 (2019). https://doi.org/10.4018/IJCRE.2019070104
8. Latif, S., Qadir, J., Farooq, S., Imran, M.: How 5G wireless (and concomitant technologies) will revolutionize healthcare?. Future Internet **9**(4), 93 (2017). https://doi.org/10.3390/fi9040093
9. ETSI TS.123.501 v15.8.0 technical specification: 5G; System Architecture for the 5G System (5GS) (3GPP TS 23.501 version 15.8.0 Release 15) (2020). https://www.etsi.org/deliver/etsi_ts/123500_123599/123501/15.08.00_60/ts_123501v150800p.pdf
10. OpenStack cloud software: Official documentation. https://www.openstack.org/. Accessed 30 Mar 2021
11. Docker container technology: Official documentation. https://www.docker.com/. Accessed 30 Mar 2021
12. Kubernetes container orchestration platform: Official documentation. https://kubernetes.io/. Accessed 30 Mar 2021
13. Barakabitze, A.A., Ahmad, A., Mijumbi, R., Hines, A.: 5G network slicing using SDN and NFV: a survey of taxonomy, architectures and future challenges. Comput. Netw. **167**, 106984 (2020). https://doi.org/10.1016/j.comnet.2019.106984. ISSN 1389-1286
14. Dzogovic, B., Do, T.V., Santos, B., Jacot, N., Feng, B., Thuan, D.V.: Secure healthcare: 5G-enabled network slicing for elderly care. In: 2020 International Conference on Computer and Communication Systems (ICCCS), Shanghai, China, pp. 864–868 (2020). https://doi.org/10.1109/ICCCS49078.2020.9118583
15. 3GPP Specification TR 38.801: Study on new radio access technology: Radio access architecture and interfaces (2018). https://portal.3gpp.org/desktopmodules/Specifications/SpecificationDetails.aspx?specificationId=3056
16. Dzogovic, B., Thuan, D.V., Santos, B., Do, T.V., Feng, B., Jacot, N.: Thunderbolt-3 backbone for augmented 5G network slicing in cloud-radio access networks. In: 2019 IEEE 2nd 5G World Forum (5GWF), Dresden, Germany, pp. 415–420 (2019). https://doi.org/10.1109/5GWF.2019.8911710
17. OpenAirInterface5G: OpenAirInterface Software Alliance. https://openairinterface.org/. Accessed 02 Feb 2021

18. Open5GS: Open-source project of 5GC and EPC Release-16. https://open5gs.org/. Accessed 02 Feb 2021
19. OpenStack project Tacker: VNF Forwarding Graphs. https://docs.openstack.org/tacker/latest/user/vnffg_usage_guide.html. Accessed 02 Feb 2021
20. OpenStack project Tacker: ESTI NFV-SOL, Experimenting CNF with Kubernetes VIM. https://docs.openstack.org/tacker/latest/user/index.html. Accessed 02 Feb 2021
21. RedHat OpenShift: About Single Root I/O Virtualization (SR-IOV) hardware networks. https://docs.openshift.com/container-platform/4.4/networking/hardware_networks/about-sriov.html. Accessed 02 Feb 2021
22. OpenStack SR-IOV: OpenStack Neutron SR-IOV functionality. https://docs.openstack.org/neutron/pike/admin/config-sriov.html. Accessed 02 Feb 2021
23. Juniper Networks: LTE Security for Mobile Service Provider Networks (White Paper) (2015). https://www.juniper.net/us/en/local/pdf/whitepapers/2000536-en.pdf
24. Liyanage, M., Gurtov, A.: Secured VPN models for LTE backhaul networks. In: 2012 IEEE Vehicular Technology Conference (VTC Fall), Quebec, Canada, pp. 1–5 (2012). https://doi.org/10.1109/VTCFall.2012.6399037
25. Farrel, A.: What is ACTN framework. Metro-Haul Project. https://metro-haul.eu/2018/08/30/what-is-actn/. Accessed 08 Feb 2021
26. 3GPP specification TS 28.530: management and orchestration; concepts, use cases and requirements, version 16.4.0 (2020). https://www.etsi.org/deliver/etsi_ts/128500_128599/128530/16.04.00_60/ts_128530v160400p.pdf
27. Open-RAN: Alliance for Open Radio Access Networks. https://www.o-ran.org/. Accessed 30 Mar 2021
28. Data Plane Development Kit: Official documentation. https://www.dpdk.org/. Accessed 30 Mar 2021
29. 5G Infrastructure Public Private Partnership (5GPPP): View on 5G Architecture, version 3.0. URL: https://5g-ppp.eu/wp-content/uploads/2019/07/5G-PPP-5G-Architecture-White-Paper_v3.0_PublicConsultation.pdf (2019).
30. 3GPP specification TS 38.300: Technical specification group radio access network; NR; NR and NG-RAN overall description; stage-2, Release 16. Version 16.4.0 (2020). https://www.etsi.org/deliver/etsi_ts/138300_138399/138300/16.04.00_60/ts_138300v160400p.pdf
31. GSMA: An Introduction to Network Slicing, white paper (2017). https://www.gsma.com/futurenetworks/wp-content/uploads/2017/11/GSMA-An-Introduction-to-Network-Slicing.pdf
32. 3GPP specification TS 33.126: Lawful Interception Requirements (Release 16), version 16.3.0 (2021). https://www.etsi.org/deliver/etsi_ts/133100_133199/133126/16.03.00_60/ts_133126v160300p.pdf

Social Considerations of Technology

GuideSwarm: A Drone Network Design to Assist Visually Impaired People

Görkem Sakarya$^{(\boxtimes)}$, Talip Tolga Sari, and Gökhan Seçinti

Istanbul Technical University, Istanbul, Turkey
{sakaryag,sarita,secinti}@itu.edu.tr

Abstract. Today, most of the metropolitan areas lack necessary infrastructure to guide visually impaired people. Even with an existing infrastructure, it is nearly impossible to ensure the safety of visually impaired people in dense/crowded urban areas. In this paper, we propose aerial swarm framework, namely GuideSwarm, cooperatively utilizing multiple drones to provide assistance to visually impaired people in crowded urban environments. In this manner, GuideSwarm first formally structures allocation and scheduling problems by defining different sets of assistance missions. Then, we form an optimization problem with the objective of minimizing average waiting time for the users and propose a heuristic method solving the defined optimization in $O(n^2)$ time complexity. Compared to the greedy approaches, our solution provides 19% less waiting time for users demanding assistance.

Keywords: UAV · Task scheduling · Visually impaired

1 Introduction

In World Report on Vision by World Health Organization [1], it is stated that there are 2.2 billion visually impaired people in the world and a significant number of these people suffer from either complete or nearly complete vision loss.

Visually impaired people have lots of troubles in their daily lives due to the lack of awareness of their surroundings. Streets in urban areas, crowded public transportation, shopping malls are only few of the examples, in where it is extremely inconvenient and stressful for people with such impairments to be. Such places/locations require solid infrastructure and dynamic control systems to guide these people through. Even today, most of the major cities still lack tactile pavements to help visually impaired people to follow sidewalks using white canes. In such places (where there is limited to none infrastructure), using guide dogs looks like a promising solution. Unfortunately, this is not a cost-effective solution due to high cost and effort in breeding, training and maintain these animals. In addition, they are prone to other people's reactions/interactions, where some people may naively try to pet them without realizing they are working animals and easily distract/disorient the people these animals are guiding.

© ICST Institute for Computer Sciences, Social Informatics and Telecommunications Engineering 2021
Published by Springer Nature Switzerland AG 2021. All Rights Reserved
I. M. Pires et al. (Eds.): GOODTECHS 2021, LNICST 401, pp. 139–152, 2021.
https://doi.org/10.1007/978-3-030-91421-9_11

In this paper, we propose to use Unmanned Aerial Vehicles (UAVs) to guide visually impaired people in large cities. In the system model we devised, multiple UAVs are located at different locations within the city, where they can be conveniently deployed for real-time assistance of visually impaired people. Inside a coverage area, our main purpose is providing assistance to user as soon as possible, where multiple users may request assistance simultaneously, which requires effective scheduling of multiple Unmanned Aerial Devices at different locations.

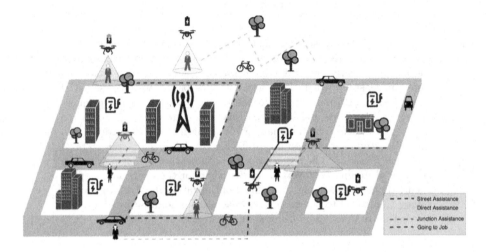

Fig. 1. System model

Figure 1 visualises the use cases we addressed in this paper. It shows the different types of assignments and the main principles of the system. All different assignment types are represented with dashed lines in different colors. The charge stations and representative current battery level are shown in the figure. Also the interchange between different assignment types are simulated. In order to solve the problem introduced above, we basically proposed a new scheduling algorithm in order to complete maximum number of tasks with minimum average waiting time for users. To this end, we formulate an optimization problem, with the constraints such as to satisfy power consumption and batter capacity limitation of UAVs as well as to assign suitable drone for awaiting tasks.

After we formulate the optimization problem, we employed several well-known scheduling algorithms, such as which are "First in First Out" and "Shortest Time First", in order to address the formulated allocation problem. Then, we devised a new heuristic algorithm in order to achieve a higher efficiency of obtaining smaller average waiting time than the other algorithms. The new heuristic gives better results for the optimization. The total of the time for going to task, doing the task and returning to the charging station for UAVs, either working or waiting, is used as a parameter. Also, while choosing the best UAV for the user, distance between UAVs' charging station, users' position and the target point are considered. Lastly, the UAV which have the minimum total time, is assigned to the user and this match enables us to have minimum average waiting time.

The main working principle is that, according to the optimization problem, the UAVs are being assigned to jobs. After this assignment, the assigned UAVs wait until the users are ready to work with UAV. After that the UAVs go to the users in coordination. When the user and the UAV is at the same location, they start to move together. While they are moving together, UAV will give some directives to the user in order to assist him/her. After they reach the target coordinates, the UAV returns to its own charging station. On the other hand, a UAV can be assigned to multiple jobs at different times. However, before starting to a new job, the drone must be charged to have enough charge level to meet the battery consumption of the next job. Also, UAVs have a safety threshold for being able to reach their charging stations before their charge finishes. When all of the waiting jobs are finished, all UAVs go to their stations and the program terminates.

This paper offers three main contributions as follows:

- We designed a system that provides assistance to visually impaired people. While providing this assistance, we have more than one UAV and multiple users in our scope.
- We formulate an optimization problem for scheduling the system according to the case that includes multiple task and multiple device.
- We implemented an algorithm that applies the optimization problem to the assistance system. We decreased the average waiting time of the user in the system by using this algorithm.

In Sect. 2, we examined some researches on both visually impaired assistance with different devices and applications of different types of task scheduling algorithms and in Sect. 3, we defined our optimization problem and explained the main structure of our project. In Sect. 4, we mentioned about our results and lastly in Sect. 5, we conclude our project briefly.

2   Related Work

There are various studies and products targeting visually impaired people, which recently include UAVs as well as other flourishing robotic technologies and equipment. These studies vary from, utilizing indoor robotic assistance for blind people [2], offering mobile robots to assist visually impaired people [11], and building drone-based navigation system for visually impaired person [5], to flying guide drones for runners [6]. Some of these studies rely on multiple agents to work in collaboration, where efficient task scheduling and allocation methods are required. There are various researches on Task Scheduling and one of them is, collaborative task allocation for multiple UAVs [8] and also some researchers work on control of multiple UAVs some of them are, algorithms and tests of controlling multiple UAVs [15], managing disaster with the help of UAVs [14]. Lastly, some researches with UAVs and/or task allocation which construct the base of our project are machine learning methods to communicate with UAVs [9] and task allocation for multiple robots by applying clustering [12]. The researches that work with reinforcement learning are using reinforcement learning for designing a project that schedule the UAV clusters [10] and applying multi-agent reinforcement learning techniques for dynamic task allocation [13].

Researchers have been working on different technological developments, and using some different devices for visually impaired people. Some of the researchers are using robots for assisting visually impaired people. Kulkarni et al. [2] developed an indoor robotic assistance for visually impaired people to follow the robot for avoiding obstacles and finding their ways. Also, in their research [3], Kulkarni et al. developed a mobile robot to assist visually impaired people more interactively using small robots. In an older research, Mori and Kotani [11] developed a mobile robot that assists visually impaired people by image processing and used some range sensors. As a different solution for visually impaired people, Simoes et al. [4] propose a wearable low-cost device for guiding visually impaired people in an indoor environment. They implemented an assistance system using a pair of glasses that contains cameras and sensors. Our Project also aims to apply different techniques and use UAVs for assisting visually impaired people and while doing this, we try to find more convenient ways to give them the opportunity to use this technology without need to hold something on hand or on them.

Similar to our project, there are some researches that are using Unmanned Aerial Devices to guide virtually impaired people. As one of these, Avila et al. [5] found a stable and reliable solution for the guidance system for visually impaired people. They developed a system by using a small drone to navigate virtually impaired people within an indoor area. Another UAV solution for blind people, Zayer et al. [6] proposed a UAV based assistance system for blind navigation. It provided a feasible system for UAV assistance by which visually impaired people could run by following the UAV. Unlike the other projects that project provided an outdoor solution. The main difference between our project and these researches is that we work on multiple UAV and multiple user domain. By applying the assistance in this way, we needed to deal with task allocation and coordination. In the paper by Trotta et al. [7] researchers have an approach to use multiple UAVs in coordination. They proposed a network architecture for being able to manage UAVs around a city. In this project we are also inspired from that approach to use multiple UAVs for visually impaired people's assistance within a city.

In addition to UAV assistance, our research focuses on the task allocation method for the UAVs. The projects that make task allocation vary according to their constraints and features. Some of these researches have been examined for having a background for our project. Fu et al. [8] studied an allocation problem to find the best allocation algorithm for their multi-UAV system and they presented a method. Like this research, there are lots of researches on multiple UAV collaboration and one of them is Nigam et al. [15] that tries to organize multiple UAVs and control them simultaneously. Erdelj et al. [14] also developed a system that works with multiple UAVs to help and coordinate on disasters. We also control and organize the UAVs on our simulation. While doing this, we implement some algorithms and also, we propose a new algorithm that increases the efficiency of the system.

Another research area is the application of some machine learning techniques on UAV control or task allocation. Bithas et al. [9] made a survey on different machine learning techniques to communicate with UAVs and while doing that they try different types of task allocation. Janati et al. [12] also stated that their proposed task allocation method increases the efficiency of task allocation on a large number of tasks and robots by applying the clustering method. Another technique to have a better task allocation is to use some reinforcement learning methods, as stated by Yang et al. [10]. They designed a Deep Q Learning method on UAV clusters to optimize the task schedule. Like this research, Noureddine et al. [13] proposed a method for dynamic task scheduling that is based on reinforcement learning and they improved the Deep Q learning method by adding some features for their purpose, and their method makes the cooperative task allocation. We planned to develop an agent based on reinforcement learning as a future work.

Briefly, our project combines some different methods from researches that work on the use of UAVs for the assistance of visually impaired and to achieve the necessary task allocation for this purpose. As a combination of all of these, we propose an optimization problem that is designed for multiple UAVs and multiple users and a new customized task allocation method to increase efficiency of the project.

3   System Model and Proposed Approach

Our project consists of two main phases to accomplish UAV assistance system for visually impaired people by implementing a task allocation. First, we construct an optimization problem to specify the main way to reach the purpose and to realize all of the limitations and constraints for this project. Following this, we propose a task allocation algorithm by using these constraints then, compared several different algorithms. As a result of these comparisons, we proposed an adapted task scheduling algorithm (Table 1).

Table 1. Symbol list

Symbol	Refers
α	Unit discharge rate for street assistance
β	Unit discharge rate for direct assistance
γ	Unit discharge rate for junction assistance
θ	Charging rate
δ	Discharge rate when moving
ζ	Discharge rate when moving
m	Total number of Jobs
a_i	Assign Time of job i
t_i	Arrival time of user i
d_i	Duration of Job i
E_i	Whether there is street assistance for job i
D_i	Whether there is direct assistance for job i
J_i	Whether there is junction assistance for job i
R_{ij}	Whether drone j returning from job i
G_{ij}	Whether drone j going to job i
$IDLE_i$	Whether drone i is idle
$C_j(t)$	Charge level of jth drone at time t
$Ch_j(t)$	Whether drone j is charging at time t
Q_i	Whether job i is in the queue
W_{ij}	Whether drone j is assigned to job i
MB	Maximum Battery Size

3.1 Optimization Problem

The main objective is to minimize average waiting time which is the difference between the assign time and arrival time of user. The minimization function in order to achieve this objective is shown in below expression.

$$\min \frac{\sum_{i=0}^{m}(a_i - t_i)}{m} \tag{1}$$

$$\text{subject to: } E_i + D_i + J_i + Q_i \leq 1 \qquad \forall i \in Job \tag{2}$$

$$W_{ij} = 1 \implies$$
$$a_i = min\{t | C_j(t - g_{ij}) > (g_{ij} \times \delta + CNP_i + r_{ij} \times \delta + \zeta) \wedge (t - g_{ij} \geq t_i)\} \, \forall t \tag{3}$$

$$W_{kj} = 1 \wedge W_{lj} = 1 \implies$$
$$(a_k < a_l \wedge a_k + d_k + r_{kj} + ct_i < a_l - g_{lj}) \vee$$
$$(a_l < a_k \wedge a_l + d_l + r_{lj} + ct_i < a_k - g_{kj}) \tag{4}$$

$$Ch_j(t) = 1 \implies ((a_i - g_{ij} > t) \wedge (t > a_i + d_i + r_{ij})) \vee (a_i - g_{ij} < t) \quad (5)$$

Function (1) minimizes the average waiting time by using 3 variables, where a_i defines the assign time of the job to drone, t_i represents the arrival time of the user to the system and m stores the number of jobs. The minimization function meets the following constraints. The first constraint (2) implies that a job could be assigned to one of these variables at a time. For example, when a job is assigned to an street assistance it cannot be assigned to direct assistance. Another constraint (3) indicates that when i^{th} job assigned to j^{th} drone, the assign time of the ith job will be the minimum time that satisfies the condition is that the capacity of the jth drone at the starting time of the ith job will have higher capacity than the sum of going, processing and returning time and the safety threshold.

Lastly, constraint (4) is created to imply that if two jobs assigned to same drone, the time to work with the drone is not overlap. This expression creates the time to the drone for going to the user's location by subtracting this time from the assign time. For example, if k^{th} job assigned before, the first assign time of lth cannot be earlier than the finish of the kth job. The last constraint 5 that we have created is for charging time of the drone. The charging time of the jth drone must be before a job assignment or after the assignment.

Definitions. The first part of the project is preparing an optimization problem and we developed our problem based on the features that we have decided. The main purpose of our project is to develop a UAV assistance for visually impaired people. Consequently, we defined Job and Resource variables. The Job stores the values for the users request as an array. While a user could have several job requests, one row of an array consists several values of a job which is a vector that specifies the path from the initial coordinate to target. It also has a variable which stores the assistance type and 3 variables that stores different times. These are duration, assigning time and arrival time of job. The assign time is defined with initial value -1 and when it is overwritten for assignment the assign time is assigned after the drone arrives to job location. The information about jobs stored in a two dimensional array that is called Jobs. The Jobs array consists all jobs with their information in 5 branches, where vector stores start and finish coordinates, type stores the type of job as Street, Direct or Junction assistance, d_i stores the job duration, a_i defines the assign time of the job to drone, t_i represents the arrival time of the user to the system.

Type of the Job depends on user requirements and it has 3 different types which are Street, Junction and Direct assistance. The defined types correspond to the assistance of the UAVs. When the UAV assists the user while it is following a street in an environment, Junction assistance may contain multiple UAVs to help user to be able to pass the junctions. Direct assistance is the assistance method to users while they do not have a specific path like tactile paving. The features for assistance type are not considered for this project, they are only defined as a structure. Job types are defined as a boolean value that represents whether the user requests the corresponding type of Job.

On the other hand, the UAVs have some different features, definitions and status values. UAVs have 4 different statuses during the operations. These are Going to Job, Returning From the Job, Charging and IDLE. In the equation given below, these variables are defined with boolean type. The G_{ij} is defined for the status that shows whether the drone is assigned to go to the user. If the value equals to 1, that means the jth drone assigned to i^{th} job and drone started to go to the start position of the job from the base coordinate of itself. R_{ij} is defined to specify that whether the drone assigned to return to base. If the value is equals to 1 the jth UAV completed i^{th} job and returning from the target location of the job to the base location of itself. Ch_j shows if it is equals to 1 the jth drone is charging. The last status is $IDLE_j$ and which indicates that the UAV is ready to assign to a job. The structure of the Drone Status is given below.

$$UAV\_Status_{ij}(t) = \begin{cases} R_{ij} = 1, & j^{th} \; drone \; returning \; from \; i^{th} job \\ \\ G_{ij} = 1, & j^{th} \; drone \; going \; to \; i^{th} job \\ \\ IDLE_j = 1, & Drone's \; Status \; is \; IDLE \\ \\ Ch_j(t) = 1, & Charging \; at \; time \; t \end{cases} \tag{6}$$

Also, there are some specifications for the UAVs which are Base Coordinates of the drones and Capacity of drones. These variables are stored and used for some constraints and functions. The Base coordinates stores a tuple that consists X and Y coordinates of the base station of corresponding drone into an array. Also, the capacity of drones stores the current battery level of the drone for tracking the capacity for planning and creating safety threshold. The $C_j(t)$ function gives a result, that shows the capacity level between 0 and 100, at time t.

Some of the definitions for the other variables are given below. The Q_i is defined for show the status of a job. If the value equals to 1, that means the ith job is assigned to a UAV but it is waiting its starting time in a queue. W_{ij} is a multi-dimensional list that stores the assignment of the user and job. When i^{th} job assigned to j^{th} job the corresponding value of W_{ij} is assigned as 1. This variable is storing for tracking the assignments whether all jobs are finished or not.

$$Q_i = \begin{cases} 1, & i^{th} \; job \; is \; in \; queue \\ 0, & processing \; or \; not \; assigned \end{cases} \tag{7}$$

$$W_{ij} = \begin{cases} 1, & j^{th} \ drone \ assigned \ to \ i^{th} \ job \\ 0, & no \ relation \end{cases} \tag{8}$$

Functions. There are several functions to prepare the optimization function for implementation. These functions use the variables which are described before and store their values. The first function is calculating flying time from a location to another. As stated below, by dividing the path length to velocity of the jth drone the flying time is calculated. Going and returning times are calculated with this formula and task allocation will be done according to these variables.

$$FT(vector_i(start/end), BC_j) = \frac{Path}{V_j} \tag{9}$$

$$r_{ij} = FT(vector_i(end), BC_j) \tag{10}$$

$$g_{ij} = FT(vector_i(start), BC_j) \tag{11}$$

The consumption function below shows the total expended energy. As stated, before α refers the unit energy expended for street assistance, β for direct assistance and γ for junction assistance. And the consumption is calculated by multiplying these values with duration of job. At least one of the summing parts in the consumption function is not zero, because of the corresponding constraint that is given in the Eq. 7. The formula for consumption is given below.

$$CNP_i = \begin{cases} (\alpha \times d_i), & E_i = 1 \rightarrow \ street \ assistance \ to \ i^{th} job \\ (\beta \times d_i), & D_i = 1 \rightarrow \ direct \ assistance \ to \ i^{th} job \\ (\beta \times d_i), & J_i = 1 \rightarrow \ junction \ assistance \ to \ i^{th} job \end{cases} \tag{12}$$

Another function to our problem calculates the charging time after a job. The result of consumption function for i^{th} job, divided by θ that stores the constant for charging amount within unit time.

$$ct_i = \frac{CNP_i}{\theta} \tag{13}$$

The last function calculates the capacity of drone at a time. Also in the function given below, the total consumption is calculated. This function have several conditions which calculate consumption during different states of drones. It calculates total_consumption in 6 cases, first and last cases occur when a drone has not an assigned job and it is ready to be assigned, there is no consumption. Second and fourth cases are specified for the consumption while going to job and returning from job. Third case also shows the consumption during the job and lastly fifth case shows the charging.

$$
J_{ij}(t) = \begin{cases}
0 \ , \ job \ is \ not \ assigned & t < a_i - g_{ij} \\[2ex]
UAV\_Status_{ij}(t) \times \delta \ , \ going \ to \ user & a_i - g_{ij} \leq t < a_i \\[2ex]
\dfrac{W_{ij} \times CNP_i}{d_i} \ , in \ job & a_i \leq t < a_i + d_i \\[2ex]
UAV\_Status_{ij}(t) \times \delta \ , \ returning & a_i + d_i \leq t < a_i + d_i + r_{ij} \\[2ex]
-UAV\_Status_{ij}(t) \times \theta \ , \ charging & t < a_i + d_i + r_{ij} + ct_i \\[2ex]
0 \ , \ IDLE & t \geq a_i + d_i + r_{ij} + ct_i
\end{cases}
\tag{14}
$$

The last function calculates the capacity of drone at a time. In this function the charge level is calculated by subtracting the sum of total_consumption of all jobs from the maximum battery level.

$$
C_j(t) = MB - \sum_{i=0}^{n} \sum_{s=0}^{t} J_{ij}(s)
\tag{15}
$$

3.2 Task Allocation Methods

Following the problem construction, we developed a task allocation algorithm to apply the optimization problem. This task scheduling algorithm makes the match between the job and drone, while doing this match it considers the main objectives of our optimization function and fits with the constraints. Although not all parts of the optimization problem are designed on the algorithm, it implements the main structure. It tries to decrease the average waiting time for randomized values. All of the values like, job number, job location, drone number and drone locations are selected randomly and the results are compared.

We researched lots of algorithms which could give better results on our project, and lastly, we decided to use Shortest Time and First Come First Serve scheduling algorithms. These algorithms are adapted to our optimization problem and coded in Python.

We implemented the First Come First Serve(FCFS) algorithm for our optimization problem and the main structure is built by selecting a drone for a job in a sequence while the time is being iterated. The sequence is determined according to the arrival time that is given at the 5th column of the array for the corresponding job. Also, the shortest time algorithm is implemented and the Job array is sorted according to their duration and after the sort, it is iterated over time. The shortest time algorithm worked with a queue to take the sorted order at a time.

On the other hand, we proposed an algorithm that decreases the average waiting time of the jobs. This algorithm is developed by aiming to decrease average waiting time and for being able to do that it uses a priority queue. The priority queue is designed to return the id of job which will be finished earlier. The time includes both the drone's coming and returning time and the job duration. Because of that, the minimum time priority also avoided from selecting smaller jobs. Time is iterated in the algorithm to find assign time and it is checked with the arrival time of the job for avoiding to assign drones to jobs which are not arrived. However, this algorithm enables system to wait the jobs which could decrease average waiting time. Briefly, our method enables the system to select best job for a drone. We designed and tested this algorithm with different cases and the pseudo code of our algorithm is given below.

Algorithm 1: New Scheduling algorithm

1: **for all** $Jobs : Job_y$ **do**
2:     **for all** $Jobs : Job_x$ **do**
3:         **for** $Time : T$ **do**
4:             **if** Job_x is not $assigned$ **then**
5:                 **if** $Drone(Y\%NumDrone)$ $available$ at $(T, T + Work)$ **then**
6:                     **assign** max $arrival$ $time$ and $T- > temp\_assign\_time$
7:                     **push** $temp\_assign\_time$ $- > Priority\_Queue$
8:         **assign** $Priority\_Queue(Min\ Finish\ Time)$ $- > Assign\_Time$
9:         **assign** Job_x to $Drone(Y\%NumDrone)$

---

4   Experimentation Environment and Experiment Design

We tested the implementation and examined the possible results in different cases. First Come First Serve algorithm gives bad results for the average waiting time because of the obscurity. Although, Shortest Time algorithm generally gives better results than FCFS, it gives too much waiting time for longer jobs. Also, the assignments could be inefficient because the distances between jobs and drones are not taken into account in these two algorithms. On the other hand, in lots of different cases our proposed heuristic gives better results than all of the other algorithms. In these cases, 4 drones are assigned to different number of users and according to the task scheduling method average waiting time is calculated and compared with each other A chart for different cases is given below (Fig. 2).

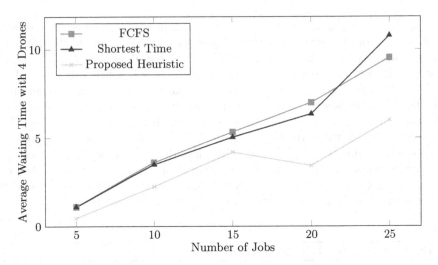

Fig. 2. Comparison of minimization functions.

For testing the program random values assigned to the variables of jobs and drones. This chart is created by using 4 drones and different number of jobs. The position of jobs and drones selected randomly. Also another graph that visualize the change of the average waiting time according to map size. While the map size increasing, the average waiting time of proposed heuristic increases less than the others. This test case created by using Poisson Distribution to arrival times and Gaussian Distribution to duration. While creating this chart 4 drones and 50 jobs are defined within the different maps (Fig. 3).

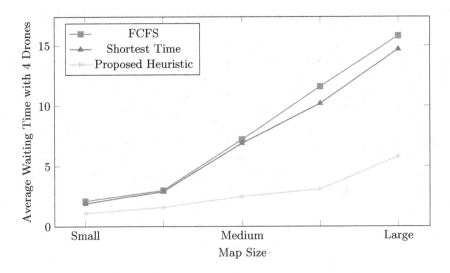

Fig. 3. Comparison of minimization functions on different map sizes

5   Conclusion and Future Work

Briefly, we designed a task allocation system for assisting the visually impaired people by cooperatively working multiple Unmanned Aerial Vehicles. The main purpose is making some sequence of operations to assist visually impaired people and this sequence is matching the distributed UAVs around the environment and the jobs which are created by the users. While doing this match, the task scheduling algorithms are being used to get better results. The results and the variables of task allocation algorithms depend on the optimization problem. Our optimization problem is constructed for minimizing the average waiting time of the jobs given the constraints. After comparing several task scheduling algorithms, a new algorithm has been proposed for the optimization problem. All of the experiments showed that using this algorithm decreases the average waiting time.

We determined some future works for the project. One of them is working on an agent that learns to schedule the jobs by using reinforcement learning and minimize the average waiting time. The other planned future work is calculating the energy consumption of the UAVs more accurate.

References

1. World Health Organization. World report on vision. https://www.who.int/publications/i/item/world-report-on-vision
2. Kulkarni, A., Wang, A., Urbina, L., Steinfeld, A., Dias, B.: Robotic assistance in indoor navigation for people who are blind. In: 2016 11th ACM/IEEE International Conference on Human-Robot Interaction (HRI), pp. 461–462. IEEE (2016)
3. Kulyukin, V., Gharpure, C., Nicholson, J., Osborne, G.: Robot-assisted wayfinding for the visually impaired in structured indoor environments. Auton. Robot. **21**(1), 29–41 (2006). https://doi.org/10.1007/s10514-006-7223-8
4. Simôes, W.C., De Lucena, V.F.: Blind user wearable audio assistance for indoor navigation based on visual markers and ultrasonic obstacle detection. In: 2016 IEEE International Conference on Consumer Electronics (ICCE), pp. 60–63. IEEE (2016)
5. Avila, M., Funk, M., Henze, N.: Dronenavigator: using drones for navigating visually impaired persons. In: Proceedings of the 17th International ACM SIGACCESS Conference on Computers & Accessibility, pp. 327–328 (2015)
6. Al Zayer, M., Tregillus, S., Bhandari, J., Feil-Seifer, D., Folmer, E.: Exploring the use of a drone to guide blind runners. In: Proceedings of the 18th International ACM SIGACCESS Conference on Computers and Accessibility, pp. 263–264 (2016)
7. Trotta, A., Andreagiovanni, F.D., Di Felice, M., Natalizio, E., Chowdhury, K.R.: When UAVs ride a bus: towards energy-efficient city-scale video surveillance. In: IEEE Infocom 2018-IEEE Conference on Computer Communications, pp. 1043–1051. IEEE (2018)
8. Fu, Z., Mao, Y., He, D., Yu, J., Xie, G.: Secure multi-UAV collaborative task allocation. IEEE Access **7**, 35579–35587 (2019)
9. Bithas, P.S., Michailidis, E.T., Nomikos, N., Vouyioukas, D., Kanatas, A.G.: A survey on machine-learning techniques for UAV-based communications. Sensors **19**(23), 5170 (2019)

10. Yang, J., You, X., Wu, G., Hassan, M.M., Almogren, A., Guna, J.: Application of reinforcement learning in UAV cluster task scheduling. Futur. Gener. Comput. Syst. **95**, 140–148 (2019)
11. Mori, H., Kotani, S.: Robotic travel aid for the blind: HARUNOBU-6. In: European Conference on Disability, Virtual Reality, and Assistive Technology (1998)
12. Janati, F., Abdollahi, F., Ghidary, S.S., Jannatifar, M., Baltes, J., Sadeghnejad, S.: Multi-robot task allocation using clustering method. In: Kim, J.-H., Karray, F., Jo, J., Sincak, P., Myung, H. (eds.) Robot Intelligence Technology and Applications 4. AISC, vol. 447, pp. 233–247. Springer, Cham (2017). https://doi.org/10.1007/978-3-319-31293-4_19
13. Noureddine, D.B., Gharbi, A., Ahmed, S.B.: Multi-agent deep reinforcement learning for task allocation in dynamic environment. In: ICSOFT, Chicago, pp. 17–26 (2017)
14. Erdelj, M., Natalizio, E., Chowdhury, K.R., Akyildiz, I.F.: Help from the sky: leveraging UAVs for disaster management. IEEE Pervasive Comput. **16**(1), 24–32 (2017)
15. Nigam, N., Bieniawski, S., Kroo, I., Vian, J.: Control of multiple UAVs for persistent surveillance: algorithm and flight test results. IEEE Trans. Control Syst. Technol. **20**(5), 1236–1251 (2011)

LISA - Lingua Italiana dei Segni Accessibile: A Progressive Web App to Support Communication Between Deaf People and Public Administrations

Celeste Zhilla[1,2], Giulio Galesi[1], and Barbara Leporini[1(✉)]

[1] ISTI-CNR, Pisa, Italy
{giulio.galesi,barbara.leporini}@isti.cnr.it
[2] University of Pisa, Pisa, Italy

Abstract. Most deaf people use Sign Language (SL) to communicate. This usually requires the presence of an SL interpreter to mediate and decode the communication with a non-deaf person. However, the presence of an SL interpreter to support a deaf person can be very difficult, expensive and not always possible, for example during the COVID-19 pandemic which requires limiting contact between people in presence. This work proposes a Progressive Web Application (PWA), called LISA, as a solution to facilitate communication between a deaf citizen and a non-deaf person, thanks to a remote Sign Language Interpreting Service (SLIS). The LISA prototype is designed to promote the communication of deaf citizens with the Public Administrations (PA). This real-time SLIS can be used flexibly on different types of devices (i.e. mobile and desk). This allows PA operators to easily respond to the needs of deaf citizens. Furthermore, to facilitate written communication and to overcome the difficulties encountered by deaf people in writing text messages, the LISA system integrates a text/SL gateway. The user selects items from a gallery of GIF images that represent simple pre-set phrases and words in SL, and the system can also convert them into text. This improves accessibility by offering a more suitable messaging tool than a text chat for the needs of the target population.

Keywords: Deaf people · Sign language · Communication tools

1 Introduction

According to World Health Organization (WHO), approximately 466 million people worldwide suffer from disabling hearing loss and approximately 95% deaf/deaf children are born to hearing impaired parents. WHO estimates that 900 million people will suffer from hearing loss in 2050[1]. According to the Italian Association for Deafness Research (AIRS), in Italy about seven million people suffer from hearing disorders, more

---

[1] https://www.who.int/news-room/fact-sheets/detail/deafness-and-hearing-loss.

© ICST Institute for Computer Sciences, Social Informatics and Telecommunications Engineering 2021
Published by Springer Nature Switzerland AG 2021. All Rights Reserved
I. M. Pires et al. (Eds.): GOODTECHS 2021, LNICST 401, pp. 153–162, 2021.
https://doi.org/10.1007/978-3-030-91421-9_12

or less severe. Most of them use the visual-gestural communication channel, through the Italian Sign Language (LIS), to communicate. The LIS, like any other Sign Language (SL) in general, is a visual language that uses hand shapes, facial expressions, gestures and body language, consisting of a structured and organized set of signs, with grammar, syntax, and its own morphology. It is important to note that deaf people who use SL to communicate, rarely wear advanced cochlear implants. As a result, they often encounter serious difficulties in interacting with the auditory world. Furthermore, a survey conducted by the Gallaudet Research Institute (GRI) showed that most deaf people also have an additional disability; among these the most common are intellectual or learning disabilities, visual impairments and cerebral palsy [1]. As a result of the presence of coexistent or comorbid disorders, the effects of a disability can be aggravated, creating specific and unique needs for the individual who has a further disability in addition to deafness. Communication is one of the most affected areas by the interaction of these needs [2].

In this context, simple daily activities can be difficult for people with severe hearing problems due to the considerable communication effort required. A deaf person or a person with severe hearing loss can face hard challenges in daily communication. For example, they may not be able to hear announcements in public spaces such as train stations, bus stops, airports; attending an interview to get a job may be very difficult; entertainment resources such as public theatres and movies may not be very valuable, not all restaurants, banks, hospitals, shopping malls provide teletypewriters, interpreters or visual warning systems [3]. Hence, simple daily life interactions, such as an administrative or medical interview, may become significantly difficult for a deaf person who is constrained to rely on the use of SL to communicate. This is especially true for deaf people who primarily use SL to communicate. In this case, an SL interpreter is usually needed to support communication between a hearing person and a deaf person. SL interpreters are professionally qualified to translate between national language and SL. Interpreters are booked for professional meetings, interviews, training and conferences. The cost of an interpreter varies depending on the interpreter, the agency and the place where the service is requested. A minimum number of hours and travel expenses must be covered.

In recent years, the need for the Public Administration (PA) to be accessible and inclusive has become more and more a priority. Therefore, having tools and services that can be used to enable deaf citizens to communicate easily is becoming increasingly crucial [4]. For deaf people who only use SL to communicate, an SL interpreter should always be present to support communication with a hearing person. However, having an SL interpreter available in presence at any time is a challenge for a deaf person, for both logistical and cost-effective reasons [5].

For the PA, a live SL interpreting service available at any time would be very useful and inclusive for deaf citizens. However, the presence of an SL interpreter in the PA offices cannot always be guaranteed. As a result, they can only offer limited access to their services since an SL interpreter is missing, unless the deaf citizen is accompanied by a personal interpreter. Furthermore, due to the restrictions on the Covid-19 pandemic, a limited number of persons is allowed in presence in a room. This could lead to additional difficulties for people with severe hearing problems. In this context, new technologies and network communication infrastructures can play an essential role in improving communication between deaf and hearing people.

In this work, we propose a communication tool to support deaf people and people with severe hearing problems in daily activities and in communication services. In particular, we present the LISA (Lingua Italiana dei Segni Accessibile - Accessible Italian Sign Language) prototype, which has been specially designed to be used in a PA context. This tool allows communication between a deaf citizen and a PA operator by establishing a remote SLIS. Thanks to this tool, a remote communication is arranged between three people: the deaf citizen, the PA operator and the SL interpreter. Indeed, the deaf citizen and the operator can meet at the PA office while the SL interpreter can reach them via the Internet, being connected remotely. Usually, a deaf person requires to be accompanied by an SL interpreter to interact and communicate with a PA operator. LISA aims to overcome this aspect, offering a remote SLIS to facilitate the deaf citizen's interaction with the PA office, guaranteeing real-time interpretation in compliance with Covid-19 restrictions.

2   Related Work

Interaction in a verbal world is a challenge the deaf person faces every day in a predominantly hearing society that often limits their personal contacts and activities. Investigations into ICT solutions for communication between deaf and hearing people are on the rise to explore possible assistive tools [6]. The video communication system E-LISIR (Evolution of the Italian Language Signs with Interpreter on the Net[2]) offers a video call connection service to a video center where SL interpreters can translate in real time from the LIS to the spoken language and vice versa. E-LISIR is a free service that can be activated via an application on a set of preconfigured tablets (located in Rome, at the university and in the main hospital). The number and location of available tablets represent the main limitations of this application. In fact, only deaf users who live in Rome and visit predefined locations can access and benefit from this application.

CGS - Global Communication for the Deaf[3] (Comunicazione Globale per Sordi) is very similar to the E-LISIR app: it offers limited service to deaf people living in Rome. Unlike the E-LISIR app, the user can install the CGS app on their mobile device. However, the CGS app has some critical issues: the user is out of control since there is no navigation menu and some usability problems have been detected by users.

Another video interpreter service with a remote interpreter is Veasyt Live![4]. This tool offers interpreting service in twenty-five vocal languages including LIS. The interpreter can be contacted via (1) the "Immediate Service", an interpreter is available in a few minutes; (2) by booking for the next few days. This service can be used via web and mobile apps.

To facilitate communication between hearing and deaf people, there is considerable research in the development of wearable tools and automatic translation systems from

---

[2] https://www.leggo.it/societa/sanita/app_e_lisir_sordita_ospedale_bambino_gesu_roma-172 3677.html.

[3] https://cgs.veasyt.com/.

[4] https://live.veasyt.com/.

verbal language to SL [6]. However, these systems often operate in a very narrow domain (for example, systems designed to assist in the completion of a transaction between a post office (PO) employee and a deaf customer) [7] or wearable technologies often mean that the deaf person should wear numerous or very conspicuous devices (e.g., gloves with sensors, helmet having a camera with infrared filters) [8, 9]. This could potentially pose a stigma to the hearing impaired person.

Our prototype aims to be a tool that can be used freely in any place, accessible from any platform regardless of the operating system of the different devices available to the deaf user, without the need for advanced digital skills. Also, PAs usually don't use mobile devices to work. Therefore, a cross-platform application can bring benefits to different contexts and users.

3 Use Scenarios

To show the possible use of the LISA application, some scenarios describing possible real situations are reported in the following.

Scenario 1. Alan is a deaf user who goes to a municipal office to ask some questions. Alan does not use any smartphone or tablet. In this scenario, the municipal employee will have to start the video connection with a remote interpreter. The following steps are required: (1) Log in to the LISA application on the PA staff's device using their credentials (defined in a previous account registration). (2) Request an SL interpreter via the app. (3) As soon as the interpreter is available, the audiovisual connection will take place.

Scenario 2. Betty is a deaf user who goes to a municipal office to ask a few questions. She brings her smartphone with (possibly) the pre-installed LISA app. In this scenario, the municipal employee will have to perform the following operations: (1) Provide (if necessary) the user with an information leaflet with instructions to access the application from their device. (2) Wait for the user to initiate the video connection with a remote SL interpreter. Betty, on the other hand, must: (1) log into the app from their smartphone using the credentials created during the account registration; (2) request the availability of an SL interpreter through the application. As soon as an interpreter is available, the audio-video call will take place. Alternatively, Betty could have booked an SL interpreter for this appointment (i.e. for a specific day and time).

Scenario 3. Charly is a deaf person who goes to the PA offices bringing his tablet with him. Some days before going to the appointment, Charly books an interpreting service for the specific day at the specific time using the LISA tool. The day before going to the office, he wants to ask the booked interpreter a few simple questions in advance. So, the deaf user has already registered an account in the app and has already booked an interpreter for his appointment. Now, Charly wants to contact the booked interpreter via short messages, but, unfortunately, he is not familiar with the written text. So, Charly would like to communicate via SL. Thanks to LISA, he can use the chat service based on simple SL words. Therefore, he can: (1) log into the application; (2) open the appointment section showing the booking with the interpreter; (3) write a message to the interpreter using GIFs that represent words or phrases in SL (see next section for more details).

4   LISA Prototype

LISA is a multiplatform application designed to be used on both a mobile and desktop operating system. The prototype was developed as a Progressive Web App (PWA) in order to have a single application that can be installed on both mobile and desktop platforms while maintaining a single version. This type of solution can be very useful and relevant for PA offices that usually do not use mobile devices, while the citizen or the SL interpreter use their mobile device. This feature makes LISA different from the tools we previously analysed in our study.

The LISA PWA prototype can be used both from the user's mobile device and from the work device of PA operators. The main functions offered to the deaf user can be summarized as: (1) booking an appointment with an SL interpreter; (2) writing short SL messages to an interpreter; and (3) make a video call with a previously booked SL interpreter or available upon request. A PA operator can (1) call an interpreter when a deaf person arrives at the office without any assistance.

4.1   The Prototype Design

The progressive structure allows you to combine the experience and skills to which users are accustomed to on native web apps, leveraging the strengths of both: the user can install the LISA PWA on the home screen of the device and access the app without using the browser, providing a full-screen interface. The LISA PWA is, therefore, able to function independently of an operating system, browser or device type and automatically adapts to the graphical user interface (GUI) of the device.

A basic style of flat web design was used in designing the GUI: a minimalist template with simple elements, typography and flat colors.

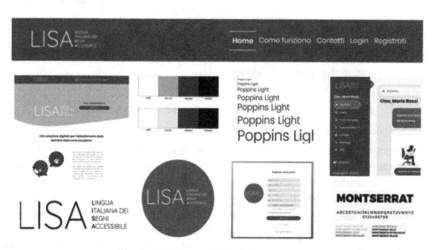

Fig. 1. LISA material design components

The layout of LISA is well structured to encourage users to focus only on the content and their goals, avoiding elements of distraction. As shown in Fig. 1, particular attention was paid to the choices of colors, fonts and navigation systems in order to inspire users with confidence, promote readability and complete understanding of the information while remaining visually appealing and accessible [10].

4.2 Booking an Appointment

The LISA PWA allows the deaf citizen to make a remote video connection with an SL interpreter, who translates in real-time SL into verbal language and vice versa, i.e. the conversation between the deaf user and the PA employee. To this end, different roles are defined in the LISA tool.

The LISA prototype offers a multi-role environment: the user can select the appropriate role when accessing the app: "user", "interpreter" and "operator".

After logging in, the user is redirected to their Dashboard which provides an overview of the available sections/actions. As shown in Fig. 2, these sections (accessible via shortcuts) allow the user to interact with the system and perform operations.

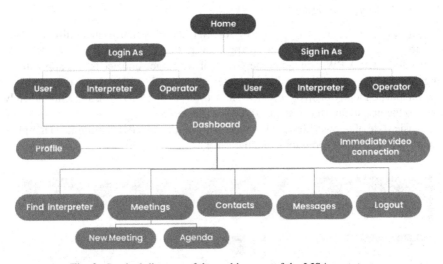

Fig. 2. Logical diagram of the architecture of the LISA prototype

For example, in the "Find an Interpreter" section, the user can get an overview of the interpreters registered in the system. As a result, the user can select the desired SL interpreter, for example an expert in a particular field or topic. For this reason, a filter by areas has been provided which, based on the scope of the selected appointment, retrieves interpreters with the corresponding area of expertise. Areas of expertise include legal, medical, educational, cultural, economics, tourist, technological. Once an interpreter has been selected, the user can read their profile, write a message or book an appointment with that interpreter. In summary, the deaf citizen (user) can book an appointment with the selected and available SL interpreter in order to receive an SL translation for a particular topic (legal, economic, educational, health, cultural, tourism, technology), on a certain day, at a given time via a videoconference meeting.

4.3 Chat Functions

In addition to the booking function, LISA provides users with a chat tool (Fig. 3) to communicate in real time with the interpreter. An innovative feature of this tool is that it allows the deaf user to communicate, in addition to the written mode, using GIFs that represent words and phrases in LIS [11]. This format was chosen because it has the ability to reproduce the visual-gestural characteristics of SL in an infinite and silent loop [12].

The development of this chat tool takes into account the difficulties related to the production of writing by deaf users (with or without additional pathologies). In light of the fact that further methods may be needed that seek to reduce, moderate and compensate for temporary or permanent difficulties of people with severe communication disorders, both on the expressive and receptive front, the use of the Augmentative Alternative Communication (AAC) methodology can overcome communication problems and related barriers and help these users in their social needs in life [13].

In particular, for deaf people, a functional technique of AAC Representational Systems is the Picture Exchange Communication System (PECS), which is a communication strategy based on the exchange of PECS images to compose a sentence [14]. PECS is used to remedy the discrepancy in communication methods of people with deafness and one or more intellectual disabilities (mild or moderate) who communicate through SL and those who do not use it [15]. In this way, the studies, proposing illustrated dictionaries to facilitate the writing of messages intended for their communication partners, have shown that, with adequate preparation for the rules of use, the subjects have been able to successfully use these tools and have had the role of facilitating writing [16].

In this perspective, we propose the use of a way of communicating with short and silent moving images, the Graphics Interchange Format (GIF) [17] to facilitate written communication via chat, according to the representational assisted AAC methodology. The prototype (better described in [11]), as mentioned, has a set of GIFs representing sentences and words expressed in SL that can be selected and sent to the recipient by the user. This set, although limited, is a representative example of the proposed methodology for chat communication of deaf and non-deaf people. Further studies are needed to extend the basic idea to the various existing sign languages (and will take into account the interface localization so that the gif gallery is shown in the selected language) and to overcome the limitations described above as well.

4.4 Operator and Interpreter Functions

The operator and interpreter interfaces have been implemented in a user-like way:

- the operator can use the same functions available for the user role. During the registration phase, however, the user is asked to indicate the affiliation, in addition to personal data. The PA operator can search for an "available interpreter" for an immediate call. This is necessary when a deaf citizen comes to the office at any time without assistance.
- The interpreter cannot search for and book other interpreters. An interpreter can set its immediate or future availability (to be booked for an appointment). The "immediate

Fig. 3. Main components of LISA chat tool

mode" allows to receive video calls without an appointment. An interpreter can also manage their own appointments (accept, decline, and simply get information).

5 LISA Architecture

The structure of the LISA PWA has the same three tiers of a web application, with the addition of two elements: The Manifest and the Service worker (Fig. 4).

Fig. 4. LISA Architecture showing the interconnections between the five tiers

1. Presentation tier: it is the user interface of the web application; the technologies used are HTML5, CSS3, JavaScript and its jQuery library; and Bootstrap, which contains design patterns based on HTML, CSS, and JavaScript, used for the various components of the interface.
2. Logic tier: this is the application processing component. The main technology used is the PHP programming language.
3. Data tier: it allows you to manage and shape the information content of the app; the technologies used, contained in the WAMP multiplatform, are MYSQL database and Apache.

To make LISA tool a progressive web app (PWA), the Manifest and the Service Worker components are required:

- The Manifest is a JSON file that describes to the browser the application structure and elements, and the tasks to carry out when the app will be installed on the home screen of a mobile device. So, the manifest includes information such as the name of the app, the icons to use to install it, and the main address to start it.
- The Service Worker is a JavaScript file performed by the browser in the background, which performs background synchronization and network request management operations via the cache.

6 First Evaluation

The design of the prototype was based on requests and suggestions provided by a group of people from the local Deaf Association. The same group evaluated the first app prototype. The evaluation tests focused on the functions developed (registration, interpreter booking for an appointment, video call). In particular, the people involved have appreciated the new AAC-based system proposed for short messaging (chat), as it takes into account the needs of those who have difficulty with written texts and therefore prefer to communicate with SL. So, even though the chat system offers simple words and phrases, the idea was assessed positively. As for the functions of the prototype, users stated that a completely remote connection for the three people would be very interesting.

7 Conclusions and Future Work

In this work, we present a possible application that supports communication between the deaf citizen who uses SL to communicate and the hearing person who uses natural language. The proposed solution aims to promote communication and inclusion of the deaf person in everyday life scenarios, through: 1) a remote SLIS (videoconference) both instant and on demand (booking), and 2) written communication through an assisted chat system accessible and usable by the community of people who use SL.

Starting from previous research on possible ICT solutions for overcoming the communication barriers existing between deaf and hearing people, this work aims at providing a further step forward in the field by proposing the LISA tool.

The LISA tool was developed as a Progressive Web App (PWA), to offer a multi-device service that facilitates communication between PA and deaf citizens. However, although the context considered in this work is related to PAs, the proposed application can be adapted to many other contexts where communication between deaf signers and hearing people is needed. The PA has been selected as a potential scenario because the local Association for the Deaf suggested this use of context. However, the application can also be used to enhance private and personal contexts.

The GIF-based chat messaging service was really appreciated by the users involved in the evaluation. We have proposed an AAC-based system for writing very short messages accessible to deaf people who have problems with written texts and rely mainly on sign language communication.

Future work will include further development of the gateway-based chat system for automatic translation between chats from written text to GIF in LIS and vice versa, to make written communication between a deaf person and an auditory interlocutor more effective and satisfying. This can be implemented for simple text but could be interesting for more complex communications. Another possible improvement could affect the booking functionality: the deaf user could book an appointment with both the PA operator and the SL interpreter, and possibly carry out the videoconference completely remotely, as suggested by some users during the evaluation.

References

1. Gallaudet Research Institute: Regional and national summary report of data from the 2007–08 annual survey of deaf and HoH children and youth. Gallaudet University, Washington, D.C. (2008)
2. Davis, T.N., Barnard-Brak, L., Dacus, S., Pond, A.: Aided AAC systems among individuals with hearing loss and disabilities. J. Dev. Phys. Disabil. **22**, 241–256 (2010)
3. Dhanjal, A.S., Singh, W.: Tools and techniques of assistive technology for hearing impaired people. In: International Conference on Machine Learning, Big Data, Cloud and Parallel Computing (COMITCon), Faridabad, India, pp. 205–210 (2019)
4. Cuevas Valenzuela, H.: Governing the deaf: the educational apparatus. Rev. Ciencia Polit. **33**, 693–713 (2013)
5. Kirkpatrick, K.: Technology for the deaf. Commun. ACM **61**(12), 16–18 (2018)
6. Tilano, L., et al.: Tools facilitating communication for the deaf. Educ. Educad. **17**, 468–480 (2014)
7. Cox, S., et al.: TESSA, a system to aid communication with deaf people. In: Annual ACM Conference on Assistive Technologies, Proceedings, pp. 205–212 (2002)
8. Gollner, U., Bieling, T., Joost, G.: Mobile lorm glove: introducing a communication device for deaf-blind people (2012)
9. Caporusso, N., Biasi, L., Cinquepalmi, G., Trotta, G.F., Brunetti, A., Bevilacqua, V.: A wearable device supporting multiple touch- and gesture-based languages for the deaf-blind. In: Ahram, T., Falcão, C. (eds.) AHFE 2017. AISC, vol. 608, pp. 32–41. Springer, Cham (2018). https://doi.org/10.1007/978-3-319-60639-2_4
10. Krug, S.: Don't Make Me Think! A common Sense Approach to Web Usability, II edn. New Riders, Berkeley (2006)
11. Zhilla, C., Galesi, G., Leporini, B.: Sign language GIFs exchange communication system: a PECS-based computer-mediated communication tool for the deaf. In: Ardito, C., et al. (eds.) INTERACT 2021. LNCS, vol. 12936, pp. 490–494. Springer, Cham (2021). https://doi.org/10.1007/978-3-030-85607-6_64
12. Eppink, J., Portwood-Stacer, L., Nooney, L.: A brief history of the GIF (so far). J. Vis. Cult. **13**(3), 298–306 (2014)
13. Koul, R.K., Lloyd, L.L.: Survey of professional preparation in augmentative and alternative communication (AAC) in speech-language pathology and special education programs1. Am. J. Speech Lang. Pathol. **3**(3), 13–22 (1994)
14. Malandraki, G.A., Okalidou, A.: The application of PECS in a deaf child with autism: a case study. Focus Autism Other Dev. Disabil. **22**(1), 23–32 (2007)
15. Bondy, A.S., Frost, L.A.: The picture exchange communication system. Semin. Speech Lang. **19**, 373–389 (1998)
16. Allgood, M., Kathryn, H., Easterbrooks, S., Fredrick, L.: Use of picture dictionaries to promote functional communication in students with deafness and intellectual disabilities. Commun. Disord. Q. **31**, 56–64 (2009)
17. Erdem, E.: Graphics interchange format (GIFs) as micro movies. Master's thesis, İhsan Doğramacı Bilkent University, Department of Communication and Design, Ankara (2015)

Building Emotionally Stable, Inclusive, and Healthy Communities with ICT: From State of the Art to PSsmile App

Margherita Bortoluzzi[1], Teresa Maria Sgaramella[1(✉)], Lea Ferrari[1], Vida Drąsutė[2], and Vaiva Šarauskytė[2]

[1] University of Padova, Padova, Italy
teresamaria.sgaramella@unipd.it
[2] Kaunas University of Technology, Kaunas, Lithuania

Abstract. There is an increasing interest in Social and Emotional learning (SEL) of youth across the world as testified by many international organizations and institutions. Research clearly shows that higher SEL is linked to successful participation in school life, better health, positive youth development. The COVID-19 pandemic has brought the essential role of SEL into focus and has drawn attention to the need to take a more holistic approach to contrast unexpected and challenging situations. To pursue these goals, it is mandatory that adults acquire and apply knowledge, skills, and attitudes enhancing Social and Emotional competences. To enhance their contribution to social goods, ICTs applications should align with this perspectives' taking. After providing a picture of main currently available tools, the paper presents the Erasmus+ PSsmile project, aimed at developing Social and Emotional competencies and contribute to building emotionally stable, inclusive, and healthy communities. PSsmile is also the name of the mobile application described in the paper with its five weeks program. It is based on the most relevant outcome within SEL studies, and recent theoretical approaches. It is aimed at raising parents and teachers' awareness, promoting and strengthening their personal Social-Emotional competences making them more effective agents of positive growth for children and for their communities.

Keywords: Social and emotional learning · Adult education · PSsmile mobile app

1 Introduction

Social and Emotional Learning (SEL) is the process through which we learn to recognize and manage emotions, care about others, avoid negative behaviors and make good decisions, behave ethically and responsibly, develop positive relationships [1]. It

PSsmile project has been co-funded by the European Commission through the Erasmus+ Programme. This paper reflects the views only of the authors, and the Commission cannot be held responsible for any use which may be made of the information contained therein.

I. M. Pires et al. (Eds.): GOODTECHS 2021, LNICST 401, pp. 163–178, 2021.
https://doi.org/10.1007/978-3-030-91421-9_13

is considered as the learning that unites all areas of human life since its beginning: social, emotional, academic, cognitive, physical, etc. On the other hand, social emotional competence refers to the ability to use social and emotional skills and knowledge to be resourceful, adapt to, respect, and work well with others, and take personal and collective responsibility.

Within the most well-known model of SEL, these skills are organized as five interacting components: self-awareness (the ability to understand one's own emotions, personal goals and values); self-management (the ability to regulate affect and calming oneself down); social awareness (the ability to understand others and take the perspective of those with different backgrounds and cultures, and to act with empathy and compassion); relationship skills (the ability to communicate clearly, to negotiate and to seek help, when needed) and the ability to take responsible decisions [2, 3].

Addressing Social and Emotional competences has important reference to and implications for educational policy and practice. The term 'Social and Emotional Education' (SEE) refers, in fact, to the educational process by which an individual develops social and emotional competence for personal, social and academic growth and development through curricular, embedded, relational and contextual approaches [4].When we promote social and emotional skills, we build skills that can offset the effects of differences, promote participation of all in several contexts. The numerous benefits of SEL (e.g., increased chance of academic and workplace success, reduced emotional distress, reduced risk of behavioral problems, improvement of scholastic environments, etc.) are more and more recognized [5] and suggest that Social and Emotional Capacity Building contribute to Social Inclusion, to the process that develops along the domain of participation, connection and citizenship.

1.1 Threats and Challenges to Social and Emotional Competences

Although Social and Emotional Competences change over time (Campbell et al., 2016), their components do not evolve in insolation. The course of social-emotional development—whether healthy or unhealthy—depends on the quality of relationships that a child has the possibility to experience in different settings, including their families, schools, and communities, with each context playing an important role throughout childhood and adolescence [6].

The COVID-19 pandemic has brought the essential role of SEL into focus and has drawn attention to the need to take a more holistic approach to students' learning and development. SEL may have relevance in the contexts where even greater challenges have been faced in supporting students' distance learning.

The pressing need to bring SEL, mental health, and wellbeing to the fore in children's learning and development, stems from some consequences of the global pandemic. During school closures arising from the pandemic, support for learning through distance education did not reach all students. It may have impacted different groups of students in different ways, with those who are most marginalized experiencing the most adverse effects. Emerging evidence suggests that the pandemic may have exacerbated existing inequalities and created new inequalities. Students who are disadvantaged—including children from poor families, girls, children with disabilities, and those living in rural and disadvantaged regions—may have faced the biggest challenges both in terms of continuing their learning and of maintaining social and emotional contact [7].

1.2 Social and Emotional Learning in Action: Current Findings and Choices Promoting Change

Social-Emotional Learning (SEL) curricula are now booming, as more and more countries are including Social and Emotional Skills (SEC) in their national educational strategies [8] and international organizations, such as the Organization for Economic Co-operation and Development (OECD) and the World Economic Forum WEF), are promoting their dissemination [9, 10].

Social-emotional competence programs conducted in schools have shown to be effective in several directions [11, 12]:

- promotes positive, behavioral, and academic results that are important for healthy development
- predicts important results related to the future
- can be improved with feasible and cost-effective interventions
- plays a critical role in the behavior change process.

For instance, school-based programs effective in preventing school violence, including bullying, are intrinsically linked to youth's ability to manage emotions, regulate emotions, and to communicate and problem-solve challenges and interpersonal conflicts [13].

Schools can be seen as an ideal place to provide everyone learning activities designed to help them achieve their best leadership chances, happy, healthy, and independent lives, and reach their unique career potential [14]. Fostering SEL requires implementing practices and policies that help not only students but also adults acquire and apply knowledge, skills, and attitudes that enhance personal development, social relationships, ethical behaviours, and effective, productive work [15–17].

Moreover, participation of significant caregivers (e.g., parents, grandparents, stepparents, foster parents) in the educational process characterized quality of the learning experience from the learner perspective [18]. For a full participation of all to the educational process, the involvement of both the meso (family, school, or classroom) and micro (individual learner) levels should be then considered [19]. SEL development for teachers to support high-quality instruction is considered fundamental for the school of the future [13]: higher SEL competences benefit class management and students' school and personal development [20]. As concern parents, evidence exists that positive parenting roles and SEL practices support children's efforts in school and lead to academic achievement and social skills improvement [21, 22]. Moreover, an effective school-family partnership has been shown to be effective in supporting and improving children's learning. Additionally, benefits for children, teachers and families are achieved through positive changes in social skills and adaptive children's behaviors [23].

1.3 The Proposal

The European project PSsmile (Social-Emotional Capacity Building in Primary Education, http://smile.emundus.lt/) is the premise for the proposal presented in this work and the app development. Beginning in 2019, it involves teams from Bulgaria, Greece, Italy, Lithuania, and Portugal. This project has its pillars in the SE education as a capacity building process that involve all children, especially those from low-income, underrepresented backgrounds, and high-risk populations. The pandemic caught partners in a specific phase of the project development, that is when we were ready to start the development of the training programs both for educators and students. The school closing and the many challenges both students, teachers and families were experiencing required us to focus on understanding how our project could address some of them and be timely.

Based on the Positive Youth Development approach [24] the project develops along some key goals. A first aim is in developing a training program for primary school teachers; the second one is to develop a training program for children to promote their SE skills to make them more ready to think about their future and facilitate school transitions. A third aim, specifically relevant for this work, is to provide teachers and parents a tool aimed at fostering their SE skills, that is a specific app.

Following recent theoretical studies and challenges to everyone's wellbeing, promoting social-emotional competence in our view requires some methodological choices and actions:

- *Adopt a perspective where both emotional and social dimensions are considered.* It is mandatory to encourage and reinforce social skills such as greeting others, taking turns, cooperation and resolving conflicts, devoting a specific space to emotions and behaviors, knowledge and action level, awareness and management skills.
- *Adopt a future oriented perspective.* This choice is proposed because of the relevance of looking at present and future objectives and undertaking a positive approach, emphasizing the role of decision making in the domains and in all proposed activities.
- *Care for the significant adults, both teachers and parents.* Creating an environment where adult take care of their Social and Emotional Wellbeing and in which children feel safe to express their emotions with the contribution of teachers and family is essential for healthy social-emotional outcomes in young children because attitudes and beliefs of meaningful adults play a key role [25].
- *Promote SECs outside schools* Social-emotional exercises outside of school hours could be of great help in strengthening these competences with repeated exposure in real life contexts and with persons with whim they have a meaningful relationship.
- *Apply new technologies.* Information and Communication Technologies can support Social-Emotional Competencies (SECs) development by providing innovative tools (see, videogames and mobile apps) designed to teach self-management exercises [26] and delivering fast and easily accessible courses and materials (webinars, video training, synchronous/asynchronous lessons, online resources, and many other tools [27].

2 Previous Research

Although at an early stage, research addressing the relationship between SEL and technologies shows a new trend in the use of educational technologies (ed-tech), aimed at broadening their scope of action, providing greater support to teachers and innovating the school experience. Because it involves such a broad field of action, SEL curricula need new and specific tools, technology can be a useful ally in the design of these programs.

An image of the current state of the art was provided by Stern and colleagues who, after presenting a historical account of the reflections that accompanied the technological development and the emergence of the SEL studies, divided the technologies adopted for SEL into three categories: Established (webinar, Online libraries, Software supports, etc.) Emerging (Remote video coaching, podcast, digital teacher manuals, etc.) Future (SEL focused videogames, mobile apps, avatar, etc.) [28].

Morganti and colleagues further developed this tripartite division by focusing on the current field of application of these technologies [27]. They identified 4 possible applications for the SEL domains: teacher training by delivering fast and easily accessible courses; Support to the didactic implementation of SEL activities at school through didactic platforms that also allow to establish a connection between teachers; Involvement of parents who can support their children and their social and emotional learning and provide opportunities for meaningful family time [26]. Assessment of skills acquired by students by transferring some examples of protocols and guidelines on how to assess social-emotional skills from physical to digital format.

The World Economic Forum (WEF) report, in 2016, included cutting-edge technologies such as wearable devices, cutting-edge apps, virtual reality, advanced analytics and machine learning, affective processing as tools that could play an important role for SEL in the next future. Certainly, EdTech is an excellent resource for helping teachers and parents and students to meet social-emotional needs, as tools we can also use to support other methods used daily in school such as hands-on activities, outdoor learning and creative play. CASEL and Elias (2016), emphasizing the need to promote SEL learning by providing children with consistent and ongoing learning opportunities to practice their skills, go beyond the simple presentation of information to focus on repeated practice. The authors also report how essential it is to involve people inside and outside the school, who "walk together" towards achieving the same goals [15].

We will go through some of the most well-known tools available to describe the current state of the art, to highlight strengths and limits that motivate the choices underlying the PSsmile app. We will describe first the apps for children and, then those for adults.

Table 1 describes the main aspects of these tools that can be summarized as follows:

Dimensions Addressed: Not all apps consider both awareness and management (5/8).

Users' Characteristics: Often the age range is too broad or not classified in terms from age-to (4/8). Only 2 apps foresee a progression in the difficulty of the activities (2/8). None of the apps summarized identify or describe possible manipulations to make activities suitable for younger or older children.

Ecological Validity: A key aspect is the type of task used and their ecologic validity. An ecologically valid tool is one that has characteristics of "topographical similarity"

Table 1. Dimensions and key aspects addressed by the main apps created for primary school

Awareness	Management	Domains	Ecologic	Parents
EMOTIONS -AVOKIDDO (Age: 4+) https://play.google.com/store/apps/details?id=andy.emotions&hl=it&gl=US				
○ Put names to emotions and re-actions ○ Connecting the animals' emotions to their causes	○ Exploring cause and effect relationships ○ Empathy ○ Understanding & care for other creatures	emotional and social	Creative expression through pretend play	
POSITIVE PENGUINS (Age: 4+) https://apps.apple.com/us/app/positive-penguins/id570371342				
○ Help you understand that feelings arise from your thinking ○ Presents emotions to choose	○ Challenge negative thoughts successfully to see things in a more realistic and optimistic way ○ Relational problem-solving situations.	emotional and social	You can choose your penguin	Info for teachers and parents
THE MIDDLE SCHOOL CONFIDENTIAL SERIES BUNDLE (Age 8-14) https://apps.apple.com/us/app-bundle/middle-school-confidential-series/id917713588				
	○ Self-confidence ○ Communication problems ○ Conflict resolution ○ Out of control emotions ○ Friendship issues	social	Interactive quizzes that let readers choose how they would handle thes situations	
THE SOCIAL EXPRESS PROGRAM (Age 5-14) https://www.educationalappstore.com/app/the-social-express				
○ Self managment ○ Non-Verbal Communication ○ Relationship	○ Attentive Listening ○ Conflict Resolution ○ Conversations ○ Critical Thinking	emotional and social	Real life situations	Teachers tools
TOUCH AND LEARN - EMOTIONS (Age 4+) https://apps.apple.com/us/app/touch-and-learn-emotions/id451685022				
○ Read body language and understand emotions		emotional		Customize: introduce new emotion and hearing parent's voice
OK PLAY (Age 3-8) https://play.google.com/store/apps/details?id=com.okco.okplay&hl=it&gl=US				
○ Explore new worlds, experiences, and understanding emotion ○ Build persistence ○ Build new plan	○ Regulating emotion ○ Turn taking ○ Supporting other ○ Build empathy and kindness	emotional and social		Share the game with parents; Blog with articles

to the skills or behaviors required in the child's natural environment and has value in predicting daily function (Franzen & Wilhelm, 1996). Five out of 8 apps present real-life situations or use a fantasy world to represent everyday situations (e.g., animals are used to avoid gender definitions or language).

Parent's Involvement: 4 out of 8 apps have a "tips" section for parents or teachers; 3 of these 4 the involvement of parents is thought in terms of "playing with the children". None of the apps includes activities in which the parent works on their knowledge and skills. None of the apps consider the involvement of both parents and teachers to build shared knowledge.

Future Time Perspective: only one app includes activities about future, and in terms of building new plans.

We then addressed tools developed for adults' education and learning (Table 2). In this case, again, some main aspects emerge:

Dimensions Addressed: Most apps consider both self-awareness and self-management (7/9) and only 2 (out of 9 apps) consider social dimension, in terms of strategy to manage conflict or strengthen a relationship;

Users' Characteristics: only *Smiling mind* provides the opportunity to share similar activities with other adults;

Ecological Validity: 6 out of 9 apps present real-life situations or use a chatbot that simulate a conversation;

Future Time Perspective: only 2 apps include activities about future, in terms of planning actions.

In more general terms, apps that support SEL align with the skills outlined by CASEL. However, most of these apps do not cover the full range of SEL categories (self-awareness, social awareness, self-management, relationship skills, responsible decision making) and leave parents out. Offering them the possibility to become more competent in SEL skills with a tool that join them to teachers is a way to engage them and realize the school to home collaboration. Since their value is recognized, their self-perceptions and parenting skills are fostered.

3   The PSsmile App: Its Development and Use

PSsmile Mobile App has been developed as an intellectual output from the Erasmus+ project "Social-emotional Capacity Building in Primary Education". It can be seen as an opportunity to apply the most relevant outcome within SEL studies, portraying a viable solution for those problems that have been often indicated in SEL curricula. Its main aim is to raise adults' awareness of SEL's importance and develop the target social-emotional skills, to contribute to building emotionally stable, inclusive, and healthy

Table 2. Dimensions and key aspects addressed by the main apps created for adults

Awareness	Management	Domains	Ecologic	Parents
SMILING MIND https://play.google.com/store/apps/details?id=com.smilingmind.app&hl=it&gl=US				
◦ Meditation and mindfulness exercises	◦ Dealing with the pressure, stress, and challenges of daily life	emotional	Characters mirror humans	
MITRA track what matters most https://play.google.com/store/apps/details?id=com.mitrapp.mitra&hl=es_GT				
◦ Learn how emotions impact your ability to live ◦ Build awareness of values and emotions ◦ Stay true to your personal values	◦ Reflect on and record what contributed to your day's value alignment and emotion rating, view the "Analytics" screen to see your improvement over time	emotional	Chatbot	
PARADYM: emotional wellbeing https://www.appannie.com/en/apps/ios/app/paradym-love-yourself/				
◦ Identify emotional patterns ◦ Mind-body connection ◦ Confidence, value and identity ◦ Stress	◦ Guidance to help you break negative patterns ◦ Relationship ◦ Team player or solo player	emotional and social	Chatbot	
WYSA: anxiety, depression & sleep therapy chatbot https://apps.apple.com/us/app/wysa-sleep-depression-support/id1166585565				
◦ Build confidence, reduce self-doubt and improve your self-esteem	◦ Keep track of mood ◦ Mindfulness exercises for effective anxiety relief, depression and stress management ◦ Manage anger, worry and tiredness ◦ Manage conflict at work, school, in relationships	emotional and social	Diary	
DAYLIO: Diary, Journal, Mood Tracker https://play.google.com/store/apps/details?id=net.daylio&hl=en_US&gl=US				
◦ Private journal with your mood and activity of the day	◦ Monitoring data ◦ Track and improve your mood	emotional	Empathetic Artificial Intelligence (chat)	

(continued)

Table 2. (*continued*)

YOUPER AI therapy for anxiety & depression
https://play.google.com/store/apps/details?id=br.com.youper&hl=it&gl=US

◦ Understand yourself	◦ Track and improve your mood	emotion-al

SUPERBETTER
https://play.google.com/store/apps/details?id=com.superbetter.paid&hl=it&gl=US

	◦ Build resilience, achieve goals, tackle challenges (anxiety, depression, stress, chronic pain...) ◦ Adopt a new habit, learn or improve a skill, strengthen a relationship, make a physical or athletic breakthrough, complete a project, or pursue a lifelong dream ◦ Overcome a life challenge	social	Bringing the same mindset and psychological strengths naturally displayed when playing games	Project and lifelong dream

MOOD METER
https://play.google.com/store/apps/details?id=com.reliablecoders.moodmeter

◦ Identify emotions throughout the day, supports when shifting to a different emotion ◦ Expand emotional vocabulary, discover emotional nuances	◦ Discover what causes you to feel the way you do and see patterns over time ◦ Learn effective strategies to help you regulate your feelings and enhance the way you manage your life each day	emotion-al

communities where significant adults, namely parents and teachers, take care of their own social-emotional functioning and support its development in children.

We will describe and provide details on the app including the general idea, the explanation of the programme, some screenshots and a first activity. Then we will address how this programme was implemented from IT side, how to use the app for the user and what information will be collected.

3.1 Basic Choices

The app includes a great deal of daily exercises, a thorough and accurate explanation of the theoretical background on which SEL is based, infographics showing the progress made by the users, and a questionnaire for feedbacks, providing relevant data for research and the opportunity to improve the app, making it more suitable for the users. This division has been adopted to escort the learners through the entire course, building their social-emotional skills in an incremental way, one that adapts itself to the needs of the trainee.

The app has been designed to deliver adult training, both for parents and teachers, who have their own dedicated sections and activities, since they play different and specific roles in children's social-emotional development. Additionally, PSsmile app is unique because it can also be used by parents and teachers simultaneously. The app was in fact realized specifically for having these two groups no longer neglected as active agents of change and supporting for a positive development [29].

3.2 The Five-Week Program and Its Content

In essence, *PSsmile Mobile App* is an innovative social and emotional learning guide structured to be a five-week-long programme (Fig. 1).

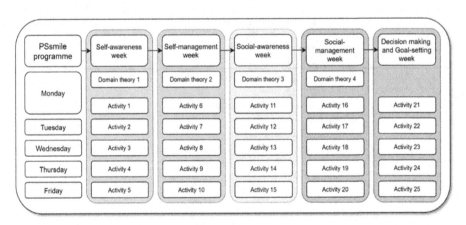

Fig. 1. PSsmile programme structure

The first four weeks are dedicated to getting acquainted with all the SEL domains, Self-awareness, Self-management, Social-awareness, Social-management, respectively.

The fifth week is dedicated to learning to take responsible decisions and thinking about the future.

3.3 Structure of the PSsmile App

The first thing a new user sees after logging in is a page containing the rules of the five-week *PSsmile Mobile App* and here user can get acquainted with the SEL domains by reading more about them (Fig. 2).

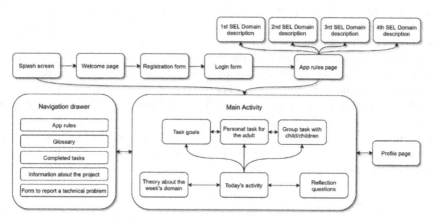

Fig. 2. Individual components of the program

After agreeing to the programme rules, the users finally see the Main activity. Main Activity has a bottom navigation bar connecting it to Theory and *Reflection Questions* sections, as well as a *Profile* page button at the top right corner (Fig. 3).

Fig. 3. App navigation drawer and registration page

If they did not download the app on a Monday, a notification on this screen will invite the users to come back on Monday or start learning about SEL in the Theory section. The best practice for the users is always to read more about the week's domain in the Theory section on Monday, before doing the first task of the week.

Each day of the week, form Monday to Friday, this page displays a unique SEL activity, related to the week's domain. The daily activity section is divided into three tabs – the first one contains the name, instructions, and goals of the daily task, usually paired with a visual; the second one contains a detailed description of the task that the adult must do alone; and the third one contains a detailed description of the task the adult must complete with a child or children.

To score points, the user must click completion confirming buttons in second and third tabs and answer all the three reflection questions.

For the users' convenience, the *Main Activity* also contains a navigation drawer in the top left corner. Here the user finds the rules of the five-week programme, a glossary with more complex definitions presented in the content, a section to review already completed tasks, a section to read more about the *PSsmile* project, as well as a form to report a technical problem.

The application was implemented using Android Studio.

When users open the application, they are always greeted with a Splash screen – a colorful loading screen containing the project logo. If it is their first time using *PSsmile* application, they will be directed to a Welcome page, which invites them to use this innovative social-emotional learning tool.

The first thing the users must do is register or log in if they already have an account from earlier (Fig. 4). For this aim they must provide some basic information, such as their name or nickname, if they are a teacher or a parent, email, and chosen password.

After registration the users receive an email confirmation letter. The users must open it and validate their email before logging in. After this process is completed, the users can log in using their email and password. Although, it is important to note, that the registration using email and password feature will only be active during the research data collecting period.

3.4   Using the Program

Preferably, the user should start using the *PSsmile Mobile App* at the beginning of the week. Every Monday morning the user should read the theory to learn more about the week's domain. In addition, each working day the user should read the first part of the daily task in the morning. After that, during the day, at any convenient time the adult should mindfully do the personal task, and only after that experience the task with a child or children. It is evident that adult should first learn more about SEL skills and test them on themselves before practice with children.

Weekends are meant for resting or if one wishes – reading more about SEL, repeating some of the activities.

3.5   A Closer Look to the Activities: The First Activity in PSsmile App

When the users start to use the *PSsmile Mobile App*, they will first encounter a description of the first domain – Self-management – and then the first activity, titled the Tree of emotions (Fig. 4). With this task the users start their social and emotional learning journey with improving how to better express emotions verbally.

3.6   Data Collection and Participant Profile

For each user the following basic information (name or nickname, gender and age group), were collected:

- Status (parent or teacher)

Fig. 4. Screenshots from day 1

- Activities completed
- Domain and Final score
- Answers to *Reflection Questions* the participant answers after each activity
- Answers to the App Evaluation Questionnaire.

The reflection questions represent an important section for users to self-monitoring their learning across the five domains. They could increase their awareness on domains where they experienced more difficulties or reached higher goals, where they gained more benefits in everyday life. This section also provides useful information on the activities that have an impact on the users, which ones were disregarded. For the same reason, the tool includes the App Evaluation Questionnaire with the following questions:

1. *The programme I participated in was unique, positively different from other experiences I have had.*
2. *Information was presented in a clear way.*
3. *Interacting with the app was simple.*
4. *The navigation structure was easy to use.*
5. *Application interface was visually appealing.*
6. *Do you have any suggestions to the creators?*

Respondents are required to provide an answer using a Likert scale ranging from 1 (Strongly disagree) to 5 (Strongly agree). This questionnaire will be used only during the piloting with the aim of knowing details on the performance and improving the application.

4   Conclusions

Thanks to the basic choices underlying the application, the attention in choosing significant activities as well as feedback from preliminary data collected, we expect the use of *PSsmile Mobile App* will help moving "towards building emotionally resilient individuals who are able to navigate the complex landscape of conflicting goals and dissonance, to one of prosocial behavior that promotes human flourishing and the attainment of the Sustainable Development Goals" (UN Sustainable Development Goals). More specifically, since the COVID-19 pandemic has highlighted the important role that schools, and contexts will play in supporting a whole children's development, it will be useful in ensuring that all members of the community- and children in the first line- receive the support that they require, first from the closer significant adults in their life, that is from teachers and parents.

As Iyengar recently argued, "education is the path to a sustainable recovery from COVID-19" [30]. We hope that a systemic approach can go further to not only support children currently and during future school disruptions, but also all individuals as educators, parents and responsible adults that take care of their personal and community members wellbeing.

References

1. Donoso, M., Collins, A.G., Koechlin, E.: Foundations of human reasoning in the prefrontal cortex. Science **344**(6191), 1481–1486 (2014)
2. Collaborative for Academic, Social, and Emotional Learning: Effective social and emotional learning program. CASEL Guide (2012)
3. Durlak, J.A.: Handbook of Social and Emotional Learning: Research and Practice. Guilford Publications, USA (2015)
4. Cefai, C., Cavioni, V.: From neurasthenia to eudaimonia: teachers' well-being and resilience. In: Cefai, C., Cavioni, V. (eds.) Social and Emotional Education in Primary School, pp. 133–148. Springer, New York (2014). https://doi.org/10.1007/978-1-4614-8752-4_8
5. Fischer, S.N.: Teacher perceptions of the social emotional learning standards (2017)
6. Cefai, C., Cooper, P.: Emotional education: connecting with students' thoughts and emotions (2009)
7. Mascheroni, G., et al.: La didattica a distanza durante l'emergenza COVID-19: l'esperienza italiana (No. inorer1191) (2021)
8. Cefai, C., Bartolo, P.A., Cavioni, V., Downes, P.: Strengthening social and emotional education as a core curricular area across the EU: A review of the international evidence. Analytical report. Publications Office of the European Union, Luxembourg (2018)
9. Organisation for Economic Co-operation and Development: Skills for social progress: The power of social and emotional skills. OECD Publishing (2015)
10. World Economic Forum. New vision for education: Fostering social and emotional learning through technology. World Economic Forum, Geneva, March 2016
11. Domitrovich, C.E., Durlak, J.A., Staley, K.C., Weissberg, R.P.: Social-emotional competence: an essential factor for promoting positive adjustment and reducing risk in school children. Child Dev. **88**(2), 408–416 (2017)
12. Pomerance, L., Greenberg, J., Walsh, K.: Learning about learning: what every new teacher needs to know. National Council on Teacher Quality, Washington, D.C. (2016)
13. Dusenbury, L., Zadrazil, J., Mart, A., Weissberg, R.: State learning standards to advance social and emotional learning. CASEL, Chicago (2011)
14. Patton, W., McMahon, M.: The systems theory framework of career development: 20 years of contribution to theory and practice. Aust. J. Career Dev. **24**(3), 141–147 (2015)
15. Elias, M.J., Leverett, L., Duffell, J.C., Humphrey, N., Stepney, C., Ferrito, J.: Integrating SEL with related prevention and youth development approaches (2015)
16. Weissberg, R.P., O'Brien, M.U.: What works in school-based social and emotional learning programs for positive youth development. Ann. Am. Acad. Pol. Soc. Sci. **591**(1), 86–97 (2004)

17. Zins, J.E., Elias, M.J., Greenberg, M.T.: School practices to build social-emotional competence as the foundation of academic and life success. Educ. People Emot. Intell. 79–94 (2007)
18. Ainscow, M.: Diversity and equity: a global education challenge. N. Z. J. Educ. Stud. **51**(2), 143–155 (2016)
19. Ramberg, J., Watkins, A.: Exploring inclusive education across Europe: some insights from the European Agency Statistics on Inclusive Education. In: FIRE: Forum for International Research in Education, vol. 6, no. 1, January 2020
20. Jennings, P.A., Doyle, S., Oh, Y., Rasheed, D., Frank, J.L., Brown, J.L.: Long-term impacts of the CARE program on teachers' self-reported social and emotional competence and well-being. J. Sch. Psychol. **76**, 186–202 (2019)
21. Sheridan, S.M., Witte, A.L., Holmes, S.R., Wu, C., Bhatia, S.A., Angell, S.R.: The efficacy of conjoint behavioral consultation in the home setting: outcomes and mechanisms in rural communities. J. Sch. Psychol. **62**, 81–101 (2017)
22. Smith, T.E., Reinke, W.M., Herman, K.C., Huang, F.: Understanding family–school engagement across and within elementary-and middle-school contexts. School Psychol. **34**(4), 363 (2019)
23. Sheridan, S.M., Smith, T.E., Moorman Kim, E., Beretvas, S.N., Park, S.: A meta-analysis of family-school interventions and children's social-emotional functioning: moderators and components of efficacy. Rev. Educ. Res. **89**(2), 296–332 (2019)
24. Lerner, R.M., et al.: Positive youth development: processes, programs, and problematics. J. Youth Dev. **6**(3), 38–62 (2011)
25. Oluremi, F.D.: Attitude of teachers to students with special needs in mainstreamed public secondary schools in southwestern nigeria: the need for a change. Eur. Sci. J. **11**(10) (2015)
26. Gillespie, C.:10 apps to help kids control their emotions. Mashable (2018)
27. Morganti, A., Pascoletti, S., Signorelli, A.: Per un'educazione inclusiva: la sfida innovativa delle tecnologie per l'educazione socio-emotiva. Form@ re **16**(3) (2016)
28. Stern, R.S., Harding, T.B., Holzer, A.A., Elbertson, N.A.: Current and potential uses of technology to enhance SEL: what's now and what's next. Handb. Soc. Emot. Learn.: Res. Pract. 516–531 (2015)
29. Sgaramella, T.M., Ferrari, L., Drąsutė, V.: 2020 Social and emotional education: a review of applied research studies and curricula and proposal for an integrative approach. Appl. Psychol. Around World **77**, 77 (2020)
30. Iyengar, R.: Education as the path to a sustainable recovery from COVID-19. Prospects **49**(1–2), 77–80 (2020). https://doi.org/10.1007/s11125-020-09488-9

Links to the Apps:

31. EMOTIONS -AVOKIDDO. https://play.google.com/store/apps/details?id=andy.emotions&hl=it&gl=US
32. POSITIVE PENGUINS. https://apps.apple.com/us/app/positive-penguins/id570371342
33. THE MIDDLE SCHOOL CONFIDENTIAL SERIES BUNDLE. https://apps.apple.com/us/app-bundle/middle-school-confidential-series/id917713588
34. THE SOCIAL EXPRESS PROGRAM. https://www.educationalappstore.com/app/the-social-express
35. TOUCH AND LEARN – EMOTIONS. https://apps.apple.com/us/app/touch-and-learn-emotions/id451685022
36. OK PLAY. https://play.google.com/store/apps/details?id=com.okco.okplay&hl=it&gl=US
37. SMILING MIND. https://play.google.com/store/apps/details?id=com.smilingmind.app&hl=it&gl=US

38. MITRA track what matters most. https://play.google.com/store/apps/details?id=com.mitrapp.mitra&hl=es_GT

39. PARADYM: emotional wellbeing. https://www.appannie.com/en/apps/ios/app/paradym-love-yourself/

40. WYSA: anxiety, depression & sleep therapy chatbot. https://apps.apple.com/us/app/wysa-sleep-depression-support/id1166585565

41. DAYLIO: Diary, Journal, Mood Tracker. https://play.google.com/store/apps/details?id=net.daylio&hl=en_US&gl=US

42. YOUPER AI therapy for anxiety & depression. https://play.google.com/store/apps/details?id=br.com.youper&hl=it&gl=US

43. SUPERBETTER. https://play.google.com/store/apps/details?id=com.superbetter.paid&hl=it&gl=US

44. MOOD METER. https://play.google.com/store/apps/details?id=com.reliablecoders.moodmeter

Management Technology for Institutional Environment in Pandemic Times

Maria Eduarda Aragão[1]([✉]), Maria Alice Lopes[1], Gustavo Neves Miranda[1],
José Morgado[1], Francisco Miguel Morgado[2], and Ivan Miguel Pires[1,3,4]

[1] Computer Science Department, Polytechnic Institute of Viseu, 3504-510 Viseu, Portugal
`{estgv18545,estg18491,estgv19191}@alunos.estgv.ipv.pt`,
`fmorgado@estgv.ipv.pt`
[2] Computer Science Department, Universidade de Aveiro, 3810-193 Aveiro, Portugal
`fmpfmorgado@ua.pt`
[3] Instituto de Telecomunicações, Universidade da Beira Interior, 6200-001 Covilhã, Portugal
`impires@it.ubi.pt`
[4] UICISA:E Research Centre, School of Health, Polytechnic Institute
of Viseu, 3504-510 Viseu, Portugal

Abstract. Regarding the current social state and the benefits of social distancing, this paper intends to use technology, namely mobile and web applications, to control the flow of people in institutional spaces, namely the management of students at Polytechnic Institute of Viseu. The idea is to use QR codes distributed in spaces (classrooms, libraries) so that it is possible to carry out monitoring in real-time. When a professor or student attends a specific room, information about the number of people in that location will be updated in the app. Thus, it will be possible to count the number of students present in each space and carry out the automatic registration of students' attendance per class, removing the professor's concern about registering them. The application will also be able to effectively control the sanitation of each space since alerts will be issued at the end of each class to the administrator of the web application. As for the web part, the responsible institution will be able to make the schedules of the different shifts available to students via the website to enroll in these shifts and access information regarding the number of people who intend to attend a specific class. In this way, it will possibly be better to manage academic sites in terms of social distance.

Keywords: Management · Academic environment · Social distancing

1 Introduction

A technological project is being held at the Polytechnic Institute of Viseu [35] to contribute to the current social situation in Portugal [8], with the help of professors, aimed at the development of a mobile and web application that results in an optimized administration of classes and internal spaces inside an academic institution [14].

In this way, the system works to facilitate access to the acquisition of information by the student regarding the number of people present in a specific room during a class

I. M. Pires et al. (Eds.): GOODTECHS 2021, LNICST 401, pp. 179–193, 2021.
https://doi.org/10.1007/978-3-030-91421-9_14

and giving the professor the possibility of getting feedback from the students about their courses as well, where they will be able to evaluate 1 to 5 stars [22]. A QR code is a two-dimensional symbol invented in 1994 by Denso [12]. One of the primary group companies, i.e., Toyota counts the number of people [27]. QR codes can support higher data density and can be used free of charge, making them a perfect choice for the project [20].

The study's primary purpose is to allow a student to perform the scan available physically at the university classroom door. In this way, their entry will be counted in the database, making this information available to the administrator, professor, and other students, all related to the class.

Likewise, at the end of the class, the student will scan the QR code from inside the room. The professor will have the option to end the lesson, receiving a list of attendance with the names and numbers of each student present. The university manager will administer the web, where he will have options to insert students and professors, remove them, manage disinfection alerts for places after classes and keep track of general data.

The development of this management tool arose, intending to return to the universities' classroom classes, it is possible to manage the number of students in specific classrooms during certain courses [6]. Thus, it facilitates the teacher's registration of presences and gives information on the number of students present in a room.

2 Background

As we know it today, the Internet was started as a military project between the 1960s and 1970s to share information between the bases in a safe way [1]. In this sense, Velloso [32] brings the definition of the Internet that nowadays is employed as the most prominent electronic communication network, operating in all parts of the world in millions of computers.

Over time, the Internet underwent significant changes until it reached its commercial use in the mid-1990s [33]. The same, which was previously private to the United States of America citizens, was disseminated in other countries, similarly entering society to electricity at the end of the 19th century [28].

We live in the so-called "information age", where we are updated concerning the latest events worldwide and almost instantaneously, thanks to the Internet, which enables socialization and communication between people from different places of the world [10, 30].

Then, it is perceived that the Internet is increasingly present in a globalized context [18]. Its presence is even more on the agenda in the current social and economic scenario that we find during the period of isolation, the result of the pandemic caused by the virus SARS-CoV-2 discovered in 2019 in China, Wuhan, causing instant lockdown by the authorities and thousands of deaths [7, 31].

The discovery of this new type of virus has brought a turnaround in the way we organize ourselves. Different areas, such as education and business institutions, have had to, more than ever, resort to the Internet, migrating all their activities to online platforms [21].

Regarding the transition of schools and universities, they had to abruptly organize themselves to find a way to migrate their entire teaching and learning system to be condensed into classes held using electronic devices [23]. Online learning is nothing but the use of the Internet applied to educational purposes [29].

In this way, students at all levels of education were also affected by the rapid change in teaching standards known as "remote learning" [16]. As a result, they will not complete their school curriculum and assessment in the usual way, and, in many cases, they have been torn away from their social group almost overnight [9].

Indeed, the transition from conventional teaching methods to online methods has pros and cons [11]. On the one hand, it causes the lack of contact between instructor and student that, for some students, can be crucial due to lack of attention and concentration in classes [11]. Because it depends entirely on electronic devices and the Internet, online learning can jeopardize both teachers and students who have a bad Internet connection or out-of-date devices [34]. On the other hand, online classes promote studies in environments more conducive to student comfort, which can be seen as a disadvantage or advantage [15]. In addition, it is providing a safer environment because we do not have to physically move to attend classes, reducing the risk of contamination of the virus [17].

Also, as expected, not all universities and schools could, both financially and technologically, migrate their education and learning systems to online platforms [24]. In this way, many students worldwide, more specifically in underdeveloped countries, while was directly impacted by lockdown and rapid lifestyle change, have been jeopardized for months without access to classes, whether face-to-face or online [13]. Consequently, they will graduate after an extended period, in addition to future challenges in the labor market, as Sahu states that the graduates are going to face the severe recession of the global recession caused by the COVID-19 crisis [4].

It is, in fact, an overwhelming situation, because on the one hand, online learning is currently saving us during this pandemic period [5]. On the other hand, however, there are still universities and educational institutions that need face-to-face access to education due to the financial conditions of the institution and students [3].

3 Materials and Methods

3.1 Requirement Analysis

Requirement analysis is an essential aspect of project management, as it aims to document the steps that the software will perform. It consists of recognizing and evaluating the problem, deconstructing it into smaller parts, modeling data, and consolidating functions and interfaces.

When applied to software development, this step can predict the behavior of the system, including any unexpected problems, as it also makes it easier to add new features to a project already under development, meaning less investment and human resources.

It is noteworthy that the requirements are fundamental for modeling, design, implementation, testing, and maintainability, as they are separated into two main aspects: functional and non-functional requirements.

3.2 Functional Requirements

According to Ruth Malan, functional requirements describe what the system does or does not do by defining services and tasks. That is, all the needs, features, and functionalities are expected in a process that the software can meet. Functional requirements, in short, refers to what the system must do, and as they cannot be measured, they are specific actions or behaviors of the system [19].

Regarding the mobile app, it will be developed so that professors and students can access it. This way, it will be divided into two parts: the students and the professors. For the functional requirements of the mobile app, Table 1 describes the most relevant ones.

Table 1. Functional requirements (student perspective app)

#	Description for the app - student	Priority
1	It should be possible for the user to request a reset of their password, informing the e-mail address	HIGH
2	The system must provide a list of upcoming classes for the user	HIGH
3	The system only accepts users belonging to the email list registered by the administrator	HIGH
4	The user should see information about the class such as professor, date, time, place, other students' class rate, subject, and description	HIGH
5	The user should have access to exercises related to a specific class	HIGH
6	The system should allow the student to rate a professor's class from 1 to 5 stars	HIGH
7	The system must allow edit user data, such as name, email, and photo	MEDIUM
8	The system should display information about the number of classes taken, graphics about performance, etc	MEDIUM
9	The system must allow the user to access other user profiles	LOW

Regarding the user from the perspective of the professor, Table 2 demonstrates the most important of them.

The web application will be aimed at the university administrator to add files regarding the classes, students, professors, and classrooms. When it comes to its functional requirements, those can be found in Table 3.

3.3 Mobile App

The mobile application development is being carried out in the modern Dart programming language, developed by Google. According to [18], Dart is a general-purpose programming language designed with ease of use, familiarity to most programmers, and scalability in mind. Along with this powerful language, the Flutter framework is also being used, which allows the rapid and scalable development of mobile and web applications. Minetto explains a framework as a 'basis' from which one can develop

Table 2. Functional requirements (professor app perspective)

#	Description for the app - professor	Priority
1	It should be possible for the user to request a reset of their password, informing the e-mail address	HIGH
2	The system only accepts users belonging to the email list registered by the administrator	HIGH
3	The system must provide a list of upcoming classes for the user	HIGH
4	The user should be able to add and edit the description of the class	HIGH
5	The system must allow the user to attach exercise files to classes	HIGH
6	The system must allow the user to initiate and end classes	HIGH
7	The system must allow the user to export files containing information about the class attendance list	HIGH
8	The user should be able to publish announcements in the community area	MEDIUM

Table 3. Functional requirements of web application

#	Description for the web – university administrator	Priority
1	The system should allow registering of new users, performing the validation via a confirmation email	HIGH
2	It should be possible for the user to request a reset of their password, informing the e-mail address	HIGH
3	The user must be able to add new places that belong to the university	HIGH
4	The user must be able to add new users and classes	HIGH
5	The system must alert the administrator if a classroom is highly busy with an urgent disinfection alert	MEDIUM
6	The system must show statistics about the university (number of app users, number of internal places, etc.)	MEDIUM
7	The system must allow edit user data, such as name, email, and photo	LOW

something more significant or more specific. It collects source codes, classes, functions, techniques, and methodologies that facilitate the new software development [17].

One of the advantages of using a framework is automating tasks through internal operations that prevent unnecessary code repetition. Therefore, the Flutter framework was chosen because it is a robust, time-saving framework with multiple features that can build and maintain quality mobile applications. Figures 1, 2, 3 and 4 show the prototype developed so far regarding the student part of the application.

Fig. 1. The initial screen of the app with login buttons for the professor and student

Fig. 2. Student login screen

Fig. 3. Home page with upcoming classes and notifications

Fig. 4. Information about a class

3.4 Web Application

Regarding web pages that are available to the administrator, the front-end is being implemented using the HTML markup language, created in 1991, and the CSS style sheets, the latter being optimized using the Bootstrap framework. The language is limited and has only the function of pointing out what information should appear in the browser [4]. When talking about HTML, it is also necessary to quote a language for styles and definitions of the layout of HTML documents. In this context, there are cascading style sheets (CSS). Cascading style sheets change the way pages are organized. The user can set in a single location the formatting used by each tag [22]. CSS is a formatting mechanism, such as color insertion, fonts, spacings, among other needs, all for better interaction with the user.

Since there is a need for data storage, it is necessary to use a Database Manager System that is defined as a general-purpose software system that facilitates defining, building, manipulating, and sharing databases between multiple users and applications [28]. In other words, they are software that provides the user with the ability to guarantee and manage the integrity of the data and create and store them. For the creation of the application design, the Adobe XD the program, designated for prototyping and design, was used. Figures 5, 6 and 7 present the prototypes developed in Adobe XD for the web application.

Fig. 5. Login screen for the administrator

3.5 Survey Questionnaire

A survey was applied as a questionnaire to validate the problems found in the hypotheses raised during the project. Thus, two surveys were developed to conduct the research, which, as explained in [26], collects data from a series of pre-elaborated questions. In total, 27 professors and 52 students from the Polytechnic Institute of Viseu were interviewed. Some were having and teaching online and in-person classes when this survey was developed and tested, while others were only having online courses, as the results show.

Fig. 6. Dashboard

Fig. 7. Add new spaces to a university page

These surveys were developed for two future users of the mobile application: students and professors. The questions were designed to understand better how people are dealing with online learning and teaching and if they would find it acceptable to return to in-person classes if better management of the number of people took place. The results are described in Figs. 8, 9, 10, 11, 12 and 13.

As shown in Fig. 8, most teachers are still taking classes online, with a percentage of 88.9% in the "yes" answer. Next, as shown in Fig. 9, most teachers want to know the opinion of the students about the classes. Thus, one of the features designed to be implemented in the project's mobile application is the possibility of rating a professor's class out of 5 stars. Finally, as shown in Fig. 10, the professor likes the idea of automation in obtaining the attendance list.

Next, the questionnaires applied to the different students were analyzed, verifying that 69.2% of respondents develop more excellent content retention when participating physically and personally in the teaching process. In comparison, only 17.3% of students prefer the online methodology, as shown in Fig. 11. Furthermore, as presented in Fig. 12, 65.4% of students would like the possibility to evaluate a teacher's class. Finally, Fig. 13 shows that 61.2% of the students interviewed responded positively to whether they would

Are you currently teaching online ?

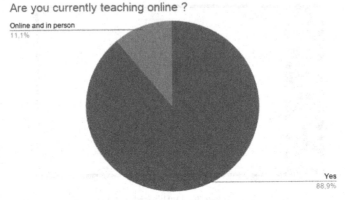

Fig. 8. Answers to the question "Are you currently teaching online?"

Would you like to know what your students have to say about your classes?

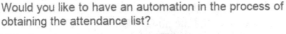
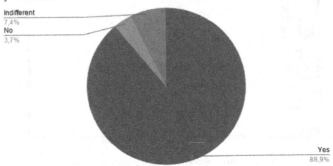

Fig. 9. Answers to the question "Would you like to know what your students have to say about your classes?"

Would you like to have an automation in the process of obtaining the attendance list?

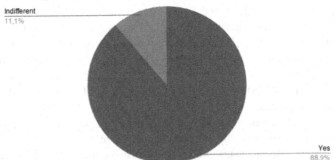

Fig. 10. Answers to the question "Would you like to have automation in the process of obtaining the attendance list?"

feel safer and more comfortable if there were better management of the number of people within a classroom.

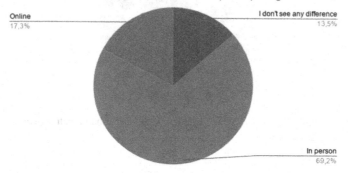

Fig. 11. Answers to the question "Which teaching methodology do you have the easiest learning, attention, and knowledge retention when participating in?"

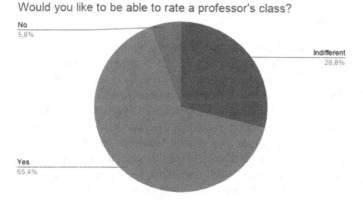

Fig. 12. Answers to the question "Would you like to be able to rate a professor's class?"

Through this short survey, it was found that the data presented in the charts both students and teachers are willing to test new technologies regarding the best student-professor relationship in the educational field, and mainly some relevant points were noted for the construction of the solution.

Initially, the survey of the functional and non-functional requirements of the system was distributed. According to [25], non-functional requirements, unlike functional ones, do not express any function performed by the software but rather behaviors and restrictions that this software must satisfy. Thus, it is a software engineering step in which development paradigms are constructed from the functionalities that the system must perform.

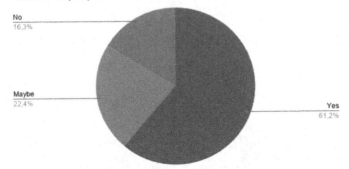

Fig. 13. Answers to the question "Would you feel safer if you had a better management of the number of people in a classroom?"

Among the functional requirements, the following stand out: evaluation of teachers, feedback of classes by students, registration of places in the institution by the administrator, among others.

3.6 Use Case Diagram

In system analysis, a use case diagram helps the team understand how a user might interact with the system that is being engineered. Ivar Jacobson designed this diagram in 1986. It consists of a methodology that can also be used outside software engineering with a few adjustments and helps identify all system requirements [2].

There are four main components in a Use Case Diagram: actors (1): the users who interact with the system. The actor can be an external person, organization, or system that interacts with your application or system. However, they must be external objects that produce or consume data. (2) System: a specific sequence of actions and interactions between the actors and the system. The system can also be called a scenario. (3) Goals: the result of most use cases. A correctly created diagram should describe the activities and variants used to achieve the goal. (4) Use case: horizontal oval shape and representing the different uses that a user can have. (5) Associations: a line between actors and use cases. In complex diagrams, it is essential to know which actors are associated with which use cases.

In Fig. 14, there is a simple use case diagram to illustrate the system overview.

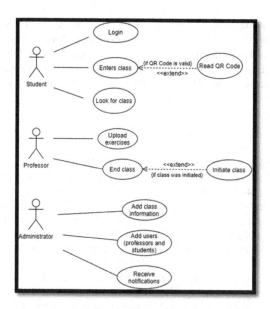

Fig. 14. Use case diagram for overall system

4 Discussion and Conclusions

It is undeniable how fast every aspect of living changed after the world breakout in 2020, including teaching methods. Yet, until this day, every time a school or university tries to open doors, it immediately shuts down after a few days, commonly because of the virus outbreak.

Given this issue, there is a need to manage university institutions and the use of technological applications to do so, thus ensuring the security conditions to minimize the contagious caused by SARS-CoV-2 in these environments. Therefore, we aim to make it possible, enabling the use of digital presences and functionalities that allow the student to give feedback on the classes attended, increasing the proximity between professors and students.

After the data, we could gather it by carrying out the survey. We could state that both professors and students are open-minded about the application we intend to develop. For example, informing the users of the number of people present in a room will be beneficial to the administrators to create a greater sense of space and disposition of students in a classroom. In addition to giving the professor automation in obtaining the attendance list of a particular student in their class to improve his didactics based on the feedback that his students will provide on the platform, to improve their teaching techniques.

Acknowledgements. This work is funded by FCT/MEC through national funds and co-funded by FEDER – PT2020 partnership agreement under the project **UIDB/50008/2020** (*Este trabalho é financiado pela FCT/MEC através de fundos nacionais e cofinanciado pelo FEDER, no âmbito do Acordo de Parceria PT2020 no âmbito do projeto UIDB/50008/2020*). This work is also funded by National Funds through the FCT - Foundation for Science and Technology, I.P., within the scope of the project **UIDB/00742/2020**. This article is based upon work from COST Action IC1303–AAPELE–Architectures, Algorithms and Protocols for Enhanced Living Environments and COST Action CA16226–SHELD-ON–Indoor living space improvement: Smart Habitat for the Elderly, supported by COST (European Cooperation in Science and Technology). More information in www.cost.eu. Furthermore, we would like to thank the Politécnico de Viseu for their support.

References

1. Abbate, J.: Inventing the Internet. MIT Press, Cambridge (2000)
2. Aleryani, A.Y.: Comparative study between data flow diagram and use case diagram. Int. J. Sci. Res. Publ. **6**, 124–126 (2016)
3. Ali, W.: Online and remote learning in higher education institutes: a necessity in light of COVID-19 pandemic. High. Educ. Stud. **10**, 16–25 (2020)
4. Aristovnik, A., Keržič, D., Ravšelj, D., Tomaževič, N., Umek, L.: Impacts of the COVID-19 pandemic on life of higher education students: a global perspective. Sustainability **12**, 8438 (2020)
5. Bozkurt A, et al.: A global outlook to the interruption of education due to COVID-19 pandemic: navigating in a time of uncertainty and crisis (2020)
6. Carroll, A.B.: Responsible management education: the role of CSR evolution and traditions. SAGE Handb. Responsible Manag. Learn. Educ. 73 (2020)
7. Cheval, S., Mihai Adamescu, C., Georgiadis, T., Herrnegger, M., Piticar, A., Legates, D.R.: Observed and potential impacts of the COVID-19 pandemic on the environment. Int. J. Environ. Res. Public Health **17**, 4140 (2020)
8. Correia, P.M.A.R., de Mendes, I.O., Pereira, S.P.M., Subtil, I.: The Combat against COVID-19 in Portugal: how state measures and data availability reinforce some organizational values and contribute to the sustainability of the national health system. Sustainability **12**, 7513 (2020). https://doi.org/10.3390/su12187513
9. Daniel, S.J.: Education and the COVID-19 pandemic. Prospects **49**(1–2), 91–96 (2020). https://doi.org/10.1007/s11125-020-09464-3
10. Davidson, C.N., Goldberg, D.T.: The Future of Learning Institutions in a Digital Age. The MIT Press, Cambridge (2009)
11. Dhawan, S.: Online learning: a panacea in the time of COVID-19 crisis. J. Educ. Technol. Syst. **49**, 5–22 (2020)
12. Din, M.M., Fazal Fazla, A.: Integration of web-based and mobile application with QR code implementation for the library management system. J. Phys. Conf. Ser. **1860**, 012018 (2021). https://doi.org/10.1088/1742-6596/1860/1/012018
13. Dubey, S., et al.: Psychosocial impact of COVID-19. Diabetes Metab. Syndr. Clin. Res. Rev. **14**, 779–788 (2020)
14. Engzell, P., Frey, A., Verhagen, M.D.: Learning loss due to school closures during the COVID-19 pandemic. Proc. Natl. Acad. Sci. **118**, e2022376118 (2021). https://doi.org/10.1073/pnas.2022376118
15. Fatonia, N.A., et al.: University students online learning system during Covid-19 pandemic: advantages, constraints, and solutions. Syst. Rev. Pharm. **11**, 570–576 (2020)
16. Garbe, A., Ogurlu, U., Logan, N., Cook, P.: COVID-19 and remote learning: experiences of parents with children during the pandemic. Am. J. Qual. Res. **4**, 45–65 (2020)
17. Jones, E., et al.: Healthy schools: risk reduction strategies for reopening schools. Harv TH Chan Sch Public Health Healthy Build Program (2020)
18. Lin, H.-F.: Understanding behavioral intention to participate in virtual communities. Cyberpsychol. Behav. **9**, 540–547 (2006)

19. Malan, R., Bredemeyer, D.: Functional requirements and use cases. Bredemeyer Consult (2001)
20. Mohamed, S.: Initiating mobile phone technology using QR Codes to access library services at the University of Cape Town. Inf. Dev. **30**, 148–158 (2014)
21. Platje, J., Harvey, J., Rayman-Bacchus, L.: COVID-19–reflections on the surprise of both an expected and unexpected event. Cent. Eur. Rev. Econ. Manag. **4**, 149–162 (2020)
22. Relkin, E., de Ruiter, L.E., Bers, M.U.: Learning to code and the acquisition of computational thinking by young children. Comput. Educ. **169**, 104222 (2021). https://doi.org/10.1016/j.compedu.2021.104222
23. Riter, L.: Entrepreneurial Educators: a narrative study examining professional transition experiences of educators who have experimented with the launching of an educational activity. Northeastern University (2020)
24. Rizvi, Y.S., Nabi, A.: Transformation of learning from real to virtual: an exploratory-descriptive analysis of issues and challenges. J. Res. Innov. Teach. Learn. (2021)
25. Sampaio, D.: Ninguém morre sozinho: o adolescente e o suicídio. 3rd edn. Caminho, Lisboa (1991)
26. Soares, G.L.C.: Práticas pedagógicas e percepção dos professores alfabetizadores sobre o processo de alfabetização (2020)
27. Soon, T.J.: QR code. Synth. J. **2008**, 59–78 (2008)
28. Stankiewicz, A.E.M.A., Amburgy, P.M., Bolin, P.E.: Questioning the Past: Contexts, Functions, and Stakeholders in 19th-Century Art Education. Routledge (2004)
29. Suryaman, M., et al.: COVID-19 pandemic and home online learning system: does it affect the quality of pharmacy school learning? Syst. Rev. Pharm. **11**, 524–530 (2020)
30. Sussman, G.: Communication, Technology, and Politics in the Information Age. Sage (1997)
31. Tabish, S.A.: COVID-19 pandemic: Emerging perspectives and future trends. J. Public Health Res. **9** (2020)
32. Velloso, F.: Informática: Conceitos Básicos. Elsevier, Brazil (2014)
33. Xiang, Z., Wang, D., O'Leary, J.T., Fesenmaier, D.R.: Adapting to the internet: trends in travelers' use of the web for trip planning. J. Travel Res. **54**, 511–527 (2015)
34. Yang, N.: eLearning for Quality Teaching in Higher Education. Springer, Heidelberg (2020). https://doi.org/10.1007/978-981-15-4401-9
35. Polytechnic Institute of Viseu: Instituto Politécnico de Viseu. https://www.ipv.pt/guide/. Accessed 12 May 2021

Technology and Ageing

Augmented Reality, Virtual Reality and Mixed Reality as Driver Tools for Promoting Cognitive Activity and Avoid Isolation in Ageing Population

Maria Victoria Gómez-Gómez[1]([✉]), María Victoria Bueno-Delgado[2],
Cristina Albaladejo-Pérez[2], and Volker Koch[1]

[1] Building Lifecycle Management, Karlsruhe Institute of Technology,
Englerstr. 7, 76131 Karlsruhe, Germany
{Maria.gomez,volker.koch}@kit.edu
[2] Department of Information and Communication Technologies, Universidad Politécnica de
Cartagena, Plaza del Hospital, Cuartel de Antigones, 30202 Cartagena, Spain
{mvictoria.bueno,cristina.albaladejo}@upct.es

Abstract. In this work, the Augmented Reality (AR), Virtual Reality (VR) and Mixed Reality (MR) technologies are presented as candidate tools for promoting cognitive and physical activity and for avoiding social isolation in ageing population. The work includes a desk-research, focused on the software/hardware solutions, innovations and challenges. An experimental study in ageing population has been conducted to get preliminary results about the benefits and drawbacks of these technologies for elderly. The positive feedback received open the door to extend the study with specific key performance indicators (KPIs) that can help to better measure the improvements of cognitive and physical activity through continuous training, and e.g. to study the benefits on ageing population with specific impairments or degenerative diseases like dementia, Parkinson or Alzheimer.

Keywords: Augmented reality · Virtual reality · Mixed reality · Ageing population

1 Introduction

The increasingly exponential growth of ageing population and the lack of resources to manage their needs has stimulated the creation of new frameworks and solutions, where the Information and Communication Technologies (ICT) have an important role in them. The pandemic of covid-19 has also served to reinforce the fact that the ICT can help to avoid isolation, permitting social interaction when the mobility of population is reduced or restrictions by lockdown are applied. But ICT are also promoted in ageing population for helping them in healthcare needs, e.g. to combat cognitive ageing. In this regard, immersive technologies like Augmented Reality (AR), Virtual Reality (VR) or Mixed

© ICST Institute for Computer Sciences, Social Informatics and Telecommunications Engineering 2021
Published by Springer Nature Switzerland AG 2021. All Rights Reserved
I. M. Pires et al. (Eds.): GOODTECHS 2021, LNICST 401, pp. 197–212, 2021.
https://doi.org/10.1007/978-3-030-91421-9_15

Reality (MR) offer older people the opportunity to be stimulated, and to live, in a virtual reality environment, simulating activities or physical exercises that they used to do or cannot do now due to illness or physical/mental impairments.

VR, MR and AR are immersive media technologies that provide new scenarios and applications to education, healthcare, business and society, enabling new ways of learning, interacting, communicating, enjoying and working. Although numerous applications have been or are being developed for the immersive media AR, MR and VR, uniform technical and legal standards and the methods for workflows to develop content and products are still missing for mass market maturity. Distribution channels through which larger user groups can use these media are just emerging as well. In short, AR, MR and VR are innovative technologies that are still in an early stage of development [1] (Fig. 1).

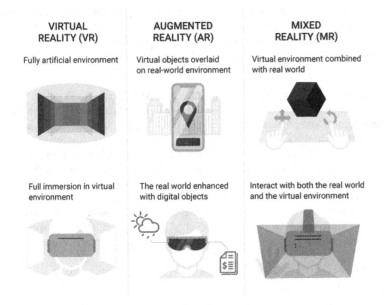

Fig. 1. Differentiation of VR, AR and MR [2]

One of the biggest differences between AR/MR and VR (at the current time) is that AR or MR is more of an individual experience, whereas in VR enables an easier communication and collaboration with other avatars, like in multiplayer video games. However, according to recent reports [3–5], AR will also soon move towards collaboration. Nevertheless, AR/MR and VR should not be seen as competing products, as both have individual potential uses with advantages and disadvantages.

In this work, the AR, VR and MR technologies are introduced in depth, identifying the state of art, research, innovations and challenges of these for ageing population. The research is focused on the software/hardware solutions existing that can be applied in an extended Ambient Assisted Living (AAL) where intelligent furniture and living habitat of the ageing population is expected. The research also includes an experimental study carried out with AR and VR, to show the benefits of using these technologies in ageing population.

This contribution is organized as follows: Sect. 1 introduces the work. Section 2 defines VR, AR and MR technologies, reviews the most popular devices and applications that are found in the state of art and market. Section 3 explores the development and application tools of AR, VR and MR that could be useful for ageing population. Section 4 explains the experimental study carried out to make a first assessment of the suitability of using AR and VR technologies for stimulation in elderly people. Finally, Sect. 5 presents the conclusions and future work.

2 AR, VR and MR: Definition, Devices and Development Tools

2.1 Virtual Reality

VR, from a technology-centered perspective, is a set of computer systems that create immersive and interactive environments through appropriate hardware such as stereo displays. VR is also defined as a methodology for giving users the experience of inclusion in an illusory reality. The goal is not necessarily to achieve a perfect VR in which virtuality and reality can no longer be distinguished. Peculiarities of human perception such as the "Suspension of Disbelief" can be used to create effective virtual environments for people and to give them the feeling of being present in VR. This can serve different purposes: research (e.g. human perception), education, entertainment, supporting communication, visualising simulation results or economic goals (e.g. prototyping to increase efficiency or save costs). The goal of VR is mainly focused on creating innovative interfaces between humans and computers [6].

VR experiences can have different levels of immersion, understood as the capacity of a system to generate an environment that emulates experience of presence in the real world. Depending on the degree of immersion, VR are classified as:

- **Non-immersive:** They show the virtual world through a combination of three-dimensional images on screen, sounds and a high degree of interaction with the simulated virtual world. The hardware used is low cost and easy to install. A clear example is the desktop personal computer and 3D video games. Although they are not immersive systems per se, they are capable of generating a high degree of attraction of the user's attention, producing strong emotional responses.
- **Semi-immersive:** These generally comprise a projection system that displays the virtual environment on the walls and floor of a room. They also have a system that tracks the user's head movements in order to adjust the simulation accordingly, and in most cases, they incorporate a handheld device to interact with the virtual world. This type of system has a multi-user capability, where several people can enjoy the virtual experience, which makes them very interesting in collaborative work environments. These systems require a large space for their installation and their cost is high.
- **Immersive:** They offer the highest degree of immersion, making the user's perception of the virtual world as close as possible to the human relationship with the real world, blurring the line between the physical world and the digital or simulated world. These systems are generally comprised of a helmet with a stereoscopic vision system that

allows the user to visually perceive the three-dimensional virtual world in a way that is identical to how the real world is perceived. The helmet also incorporates position and movement sensors that synchronise the user's position and perspective with the virtual world in real time, as well as headphones that reproduce a surround sound environment and various input devices, such as joysticks or gloves, that allow interaction with the virtual world. The cost of these systems varies from medium to high, depending on the system chosen and its peripherals.

The most popular devices that enable a VR experience are the VR goggles with headphones. They enable virtual or visual experiences. In virtual experiences, the user does not interact with the real world, and is immersed in a virtual environment with an avatar. The user can manage it with gestures, controllers or a special suit via motion tracking. In visual experiences, the user is immersed in the virtual environment only with visual role, e.g. when playing Minecraft or visiting a virtual world such as Second Life by means of a computer screen [7] (Figs. 2, 3, 4 and 5).

Fig. 2. VR traking [8]

Fig. 3. HTC vive tracker [9]   **Fig. 4.** Cybershoes [10]   **Fig. 5.** VR glasses [38]

2.2 Augmented Reality

AR is defined as a set of tools that offer a user experience in which the real world that the user perceives is enriched by additional information, usually generated by a computer. Then, AR can be understood as an integration of the virtual world into the real world. The real world can be augmented by one or several senses, which means that visual, sound, tactile and even olfactory AR experiences can be achieved, separately or a combination of them.

AR experiences with a visual component can be classified according to their levels of immersion, with the following degrees or levels:

- **Non-immersive:** These monitor the user's orientation by means of sensors and capture the real world through a camera, which in turn is shown to the user through a screen. It is in this interface where the integration of the real world with the virtual elements takes place, which are oriented according to the data received by the sensor system. Currently, most of mobile devices in the market (smartphones and tablets) are compatible with these developments, and are used as tools for capturing, processing and projecting the augmented experience. This is a low cost solution for enjoying the AR experience.
- **Immersive:** These are the same as in VR experiences, but with the use of a set of cameras that capture the real world and transfers it to the helmet's vision system. The experience reproduced has a strong immersion, by combining its stereoscopic vision system, together with the advanced sensor system and controls for interaction with the virtual elements.

The most popular devices for VR are the smart glasses such as Google Glass or slightly futuristic-looking glasses like Microsoft's HoloLens, which also make it possible to superimpose virtual elements in the real world [7].

AR can be enjoyed also through smartphones with camera and apps such as Aurasma [11], which superimposes content on the smartphone screen over the images that come from the camera; e.g. info about historical monuments placed in the street, or translating text captured by the camera in real time. One popular AR example is the smartphone game Pokémon GO, in which Pokémons are superimposed on the user's current surroundings [1] (Fig. 6).

Fig. 6. Aurasma [8]

2.3 Mixed Reality

MR belongs to the continuous spectrum of virtuality, integrating the virtual world with the real world but one step further, allowing the physical elements of the user's environment to be components of interaction with the virtual elements. This allows the creation and modification of virtual objects through data obtained from the real world and a better integration of the virtual elements in the real world, by being able to calculate how they are affected by the real physical environment in which they are incorporated, e.g. to adapt the shadows and reflections to the physical environment, to modify the lighting of the object depending on the luminosity of the scene, to limit their movements to the real environment, etc.

MR systems can be classified analogously to AR systems: non-immersive systems and immersive systems, as AR systems were taken as the basis for further research and development in MR technologies.

The term MR is often used synonymously with AR and associated with data glasses such as the HoloLens. Since both cases involve the expansion of the real-physical environment through the integration and overlapping of virtual objects, the terms MR and AR are used synonymously in this work.

MR is currently in a development phase and requires a boost in research at both software and hardware level, making it necessary to explore improvements in the algorithms for interpreting the real world and perfecting the capabilities of components and systems for immersive technologies.

3   AR and VR Tools for Stimulating and Motivating Ageing People

AR and VR can be used as a driver technology for avoiding isolation, stimulating and motivating ageing population, tools to support active ageing [12].

With AR, it is possible to superimpose a lot of information in text, graphics, video and audio into a real time environment. Elderly people can participate interactively with the environment, exploring and learning details of each significant area of the event site [13]. With AR is also easy to design interactive paper worksheets to be used in workshops for adults and ageing population. The work is done by uploading the triggers (objects such as pictures that are recognized by an AR app when users look at it through the camera). The AR app (e.g. Aurasma) enables to add overlays. When a user scans the worksheet with the AR app, tips, learning videos or additional tasks are plotted [14].

The AR interface can reduce cognitive load and provide correct spatial information, promoting the spatial visualisation ability of older adults [15]. Some AR gaming applications have also proven to be useful for early detection of dementia and cognitive training [16].

At present, we can find some interesting applications and services for creating interactive AR contents for different purposes. Thinking on elderly people, a set of tools are identified as suitable candidates for cognitive and physical stimulation. They are listed in Table 1.

On the other hand, VR allows users to interact with all manner of objects and systems, including those that are too small, too large, or perhaps too dangerous to experience in real life. With VR, elderly people can work in stimulating tasks, such as assemble, disassemble, manipulate and modify objects and environments in ways that have not been possible previously. VR can also help ageing population to expand their knowledge about complex concepts that cannot be explained otherwise.

VR enables to engage the senses, emotions and cognitive functions of the brain, harnessing the most powerful aspects of retention. Now, from manufacturing to customer service, organizations are jumping on the bandwagon, realizing that virtual visits in training can really affect their bottom line. VR, delivered through immersive headsets, offers the opportunity for interventions to improve physical, mental and psychosocial health outcomes in older adults [17].

Nowadays we can find applications that allow health professionals and caregivers to create their own content for VR glasses, focused on ageing population. One of the most popular is the tool provided by Google, which enables virtual field trips with its Google Cardboard and Google Expeditions apps. Others are also coming onto the market with higher-priced glasses such as the Oculus Rift or the HTC Vive [18].

A set of interesting applications have been identified that could be beneficial for stimulating elderly people, even although some of them were primarily designed for educational purposes. They are summarized in Table 1.

Table 1. List of suitable AR/VR tools and apps for being used for stimulating elderly people

AR tools/apps	VR tools/apps
Quivervision Education [19]	Boulevard [20]
Mirage [21]	Tilt Brush [22]
Sky Map [23]	Nature Treks VR [24]
Google Expedition AR [25]	Google Expedition [26], Google Earth VR [27], Google Arts & Culture [28]
FaceRig [29]	YouTube VR 2021 [30]
Aurasma [11]	Oculus Room [31]
Star Walk 2 [32]	Renderver [33]

4 Experimental Study of Immersive Experience of Ageing Population with AR/VR

There are numerous works that present different applications of AR and VR to improve the quality of life of older people, e.g., on how to improve spatial vision [15], medication management [34], early detection of dementia and cognitive training [16], fall prevention [35], etc. But only a few show results of using these technologies already implemented, freely available and easily accessible tools.

In this context, in this work an experimental study was carried out with elderly people to measure if immersive experiences using AR and VR could be beneficial to them. The candidates were 10 people over range of 73–80 years old, without mental/physical impairments or diseases, living alone or with a partner. Six of them are women and four are men.

This study was conducted during the month of April 2021 in Spain, so the global covid-19 pandemic situation prevented a larger number of participants, as the study candidates belong to the at-risk population. In addition, the restrictions and security measures resulting from the pandemic also influenced both the development and the number of participants. It should be noted that all necessary distancing and hygiene measures were complied with and the activities ran smoothly.

The candidates were invited to enjoy two different experiences: to use AR app using smartphones and to use VR glasses in which they watched 360 videos on topics of interest to them and to try out. The VR experience consisted of watching or visiting one of the following list of possibilities: (1) Machu Picchu, (2) The Maldives, (3) Manhattan, (4) Seeing a pride of lions and (5) Wild dolphins. Six of them decided to enjoy an experience of virtual travel and four of them to watch animals. For the VR experience, REDSTORM VR glasses [36] with built-in headphones for a more immersive experience, and adjustable grip were used. The ARLOOPA [37] application was used for AR, giving them the opportunity to overlap some virtual elements on their real environment.

After enjoying both experiences, the users filled a questionnaire to gather key information that could help us to primarily evaluate the suitability in the use of immersive technologies in the elderly population. The questionnaire was designed to capture also two KPIs:

- Positive or negative feelings with the experience.
- Weaknesses in the use of the devices, technologies and environment (Figs. 7, 8, 9, 10, 11, 12, 13 and 14).

Fig. 7. Virtual experience Machu Picchu.

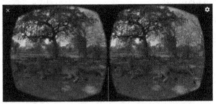

Fig. 8. Virtual experience Pride of lions.

Fig. 9. Virtual experience Manhattan.

Fig. 10. Virtual experience Maldives.

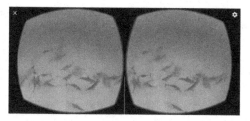

Fig. 11. Virtual experience wild dolphins.

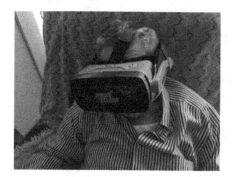

Fig. 12. Virtual visit to Machu Picchu.   **Fig. 13.** Virtual visit to the bottom of the sea with wild dolphins.

Fig. 14. ARLOOPA app – screenshots.

For reasons of data protection, only the gender and age of the respondents were collected as personal data. The age of the respondents is between 73 and 80 years old, 40% man, 60% woman.

They were asked about overall rating of the AR experience. The results were very positive, 60% 9 points over 10, 40% 10 points over 10 (Fig. 15). The users were also

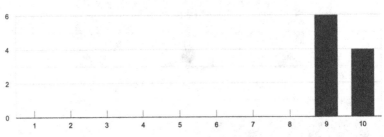

Fig. 15. Rating of AR experience.

asked about their emotions during the AR experience. The answers (Fig. 16) reflected that they felt closer to the young population, being enthusiastic and excited to be able to use these technologies.

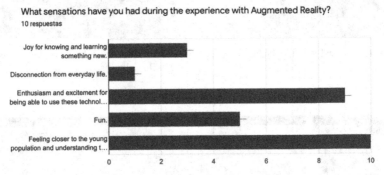

Fig. 16. Feeling during the AR experience.

They were asked about the AR experience lived. Most of them declared it was fun and moving. They also stated that to see the information superimposed on their environment was impressive and exciting. They were entertained and showed interest in continuing to play with the application and its different functions. A summary of the answers gathered is shown in Fig. 17.

Regarding augmented reality, what did you think about what you were able to see through the mobile phone at home?

I found it very amusing to see how an elephant appeared in the room. And I really enjoyed seeing the Mona Lisa painting in my living room.

I was very impressed to see the eagle, it looked very real.

I enjoyed playing with placing furniture in different places in the living room.

I found it a very moving experience. I liked on the mobile screen how the animals moved in my house.

I found the experience very fun and entertaining.

I loved to see the eagle flying on my balcony, it was very beautiful.

I found it very interesting, I liked it, now I understand my grandchildren better and why you spend so much time playing with the mobile phone, but I still think that the mobile phone is only for a short time a day.

I really enjoyed seeing the animals in my house and choosing new furniture and placing it in my living room.

I liked it, but I prefer to go to the countryside and see the real animals and breathe fresh air.

I liked it and I was entertained for a while.

Fig. 17. Synthesis of the AR experience.

On the other hand, the overall evaluation of the VR experience was also very positive, with 50% giving the experience the highest score and the other 50% giving it a 9 out of 10 (Fig. 18).

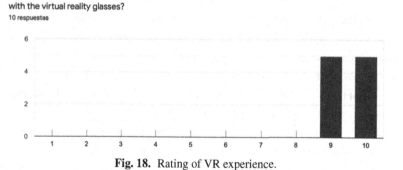

Between 1 and 10 (one being the lowest and 10 the highest) How would you rate the experience with the virtual reality glasses?
10 respuestas

Fig. 18. Rating of VR experience.

In order to synthesize the emotions experienced with VR, we provided them with a list of 6 statements (Fig. 19). Most of them stated that they felt disconnected from their everyday life, felt that for a short period of time they were away from home and had interest in the places they were visiting virtually. The experience was fun both for learning and getting to know something new and for feeling integrated by being able to use this technology.

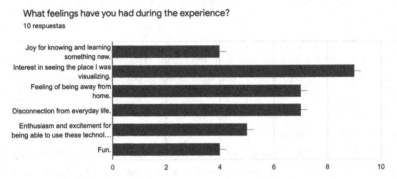

Fig. 19. Feelings during the immersive experience.

They were also asked for the positive things of using VR. All of them answered to have had an enriching and immersive experience. The feeling of doing something different for the first time and feeling integrated, both for the experience and for the use of the devices and technology. The list of the answers gathered is shown in Fig. 20.

What is the best thing you can say about this experience?

It seemed like I was really in Machu Picchu. The scenery was beautiful, and all this sitting on the sofa in my house.

I liked everything. And I had a very fun time.

Have the feeling of being in the jungle with the lions. To be able to turn around and see everything around me.

Some of the images were a bit blurry, but I really enjoyed seeing the dolphins in the sea.

Feeling like I was away from home in a different country, and seeing beautiful places.

I really enjoyed the scenery I saw even though the glasses were a bit heavy and uncomfortable.

Seeing and listening at the same time made me feel that I was really in this place.

The feeling of freedom and disconnection, watching TV is very boring at times, I really enjoyed the experience and the feeling of being somewhere else.

Being able to turn around and see everything was a new and very exciting experience, everywhere I looked I had things to see. It felt like I was present at the site of the video.

Seeing the family of lions, one of them looked like it wanted to greet me and I reached out to try to touch it.

Fig. 20. Synthesis of the experience with VR.

Some problems were also detected during the experiment. Eight of the ten participants encountered some problems with the use of the glasses due to the weight of the glasses and the lack of sharpness in the images. With more modern and higher quality devices these sensations can be reduced considerably. Figure 21 summarizes the list of drawbacks.

Have you had any discomfort while using the goggles?

No

The glasses bothered my nose a bit.

The image was not very sharp and the glasses were a little annoying.

I got a little dizzy.

I had to take off my glasses to be more comfortable with the device and I couldn't see very clearly.

The glasses are a bit heavy and they bothered me a bit.

A little dizzy when I took the device off.

No, everything has been fine.

I've had a weird feeling about having those big glasses on my face, they're not very comfortable.

Fig. 21. Discomfort while using VR glasses.

Figure 22 shows participants' ratings of their experiences with VR and AR according to gender. As can be seen in the graph in Fig. 23, there is hardly any difference, despite the fact that women rated them higher, both sexes rated the experiences above 9.

Age	Gender	Between 1 and 10 (one being the lowest and 10 the highest) How would you rate the experience with the virtual reality glasses?	Between 1 and 10 (one being the lowest and 10 the highest) How would you rate the experience with augmented reality?
73	Woman	9	9
78	Woman	10	10
74	Woman	10	9
75	Woman	9	10
78	Woman	10	10
75	Woman	10	9
79	Man	10	10
80	Man	9	9
79	Man	9	9
73	Man	9	9

Fig. 22. Data collected on VR and AR experience ratings.

Moreover, the trainers of the study also detected that most of candidates presented other problems during the experiment. Most of them were related to the difficulty candidates had in handling the devices, visualizing buttons or commands, need of training and help in its use. Finally, the high cost of some of the devices and applications for AR and VR, not mentioned during the experimental study, could be a handicap for their massive adoption for ageing population.

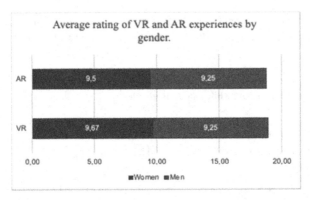

Fig. 23. Average rating of VR and AR experiences by gender.

5   Conclusions

In this work, the AR, VR and MR technologies have been introduced as suitable tools for promoting cognitive and physical activity and for avoiding social isolation in ageing population. The work has included a review of the most popular hardware and software solutions found in the state of art and market and the use of them for specific activities focused on elderly people. An experimental study has been also carried out to get a preliminary feedback about the benefits and drawbacks of these technologies for elderly. Although the technologies used in the study were very welcome by the candidates, reflecting positive feelings and experiences, some drawbacks were exposed, most of them related to the convenience of the devices. Trainers in the study also detected that elderly population need specific training for the use of these technologies. The positive balance in the experimental study opens the door to extend the study with specific KPIs that can better measure the improvements of cognitive and physical activity through continuous training, and e.g. to study the benefits for ageing population with specific impairments or degenerative diseases like dementia, Parkinson or Alzheimer.

Acknowledgments. We thank all participants in the experimental study, especially a loving memory to Mr. Gómez, who passed away in August 2021.

This work has been partially funded by the European Union's Horizon 2020 research and innovation programme under grant agreement No 857188 – Pharaon Project, and Spanish National Project ONOFRE-2, ref. TEC2017-84423-C3-2-P (MINECO/AEI/FEDER, UE).

References

1. Langer, E.: Medientinnovationen AR und VR. Springer, Berlin (2020)
2. RubyGarage. https://rubygarage.org/blog/difference-between-ar-vr-mr. Accessed 7 Apr 2021
3. Vidal-Balea, A., Blanco-Novoa, O., Fraga-Lamas, P., Vilar-Montesinos, M., Fernández-Caramés, T.M.: Creating collaborative augmented reality experiences for industry 4.0 training and assistance applications: performance evaluation in the shipyard of the future. Appl. Sci. **10**(24), 9073 (2020). https://doi.org/10.3390/app10249073

4. Sereno, M., Wang, X., Besancon, L., Mcguffin, M.J., Isenberg, T.: Collaborative work in augmented reality: a survey. IEEE Trans. Vis. Comput. Graph. https://doi.org/10.1109/TVCG.2020.3032761

5. Shyshkina, M.P., Marienko, M.V.: Augmented reality as a tool for open science platform by research collaboration in virtual teams. In: Proceedings of the 2nd International Workshop on Augmented Reality in Education (2020)

6. Döner, W.R.: Virtual undd Augmented Reality (VR/AR). Springer, Berlin (2019)

7. Wössner, S.: Landesministerium Badenwürttemberg. LMZ-BW. https://www.lmz-bw.de/medien-und-bildung/medienwissen/virtual-und-augmented-reality/ueberblick/#c35727. Accessed 23 Apr 2021

8. 4Experience. https://4experience.co/vr-tracking-meet-degrees-of-freedom/. Accessed 8 Apr 2021

9. Corporation, H.: Vive. https://www.vive.com/uk/accessory/tracker3/. Accessed 8 Apr 2021

10. Cybershoes: Cybershoes. https://www.cybershoes.com/us/. Accessed 10 Apr 2021

11. AURASMA, AURASMA. http://aurasmaproject.weebly.com/. Accessed 5 Apr 2021

12. Hughes, S., Warren-Norton, K., Spadafora, P., Tsotsos, L.E.: Supporting optimal aging through the innovative use of virtual reality technology. Multimodal Technol. Interact. 1(4), 23 (2017). https://doi.org/10.3390/mti1040023

13. Lubrecht, A.: Augmented Reality for Education. Digital Union, The Ohio State University (2012). http://en.wikipedia.org/wiki/Augmented_reality#cite_note-74. Accessed 12 Apr 2021

14. Wössner, S.: Landesmeddienzentrum Baden – Württemberg. LMZ – BW. https://www.lmz-bw.de/medien-und-bildung/medienwissen/virtual-und-augmented-reality/augmented-reality-unterrichtsbeispiele/. Accessed 23 Apr 2021

15. Chang, K.-P., Chen, C.-H.: Design of the augmented reality based training system to promote spatial visualization ability for older adults. In: Shumaker, R., Lackey, S. (eds.) VAMR 2015. LNCS, vol. 9179, pp. 3–12. Springer, Cham (2015). https://doi.org/10.1007/978-3-319-21067-4_1

16. Boletsis, C., McCallum, S.: Augmented reality cubes for cognitive gaming: preliminary usability and game experience testing. Int. J. Serious Games 3(1) (2016). https://doi.org/10.17083/ijsg.v3i1.106

17. Dermody, G., Whitehead, L., Wilson, G., Glass, C.: The role of virtual reality in improving health outcomes for community-dwelling older adults: systematic review. J. Med. Internet Res. 22(6), e17331 (2020)

18. Wössner, S.: Landesmedienzentrum Baden-Wüettemberg. LMZ –BW. https://www.lmz-bw.de/medien-und-bildung/medienwissen/virtual-und-augmented-reality/geschichte-der-virtuellen-realitaet/. Accessed 20 Apr 2021

19. QuiverVision. QuiverVision. https://quivervision.com/education-coloring-packs. Accessed 7 Apr 2021

20. Boulevard. Boulevard. https://www.blvrd.com/. Accessed 10 Apr 2021

21. Mirage, Mirage studios. https://www.miragestudiosar.com/augmented-reality/. Accessed 7 Apr 2021

22. Google: Tilt Brush. Google. https://www.tiltbrush.com/. Accessed 10 Apr 2021

23. Google Sky Map: Google. https://play.google.com/store/apps/details?id=com.google.android.stardroid&hl=en_US&gl=US. Accessed 7 Apr 2021

24. Google Games: Nature treks VR. https://naturetreksvr.com/. Accessed 10 Apr 2021

25. Google Expedition, Google. https://edu.google.com.au/expeditions/ar/#about. Accessed 7 Apr 2021

26. Google Expedition: Google. https://edu.google.com.au/expeditions/ar/#about. Accessed 10 Apr 2021

27. Google: Google Earth VR. https://arvr.google.com/earth/. Accessed 10 Apr 2021
28. Google: Google Arts&Culture. Google. https://artsandculture.google.com/. Accessed 10 Apr 2021
29. Holotech Studios: FaceRing Software. Holotech Studios. https://facerig.com. Accessed 7 Apr 2021
30. YouTube: YouTube VR. YouTube. https://vr.youtube.com/. Accessed 10 Apr 2021
31. Oculus: Oculus rooms. https://www.oculus.com/experiences/go/1101959559889232/. Accessed 10 Apr 2021
32. Vito Technology Inc.: Star walk 2: the night sky map. https://apps.apple.com/ee/app/star-walk-2-the-night-sky-map/id892279069. Accessed 7 Apr 2021
33. Renderver. Renderver. https://www.rendever.com/. Accessed 10 Apr 2021
34. Guerrero, E., Lu, M.-H., Yueh, H.-P., Lindgren, H.: Designing and evaluating an intelligent augmented reality system for assisting older adults' medication management. Cogn. Syst. Res. **58**, 278–291 (2019)
35. Bianco, M.L., Pedell, S., Renda, G.: Augmented reality and home modifications: a tool to empower older adults in fall prevention. In: Proceedings of the 28th Australian Conference on Computer-Human Interaction, pp. 499–507 (2016)
36. Redstorm. https://www.amazon.de/dp/B0915PX157?tag=strawpollde-21&linkCode=osi&th=1&psc=1. Accessed 10 Apr 2021
37. Arloopa: Arloopa. https://arloopa.com/. Accessed 10 Apr 2021
38. Oculus. www.oculus.com. https://www.oculus.com/compare/. Accessed Mar 2021

Ageing@home: A Secure 5G Welfare Technology Solution for Elderlies

Boning Feng[1], Birgitta Langhammer[1], Van Thuan Do[1,2], Niels Jacot[2],
Bernardo Santos[1], Bruno Dzogovic[1], Per Jonny Nesse[3], and Thanh van Do[1,3(✉)]

[1] Oslo Metropolitan University, Pilestredet 35, 0167 Oslo, Norway
{boning.feng,birgitta,bersan,bruno.dzogovic}@oslomet.no
[2] Wolffia AS, Haugerudvn. 40, 0673 Oslo, Norway
{vt.do,n.jacot}@wolffia.net
[3] Telenor ASA, Snarøyveien 30, 1331 Fornebu, Norway
{per-jonny.nesse,thanh-van.do}@telenor.com

Abstract. The world population is ageing at a fast pace and to enable elderly to age at home can become a viable solution both economically and socially speaking, leading also to the overall improvement of the elderly's well-being and comfort. There are currently a few AAL (Ambient Assisted Living) systems which although operational are not yet optimal in terms of efficiency and security. This paper proposes a welfare technology solution called Ageing@home which aims at enabling newly hospitalized elderlies to come home earlier by making use of a dedicated 5G network slice for health care system. Such an isolated logical network will provide adequate security, privacy and reliability for the selected welfare technologies and services deployed at the elderly home. The proposed solution allows the selection and customization of needed welfare technologies and services and promotes the re-allocation and re-use of equipment. Validation methods and a business plan have been presented as well as a thorough description of a proof-of-concept implementation.

Keywords: 5G mobile networks · Network slicing · Assisted living · Home based elderly care · Welfare technology

1 Introduction

Ageing population is taking place across all countries of the world, raising major issues for the direction of social policy [1]. The proportion of those aged 60 years and older in the Global North is expected to reach 32% in 2050. In the Global South, the share of older persons increased slowly between 1950 and 2013, from 6% to 9%, but is expected to accelerate in the coming decades, reaching 19% in 2050 (United Nations, 2014a). This can lead to significant challenges such as increased dependency rates, overload of the healthcare systems, lack of elderly homes to provide support, etc. Enabling elderly people to stay and live in the comfort of their own homes as much as possible is a good solution to address those problems, as it puts less pressure on the current healthcare systems

© ICST Institute for Computer Sciences, Social Informatics and Telecommunications Engineering 2021
Published by Springer Nature Switzerland AG 2021. All Rights Reserved
I. M. Pires et al. (Eds.): GOODTECHS 2021, LNICST 401, pp. 213–229, 2021.
https://doi.org/10.1007/978-3-030-91421-9_16

and is by far more cost efficient than elderly homes. It is important nonetheless to be able to monitor the senior citizen's well-being and to provide appropriate guidance and assistance in this process. In Europe, the Ambient Assisted Living (AAL) Programme [2] has as an objective the development and use of new technologies to allow elderly and disabled people to live comfortably at home, improving their autonomy, facilitating daily activities, ensuring better security, monitoring and treating sick people. Similarly, in the Nordic countries including Norway, welfare technologies [3] have been proposed to provide better services for the elderly living at home and in nursing homes.

Unfortunately, the state-of-the art welfare technologies are still suffering from many major limitations [4], such as: operation instability, deployment difficulties, poor usability and high costs which hinder their adoption and use [5]. One of the root causes lies on the use of WLAN (Wireless LAN) as connectivity technology, which suffers of disadvantages like poor security, complex configuration, limited portability, dependency on electricity, etc. Indeed, it could be quite challenging at deployment to configure and obtain optimal connectivity with WLAN. To remedy the mentioned shortcomings, we propose Ageing@home, a 5G-based solution, which makes use of the concept of network slicing to provide simple and quick deployment, simple recollection and re-use of allocation of equipment and service adaptability and extensibility. This solution is a further refinement of Home-based Elderly Care solution realized at the Secure 5G4IoT lab in Oslo [6] which enables the elderly who just had an operation at hospitals to come home by tailoring and deploying technology equipment e.g., sensors, actuators, monitoring devices, etc. necessary for a remote follow-up and assistance by healthcare personnel. Network slices (dedicated logical networks) will be allocated to the Ageing@home solution to connect in a secure way all the health sensors, devices and all caregivers to the Health Care application running on the cloud. The proposed solution will ensure higher level of security and privacy while facilitating the caregiver's assistance to the elderly in need.

The paper starts with a brief summary of state of the art of digital solutions to smart living environments for ageing people. A brief introduction of the 5G mobile network slicing is included before the main part of the paper, which is the detailed description of the proposed Ageing@home solution. To validate the implementation of the proof-of-concept, validation methods are elaborated and described in the following section. Next is the business plan which aims to ensure the successful adoption of Ageing@home as well as the description of the proof-of-concept implementation at the Oslo Metropolitan University's Secure 5G4IoT lab. To conclude, the paper presents some final remarks with some suggestions for future works.

2   State of the Art of Digital Solutions to Smart Living Environments for Ageing People

There are currently many research activities both in EU and the Nordic countries. As umbrella programmes there are Active & Assisted Living (AAL) programme, a European Innovation Partnership with 19 countries and Nordic Ambient Assisted Living coordinated by the Nordic Council of Ministers. In addition to numerous national projects in European countries there are also multiple COST and H2020 projects such as Sheld-on,

Activage, Phara-on, Ghost-IoT, etc. Unfortunately, so far, the AAL Digital solutions has still quite low uptake due to the following limitations:

- **Low technology maturity** [7]

  - *Instability:* Most solutions using Wireless LAN 802.11 experience occasional loss of connection due to interference, channel collision, coverage variation, etc.
  - *Configuration problems:* The usage of Wireless LAN also requires the configuration of several parameters for each installation, which is error prone. Further, security protection requires considerable knowledge and efforts.
  - *Installation difficulties:* The installation of sensors and devices at the elderly home could be difficult due to the furniture, time consuming and hence annoying to the users.

- **Fragmentation:** The current digital solutions are "silos" applications that operating in isolation without interworking and interoperability with each other. Consequently, the introduction of additional services will require a full installation of hardware and software which incurs high cost and disturbance to the elderly.
- **Technology oriented:** The current digital solutions are too much technology oriented [8] consisting of a bunch of technologies that are put together and offered to the elderly without sufficient considerations of the elderly user preferences or the health personnel's opinions [9].
- **Security and Privacy issues:** Although it is necessary to collect data to provide effective services to the elderly these data are personal which illegal access constitutes a privacy violation [10]. Unfortunately, the protection of personal data is currently not adequate. Further the use of video camera has been considered as obtrusive by elderly who feels watched.

3 Brief Introduction to 5G Network Slicing

The 5th generation mobile network (5G) [12] is well known for its significant advantages compared to 4G in terms of performance, coverage and quality of service and the promise of an enhanced mobile broadband (eMBB) with higher data speed and the support of a wide range of applications and services ranging from massive machine-type communications (mMTC) to ultra-reliable and low-latency communications (URLLC). Less known but not less important is the fact that 5G is a softwareized and virtualized network [13] (Fig. 1).

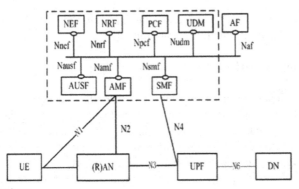

On the User plane:
- **UE** (User Equipment): is the user's mobile phone.
- **(R)AN** (Radio Access Network): is the Access Network Function which provides connectivity to the mobile phone.
- **UPF** (User Plane Function): handles the user plane traffic, e.g., traffic routing & forwarding, traffic inspection and usage reporting. It can be deployed in various configurations and locations depending on the service type.
- **DN** (Data Network): represents operator services, Internet access or 3rd party services.

On the Control plane:
- **AMF** (Access and Mobility Management Function): performs access control, mobility control and transparent proxy for routing SMS (Short Message Service) messages.
- **AUSF** (Authentication Server Function): provides authentication functions.
- **UDM** (Unified Data Management): stores subscriber data and profiles. It has an equivalent role as HSS in 4G but will be used for both fixed and mobile access in 5G core.
- **SMF** (Session Management Function): sets up and manages the PDU session according to network policy.
- **NSSF** (Network Slice Selection Function): selects the *Network Slice Instance* (NSI), determines the allowed *network slice selection assistance information* (NSSAI) and AMF set to serve the UE.
- **NEF** (Network Exposure Function): exposes the services and capabilities provided by the 3GPP network functions.
- **NRF** (NF Repository Function): maintains NF profiles and supports service discovery.
- **PCF** (Policy Control function): provides a policy framework incorporating network slicing, roaming and mobility management and has an equivalent role as PCRF in 4G.
- **AF** (Application Function): interacts with the 3GPP Core Network (CN) to provide services

Fig. 1. The 5G reference architecture (courtesy of 3GPP)

The software nature of the 5G network brings with it both weaknesses and strengths since it shows the same vulnerabilities as any other software at the same time as higher flexibility and dynamicity can be achieved through the logical network segments also known as Network slices.

Currently, there is no consensus on what a network slice is and how it can be realized [14]. In fact, while the 3rd Generation Partnership Project (3GPP) [15] provides a more network-focused definition stating that "network slices may differ for supported features and network functions optimizations", the 5G Infrastructure Public Private Partnership (5G PPP) adopts a business oriented view mandating that "a network slice is a composition of adequately configured network functions, network applications, and the underlying cloud infrastructure (physical, virtual or even emulated resources, RAN resources etc.), that are bundled together to meet the requirements of a specific use case, e.g., bandwidth, latency, processing, and resiliency, coupled with a business purpose [12].

In this paper we use the 5G PPP's definition that allows the support of a variety of devices. To obtain a wireless Home Networking capable of supporting a broad range of devices, the 5G network slicing concept is adopted to establish a secure 5G network for Elderly Care.

4 The Ageing@home Solution

4.1 Objectives

The main objective of Ageing@home is to enable newly hospitalized elderlies to return home earlier by providing a set of welfare technologies and services deployed at their home which provides efficient support and assistance from the healthcare personnel. Ageing@home solution can also be used permanently or temporarily for the time needed towards full recovery. The deployed equipment could be easily removed and recollected for re-use by other elderlies. As such, Ageing@home can be used in a dynamic and customized way for any elderly who needs assistance from healthcare personnel while living at their home.

4.2 Ageing@home Welfare Technologies and Services

The Ageing@home solution is adaptable and can be tailored to fit the demands of each individual elderly by enabling the selection and customization of the following welfare technologies and services:

- **Vital Signs Monitoring System:** allows the monitoring of vital signs such as heart rate (HR) [16], body temperature (BT), respiration rate (RR) and blood pressure (BP), etc. that are used by the medical professionals to get a good overview about the health of the elderly person.
- **Reminding System:** helps elderly citizens remembering to take their medicines as well as meals at correct time and dosage [17].
- **Automated Activity and Fall Detection System:** can distinguish between normal and abnormal activities and to detect a fall to trigger an alert, which can again result to an emergency with intervention of caregivers [18].
- **Automated Emergency Call System:** locates, contacts and directs the nearby appropriate caregiver who gives assistance to the elderly person in emergency cases [19].
- **Multimodal Communication:** provides secured remote medical check-up call with doctor/medical staff, secured interactions with health care system including notifications and alarms at the same time as it helps to combat isolation and loneliness by allowing elderly to communicate to friends and relative.

4.3 Typical Use Case

To illustrate the flexibility, adaptability and scalability of Ageing@home let us consider the case of Kari who had a successful heart surgery and is allowed to come home after 4 days instead of one week on the condition that her vital signs, glucose and breathing status are monitored and also assistance can be given on time at occurrence of incidents such as loss of consciousness, fall, heart attack, etc. In addition, Kari suffers of sleep disorder which needs to be diagnosed. Last but not least, Kari needs a secure communication facility which allows secure interactions both with the hospital and also with her family and friends.

To be safe at home, Kari will need to have the following technologies in place at her home:

- Sensors for monitoring of vital signs, glucose and breathing
- Sensors for detection of incidents such as loss of consciousness, fall, heart attack, etc.
- A tablet PC acting as a secure communication with the hospital and for contact with family and friends
- A secure and reliable connection to link the sensors and equipment to the hospital system

As the majority of elderlies, Kari does not have the necessary sensors and equipment nor the secure and reliable connection needed. But, thanks to Ageing@home all the necessary equipment and infrastructure can be identified, allocated, configured and installed at Kari's home short time before her return. The roll out consists of the following steps:

- Visit and assessment of the technology infrastructure at Kari's home by technology specialists
- Design and configuration of the necessary equipment such that they will be functioning immediately after power on without any on-site configuration:

  - 5G Sensors and devices will get installed SIM cards. The device/sensors IDs, the corresponding IMSIs (International Mobile Subscriber Identity), the corresponding ISDNs (Mobile Station International Subscriber Directory Number) will be registered and their access rights to the healthcare 5G network slice (will be described in later section) and to the healthcare system will also be set up and enabled.
  - For sensor and devices using other wireless technologies such as Bluetooth, Zigbee, WLAN, etc. 5G gateway will be used and necessary pairing to ensure security will be performed.

- Design and establishment of the connection to the Health care network slice: Depending on the availability of broadband connection at Kari's home, one connectivity alternative will be chosen among 5G Fixed-wireless Access (FWA), indoor radio unit or 5G enhance Mobile Broadband.

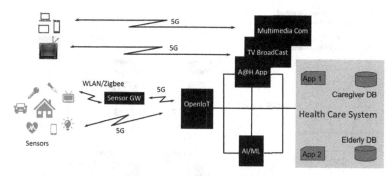

Fig. 2. The Ageing@Home conceptual model

4.4 Conceptual Architecture

To be able to accommodate all the improved welfare technologies described above in a customized, adaptable and scalable way the Ageing@Home end-to-end solution has an architecture represented by a conceptual model shown in Fig. 2.

Multiple heterogeneous sensors, both wearable aka on-body and ambient aka off-body with dedicated mission are connected to an open unifying IoT platform (OUIP) directly via 5G or indirectly, first via certain Local Area technologies such as Wireless LAN IEEE 802.11x, Zigbee, Z-wave, etc., to a Sensor Gateway and then via 5G to the OUIP. The sensors collect data and upload to the OUIP, which can then forward the collected data depending on the need to the Ageing@Home applications (Ageing@Home Apps), the Artificial Intelligence/Machine Learning (AI/ML) Platform or the Health Care System (HCS), where they are consumed in various ways. At the AI/ML Platform, the data are in multiple analytic tasks, especially the elaboration of the elderly's profile, which allows for better understanding and to respond appropriately to their needs and moods. When necessary, the data can be anonymized before being forwarded and stored.

The AI/ML Platform has interfaces with the Ageing@Home Apps and the HCS, which are then enabled to invoke various analytic tasks. The interface between the Ageing@Home Apps and the HCS enables the Ageing@Home Apps to access the HCS user and caregiver database and also other functionality, while the HCS can control the Ageing@Home Apps. The Ageing@Home Apps are essential to the implementation and provision of the targeted welfare technologies such as Digital night vision, Entertainment, Event and vital sign monitoring and detection, etc. Two Ageing@Home Apps, Broadcasting of Physical exercises and Multimodal communication, as communication apps have direct connection with their devices, i.e. TV, PC, tablets, etc.

4.5 The 5G Healthcare Network Slicing

In order to provide a connection which provides adequate protection of security and privacy at an acceptable level of reliability, a dedicated and isolated end-to-end network slice will be established. This healthcare network slice is a logical network realised by own vNFs (Virtual Network Functions) for both access network and core network as shown by Fig. 3. Only devices equipped with SIM cards own by the hospital can be

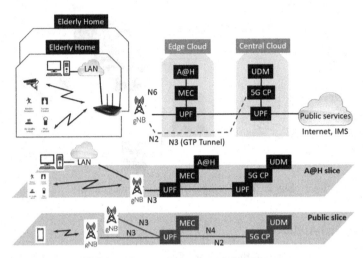

Fig. 3. Network slicing for Ageing@home

authorised to connect to this healthcare network slice. While IoT devices are in general not allowed to, some smartphones may be permitted to have simultaneous connection to the public network slice depending on the security policy of the hospital.

As shown in Fig. 3, the Ageing@Home solution consisting of OUIP (open unifying IoT platform), AI/ML (Artificial Intelligence/Machine Learning) platform and a variety of Ageing@Home applications are hosted on a MEC (Multi-access Edge Computing) host, which is located on Edge Cloud. Since the Edge Cloud is in the same area as the elderly home, very low latency can be achieved making this deployment option quite suitable for Welfare technologies, such as Broadcasting of physical exercises and mobility sessions technology. Further, both the security and privacy are considerably enhanced because communications between sensors and the Ageing@Home do not have to traverse the entire mobile network, but only a short path between the gNBs and the Edge Cloud.

5   Validation Methods

To be accepted and used it is crucial that the Ageing@Home solution not only technically functions properly but also meets all the needs and demands of the elderlies as primary users and the health care personnel as secondary users. For the technical functioning, thorough functional and performance testing will ensure the proper operation of the Ageing@Home solution.

Regarding the user acceptance it is far more challenging and not quite successful for existing welfare technologies. For example, while giving positive answers when being asked about the use of cameras in monitoring and assistance service some elderlies sabotaged the cameras by disconnecting them or taping over the lens.

Ageing@Home will make use of a combination of most efficient existing validation methods while researching and experimenting new ones as follows:

- *Outcome measures:* to measure some aspects and benefits
- *Use monitoring:* to have an overview of the use of the digital solution, which proves their usefulness
- *Questionnaires:* to gather information from a wiser group of users
- *Interviews:* to collect information from selected users. By using a structure of questions and open-ended questions it is possible to capture issues that escaped the other measurements.

5.1 Outcome Measures

- **Independence**

     The Lawton Instrumental Activities of Daily Living Scale (IADL) is an appropriate instrument to assess independent living skills (Lawton & Brody, 1969) [20] and is useful for identifying how a person is functioning at the present time and for identifying improvement or deterioration over time.

     There are 8 domains of function measured with the Lawton IADL scale: ability to use the phone, shopping, food preparation, housekeeping, laundry, mode of transportation, responsibility for own medications and ability to handle finances. Persons are scored according to their highest level of functioning in that category, scores ranging from 0 to 1. A summary score ranges from 0 (low function, dependent) to 8 (high function, independent).

- **Quality of Life /Health Related Quality of Life**

     Health related quality of life (HRQoL) refers to how health impacts on an individual´s ability to function as a multi-dimensional concept that includes domains related to physical, mental, emotional, and social functioning. A related concept of HRQoL is well-being, which assesses the positive aspects of a person's life, such as positive emotions and life satisfaction.

     The RAND-367 [21] is a 36-item questionnaire intended for use as a generic measure of HRQoL. It is developed by a non-profit organization RAND Corporation and the 36 items are identical to SF-36, described by Wade and Sherbourne (1992).

5.2 Use Monitoring

The usefulness and usability are best proven by the use of the proposed solution. For that, the Ageing@Home solution will have embedded log function which allows to record how often it is used. This method may not be usable in cases in which sensors and devices or services are constantly used.

5.3 Questionnaires and Interviews

The success of the questionnaires and interviews relies totally on the asked questions and on the views and perspectives they are focused on. So far, the sociological perspective is still neglected, and Ageing@Home project will remedy the situation by carrying out innovative research on relational perspectives on gerontechnology, i.e. technology for old age which encompasses three central dimensions:

1. The relationship between care and control
2. The relationship between autonomy and social isolation
3. The question of agency's relation to rationality, emotion and habits.

6 Business Plan

To ensure the success and adoption of Ageing@home, it is essential to have a sound commercial exploitation. A business plan must be elaborated at early stage and populated gradually with more details. The latest version of the Ageing@home business plan is shown in Table 1.

Table 1. Ageing@home business plan

Ageing@Home Business Plan
Vision: to secure smart living environments for ageing and disabled people enabling them to live a secure and comfortable life at home as long as possible.
Mission: to develop and launch a customizable and scalable end-to-end digital solution using multiple welfare technologies that offers different services to elderly people living at home. The Ageing@Home solution shall mitigate the limitations with current welfare solutions for elderly, improve the operation instability and deployment difficulties for caretakers and represent a more efficient use of resources/cost decrease for the nurseries and the municipalities.

Products/ Service Solution: Ageing@Home is an extensible and customised solution which enable the selection and customisation of the following welfare technologies as described earlier:
• Event and vital sign monitoring and detection
    ○ Basic system for abnormality detection and appropriate response
    ○ Action recognition and prediction system
    ○ Improved digital remote passive attention
    ○ Long term sleep status monitoring
    ○ Behaviour analysis system by sound, voice and communication
• Reminding System
• Multimodal communication
• Automated Emergency Call System

Customers/Market:
    • **Primary users** of Ageing@Home solutions are elderly living at home
    • **Secondary users** are healthcare personnel supporting and interacting with the elderly in their home location. Retirement homes/nursing homes may also make use of the Ageing@Home solutions. The primary and secondary users are invited to participate in workshop and demonstrations and giving feedbacks on the different solutions versions.

(*continued*)

Table 1. (*continued*)

• **Other Ageing@Home stakeholders:** Municipalities in charge of eldercare in Nordic countries and healthcare organizations in other countries are both decision makers in relation to deciding which eldercare solutions to purchase and implement In addition elderly organizations, relatives of elderly, national health authorities are also relevant stakeholders with interests in the outcome from the project. Providers of elderly solutions such as telecom operators, Internet service providers, device/terminals providers also have interest in the project outcome. • **Market:** Population ageing is taking place across all countries of the world, raising major issues for the direction of social policy. The proportion of those aged 60 years and older in the Global North is expected to reach 32% in 2050. In the Global South, the share of older persons increased slowly between 1950 and 2013, from 6% to 9%, but is expected to accelerate in the coming decades, reaching 19% in 2050 (United Nations, 2014a). According to EU, they estimate a doubling of elderly over 80 years from 5% in 2015 to 12% in 2060. Moreover, the ratio of workers to pensioners will decrease with 50% from four workers per pensioner in 2015 to 2 workers pensioner in 2060 [22]
Organization and Management: The following work after validation of the Ageing@Home solution during the pilot tests is the launch and go to market activities. Telenor as main partner of Ageing@home plans to be the actor that offers an integrated end-to-end Ageing@Home solution to the municipalities. In Norway and the Nordic market (Norway, Sweden, Denmark and Finland), this offering will be aligned with existing portfolio on welfare technology solutions. Ageing@Home solution features based on inventions, design or other intellectual work developed by sub providers related to the integrated offering from Telenor will follow an application process for IP protection managed by the responsible party in parallel with piloting and go to market process.
Go to market plan/Action plan: The major industry partners in the consortium will head their go to market plans for their respective geographical market segments. For these market segments the following actions will be executed: • **Demonstrations and promotions:** There will be presentations of the pilots and results in Norway and internationally. National demonstrations of the pilots will be carried out at Norwegian National health conferences arranged by KS and the yearly e-Health conference by Norsk Helse IT together with Nordic e-health conference [23]. • **Dissemination materials** will be brochures, posters and flyers elaborated and distributed at the demonstrations. Results from the pilots in Norway and Portugal will be planned to be demonstrated in selected EU e-Health related events, conferences, workshops and exhibitions throughout year 3 such as European conference an exhibition namely Mobile World Congress and Nordic Conference on ICT. • **Sales targets:** The market objective after launching the commercial Ageing@Home solution is to secure adoption by 25% of the roughly 250 municipalities in Norway that remains implementing Telenor's welfare technology. Whether the target is met will be measured three years after the Ageing@Home is deployed. The Ageing@Home solution will be launched in the other Telenor Nordic subsidiaries Denmark. Sweden and Finland

(*continued*)

Table 1. (*continued*)

with the same 25% target market share of the solution in municipalities. Altice and Cisco plans for similar sales strategies in their respective market segments.
• **Pricing strategy**: A fixed price for the different unified Ageing@Home solution features as well as a fixed price for the unified Ageing@Home solution including all the features. Complementary services such as training, customization, implementation, maintenance, certification and support services will be priced extra based on a combination of penetration pricing, value-based pricing and variable pricing strategies. Prices will be evaluated and determined through the project execution.
Financing and funding:
The detailed business plan from the will be developed during the project execution including estimated costs and revenues over a two to three-year period for all activities necessary to perform the further development, produce and deliver the Ageing@Home product/service for the specific Nordic, EU target markets. Required amount of funding (money and competence/persons wise) to finance (Capex/Opex) these activities will be described together with funding sources. The industry partner Telenor will together with their subproviders finance the commercialization and go to market activities. There are however options for SME/Sub providers to acquire funding of further development and testing activities in relation to pilot customers [24] as well as for commercialization activities [25] with help from public agencies such as Innovation Norway in Norway.

7   Proof-of-Concept Implementation

The network slicing for Ageing@home is achieved in a way that the users connecting to different slices will be isolated from each other and the WAN using policies and routing on-demand. In other words, separate users from slices that are not related to the healthcare system will not be able to connect to it without appropriate policies and authentication. In other case, this would open a security vulnerability that would enable adversaries to perform attacks within the slice or across network slices of the healthcare system.

Consequently, to avoid illegal actions and mitigate initial security threats, the Healthcare slice must be entirely separated from other slices, or more specifically the public enhanced Mobile Broadband slice for regular mobile communication. This implies that mobile network subscribers shall be denied access to the Healthcare slice and the assets and facilities related to it.

To complete the prerequisite, a detailed limiting network policy must be initiated at Core Networks and the C-RAN, aiming at constraining access to certain network endpoints and permitting only approved traffic.

As represented in Fig. 4, a 5G network infrastructure provisioned at the Secure 5G4IoT Lab, comprised of a Cloud Radio Access Network (C-RAN), is communicating to a cloud OpenAirInterface [26] vEPC (virtual Evolved Core Network). The deployment represents a functional split of a Baseband Unit (BBU) and the Remote Radio Heads (RRH), with the NGFI (Next Generation Fronthaul Interface). For network slicing, the

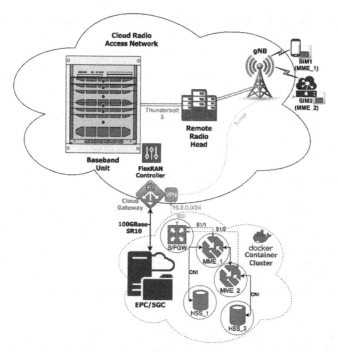

Fig. 4. 5G4IoT lab cloud radio access network slicing concept

User Equipment with SIM_1 is coupled to the Mobility Management Entity MME_1 instance, and the IoT apparatus using SIM_2 is associated with the MME_2. Both MMEs are running into Docker containers as means of virtualization and define the virtual EPC core. The other core network functions follow the same virtualization principle, with two HSS (Home Subscriber Server) databases, or more precisely HSS_1 and HSS_2 that communicate with MME_1 and MME_2 instances, respectively. The container network interface policy restricts the communication between the two HSS instances and allow only their equivalently associated MME instances to execute DIAMETER authentication in adjacent PLMN (Public Land Mobile Network) domains. Through a VPN tunneled communication, the IoT devices with SIM_2 can have a secure access to the analogous network slice via its assigned SGW (Serving Gateway) and PGW (Packet data network Gateway), establishing a route to the adjoining MME_2 and a PLMN with identifier that classifies that MME. The Service and Packet Gateways enable virtual GTP-U (GPRS Tunneling Protocol User data tunneling) tunnels between the interface of the instance to a virtual interface at the MME_1 and MME_2 successively, allowing the UE (User Equipment) to have a unique IP address and connectivity to the WAN and Internet.

The association of specific users to a specific network slice is achieved at the RAN layer, namely using the FlexRAN controller to match a particular IMSI (International Mobile Subscriber Identity) value of the UE to entries within the HSS_2. When the UE authenticates with the network, the UEs will not be able to reach other devices that are authenticated in the HSS_2, as these values are explicated in the HSS_1 and the routes are thus different for the traffic to reach the WAN via distinct Service and Packet Gateways.

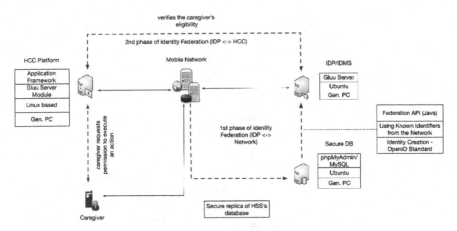

Fig. 5. Implementation of the identity management system

Allied to the described network, an identity provisioning and management system (IDMS) [27] has been implemented as shown in Fig. 5, to strengthen as well as simplify the authentication process for users (e.g. caregivers) and devices using the network by offering a single sign-on mechanism across the network and the application layers. More precisely, we inherit existing components from the network that can provide a secure way to identify a device and used it a unified way between layers.

To achieve a consensus on which parameters can be used as identifiers (**identity federation**), an API was also developed [28] to bridge between the IDMS and the network. After issuing the identities for the desired caregivers/devices, a module is created and given to the healthcare center, so that when a verification request has to occur, the healthcare center will confirm with the system as if one is eligible to provide support to an elderly person.

This identity management system is created by using an instance of the Gluu Server [29] that provides a combination of the provisioning and management tools, as well the option of deploying OpenID clients for integrations with third-party applications.

8   Conclusion

In this paper we have presented Ageing@home a welfare solution which enables newly hospitalized elderlies to come home earlier by providing a secure, privacy preserving and reliable 5G network slice and an extensible and adaptable framework allowing the selection and customization of the needed welfare technologies and services. The solution also enables the re-allocation and re-use of equipment when they are no longer needed. Validation methods and business plan are elaborated in the preparation for a future trial.

The next step of this initiative is to carry out a field trial with real elderly users living in some municipalities in Norway. Although the current proof-of-concept is working only functional and limited performance tests have been done, further tests and validations done with real users must be performed to identify weaknesses that can be improved ensuring the adoption of Ageing@home for the benefits of the elderlies. The most optimal validation would be a field trial with a limited set of elderly at one or two municipalities for a period of 6–12 months on a real 5G mobile network which is made available by the H2020 5G VINNI's facility pilot [30] in Norway. For the realization of such trial funding is required and efforts have been put to elaborate both national applications and EU project proposals. In addition, contacts and dissemination activities towards elderly organizations and municipalities should also be pursued.

Acknowledgement. This paper is a result of the H2020 CONCORDIA project (https://www.concordia-h2020.eu) which has received funding from the EU H2020 programme under grant agreement No. 830927. The CONCORDIA consortium includes 23 partners from industry and other organizations such as Telenor, Telefonica, Telecom Italia, Ericsson, Siemens, Airbus, etc. and 23 partners from academia such as CODE, university of Twente, OsloMet, etc.

References

1. United Nations, Department of Economic and Social Affairs, Population Division. World Population Ageing 2017 (ST/ESA/SER.A/408) (2017)
2. http://www.aal-europe.eu/
3. Velferdsteknologi. https://www.helsedirektoratet.no/rapporter/implementering-av-velfer dsteknologi-i-de-kommunale-helse-og-omsorgstjenestene-2013-2030/Implementering%20av%20velferdsteknologi%20i%20de%20kommunale%20helse-og%20omsorgstjenes tene%202013-2030.pdf/_/attachment/inline/cf340308-0cb8-4a88-a6d7-4754ef126db9:6f3 a196c2d353a9ef04c772f7cc0a2cb9d955087/Implementering%20av%20velferdsteknologi%20i%20de%20kommunale%20helse-og%20omsorgstjenestene%202013-2030.pdf
4. Woll, A.: Use of welfare technology in elderly care (2017). https://www.duo.uio.no/handle/10852/55537
5. Holthe, T., Casagrande, F.D., Halvorsrud, L., Lund, A.: The assisted living project: a process evaluation of implementation of sensor technology in community assisted living. A feasibility study. Disabil. Rehabil. Assist. Technol. **15**(1), 1–8 (2018)
6. Feng, B., et al.: Secure 5G network slicing for elderly care. In: Awan, I., Younas, M., Ünal, P., Aleksy, M. (eds.) MobiWIS 2019. LNCS, vol. 11673, pp. 202–216. Springer, Cham (2019). https://doi.org/10.1007/978-3-030-27192-3_16. ISSN 0302-9743, ISBN 978-3-030-27191-6, ISBN 978-3-030-27192-3 (eBook)
7. Liu, L., et al.: Smart homes and home health monitoring technologies for older adults: a systematic review. https://doi.org/10.1016/j.ijmedinf.2016.04.007
8. Memon, M., Wagner, S., Pedersen, C.F., Beevi, F.H.A., Hansen, F.O.: Ambient assisted living healthcare frameworks, platforms, standards, and quality attributes. Sensors (Basel) **14**(3), 4312–4341 (2014). https://doi.org/10.3390/s140304312
9. Offermann-van Heek, J., Ziefle, M.: They don't care about us! Care personnel's perspectives on ambient assisted living technology usage: scenario-based survey study. JMIR Rehabil. Assist. Technol. **5**(2), e10424 (2018). https://doi.org/10.2196/10424

10. Muñoz, D., Gutierrez, F.J., Ochoa, S.F.: Introducing ambient assisted living technology at the home of the elderly: challenges and lessons learned. In: Cleland, I., Guerrero, L., Bravo, J. (eds.) IWAAL 2015. LNCS, vol. 9455, pp. 125–136. Springer, Cham (2015). https://doi.org/10.1007/978-3-319-26410-3_12

11. Stefanov, D.H., Bien, Z., Bang, W.-C.: The smart house for older persons and persons with physical disabilities: Structure, technology arrangements, and perspectives. IEEE Trans. Neural Syst. Rehabil. Eng. **12**, 228–250 (2004)

12. 5G Infrastructure Public Private Partnership (5G PPP): View on 5G Architecture (Version 2.0). 5G PPP Architecture Working Group, 18 July 2017

13. ETSI: GS NFV 002 Network Functions Virtualization (NFV); Architectural Framework, v.1.1.1, October 2013

14. Dzogovic, B., Santos, B., Noll, J., Do, V.T., Feng, B., Do, T.V.: Enabling smart home with 5G network slicing. In: Proceedings of the 2019 IEEE 4th International Conference on Computer and Communication Systems ICCCS 2019, ISBN 978-1-7281-1321-0, IEEE Catalog Number CFP19D48-USB, Conf. Chair Yang Xiao, Singapore, 23–25 February 2019, pp 543–548 (2019)

15. 3rd Generation Partnership Project (3GPP): Technical Specification TS 23.501 V1.3.0 (2017–09) Technical Specification Group Services and System Aspects; System Architecture for the 5G System; Stage 2 (Release 15), September 2017

16. Park, J.-H., Jang, D.-G., Park, J., Youm, S.-K.: Wearable sensing of in-ear pressure for heart rate monitoring with a piezoelectric sensor. Sensors **15**, 23402–23417 (2015)

17. Zao, J.K., Wang, M.-Y., Tsai, P., Liu, J.W.S.: Smartphone based medicine in-take scheduler, reminder and monitor. In: Proceedings of the 2010 12th IEEE International Conference on e-Health Networking Applications and Services (Healthcom), Lyon, France, 1–3 July 2010, pp. 162–168 (2010)

18. Popescu, M., Li, Y., Skubic, M., Rantz, M.: An acoustic fall detector system that uses sound height information to reduce the false alarm rate. In: Proceedings of the 30th Annual International Conference of the IEEE Engineering in Medicine and Biology Society (EMBS 2008), Vancouver, BC, Canada, 21–24 August 2008, pp. 4628–4631 (2008)

19. Bottazzi, D., Corradi, A., Montanari, R.: Context-aware middleware solutions for anytime and anywhere emergency assistance to elderly people. IEEE Commun. Mag. **44**, 82–90 (2006)

20. Lawton, M.P., Brody, E.M.: Assessment of older people: self-maintaining and instrumental activities of daily living. Gerontologist **9**(3), 179–186 (1969)

21. https://www.rand.org/health/surveys_tools/mos/36-item-short-form.html

22. https://ec.europa.eu/economy_finance/graphs/2015-05-12_ageing_reporten.htm

23. KS – Kommunes Sentralforbund (Norwegian Association of Local and Regional Authori-ties)

24. https://www.innovasjonnorge.no/no/tjenester/innovasjon-og-utvikling/finansiering-for-inn ovasjon-og-utvikling/innovasjonskontrakter/innovation-contracts/

25. https://www.innovasjonnorge.no/no/tjenester/oppstart-avbe-drift/oppstartfinansiering/kom mersialiseringstilskudd/

26. OpenAirInterface Software Alliance (OSA): a non-profit consortium fostering a community of industrial as well as research contributors for open source software and hardware development for the core network (EPC), access network and user equipment (EUTRAN) of 3GPP cellular networks. https://www.openairinterface.org/

27. Santos, B., Do, V.T., Feng, B., van Do, T.: Identity federation for cellular internet of things. In: Proceedings of the 2018 7th International Conference on Software and Computer Applications - ICSCA 2018, pp. 223–228 (2018)

28. Santos, B., Do, V.T., Feng, B., van Do, T.: Towards a standardized identity federation for internet of things in 5G networks. In: 2018 IEEE SmartWorld 2018 Proceedings, pp. 2082–2088 (2018)

29. Gluu Server. https://www.gluu.org/. Accessed May 2019
30. 5G-VINNI: 5G Verticals INNovation Infrastructure, an European H2020-ICT-2017 re-search project which aims at accelerating the uptake of 5G in Europe by providing an end-to-end (E2E) facility that validates the performance of new 5G technologies by operating trials of advanced vertical sector services

Defining the Instruments for Zero-Measurement of Psychological Well-Being at Older Adults

Dumitru Micusa[✉] [ID]

Free International University of Moldova, Chisinau, Moldova

Abstract. Our team is working on discovering and implementing measurement instruments and practical solutions for enhancing the Psychological Well-Being of older adults. The aim is to investigate the need to ensure the continuity of social and economic activities; also, we aim to learn how to maintain, but better-improve older people's intellectual, emotional and psychological well-being. The procedural objectives of the research consist of accumulating, structuring, and retaining statistical data obtained from interviewing the groups of older people from different countries with the use of quantitative and further qualitative investigation instruments (questionnaires, tests, interviews, etc.). They are investigated, selected, and proposed recipes for better psychological well-being and social behavior towards the continuity of spiritual, intellectual, and emotional activities in the society of older people. In conclusion, if we achieve to obtain the awareness of both older adults and the employers of the fact that the continuity of activities after the retirement age, and also the understanding that practicing the proposed recipes will abundantly raise their well being, they will not leave this world unfulfilled in terms of complete knowledge of the supply of the well-being for older people.

Keywords: Older adults · Well-being · Measurement instruments

1 Introduction

By 2050 [1], the number of people in the EU aged 65 and above is expected to grow by 70%, and the number of people aged over 80 by 170% will increase demand and costs for healthcare. Integrating ICT solutions into habitats and improved building design will allow us to live at home and stay active and productive for longer despite cognitive or physical impediments. Improving accessibility, functionality, and safety at home, at work, and in society, in general, requires combining many disciplines to develop solutions that integrate ICT, ergonomics, healthcare (psychological and physical), and community design.

2 Independence in Own Homes

In the assignment of AFEdemy, within the Project "Independent Living in the rural areas of The Netherlands," 7 students from the Hanze University for Applied Sciences

© ICST Institute for Computer Sciences, Social Informatics and Telecommunications Engineering 2021
Published by Springer Nature Switzerland AG 2021. All Rights Reserved
I. M. Pires et al. (Eds.): GOODTECHS 2021, LNICST 401, pp. 230–243, 2021.
https://doi.org/10.1007/978-3-030-91421-9_17

and the University of Groningen performed research in the municipality Oldambt [2] to investigate the problem: "what do older people from 80 years and older need in their daily life, mobility, social network, and well-being to remain independent in their own homes in the villages". As a result, it was underlined [3] that "... there are several solutions to keep the elderly living longer at home, such as doorstep aids, wall brackets in the bathroom and the toilet, a second handrail a stairlift. Furthermore, the national government says that older people can live longer by adapting their current homes using new technologies. The last option is domotics (or home automation): this can make a home safer, easier to use, and can help older people stay at home for longer...".

3   What Do the Older People Need to Continue Living in Their Own House?

Two Social Work students from the Hanzehogeschool have researched the needs of older people in the township Oldambt for the organization AFEdemy [4]. The main goal of the research was to get to know what the more senior people need to continue living in their own house. The resource question is: What do older people of 80 years and older need in daily functioning, social participation, and mental well-being to keep living in their own house.

The needs of the respondents are very different. Most of them, 18 respondents, said that they have no requirements for support in any way. Most of them have an excellent social network who helps them where they need or are, despite their age, still vital and independent from others. The respondents that do need support most of the time want more contact and involvement with others. These are often people with a smaller social network and fewer skills to look for and find support in any way. Seven respondents said they feel lonely, and they said they want to go out more or have more contacts. Also, Wijnja's (2018) research outcomes said that many older people in Oldambt feel lonely. However, overall seems the respondents were satisfied with their living situation. They gave themselves a seven or eight average.

The first recommendation involves better information giving from the township Oldambt to older people, so that they know where to find the facilities in the area, especially the social facilities. The other recommendations to SociaalWerkOldambt are to recruit more volunteers and make the organization better known and accessible for older people.

4   Mobility of the Older People

The everyday outdoor mobility of older people has received increasing attention in the academic world and policy-making [5]. There are two reasons for this. The first reason is the recent and projected growth of senior citizens in (and the impacts of this on) most Western societies. Secondly, research has shown that mobility outside of the home is strongly related to well-being in later life. Therefore, older adults' experiences with outdoor mobility have been investigated by Bart Roelofs& Liselotte Vreelingsupervised by Prof. Dr. Louise Meijering and commissioned by: AFEdemy [2].

This report explores the outdoor mobility experiences of community-dwelling older people in Winschoten, the Netherlands. Specifically, it was investigated why outdoor mobility is important, what influences outdoor mobility and how they adapt to changes in mobility. In addition, it is connected to theories on age-friendly environments, outdoor mobility, independence, and well-being. The research consists of six in-depth interviews with older inhabitants of Winschoten.

The main findings indicate that outdoor mobility of older adults is diverse and subjective and is perceived to be important because it is closely related to independence. Furthermore, three interrelated dimensions are experienced to influence their outdoor mobility: personal, social, and environmental. Finally, older people seem to adapt to a decline in mobility by self-regulation. Therefore, we advise policymakers to adjust the living environment to meet the needs and capacities of older people, thus creating an age-friendly Winschoten.

5 The Age-Friendly Cities and Communities Questionnaire

The AFEdemy is co-developer of The Age-Friendly Cities and Communities Questionnaire (AFCCQ) Project [6]. In early 2020, the municipality of The Hague awarded the consortium consisting of The Hague University of Applied Sciences, Hulsebosch Advies, and AFEdemy to develop a questionnaire and run a representative survey on the perceived age-friendliness of the city among its older citizens. Part of this survey was the development of a validated questionnaire, which allows for an assessment of the perceived age-friendliness. The municipality also wanted a representative number of older Western and non-Western immigrants to be included in the sample to do justice to the super-diversity of the population of The Hague. Therefore, the consortium started to review scientific and public sources to check whether a default questionnaire was already available. The search delivered several examples of questionnaires that either lacked transparency on the development and validation or did not measure the construct of age-friendliness as a whole. Therefore, the consortium developed and validated a validated questionnaire, coined the Age-Friendly Cities and Communities Questionnaire.

The consortium used the Consensus-based Standards to select health Measurement Instruments (COSMIN) To develop the questionnaire. The development consisted of the following four phases: Development, Initial validation, Psychometric validation, and Instrument translation. The theoretical basis of the questionnaire was the Global Age-friendly Cities Guide, published by the World Health Organization in 2007, and its accompanying Checklist. This guide published a model of age-friendly cities and communities, consisting of eight domains: outdoor spaces and buildings; transportation; housing; social participation; respect and social inclusion; civic participation and employment; communication and information; and community support and health services. The features of the Checklist formed the foundation of the items for the questionnaire. Additionally, questions on technology and the financial situation were added based on the literature review.

The Age-Friendly Cities and Communities Questionnaire measures the views of older adults on the eight domains already defined by the WHO and on a relevant ninth domain, namely their financial situation. The questionnaire is open for use on every geographical level and by every public authority, civil society organization, or any other who is interested. It might be necessary to validate the questionnaire culturally.

6   The Smart Healthy Age-Friendly Environments Network

In the middle of 2020, Carina Dantas and Willeke van Staalduinen have announced [7] that "The SHAFE Stakeholders Network is happy to release its Position Paper, developed in collaboration between SHAFE partners and the participants on the COST Action Net4AgeFriendly, to present recommendations that aim to promote healthier environments for all citizens and make environments accessible, sustainable and reachable for all, with the support of ICT". The Smart Healthy Age-Friendly Environments Network will thus focus on the narrative, debate, disclosure, and knowledge translation of smart digital solutions and solutions to optimize individuals' physical and social environments in a concerted manner, bringing together the domains of health and social care.

7   Psychological Well-Being of Retired Seniors

In October–November 2020, the COST CA16226 accepted a short term scientific mission (STSM) "Measurement, maintenance and improvement of psychological well-being of retired seniors" with the scope to research the psychology of older people in the conditions of continuous activity with the emphasis of their psychological well-being supported by intellectual and emotional activities. The host institution was The AFEdemy. The researcher was PhD student Dumitru MICUȘA and mission coordinator Mrs. Willeke van STAALDUINEN.

7.1   Collaboration Between Netherlands and Republic of Moldova

The overarching aim of the STSM was to strengthen the collaboration between AFEdemy (Netherlands) and ULIM (Republic of Moldova) to improve mutual capacity to raise awareness and exchange information on the state of the art of smart, healthy age-friendly environments on national and regional levels, particularly within the topics of Responsible Research and Innovation and addressing societal challenges.

This STSM aimed to exchange information accumulated in an international environment (MoldovaNetherlands) by observing and questioning older adults, processing the data obtained to define, maintain, and improve seniors' psychological, intellectual, and emotional well-being.

To bring an instrument for measuring psychological well-being was the main object of this STSM, also monitoring the evolution of the defined psychological leaks in a multifunctional indoor environment. The scope is to meet the requirements of Europe's aging population while promoting healthy and safe aging, to identify core challenges that older adults face when aging in the workplace.

This aim is allied to the objectives of the fourth Working Group of the COST Action, which works to improve smart support furniture and habitat environments according to user's needs and further validated by these users (elderly and caretakers) for active aging.

After the mission, when the efficiency of our methodology is proved, to deliver to the host institution the new statistical method of research. In our turn, we also expect to obtain a new research method regarding the measurement of seniors' emotional/psychological/intellectual well-being, creating a portfolio of various methods to be applied to other samples during our empirical research.

7.2 Psychological Well-Being Questionnaire (PWBQ)

7.2.1 Research Methods

To test the conceptual framework, according to which the well-being of the older adults is positive, we have developed a scale method. It contains a Likert-type response scale in 7 steps – from –3 to 3. To measure the psychological well-being state at the moment of questioning, we built a Psychological Well-Being Questionnaire (PWBQ) with 30 items, five items for each of the six dimensions that we considered appropriate for the definition of psychological well-being:

i.   the feeling of being happy,
ii.   self-acceptance,
iii. control over the environment,
iv.   autonomy,
v.   positive relationships with others,
vi.   purpose and meaning of life.

Moldovan and Dutch discussed and other investigative questionnaires about elders' psychological, intellectual, and emotional well-being.

Based on the questionnaires from Moldova, the questionnaires from AFEdemy in the Netherlands, using other surveys, among other things the 36-Item Short Form Survey Instrument (SF-36) from the USA, was finished with the Psychological Well-Being Zero-Measurement instrument [9], which is ready to be applied where needed. You can find an example in Table 1 where you can notice that each of the six dimensions contains 5 questions related to the topic of the dimension.

7.2.2 Scoring

1st dimension. For scoring, we calculate the average for all 5 items. The maximum score is 3. The average score of the subjective feeling of happiness is about –0.5 to 1.0. Lower scores of –0.5 denote shared feelings of unhappiness, more significant than 1.0 - of happiness. The higher the scores are, the higher is the subjective appreciation of happiness.

2nd dimension. The scores are calculated the same as previously reported. Lower scores of –0.5 denote low self-acceptance: lack of recognition of merits, lack of positive qualities, lack of skills and aptitudes, dissatisfaction and self-disdain, more significant than 1.0 – high self-acceptance.

3rd dimension. The lower scores of –0.5 denote an inability to monitor affective states, behavior in various circumstances, the mood of others, the communication course,

Table 1. Items for measuring the subjective feeling of happiness (PWBQ).

	-3	-2	-1	0	1	2	3	

1. Generally, I consider myself

A person not too happy								Very happy

2. Compared to my colleagues / other people, I am

Less happy								Happier

3. Some people are generally pleased. They enjoy life. No matter what happens to them, they take maximum advantage of everything. To what extent does this characterization describe you?

Not at all								To the greatest extent

4. Some people are generally very unhappy. Although I am not depressed, I am never quite happy as I would be. To what extent does this characterization describe you?

To the greatest extent								Not at all

5. Every morning, I wake up with a feeling of living a happy day?

Never								Always

more significant than 1.0 – social monitoring capacity and events according to their intentions and the expectations of others.

4th dimension. Just as before, small scores denote the lack of autonomy, self-confidence, and assertiveness, features that limit the person into actions, the high ones – the ability to manifest themselves genuinely, to show initiative, actively involved in various projects and activities.

5th dimension. Small scores characterize a person with poor communication and social networking; the high ones denote potential enough adaptation to new and communicable environments and people, capable of establishing and maintaining positive relationships with others.

6th dimension. High scores are accumulated by people who recognize and accept the experience, control their present and look with optimism for the future, see the meaning of life and personal existence. On the other hand, people who accumulate small scores do not have the meaning of life, they have few or even no objectives or goals, do not see the meaning of past experiences, present, and perspectives.

8   Questioning with the Use of PWBQ

8.1   In the Netherlands

The questionnaire PWBQ [9] was adapted to the Dutch language. With the help of the PWBQ questionnaire, a group of older adults from different collectives in the Netherlands was interviewed, and information was collected about psychological well-being.

The results on each of the 6 dimensions from 12 respondents from the Dutch space are listed below in Table 2 and graphically represented in Fig. 1.

Table 2. The results of Dutch respondents (PWBQ).

Psychological well-being dimensions	Interviewed person												Total
	1st	2nd	3rd	4th	5th	6th	7th	8th	9th	10th	11th	12th	
Feeling of happiness	9	12	– 2	– 3	9	13	4	– 1	9	12	9	2	**73**
Self-acceptance	15	8	2	1	11	12	10	1	4	14	15	7	**100**
Control over environment	3	5	1	– 4	6	10	3	– 1	– 4	– 3	10	– 7	**19**
Autonomy	2	9	1	4	10	13	9	1	6	6	11	5	**77**
Positive relations with others	7	15	1	2	13	14	12	0	10	10	13	7	**104**
Purpose and meaning of life	14	12	5	1	6	5	11	3	5	9	9	5	**85**

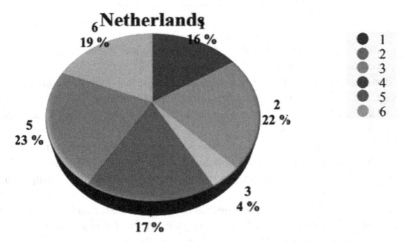

Fig. 1. Graphic representation of the results of Netherlands respondents (PWBQ).

8.2   In Moldova

The questionnaire PWBQ [9] was adapted to the Romanian language. With the help of the PWBQ questionnaire, a group of older adults from the Association "AESM Seniors" at the Academy of Economic Studies of Moldova (AESM) and associates was interviewed, and the information was collected about psychological well-being. In Table 3, you can find listed the results of Moldovan respondents and a graphical representation of the given results in Fig. 2.

Table 3. The results of Moldovan respondents (PWBQ).

Psychological well-being dimensions	Interviewed Person												Total
	1st	2nd	3rd	4th	5th	6th	7th	8th	9th	10th	11th	12th	
Feeling of happiness	15	2	10	8	8	10	15	6	8	7	5	10	104
Self-acceptance	13	8	14	10	2	10	15	15	2	10	5	8	112
Control over environment	11	− 8	11	8	2	5	15	13	2	7	− 1	5	70
Autonomy	12	− 1	10	8	− 2	10	15	12	− 2	12	7	10	91
Positive relations with others	14	7	8	10	0	9	15	13	0	12	3	12	103
Purpose and meaning of life	15	11	11	9	2	12	15	15	2	7	7	13	119

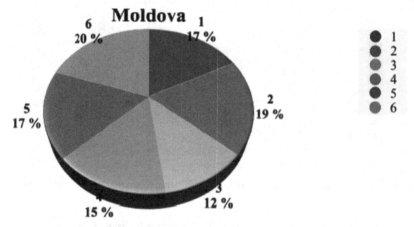

Fig. 2. Graphic representation of the results of Moldovan respondents (PWBQ).

Data from the Netherlands and Moldova were structured separately and jointly for analysis in terms of comparative evolution (Table 4, Fig. 3, Fig. 4).

Based on collected data on psychological well-being using the PWBQ questionnaire, the statistical methods of maintaining and improving the psychological excitement of the seniors were analyzed from different groups of seniors.

Collected data and analyzed methods will support the methodology and the decisions to be proposed to create a more productive, healthier, and more comfortable society for the elderly.

Also, the questionnaires, which have been implemented within the STSM, were based on the characteristics of the psychological well-being of the older adults in the sectors of psychological energy loss.

Access to local libraries and databases from the Hague, Amsterdam, Rotterdam, and AFEdemy allowed selecting and studying several work methods with investigative

Table 4. The results of Netherlands Moldovan respondents.

Dimensions	Country	
	Netherlands	Moldova
Feeling of happiness	73	104
Self-acceptance	100	112
Control over environment	19	70
Autonomy	77	91
Positive relations with others	104	103
Purpose and meaning of life	85	119

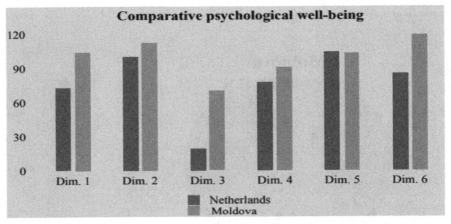

Fig. 3. Comparative data regarding psychological well-being Netherlands – Republic of Moldova.

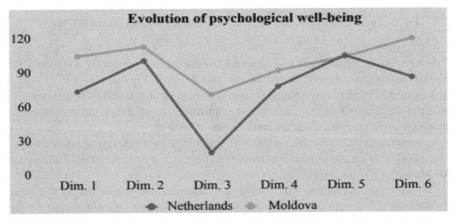

Fig. 4. Comparative data regarding the evolution of psychological well-being Netherlands – Republic of Moldova.

questionnaires. The host institution AFEdemy helped organize the groups of respondents and administer the questionnaire to the sample of respondents in Dutch space.

The information obtained from surveys resulting from the questioning seniors from selected Dutch collectives was processed, analyzed, and distributed on three age compartments to be subjected to processing using statistical methods of processing surveys. The respondents had a positive reaction to the survey, but with a remark that there are too many questionnaires to fill up everywhere nowadays (i.e., hospital, city hall, etc.). They would have much more pleasure from discussing personally with specialists sharing their stories with them. The specialists, instead, can observe from these discussions the needs of the seniors and bring them the appropriate IoT and ICT solutions.

Under the guidance of the host institution, AFEdemy was allowed to work with scientists from other Dutch institutions such as Prof. Joost van Hoof, professor of Urban Ageing from The University of Hague, and Elisabeth de Vries, and others, who helped a lot and gave suggestions on the structure of age-friendly societies and steps to take to its construction.

8.3 Portfolio of Methods for Measuring Different Aspects of Well-Being for Seniors

The STSM has been finished successfully with very good results, maybe even more than we've expected. The primary purpose of applying our instrument of zero-measurement of the psychological well being, by bringing it to the host institution for validation and appreciation, was fulfilled, so now the instrument is ready to be introduced in the portfolio of measurement instruments of the researchers from the field of Social Psychology and Sociology. Also, the host institution AFEdemy shared with us their latest Age-Friendly Cities and Communities Questionnaire, a representative survey on the perceived age-friendliness of the city among its older citizens. Part of this survey was the development of a validated questionnaire, which allows for an assessment of the perceived age-friendliness. This new instrument can be applied successfully in other countries and can also be included in our Portfolio of methods for measuring different aspects of well-being for seniors.

Interviews were held with some older adults from the Netherlands, who shared the experience of living in an age-friendly environment and some practical recommendations (for example, creating computer learning classes) for countries such as the Republic of Moldova, where age-friendly settings are not that developed. These recommendations are to be implemented.

Based on discussions with interviewees and their past experiences with different questionnaire-based surveys, the conclusion was that older respondents prefer more to participate in the interview-based surveys than filling up questionnaires. Again, it is because it gives a more personalized and qualitative response. But, even with observing these respondents' preferences, there is still no better way of questioning big groups of respondents than questionnaire-based surveys.

8.4 From Quantitative Results to Qualitative Results of Psychological Well-Being

Regarding the interviewees and representatives from the nursing homes, there is a very high level of healthcare and a suitable environment for the elderly living in the community. But, at the same time, there is still a lack of psychological services in these habitats, which is why there is a lack in measuring and maintaining psychological well-being.

A recommended solution would be to attract more psychologists to work in age-friendly habitats. This way, there would be the possibility to obtain more qualitative results through frequent interviews and conversations, rather than through the questionnaire method, which gives more quantitative results.

A better understanding of the personalized psychological needs of each individual would bring propulsion in the development of IoT Related Technology and its Impact on New ICT.

8.5 First Impressions from the International Collaboration

It has been a pleasure and an excellent collaboration with AFEdemy, as we brought to the Republic of Moldova new solutions in building age-friendly environments.

The questionnaires of the elderly, assigned and implemented for different groups of older adults in the problems of the well-being of the elderly, serve to investigate and propose other methods of maintaining and improving the psychological health of the elderly.

As part of the Medical Outcomes Study (MOS), RAND developed the 36-Item Short-Form Health Survey (SF-36). The SF-36 is a set of generic, consistent, and manageable quality of life measures. These measures are based on patient self-reporting and are now widely used by managed care organizations for routine monitoring and evaluation of care outcomes in adult patients.

It was compiled a questionnaire with 30 items to measure the degree of psychological well-being, where five things for each of the six dimensions that we considered appropriate for defining psychological well-being, where the feeling of happiness, self-acceptance, environmental control, autonomy, positive relationships with others, purpose and meaning of life - The Psychological Well Being Questionnaire (PWBQ).

After examining the questionnaire results through the short-term scientific mission at the AFEdemy Academy in Guada, the Netherlands, in October–November 2020, requires analysis of the individual's psychological situation to propose methods to maintain and ascend his well-being.

The activities of the individual to raise his psychological well-being are based, to a large extent, on the hormonal reflections of the individual. Therefore, it requires us to be aware of the hormonal reflections on which the individual's spiritual, emotional, and cognitive psychological state is based. They are component elements of the actions of the psychological survival of the elderly.

The repositories of the spiritual, intellectual, and physical procedures of intergenerational social activities represent the nucleus for elaborating the methods of the evolution of the individual's psychological well-being.

9 The Sustainability and Collaboration with Perspective

We consider this STSM was just a jumpstart of the collaboration between the Netherlands and the Republic of Moldova. For future collaborations, we express our willingness to involve Moldovan specialists in international research to develop better-personalized methods of questioning and afterward to bring solutions for the psychological assessment of older adults in the EU age-friendly habitats for SHELD-ON and AFEdemy, for improving the general level of well-being for elderly and bringing new ideas to IoT and ICT developers.

These questionnaires are also to be used on older adult samples from the Republic of Moldova with the development of different recipes for maintaining and improving the psychological well-being of the elderly. Finally, a joint estimate of the mixed survey results will be made using questionnaires of the two types. The respective conclusions will be made on the use of "Personnel Psychology" recipe warehouses, "Positive-Negative" recipe repository, together with the PWBQ recipe warehouses. These deposits will form the basis of future research into methods of maintaining and positive development of the psychological, intellectual, and emotional well-being of the elderly.

There will be investigated measures to improve the well-being of the elderly, which are primarily supported by such means as continuity of the life of the elderly through production and consumption activities, hormonal reflections, and psychological survival.

This continuing activity of the seniors has to be investigated with the thoroughgoing study of their creational and emotional, psychological performance. Therefore, most of the research is oriented to maintain and develop the seniors' progress in their activities inside their habitat and the transition process from one seniority group to another.

The results of our investigations, partly coming from the mission work carried out through this STSM project, will be implemented in the network of all the educational institutions of the Republic of Moldova and in the network of the European universities to exchange the accumulated experience.

10 Conclusion

International organizations and collectives of older adults were selected to investigate the psychological well-being characteristics of the respondents.

A set of questionnaires were researched and selected, which were included in the portfolio of questionnaires measuring the different characteristics of human ecology. These questionnaires are also to be used on older adult samples from the Netherlands and the Republic of Moldova to develop other recipes for maintaining and improving the psychological well-being of the elderly.

The PWBQ questionnaire, used in the investigation of older individuals in international collectives, was accredited as a basic questionnaire in the measurements of the psychological well-being characteristics of the respondents. The primary purpose of applying our instrument of zero-measurement of the psychological well-being, by bringing it to the host institution for validation and appreciation, was fulfilled, so now the instrument is ready to be introduced in the portfolio of measurement instruments of the researchers from the field of Social Psychology and Sociology. The databases collected in the measurement process were used for statistical analyses with sharing, comparison, and evolution methods. Based on collected data on psychological well-being using the PWBQ questionnaire, the statistical methods of maintaining and improving the psychological excitement of the seniors were analyzed from different groups of seniors.

Collected data and analyzed methods will support the methodology and the decisions to be proposed to create a more productive, healthier, and more comfortable society for the elderly.

These deposits will form the basis of future research into methods of maintaining and positive development of the psychological, intellectual, and emotional well-being of the elderly.

The statistical methods used allowed the quantitative-qualitative extrapolation of the characteristics of maintaining and developing the psychological well-being of older adults.

They are investigated, selected, and **proposed** recipes for better psychological well-being and social behavior towards the continuity of **spiritual, creative,** and **emotional** activities in the society of older people. Finally, a joint estimate of the mixed survey results will be made using questionnaires of the two types. The respective conclusions will be made on the use of "Personnel Psychology" recipe warehouses, "Positive-Negative" recipe repository, together with the PWBQ recipe warehouses.

Acknowledgments. This article is based upon work from COST Action CA16226–SHELD-ON–Indoor living space improvement: Smart Habitat for the Elderly, supported by COST (European Cooperation in Science and Technology). More information in www.cost.eu.

References

1. Dikken, J., van den Hoven, R.F.M., van Staalduinen, W.H., Hulsebosch-Janssen, L.M.T. van Hoo, J.: How older people experience the age-friendliness of their city: development of the age-friendly cities and communities questionnaire. Int. J. Environ. Res. Public Health **17**, 6867 (2020). https://doi.org/10.3390/ijerph17186867, https://www.mdpi.com/1660-4601/17/18/6867/pdf
2. Independent Living in rural areas of The Netherlands. https://www.afedemy.eu/en/il-in-rural-nl/. Accessed 10 Feb 2021
3. https://www.afedemy.eu/wp-content/uploads/2019/02/Summary,onderzoeksrapport_af_AFEdemy.pdf
4. https://www.afedemy.eu/wp-content/uploads/2019/02/Summary_onderzoeksrapport_SocialWork_CharlotteKatja_AFEdemy.pdf
5. https://www.afedemy.eu/wp-content/uploads/2019/02/Final_Report_Mobility_Anon.pdf
6. Dikken, J. van den Hoven, R.F.M., van Staalduinen, W.H., Hulsebosch-Janssen, L.M.T., van Hoof, J.: How older people experience the age-friendliness of their city: development of the age-friendly cities and communities questionnaire. Int. J. Environ. Res. Public Health **17**(18), 6867 (2020). https://doi.org/10.3390/ijerph17186867, https://www.afedemy.eu/en/age-friendly-cities-questionnaire/. Accessed 06 Feb 2021

7. https://www.afedemy.eu/en/shafe-releases-position-paper/. Accessed 21 March 2021
8. www.cost.eu. Accessed 10 March 2021
9. Rusnac, S.: Psychology PhD, applying the psychology well-being questionnaire (PWBQ) in the University environment. In: Proceedings of the 3rd Central and Eastern European LUMEN Conference NASHS 2017, pp. 223–224 (2017). ISBN: 978-973-166-461-3

DERCA Tool: A Set of Tests for Analysis of Elderly Dexterity in Information and Communications Technologies

José Paulo Lousado[1]([⊠]) [iD] and Sandra Antunes[2] [iD]

[1] Research Centre in Digital Services (CISeD), Polytechnic Institute of Viseu, Viseu, Portugal
jlousado@estgl.ipv.pt
[2] CI&DEI, Polytechnic Institute of Viseu, Viseu, Portugal

Abstract. The use of information technologies by the elderly remains a problem in today's society, which the pandemic problem by COVID-19 has highlighted, notably in the use of fixed and mobile media such as laptops, smartphones and tablets. The fight against info-exclusion and the promotion of digital literacy is not new. Still, we increasingly realize that the elderly population cannot handle the required skill. This electronic computer equipment has now become part of the daily life of the entire population, particularly the adult population, which has found itself confined and isolated, but which needs to keep in touch with family and friends. The present work began during the pandemic, constituting a set of tests that allow assessing how the continued use of information and communication technologies, namely through computers, mobile phones, and tablets with video conferencing support, the use of camera for photo manipulation, memory games, among other applications, increase the dexterity and cognitive ability of the elderly. The presented model establishes the methodology supported in the software development, a tool that makes it possible to test and evaluate the dexterity and the cognitive development and that is available for free use on various platforms. This tool is called DERCA Tool – that is a set of Analytical tests for Dexterity and Reasoning Capacity Analysis in Elderly.

Keywords: ICT · Computer systems · Mobile devices · Elderly training · Analytical tests

1 Introduction

The use of electronic equipment, such as desktops, laptops, smartphones and tablets, by people of advanced age is a problem that has greatly affected society, focused on combating info-exclusion. Several entities, such as senior universities, try at all costs to offer training to seniors, who, with greater or lesser success, are able to access content on the Internet, with particular emphasis on social networks [1, 2].

Physical training and rehabilitation, maintaining sensory stimuli in the elderly, preventing the ageing process from proceeding in an accelerated manner, in which many of the elderly would eventually lose their motor skills, in particular their mobility [3].

© ICST Institute for Computer Sciences, Social Informatics and Telecommunications Engineering 2021
Published by Springer Nature Switzerland AG 2021. All Rights Reserved
I. M. Pires et al. (Eds.): GOODTECHS 2021, LNICST 401, pp. 244–254, 2021.
https://doi.org/10.1007/978-3-030-91421-9_18

On the other hand, the role of private social solidarity institutions is unequivocally a pillar in supporting active aging, promoting playful activities, physical training, and rehabilitation, maintaining sensory stimuli in the elderly, preventing the ageing process from proceeding in an accelerated manner, in which many of the elderly would eventually lose their motor skills, namely their mobility [3].

Over the past years, corresponding to the evolution of information systems and telecommunications equipment, such as mobile phones, more or less powerful, several authors have been analyzing and evaluating people's behavior in the use of such equipment, showing that natural evolution in children and young people quickly surpasses all expectations, being naturally more able to use information and communication technologies [4, 5].

However, the assessment of dexterity and learning ability in the use of these technologies in the elderly (age > 64) has not been extensively worked, except in some studies that tested the use of tactile input devices such as touch screens, mouse computer, among others, in the execution of games and other computer programs, as referred to in [6].

Some authors have addressed other issues related to the use of technology by the elderly population, mainly in the area of domestic use of protective and safety equipment, remote monitoring, and equipment to help improve the quality of life. Particularly in [7], authors conducted a study in Australia, where they test and evaluate elderly care residents, who can no longer live independently at home due to physical or cognitive disabilities associated with aging. For this, the authors used virtual reality systems to support their playful activities and social interaction.

In another study presented in [8], the authors evaluated the impact that the use of video conferencing by Zoom had on the personal and social lives of the elderly, given the confinement dictated by the restrictions imposed by the pandemic by COVID-19, having tested and evaluated their behavior.

Other studies have focused on the evaluation of the ability of hand movements in people with various pathologies, such as dementia and Alzheimer's [9, 10], not focusing on the technology itself, but rather on how the loss of dexterity in people with these pathologies can be mitigated.

By analyzing several studies and works presented, we found that the assessment of dexterity and cognitive evolution of the elderly through the continued use of information and communication technologies has not been highlighted in the studies carried out. That is why we have focused on this aspect, with one main question: how can we evaluate the dexterity and cognitive evolution of the elderly through the continued use of information and communication technologies? To answer this question, we developed a computer tool, called DERCA Tool, an acronym for Dexterity and Reasoning Capacity Analysis for Elderly people.

2   System Concept

The proposed system in response to the question presented is based on a set of objects and concepts that are naturally associated with the use of information and communication technologies, both by children and young people, and by adults and the elderly, with particular emphasis on the latter group of individuals, aged 65 years and over. Several studies show that adults lose some faculties in terms of mobility and dexterity from this age onwards, requiring some additional therapy, in order to preserve their quality of life [11–13].

The COVID-19-derived pandemic has been causing movement restrictions in the world population, forcing the elderly population to stay at home, being the most vulnerable group to the Sars Cov-2 virus. Consequently, family distancing, leading to many institutionalized older adults who could only see their relatives through the media, by videoconference, most often with the help of support staff and geriatric technicians. This phenomenon is also present in other situations, well before the pandemic, whenever social isolation is required [8, 14]. Thus, to answer the question posed, the system we propose must respond to a set of functional and non-functional requirements, serving the population that we intend to analyze and evaluate.

2.1 Functional Requirements

The system must respond to the following set of requirements:

- Color test: considering that age, vision, and color distinction tend to decrease, a test should be created that aims to use colors, with some degree of randomness, as a differentiating element in the process of carrying out the test.
- Number test: considering that one of the most frequent current activities of the population, namely the elderly, is related to the use of numbers in accounts, dates, hours, and other matters, a test with numbers should be created with some randomness in the presentation.
- Symbol test: considering that geometric figures are present on people's days, circles, rectangles, triangles, and the combination between them, a test with symbols should be created that should appear randomly.
- Timer: the system should allow counting of the time it takes to resolve a test.
- Demo mode: the system must have the training mode, allowing users to test the application without counting time, allowing the user to familiarize themselves with the system.
- Recording of results: the values obtained for each user must be stored in memory for later viewing and archiving.

Figure 1 shows the diagram of use cases with the specific roles assigned to the actor "researcher" who can view the recorded data. The "user" actor refers to the user who will be performing the test, and the system includes the start-time mechanism whenever the user starts the test. When starting the test, the objects must be randomly arranged so that positional tampering cannot occur, avoiding bias.

2.2 Non-functional Requirements

Alongside functional requirements, we must pay special attention to non-functional requirements, such as:

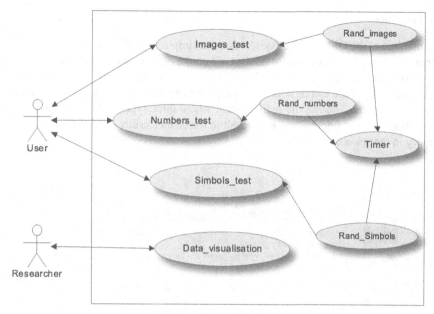

Fig.1. Use case diagram.

- Accessibility: the system must be accessible to people with different levels of movement capacity and manual dexterity.
- Usability: the system must be easy to use, bearing in mind that the system's users are elderly who will have little or no digital literacy, and therefore it must be intuitive.
- Multiplatform: The system must be multiplatform, working in different environments and operating systems, to avoid restrictions on its use.

Considering the target audience, small mobile devices are naturally not recommended for carrying out the test since they will be challenging to use in terms of pressure on graphic objects. Therefore, it is recommended to use it on tablets or computers with screens of at least 10".

3 System Prototype

In order to comply with the goals defined concerning functional and non-functional requirements, the prototype of the system was developed, to answer the question posed at the outset. Thus, with this prototype, we hope to obtain information that allows us to assess the dexterity and reasoning ability of the elderly who perform the tests.

The system will be made available free of charge in online and Windows versions. It can be used freely in studies that the scientific community intends to perform, with due reference to the authors. The full application can be freely accessed and run in http://filesjpl.000webhostapp.com/app. Additionally, the full HTML5 application can be downloaded from: http://filesjpl.000webhostapp.com/app/psico_tests_v1_en.zip.

3.1 Interface

The interface of the DERCA Tool system is quite simple, as defined in the requirements, so that elderly users do not have to read a user guide, options, parameterization, among other more complex processes. The anonymity of the electronically collected data is guaranteed, and a code can be added for each user, which will remain active throughout the session. Figure 2 shows the main screen, where three types of tests are presented: colors, numbers and figures, and it is possible to see the results obtained and stored in memory in the session.

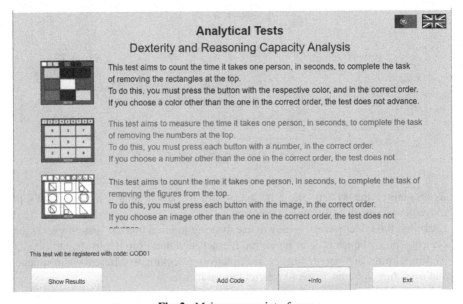

Fig. 2. Main program interface.

In Fig. 3, we show the interface of the tests related to primary and considerably different colors.

This test aims to count the time it takes one person, in seconds, to complete the task of removing the color rectangles at the top. The user must press the button with the respective color and in the correct order. If the user chooses a color other than the right order, the test does not advance.

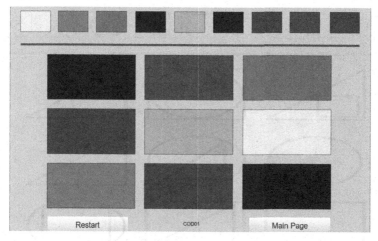

Fig. 3. Random color test interface.

Figure 4 shows the test interface with numbers, where the numerical layout is generated randomly. The order at the top is not the natural order, so there is some difficulty in memorizing. Otherwise, the test was too obvious.

Like present in the previous screen, this test aims to measure the time it takes one person, in seconds, to complete the task of removing the numbers at the top.

3	9	2	5	7	6	8	1	4

2	9	8
6	5	3
4	7	1

Restart   COD01   Main Page

Fig. 4. Random number test interface.

Figure 5 shows the test interface with figures, where the figure layout is randomly generated. This is the test with the most significant margin to be changed and may use image bank in the future.

Like present in the previous screen, this test aims to measure the time it takes one person, in seconds, to complete the task to remove figures at the top.

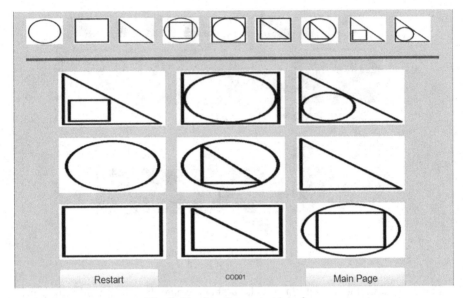

Fig. 5. Random figures test interface.

In Fig. 6, we have the interface where we can visualize the obtained data. These data can later be selected, copied, and pasted into a spreadsheet for statistical treatment, as shown in Fig. 7.

Results

codeID	Test	Value(s)
COD01	images	14
COD01	images	20
COD01	numbers	11
COD01	numbers	12
COD01	color	9
COD01	color	11
COD02	numbers	10
COD02	numbers	11
COD02	color	7
COD02	images	15

Press <Ctrl>+A and <Ctrl>+C to select the table and Copy to the memory. You can paste data directly into Excel worksheet.

Main Page

Fig. 6. Results screen, where data can be copied to the memory.

3.2 Data Analysis

After data export, the user conducting the study will have the possibility to analyze the evolution evidenced by the elderly in the use of computer tools, comparing the data obtained in two or more evaluation moments, also comparing the results with the test group and the control group.

It should be noted that the system can be easily adapted to perform dexterity and cognitive development tests using mathematical calculus and other forms of data presentation. However, in this version, we only intend to show the system's potential for the dexterity tests in the elderly population.

It should be noted that the target audience of these studies will be conditioned to a set of variables that extrapolate the objectives and goals of the proposed system, since factors such as age, the capacity of movements, or the psycho-motor capacity, among others, may condition the results, therefore the studies should be directed to the person, preferably.

This tool should be used in conjunction with other qualitative analysis tools and preferably accompanied by researchers from multidisciplinary fields, such as sociologists and psychologists, and is not a tool for obtaining isolated results from simple tests without a control group nor iterations within a time space.

	A	B	C	D	E
1	Results				
2	codeID	Test	Value(s)		
3	COD01	images	14		
4	COD01	images	20		
5	COD01	numbers	11		
6	COD01	numbers	12		
7	COD01	color	9		
8	COD01	color	11		
9	COD02	numbers	10		
10	COD02	numbers	11		
11	COD02	color	7		
12	COD02	images	15		
13					
14					

Fig. 7. Results copied to Excel spreadsheet.

4 System Validation

In order to validate the system presented we propose an application scenario, showing how a study can be conducted in the future using this tool.

4.1 Flowchart

In Fig. 8, we show the conduction flowchart of a study using the DERCA Tool.

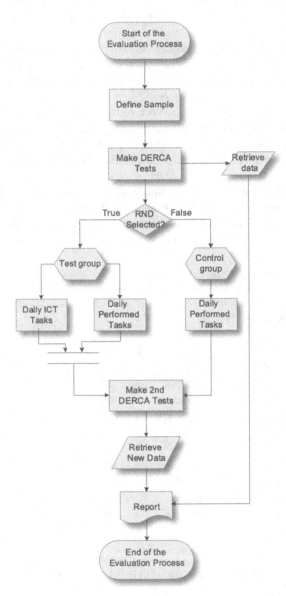

Fig. 8. Conduction Flowchart of a dexterity study with DERCA Tool.

4.2 Application Scenario

Let us consider an A entity that intends to assess the dexterity in terms of the use of computer means of the elderly who are assisted by a social solidarity institution B, to whom it plans to provide computer equipment to communicate with the family.

For this purpose, entity A selects a group of N users to whom, after having shown and explained the study's objective and collected informed consent, starts to perform the tests present in the DERCA Tool system.

Each test, of colors, numbers, and figures were performed three times to obtain the average time to complete the test tasks. Of these N users, the test group was selected with 50% at random. For two months, they began to use computer devices daily, similar to those used in the test, to perform tasks related to word processing, memory games, among others, in addition to regular maintenance and other activities.

The other 50% maintained their daily maintenance activity, physiotherapy, and recreational activities, thus constituting the control group.

At the end of these two months, entity A's team passed the tests using the same methodology for measuring the average times for carrying out the difficulties with the DERCA Tool system.

After obtaining the results, each test group member should be compared in terms of average testing times, allowing it to validate whether the skill in terms of using the computer equipment has benefited or not from the fact that, for two months, the user's test group have used computer equipment.

This application scenario will allow entity A to propose to institution B a solution in terms of the use of IT equipment, that improves users' performance in the use of this type of equipment. Information and communication technologies are currently quite useful because COVID-19 has led to a physical estrangement of institutionalized elderly persons from their other family, often being the only way to communicate.

5 Conclusion and Future Work

In conclusion, we can state that the system presented here has great potential in conducting studies based on dexterity tests in the elderly population. The natural aging process continually degrades its motor and psychic faculties, diminishing their dexterity's abilities.

On the other hand, computer illiteracy on the part of the target audience, combined with advanced age, makes this type of system and studies a real challenge for their authors, always aiming to improve people's quality of life.

The concern with making the tool available for free on various platforms is especially aimed at the management teams of social solidarity institutions, who may see this tool as an ally for decision-making in terms of adopting a specific information and communication technology.

As future work, we intend to make the application dynamic, with a test database, differentiated and stratified by sectors of activity, adapted to different target audiences, and allowing direct export of data to standard formats, namely CSV.

Also, in future terms, it is intended to implement a set of parameters that will allow a behavior adjusted to different users and various behaviors in terms of randomness.

Last but not least, to support other languages, making the application open source and with customization in this parameter can count on the collaboration of members of the community that support the opensource software.

Acknowledgments. This work is funded by National Funds through the FCT - Foundation for Science and Technology, I.P., within the scope of the project Refª UIDB/05583/2020. Furthermore, we would like to thank the Research Centre in Digital Services (CISeD) and the Polytechnic of Viseu for their support.

References

1. Teixeira, É., Galinha, S.M.G.A.: A Importância Da Universidade Sénior Para Um Envelhecimento Ativo: Universidade Sénior De Machico - Um Estudo De Caso Na Ram. Rev. da UIIPS. **5**, 142–159 (2017)
2. Oh, S.S., Kim, K.-A., Kim, M., Oh, J., Chu, S.H., Choi, J.: Measurement of digital literacy among older adults: systematic review. J. Med. Internet Res. **23**, e26145 (2021). https://doi.org/10.2196/26145
3. Liotta, G., et al.: Active ageing in Europe: adding healthy life to years. Front. Med. **5**, 8–11 (2018). https://doi.org/10.3389/fmed.2018.00123
4. Park, B., Chang, H., Park, S.S.: Adoption of digital devices for children education: Korean case. Telematics Inform. **38**, 247–256 (2019). https://doi.org/10.1016/j.tele.2018.11.002
5. Eutsler, L., Antonenko, P.: Predictors of portable technology adoption intentions to support elementary children reading. Educ. Inf. Technol. **23**(5), 1971–1994 (2018). https://doi.org/10.1007/s10639-018-9700-z
6. Wood, E., Willoughby, T., Rushing, A., Bechtel, L., Gilbert, J.: Use of computer input devices by older adults. J. Appl. Gerontol. **24**, 419–438 (2005). https://doi.org/10.1177/0733464805278378
7. Baker, S., et al.: Evaluating the use of interactive virtual reality technology with older adults living in residential aged care. Inf. Process. Manag. **57**, 102105 (2020). https://doi.org/10.1016/j.ipm.2019.102105
8. Daly, J.R., et al.: Health impacts of the stay-at-home order on community-dwelling older adults and how technologies may help: focus group study. JMIR Aging **4**, e25779 (2021). https://doi.org/10.2196/25779
9. Proud, E., et al.: Hand dexterity assessment in Parkinson's disease: construct validity of the 9-Hole peg test for the more affected hand. Disabil. Rehabil. 1–5 (2020). https://doi.org/10.1080/09638288.2020.1754474
10. Proud, E.L., Miller, K.J., Bilney, B., Morris, M.E., McGinley, J.L.: Construct validity of the 9-Hole Peg Test and Purdue Pegboard Test in people with mild to moderately severe Parkinson's disease. Physiotherapy **107**, 202–208 (2020). https://doi.org/10.1016/j.physio.2019.12.002
11. Rule, K., et al.: Purdue manual dexterity testing: a cohort study of community-dwelling elderly. J. hand Ther. Off. J. Am. Soc. Hand Ther. **34**, 116–120 (2021). https://doi.org/10.1016/j.jht.2019.12.006
12. Pew, R.W., Van Hemel, S.B.: Technology for Adaptive Aging (2004). https://doi.org/10.17226/10857
13. Pilotto, A., Boi, R., Petermans, J.: Technology in geriatrics. Age Ageing. **47**, 771–774 (2018). https://doi.org/10.1093/ageing/afy026
14. Peek, S.T.M., et al.: Older adults' reasons for using technology while aging in place. Gerontology **62**, 226–237 (2016). https://doi.org/10.1159/000430949

Building Smart Healthy Inclusive Environments for All Ages with Citizens

Willeke van Staalduinen[1]([✉]) [ID], Carina Dantas[2] [ID], Joost van Hoof[3,4] [ID],
and Andrzej Klimczuk[5] [ID]

[1] AFEdemy, Academy on Age-Friendly Environments in Europe BV, Buurtje 2, 2802 BE
Gouda, The Netherlands
willeke@afedemy.eu

[2] SHINE 2Europe Lda, Rua Câmara Pestana, Lote 3 – 1 DF, 3030-163 Coimbra, Portugal
carinadantas@shine2.eu

[3] The Hague University of Applied Sciences, Johanna Westerdijkplein 75, 2521 EN Den Haag,
The Netherlands
j.vanhoof@hhs.nl

[4] Wrocław University of Environmental and Life Sciences, ul. Grunwaldzka 55,
50-357 Wrocław, Poland

[5] SGH Warsaw School of Economics, al. Niepodległości 162, 02-554 Warsaw, Poland
aklimcz@sgh.waw.pl

https://www.afedemy.eu/, https://shine2.eu/, http://www.hhs.nl/,
http://www.sgh.waw.pl

Abstract. The paper provides an introduction to the public discourse around the notion of smart healthy inclusive environments. First, the basic ideas are explained and related to citizen participation in the context of implementation of a "society for all ages" concept disseminated by the United Nations. Next, the text discusses selected initiatives of the European Commission in the field of intergenerational programming and policies as well as features of the COST Action NET4Age-Friendly: Smart Healthy Age-Friendly Environments (SHAFE). The following sections are focused on studying and discussing examples of projects and methodologies that have been aimed at: empowering facilitators of smart healthy inclusive environments, empowering citizens to deal with health emergencies, and supporting older people's voices. The conclusion covers selected recommendations for entities of public policy on ageing (ageing policy) as well as potential directions for further research.

Keywords: Age-friendly cities and communities · Citizen participation ·
Inclusive environments · Intergenerational Programmes and Policies · Smart
Healthy Age-Friendly Environments (SHAFE) · Society for all ages

1 Introduction

Smart, healthy, and inclusive environments can help improve and support independent living throughout the course of life, regardless of age, gender, health status, disabilities,

I. M. Pires et al. (Eds.): GOODTECHS 2021, LNICST 401, pp. 255–263, 2021.
https://doi.org/10.1007/978-3-030-91421-9_19

cultural differences, and personal choices. In order to develop and design these environments, it is of the utmost importance to include the people who are to live in these designed surroundings and should ideally accept the use of the proposed solutions. In this contribution, we explore several approaches to citizen participation in order to create smart healthy inclusive solutions and environments, including solutions, programs, schemes, products, and services for all ages. The methodologies of involvement and engagement are acknowledged, and—if appropriate—success factors and lessons learned are identified. At first, a short overview of the smart healthy age-friendly environments (SHAFE) notion is given. This is followed by a paragraph on citizens' participation in the context of implementation of a "society for all ages" concept promoted by the United Nations. Thereafter, several projects are presented, methodologies of participation highlighted, results described, and conclusions drawn.

2 Defining the Smart Healthy Inclusive Environments

The challenges of various sectors, such as the information and communications technologies (ICTs) sector, the building and urban planning industry, health and social care, as well as those of citizens and their communities, are interlinked. Responding to these challenges will foster awareness and support the creation and implementation of smart, healthy, and inclusive environments for present and future generations that enable them to learn, grow, work, participate in society and enjoy a healthy life, benefiting from the use of digital innovations, accessibility solutions and adaptable support models in the European context.

The local community is the physical, social, and cultural ecosystem closest to people, which is built on relationships of trust, sharing, solidarity and intimacy, where people find social, cultural and identity references, socialise and live their daily lives. The objective conditions of the environment (maintenance, accessibility, mobility, safety, and comfort) affect the quality of life and well-being of citizens, particularly in the context of environmental challenges such as climate change and thus affect the whole community.

Thus, smart healthy inclusive environments, also described as smart healthy age-friendly environments (SHAFE), require a comprehensive approach that optimises the design of social and physical environments, which is supported by digital tools and services, which allows providing better health and social care as well as promotes not only independent living but also equity and active participation in society. This approach follows the United Nations' line-up, with the Sustainable Development Goals (SDGs) intended to be achieved by the year 2030 [1], stating that sustainable environments for all ages represent the basis for ensuring a better future for the entire world population and addressing most of the growing issues of the ageing population. They are in particular related to Goal 3 ("Ensure healthy lives and promote well-being for all at all ages") and Goal 11 ("Make cities inclusive, safe, resilient and sustainable") and can be understood as an approach broader than other ideas used in the literature such as ambient assisted living (AAL), smart and age-friendly cities and communities (SAFCC), and "ageing in place 2.0" (AIP2.0) [2].

3 Citizen Participation in the Context of Implementation a "Society for All Ages" Concept

In order to develop the above mentioned inclusive, smart, and healthy environments, citizen involvement and cooperation is particularly important. Having people's voices heard during the conceptualisation and design phases of the development of the living environment fit the objectives of the intergenerational policies related to the United Nations concept of "society for all ages" and its implementation by the World Health Organization's (WHO) Global Network on Age-Friendly Cities and Communities (GNAFCC). Citizen participation clearly pertains to the distinguished domains of age-friendliness described as buildings and housing, social participation, and social inclusion [3, 4].

Van Hoof et al. [4] took the widely used concept of the "ladder of citizen participation" by Arnstein [5] as a starting point in shaping various roles that citizens can play. Arnstein described eight roles for citizens, varying from nonparticipation (in forms such as manipulation and therapy) through tokenism to citizen power. Tokenism is divided into informing (about citizen' rights, but often the one-way flow of information), consultation (e.g., ask for opinions in surveys, neighbourhood meetings or hearings), and placation (citizens are granted a limited degree of influence in boards or commissions). Higher levels of participation grouped under the notion of citizen power are divided into partnership (shared planning and decision-making responsibilities through structures such as policy boards), delegated power (some degree of control is transferred to citizens), and citizen control (participants or residents can govern a programme or an institution and be in full charge of policy and managerial aspects).

Additional research on citizen participation by Van Hoof et al. [4] showed that involvement is not automatically a guarantee for success. For example, due to a limited number of active participants, lack of required skills to participate or not representing the target group, success can be rather limited. Van Hoof et al. further identified the factors that impact the participation of citizens in a positive manner, such as the provision of regular feedback, the full commitment of the involved organisations, and the usage of understandable and inclusive language. Having these observations in mind, the following sections are providing discussions and examples of various approaches to citizen participation related to SHAFE.

3.1 Selected Initiatives of the European Commission in the Field of Intergenerational Programming and Policies

In 2012, the European Commission announced the European Year for Active Ageing and Solidarity between Generations and took the initiative to launch a bottom-up approach to involve citizens and organisations' actions and opinions in the field of public policy on ageing (ageing policy) [6]. It led to the creation of the European Innovation Partnership on Active and Healthy Ageing (EIPonAHA) [7]. At first, it was well-received, and many parties joined the network. Over the years, the broad interest slowly faded but the main challenges recognised remained unsolved, for example, the need for scaling up and transferring across the countries, regions, and communities the best practices and solutions such as social innovations and technological innovations in ageing [8, 9]. Nevertheless, several networks that had their origin in the EIPonAHA, such as the

Stakeholders Network on Smart Healthy Age-Friendly Environments (SHAFE) [10] and the Reference Sites Collaborative Network [11], still continue to operate.

To bring the European Union (EU) citizens' involvement alive again, the European Commission, at the beginning of the year 2021, launched a new cooperation network titled the Active and Healthy Living in the Digital World. This network is a part of the Futurium platform that started already in the year 2011 as a foresight project aimed at participatory policymaking, crowdsourcing of ideas, and discussing EU policies [12]. One of the dedicated areas within this emerging network is dedicated to age-friendly environments.

On a different note, the President of the European Commission, Ms Ursula von der Leyen, also at the beginning of the year 2021, took the initiative to launch a bottom-up approach initiative: co-designing the New European Bauhaus [13]. The New European Bauhaus proposes to focus the conversations on the places that EU citizens inhabit and on the relationship with natural environments beyond the built space. It is a practical approach to discover beautiful, sustainable, and inclusive ways of living and to use them to inspire our way forward. EU citizens are invited to join the conversation and are asked to share their thoughts on future environments and places to be like. Moreover, if it was their neighbourhood, how should that look like, feel like, and work like.

3.2 COST Action NET4Age-Friendly: Smart Healthy Age-Friendly Environments

The concept behind SHAFE has inspired several projects and initiatives, including one of the most recent initiatives supported by the European Cooperation in Science and Technology: NET4Age-Friendly (2020–2024; COST Action 19136), which is an international interdisciplinary network on health and well-being in an age-friendly digital world focused on the promotion of social inclusion, independent living, and active and healthy ageing in society.

Participating scholars, practitioners, and stakeholders from the business and third sector work in four thematic groups on user-centred inclusive design, integrated health and well-being pathways, digital solutions, and large-scale sustainable implementation, and on impact and sustainability (including policy development, funding forecast, and cost-benefit evaluations). In order to synthesise and critically examine the results of these four themes and existing practices of SHAFE, a fifth working group will develop a reference framework with guidelines, standards, and practices (success factors and lessons learned) [14].

The main purpose of described COST Action is to build and nurture local, regional, or national ecosystems in each participating country. Ecosystems consist of citizens, public authorities, businesses, non-governmental organisations (NGOs), and research and development entities. These ecosystems aim to foster the implementation of SHAFE with the support of the above-mentioned working groups.

3.3 Empowering Facilitators of Smart Healthy Inclusive Environments

Erasmus+ is the EU's programme to support education, training, youth, and sport in Europe in multinational consortia [15]. These areas are key to support citizens' personal and professional development. High quality, inclusive education and training, as well as informal and non-formal learning, ultimately equip participants of all ages with the qualifications and skills needed for their meaningful participation in a democratic society, intercultural understanding, and successful transition in the labour market. Within the frame of Erasmus+, training and education is developed to empower facilitators to implement smart healthy inclusive environments in their community.

Projects such as "Hands-on SHAFE" [16], "Educational game BIG" [17], "Bridge the Gap!" [18], and "DESIgn for all methods to cREate age-friendly housing" (DESIRE) [19] supported by the Erasmus+ programme include adult learners in the field of inclusive environments. "Hands-on SHAFE" aims to deliver online training packages for informal learning experiences and hands-on tools to improve the skills of people of all ages and especially seeks to enable persons with lower skills or qualifications to choose and implement SHAFE in their own homes or neighbourhoods. In this way, the project fosters and promotes social inclusion for people of all ages and genders, including people with cognitive or physical impairments or disabilities. It also aims to enable citizens to become innovators and trailblazers in their own neighbourhoods or to become entrepreneurs in the field of SHAFE services and products.

The educational game "Building Inclusive environments for all Generations" (BIG) elaborates further on the training about SHAFE by developing an online game. The player can meet and solve the challenges of characters during the play, such as inaccessible housing for a wheelchair, loading goods in a car while taking care of a child, or visiting a restaurant with impaired sight. The project will also develop a workshop methodology to use the game in joint training settings.

The "Bridge the Gap!" project focuses on the training of older people to create and improve their own living environments to support independent living and participation in society. On the one hand, the training offers traditional means to advocate their interests. On the other hand, it will mainly focus on the capacity building of older adults to use digital skills. Such digital actions include accessing social media, building online advocacy accounts, or sharing photos to express to stakeholders and decision-makers specific local needs to improve the local living environment.

The DESIRE project is developed by an international partnership involving four countries working on a design for all (D4ALL) concept applied to age-friendly housing. DESIRE aims to provide professionals in the building industry as well as furniture and home furnishings sector with the tools and skills to apply D4ALL methods as an integral part of the design process, with the aim to create or adapt age-friendly housing as a solution for the well-being, comfort and autonomy of older adults or people in situation of dependency at home. The project will develop an innovative training course on D4ALL to meet the emotional, cognitive, and social needs of older adults while driving new opportunities in the habitat sector, fostering interactions and knowledge exchange in the design process between cross-cutting fields such as science, social sciences, and arts.

3.4 Empowering Citizens to Deal with Health Emergencies

Erasmus+ project "STEP_UP" [20] intends to develop a training tool for social care and community stakeholders, where they are introduced to the impact of behaviours in the spread of a pandemic or emergency situation and trained, through gaming strategies, to prevent and cope, being empowered to protect and promote well-being in their communities.

The core of this project will be an educational game, which can also be used as a recreational game for the common public. In "STEP_UP," the players will play with the aim to stop a pandemic from spreading. A list of measures will be displayed, and the player needs to learn about them in order to be able to choose those that would help to impede the virus spread without damaging the economy or causing societal anger. This game will also help people better understand and follow governmental measures and set aside evidence-based information and facts from myths, fake news, and other forms of misinformation or disinformation.

3.5   Case Study of Supporting Older People's Voice: Senior-Friendly the Hague

Since 2015, the municipality of The Hague is a member of the WHO's Global Network on Age-Friendly Cities and Communities [21]. Member cities of GNAFCC follow a 5-year cycle of planning, implementation, and evaluation in order to make their respective city or community age-friendly. The Hague recently finalised their first cycle by performing a broad survey among older people (65+) to express their opinions on the age-friendliness of the city. Overall, the older citizens of The Hague value the age-friendliness of their city as well as perceives it as sufficient. They give high scores to their own homes. On the contrary, outdoor spaces and buildings were scored significantly lower. People in the situation of having a lower income, health and mobility issues are less satisfied.

In order to better involve older adults in local policymaking, the municipality facilitates three ways of citizens' involvement. At first, it subsidises the overarching Older People's Council of The Hague (in Dutch: *Stedelijke Ouderencommissie*; SOC) [22–24]. Secondly, it facilitates and supports the building and maintenance of a local ecosystem titled the Knowledge Platform Age-Friendly The Hague. In this platform, older citizens, scholars, public health administration, municipal policymakers, and social enterprises (social small and medium-sized enterprises; SMEs) meet on a regular basis to exchange ongoing research and to look for cooperation opportunities in the field of the municipal Action Plan Age-Friendly The Hague (2020–2022). The final support to hear the voice of older people in The Hague is the fostering of the active involvement of an older people's panel: a broad panel of at least 1,500 older adults (out of 77,000 people aged 65 and over) who can be consulted on a large variety of municipal topics.

4   Conclusion: Citizens' Participation in Smart Healthy Inclusive Environments Explored

From this broad overview of fieldwork, it has been possible to explore various perspectives of inclusive environments, their challenges, and the needs to be addressed. Some of the lessons learned in the various projects include that citizen participation is fully recognised as essential (Table 1). However, a long way is still necessary to make it structured, constant, and comprehensive.

Table 1. The Comparison of Selected Initiatives of Citizen Participation Related to the Implementation of a "Society for All Ages" Concept

Initiatives	Strengths	Weaknesses	Challenges
European Commission's Initiatives	- Combining bottom-up and top-down approaches to ageing policy - Focus on combining population ageing with digitalisation processes and the development of diverse environments	- Unclear monitoring and evaluation of results - Dependent on funding programmes with priorities on specific sectoral policies (e.g., ICT and AI-focused economic entities)	- Scaling up of the best practices and policy transfer across the countries, regions, and communities
COST Action NET4Age-Friendly	- Bottom-up international and interdisciplinary network - Providing support in the form of guidelines, standards, and practices	- Establishing sustainability for the network after the project period	- Building multilevel ecosystems with a quadruple helix of citizens, public authorities, companies, and researchers
Projects: "Hands-on SHAFE," "BIG," "Bridge the Gap!," and "DESIRE"	- Delivering training packages and tools related to age-friendly homes or neighbourhoods - Entrepreneurship promotion	- Limited scale of innovative solutions	- Further dissemination and development of schemes
Project "STEP_UP"	- Empowering citizens to deal with health emergencies	- Monitoring and evaluation of results after the COVID-19 pandemic	- Extending focus on the fight with misinformation or disinformation
Senior-Friendly The Hague	- Broad set of initiatives to involve older people in implementation and governance of age-friendly city's idea	- Establishing sustainability of the older people's council, the knowledge platform, and an older people's panel	- Citizens' involvement is dependent on their socioeconomic status

The call for active citizenship and ownership of the transformation of society is, on the one hand, a gift to the citizens. Nevertheless, at the same time, this call is also a burden in terms of commitment and involvement, which currently, not all are prepared to deliver. To overcome these barriers, learning experiences focusing on older adults in Erasmus+ training activities and games as well as knowledge platforms and ecosystems do support the awareness of older adults to uptake and realise their own lives in their environments. The initiatives that foster more active citizenship and those who call for the participation of several age and societal groups are at the core of this citizen empowerment need, essential to create a better and fairer society for all. This development just started.

Acknowledgements. This publication is based upon work from COST Action CA19136 "International Interdisciplinary Network on Smart Healthy Age-friendly Environments," supported by COST (European Cooperation in Science and Technology). For more details go to: www.net4age.eu The publication received financial support in the form of an ITC Conference Grant awarded by the COST Action CA19136 to Andrzej Klimczuk.

References

1. United Nations: Sustainable Development Goals. www.un.org/sustainabledevelopment/. Accessed 26 April 2021
2. Klimczuk, A., Tomczyk, Ł.: Smart, age-friendly cities and communities: the emergence of socio-technological solutions in the central and Eastern Europe. In: Flórez-Revuelta, F., Chaaraoui, A.A. (eds.) Ambient Assisted Living: Technologies and Applications, pp. 335–359. The Institution of Engineering and Technology, London (2016). https://doi.org/10.1049/PBHE006E_ch17
3. World Health Organization: Global Age-Friendly Cities: A Guide. World Health Organization, Geneva (2007)
4. van Hoof, J., et al.: The participation of older people in the concept and design phases of housing in the netherlands: a theoretical overview. Healthcare 9(3), 301 (2021). https://doi.org/10.3390/healthcare9030301
5. Arnstein, S.R.: A ladder of Citizen participation. J. Am. Inst. Plan. **35**(4), 216–224 (1969). https://doi.org/10.1080/01944366908977225
6. Klimczuk, A.: Economic Foundations for Creative Ageing Policy, Volume II: Putting Theory into Practice. Palgrave Macmillan, New York, Basingstoke (2017). https://doi.org/10.1057/978-1-137-53523-8
7. European Innovation Partnership on Active and Healthy Ageing. https://ec.europa.eu/eip/ageing/home_en.html. Accessed 26 April 2021
8. Dantas, C., van Staalduinen, W., Jegundo, A., Ganzarain, J., Ortet, S.: Aging policy transfer, adoption, and change. In: Gu, D., Dupre, M.E. (eds.) Encyclopedia of Gerontology and Population Aging: Living Edition, pp. 1–6. Springer, Cham (2020). https://doi.org/10.1007/978-3-319-69892-2_216-2
9. Klimczuk, A., Tomczyk, Ł. (eds.): Perspectives and Theories of Social Innovation for Ageing Population. Frontiers Media, Lausanne (2020). https://doi.org/10.3389/978-2-88963-620-4
10. Stakeholders Network on Smart Healthy Age-Friendly Environments. https://en.caritascoimbra.pt/shafe/. Accessed 26 April 2021
11. Reference Sites Collaborative Network. https://ec.europa.eu/eip/ageing/reference-sites_en.html. Accessed 26 April 2021

12. Futurium. https://futurium.ec.europa.eu/en/. Accessed 26 April 2021
13. New European Bauhaus. https://europa.eu/new-european-bauhaus/index_en. Accessed 26 April 2021
14. COST Action 19136 International Interdisciplinary Network on Smart Healthy Age-Friendly Environments. www.net4age.eu. Accessed 26 April 2021
15. Erasmus+. https://erasmusplus.eu. Accessed 26 April 2021
16. Hands-on training and tools on smart healthy age-friendly environments. www.hands-on-sha fe.eu. Accessed 26 April 2021
17. Educational game: Building Inclusive environments for all Generations. www.big-game.eu. Accessed 26 April 2021
18. Bridge the Gap!. https://bridgethegap-project.eu. Accessed 26 April 2021
19. DESIgn for all methods to cREate age-friendly housing (DESIRE). https://innorenew.eu/pro ject/design-methods-create-age-friendly-housing-desire/. Accessed 26 April 2021
20. Stop Epidemic Growth through Learning, STEP_UP. https://stepupgame.eu. Accessed 26 April 2021
21. World Health Organization Age-Friendly World: The Hague. https://extranet.who.int/agefri endlyworld/network/the-hague/. Accessed 26 April 2021
22. van Hoof, J., van den Hoven, R.F.M., Hess, M., van Staalduinen, W.H., Hulsebosch-Janssen, L.M.T., Dikken, J.: How Older People Experience the Age-Friendliness of The Hague: A Quantitative Study (unpublished manuscript) (2021)
23. Dikken, J., van den Hoven, R.F.M., van Staalduinen, W.H., Hulsebosch-Janssen, L.M.T., van Hoof, J.: How older people experience the age-friendliness of their city: development of the age-friendly cities and communities questionnaire. Int. J. Environ. Res. Public Health 17(18), 6867 (2020). https://doi.org/10.3390/ijerph17186867
24. van Hoof, J., Dikken, J., Buttiġieġ, S.C., van den Hoven, R.F.M., Kroon, E., Marston, H.R.: Age-friendly cities in the Netherlands: an explorative study of facilitators and hindrances in the built environment and ageism in design. Indoor Built Environ. 29(3), 417–437 (2020). https://doi.org/10.1177/1420326X19857216

Healthcare

The New Era of Technology Applied to Cardiovascular Patients: State-of-the-Art and Questionnaire Applied for a System Proposal

María Vanessa Villasana[1]([envelope]) [iD], Juliana Sá[2,3] [iD], Ivan Miguel Pires[4,5,6] [iD], and Carlos Albuquerque[6] [iD]

[1] Centro Hospitalar do Baixo Vouga, 3810-164 Aveiro, Portugal
`72152@chbv.min-saude.pt`
[2] Faculty of Health Sciences, Universidade da Beira Interior, 6200-506 Covilhã, Portugal
`julianasa@fcsaude.ubi.pt`
[3] Centro Hospital e Universitário do Porto, 4099-001 Oporto, Portugal
[4] Instituto de Telecomunicações, Universidade da Beira Interior, Covilhã, Portugal
`impires@it.ubi.pt`
[5] Computer Science Department, Polytechnic Institute of Viseu, Viseu, Portugal
[6] UICISA: E Research Centre, School of Health, Polytechnic Institute of Viseu, Viseu, Portugal
`calbuquerque@essv.ipv.pt`

Abstract. The advance of technology allows daily monitoring of people with cardiovascular diseases. It enables patient empowerment, making them increasingly autonomous and responsible for their health by using digital tools and solutions. The purpose of this study is to idealize a system individualized to the patient with cardiovascular diseases, including monitoring, follow-up, treatments, and communication with healthcare professionals. A review of the existing literature was carried out, identifying the need to understand patients' needs and preferences to adapt the digital solutions. Therefore, a questionnaire was developed to characterize patients' preferences, showing that patients prefer to use their personal devices, such as mobile phones, due to their ease of use and commodity. Most patients would like to receive information through a mobile application. They also agreed that teleconsultation and telemonitoring helped to improve their health status.

Keywords: Patient-empowerment · Cardiovascular diseases · Mobile devices · Telemonitoring

1 Introduction

According to World Health Organization (WHO), cardiovascular diseases have a high prevalence worldwide, particularly in the middle- and low-income countries [24]. These diseases are mainly related to unhealthy behaviors that lead to the emergence of chronic

I. M. Pires et al. (Eds.): GOODTECHS 2021, LNICST 401, pp. 267–278, 2021.
https://doi.org/10.1007/978-3-030-91421-9_20

diseases, such as hypertension, diabetes, obesity, and cardiac failure [10]. Several reports describe the positive impact of technological equipment to promote the control of these diseases showing positive health results [4, 13], and this use is increasingly recommended for clinical practice.

Technology is currently entering daily lives, taking part in daily routines and behavior habits [5, 6]. The advancement of technology enables the possibility to monitor patients daily and promote the creation of medical assessment tools that are continuous, reliable, and accurate [1]. Thus, the medical assessment is not limited to a punctual evaluation in the clinic but translates the real values of [22]. The use of technology and telemonitoring also allows patients to have greater autonomy to manage their own health, with greater empowerment and a patient-centered approach [11, 23].

There is extensive research around this topic, but no combined technologies are used for a specific group of diseases. However, the number of studies related to remote patient monitoring, patient care using telemedicine, and the development of patient literacy is increasing [9].

Mainly, small research studies created systems for specific diseases, but they are not available in the market. For example, the authors of [16–18] argued about developing a system for blood pressure telemonitoring. They verified that it promotes the compliance to treatment, intensification, and optimization of medication use, improvement of life quality, reduction of risk of developing cardiovascular complications, and cost-saving with the help of mobile devices (i.e., Smartphones and smartwatches).

Regarding heart failure, some studies promoted the use of e-Health technologies for the telecare, remote monitoring of hemodynamic implantable devices, home monitoring of cardiovascular implantable electronic devices, and telerehabilitation, revealing robust capabilities for life-threatening deterioration, helping heart failure patients to avoid seeking medical assistance in hospitals, and revealing that home-based telerehabilitation is effective with high adherence and reduced mortality [7, 21].

Due to the high cost of the medical solutions and the rare validation of the developed solutions, the current solutions for monitoring blood pressure have limited value and benefits in hypertensive patients related to the less acceptance of these solutions [3].

This study aims to understand users' preferences in a system to monitor and control cardiovascular diseases. Furthermore, it intends to create a system as adapted as possible to patients with cardiovascular diseases, where each module can be adapted to individual patient preferences and healthcare needs. Thus, the focus is on the empowerment of patients and promote health literacy through individualized technological approaches.

2   Related Work

A literature review was performed to verify the different options for using telemonitoring technologies to promote e-Health solutions.

The study [8] proposed an electronic system for monitoring cardiac patients using the development board LinkIt ONE. It measures and analyses the cardiac pulse for the detection of arrhythmias. The system has an intelligent module that identifies the arrhythmias and activates an alarm to report the health conditions for the healthcare provider closer to the patient. The system also includes an Arduino and a GPS module connected to the virtual platform UBIDOTS by Wi-Fi. The platform provides visual information about the patient's state.

In [15], the authors recruited 80 Heart Failure patients with New York Heart Association (NYHA) functional classes II or III. The latter was hospitalized in Intensive Care patients for a study for eight weeks to compare telemonitoring intervention with usual care. The patients are separated into a control group and an intervention group. The study consisted of an educational trial to measure the application of the Iranian version of the European Heart Failure self-care questionnaire and the heart failure-related readmission rates. The mean scores showed differences between the two groups demonstrated significant differences at the baseline for self-care behaviors. Related to the covariance analysis, the differences between the groups are also significant. However, related to the readmission rates, it is low for the intervention group. Thus, it proved that telemonitoring improved self-care behaviors, but the results are not significant.

The authors of [19] implemented a telemedicine platform for pulse-wave analysis and ambulatory blood pressure monitoring. The data was recorded with a computer for the investigation, uploading it to their Web-based telemedicine platform to process the sensors' signals with proprietary mathematical algorithms. Unfortunately, a detailed analysis of the algorithms was impossible because the source code was not available.

In another work [14], the Smartphone and cardiography devices were used to identify some health rate conditions, including normal sinus rhythm, atrial fibrillation, coronary artery disease, and possibly ST-segment elevated myocardial infarction with artificial intelligence techniques. In addition, it proved that it could be used in self-monitoring systems with a mobile device.

The authors of other work [2] analyzed 340 patients with heart failure in NYHA functional class III with a remote system named CardioMEMS HF that includes a CardioMEMS PA sensor to measure Pulmonary Artery pressure. The system consists of an implantable wireless sensor with a delivery catheter, a patient and hospital electronics system, and a patient database. With this system, the medical doctors were remotely informed about the Pulmonary Artery pressure of the patients via Merlin.net. The system also evaluated the efficacy and cost-effectiveness of hemodynamic monitoring in patients with chronic heart failure. However, the authors do not report the results, and more experiments are needed to report reliable conclusions.

In other research [12], the patients with atrial fibrillation used the short continuous heart rhythm monitoring (i.e., Holter device), and the long-term intermittent heart rhythm monitoring (i.e., AliveCor Kardia device), revealing a high accuracy in the detection of the different symptoms. The authors also used the System Usability Scale and a four-item questionnaire to evaluate the system through the other patients. As a result, it was verified that long-term intermittent monitoring effectively detects atrial fibrillation recurrences after atrial fibrillation ablation. In addition, long-term periodic monitoring has more reported usability than short continuous heart rhythm monitoring. Finally, the long-term intermittent monitoring reported a high accuracy to detect atrial fibrillation.

Table 1 presents the analysis of the different studies, verifying that few studies related to telemonitoring for cardiovascular patients. However, portable devices are starting to be used with other sensors to monitor these patients constantly.

Table 1. Analysis of the related work.

Study	Data Acquisition Method	Acquired Data	Devices	Tool used for Data Analysis
[8]	Virtual platform UBIDOTS	Cardiac pulse	Arduino and a GPS module	Virtual platform UBIDOTS
[15]	Telemonitoring through phone	The Iranian version of the European Heart Failure self-care questionnaire	Mobile device	Statistical software
[19]	Web-based telemedicine platform	Pulse, blood pressure, ambulatory arterial stiffness, and central hemodynamics	Computer, BPLab device, and oscillometric BPLab device	Web-based analysis software (THOLOMEUS, Biotechmed Ltd., Somma Lombardo, Varese Italy)
[14]	Mobile application	Health rate	Smartphone and cardiography devices	Artificial intelligence techniques
[2]	CardioMEMS HF	Pulmonary Artery pressure	Implantable wireless sensor with delivery catheter and CardioMEMS PA sensor	Hospital electronics system - Merlin.net
[12]	Holter device, and AliveCor Kardia device	Heart rhythm	Holter device, and AliveCor Kardia device	System Usability Scale (SUS) and statistical methods

3 Methods

3.1 Study Design

This research started with the research about the related work using a scientific database (*i.e.,* PubMed Central) related to using technology for cardiac patients. Then, the analysis was performed with the following keywords: "cardiovascular", "e-Health", and "telemonitoring". The research was limited between 2016 and 2021, where 17 research articles were retrieved. However, only the original research articles were analyzed, which included only six studies.

A questionnaire was designed, including nine multiple-choice questions related to the patient's preferences for disease management and interaction with the healthcare provider. The questions analyzed the different studies available in the literature and previous work [20]. Patients from an Arterial Hypertension outpatient clinic voluntarily participated. Thus, 12 patients anonymously answered the questionnaire after the acceptance of the informed consent. The Ethics Committee of the Universidade da Beira Interior previously approved the study protocol with the reference CE-UBI-Pj-2021-041:ID969.

3.2 Structure of the Study

As presented in Fig. 1, this study was born from recognizing the necessity for a system to allow patient empowerment in monitoring and controlling cardiovascular diseases.

After that, the questionnaire was created and distributed to the participants. Finally, the questionnaire was designed, distributed, and analyzed to evaluate the expectations of the patients.

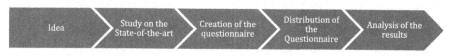

Fig. 1. Structure of the study

3.3 Statistical Analysis

Based on the data acquired, the responses were filtered and grouped by categories. Thus, the frequencies were analyzed, and different conclusions have been achieved to develop further and analyze a patient-centered innovative system for cardiovascular diseases.

4 Results

Based on the analysis of the distributed questionnaires, it was possible to verify different conclusions. The answers in the question "Which of the following instruments would you prefer to use to collect your health data?" presented in Fig. 2 show that the participants in the study do not have a consensual preference for collecting the data. We grouped

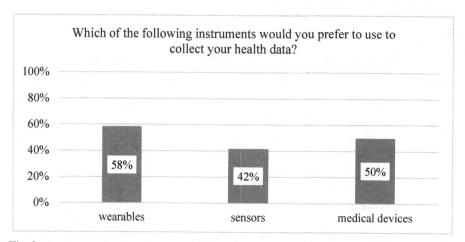

Fig. 2. Answers to the question "Which of the following instruments would you prefer to use to collect your health data?"

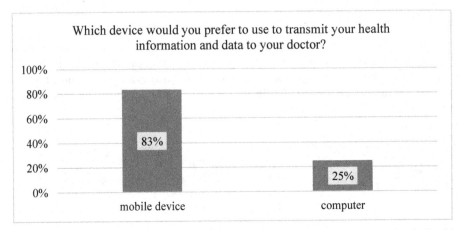

Fig. 3. Answers to the question "Which device would you prefer to use to transmit your health information and data to your doctor?"

the answers in three groups, including wearables (i.e., Smartphones and smartwatches), sensors (i.e., Clothing with built-in sensors, Sensors glued to the skin, and Sensors placed under the skin), and medical devices (i.e., blood pressure measuring device, scale, among others). A slight preference is revealed for the wearables.

Regarding the answers in the question "Which device would you prefer to use to transmit your health information and data to your doctor?", presented in Fig. 3, the answers showed a clear preference for the use of mobile devices, and only 2 of the participants do not want to use the mobile devices for this function.

Considering the answers to the question "What tools would you use to analyze/visualize your health data?" presented in Fig. 4, patients prefer mobile applications. Furthermore, only 2 participants would not like the use of mobile devices.

Regarding the question "How would you like to receive feedback from your doctor about your health status?" presented in Fig. 5, it shows a clear preference for mobile applications.

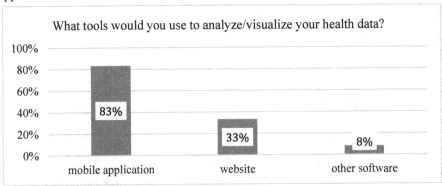

Fig. 4. Answers to the question "What tools would you use to analyze/visualize your health data?"

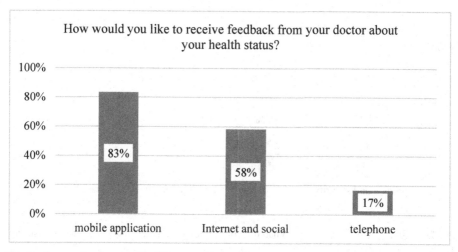

Fig. 5. Answers to the question "How would you like to receive feedback from your doctor about your health status?"

Sequentially, the question "What biological parameters do you think are important to evaluate?" presented in Fig. 6 shows that blood pressure measurement is essential for the patients. In addition, the other features critical in the patients' viewpoint for the different measures are the electrocardiographic monitoring, the peripheral oxygen saturation, and the heart rate.

Analyzing the answers in the questions "What do you value most when using medical measuring devices?" and "What do you value most in the use of computer systems in

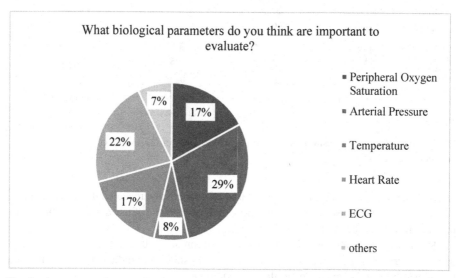

Fig. 6. Answers to the question "What biological parameters do you think are important to evaluate?"

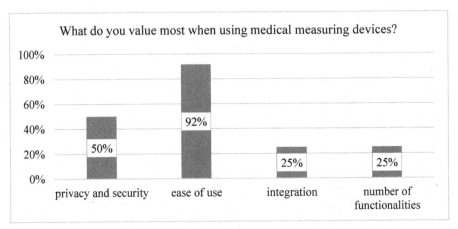

Fig. 7. Answers to the question "What do you value most when using medical measuring devices?"

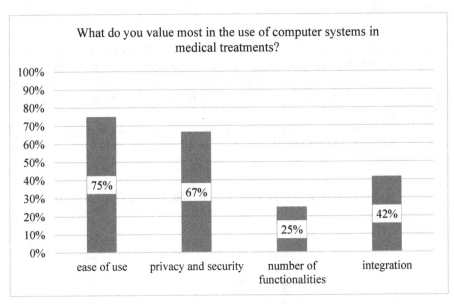

Fig. 8. Answers to the question "What do you value most in the use of computer systems in medical treatments?"

medical treatments?" presented in Figs. 7 and 8, respectively, revealed that most patients considered that the most important feature would be the ease of use and the security and privacy important for the medical treatments.

Related to the question "Would you like to contact your doctor in times of need using technology?" presented in Fig. 9, the answers showed that the patients would like to contact their doctor using technological equipment.

Finally, the question "Would you use teleconsultation/remote consultation?" presented in Fig. 10 showed that most patients would use teleconsultation/remote consultation.

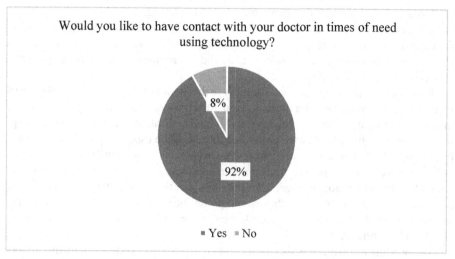

Fig. 9. Answers to the question "Would you like to have contact with your doctor in times of need using technology?"

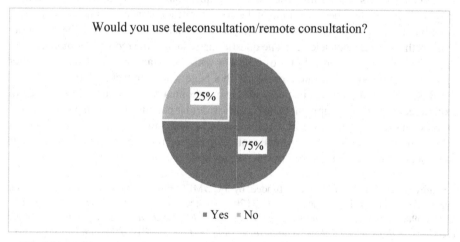

Fig. 10. Answers to the question "Would you use teleconsultation/remote consultation?"

5 Discussion and Conclusions

This study intends to analyze the use of remote technologies for improving the care of cardiovascular patients. It started with the analysis of previously developed studies regarding this subject.

The different studies analyzed were related to data acquisition and patient monitoring. However, the various authors did not present the data, applied methods, and data analysis methods. Furthermore, the different studies did not provide details about the contacts with the patients. Therefore, as part of this paper, the literature analysis was performed to plan a system for patient empowerment and monitoring, provide patient feedback, and educate the patients. However, as the significant intention of our study is related to the development of a system to promote patient autonomy, there are no studies related to this point. However, other authors already did a questionnaire to infer the patients' preferences presented in [20].

Based on the questionnaires, and similarly to the literature review, it is possible to verify that the preferred devices for the data acquisition are wearables/medical devices. Only mobile devices are chosen for data transmission, visualization, analysis, and the reception of feedback from healthcare professionals. Thus, the essential parameter selected by the patients is arterial pressure. However, two persons choose the use of computers as the preferred method of data transmission, and these persons also prefer alternative methods for visualization. However, for data visualization, one of them would like the use of mobile applications. Still, they would prefer the help of a website. Regarding the reception of feedback, one chooses mobile applications and websites to receive feedback, and the other prefers e-mails.

The previously analyzed work closely related to our work is presented by the authors of [14], which uses a standard mobile device to monitor the heart rate. In addition, other vital parameters should be monitored for the correct patient empowerment.

This study has some limitations since the questionnaire was self-administered. It may be an answer bias because some of the concepts of ignorance of some technologies' potential may not be understandable by the participants in the study. It may be one of the reasons that they are not selected. The questionnaire lacked the request for more patient data. Thus, we have a general idea of opinions with the data provided. Also, we cannot individualize the system as the knowledge about age would impact preferences.

Based on the opinions collected with the questionnaire, a system will be created to exploit technological equipment to help cardiovascular patients, promoting the patients' empowerment. The questionnaire results revealed that an informed patient would act in a specific moment of life and their treatments. Also, collecting a more significant number of subjects' variables should be considered, including technological habits.

Acknowledgements. This work is funded by FCT/MEC through national funds and, when applicable, co-funded by the FEDER-PT2020 partnership agreement under the project **UIDB/50008/2020**. (*Este trabalho é financiado pela FCT/MEC através de fundos nacionais e cofinanciado pelo FEDER, no âmbito do Acordo de Parceria PT2020 no âmbito do projeto UIDB/50008/2020*). This work is also funded by National Funds through the FCT - Foundation for Science and Technology, I.P., within the scope of the project **UIDB/00742/2020**. This article is based upon work from COST Action IC1303-AAPELE–Architectures, Algorithms, and Protocols for Enhanced Living Environments and COST Action CA16226–SHELD-ON–Indoor living space improvement: Smart Habitat for the Elderly, supported by COST (European Cooperation in Science and Technology). COST is a funding agency for research and innovation networks. Our Actions help connect research initiatives across Europe and enable scientists to grow their ideas by sharing them with their peers. It boosts their research, career, and innovation. More information in www.cost.eu. Furthermore, we would like to thank the Politécnico de Viseu for their support.

References

1. Appelboom, G., et al.: Smart wearable body sensors for patient self-assessment and monitoring. Arch. Public Health **72**, 28 (2014). https://doi.org/10.1186/2049-3258-72-28
2. Brugts, J.J., et al.: A randomised comparison of the effect of haemodynamic monitoring with CardioMEMS in addition to standard care on quality of life and hospitalisations in patients with chronic heart failure Design and rationale of the MONITOR HF multicentre randomised clinical trial. Neth. Hear. J. **28**(1), 16–26 (2019). https://doi.org/10.1007/s12471-019-01341-9
3. Choi, W.S., Choi, J.H., Oh, J., Shin, I.-S., Yang, J.-S.: Effects of remote monitoring of blood pressure in management of Urban hypertensive patients: a systematic review and meta-analysis. Telemed. E-Health **26**, 744–759 (2020). https://doi.org/10.1089/tmj.2019.0028
4. Chow, C.K., Ariyarathna, N., Islam, S.M.S., Thiagalingam, A., Redfern, J.: mHealth in cardiovascular health care. Heart Lung Circ. **25**, 802–807 (2016). https://doi.org/10.1016/j.hlc.2016.04.009
5. Consolvo, S., McDonald, D.W., Landay, J.A.: Theory-driven design strategies for technologies that support behavior change in everyday life. In: Proceedings of the 27th International Conference on Human Factors in Computing Systems - CHI 09, p. 405. ACM Press, Boston, MA, USA (2009)
6. Cook, D.J., Augusto, J.C., Jakkula, V.R.: Ambient intelligence: technologies, applications, and opportunities. Pervasive Mob. Comput. **5**, 277–298 (2009). https://doi.org/10.1016/j.pmcj.2009.04.001
7. Di Lenarda, A., et al.: The future of telemedicine for the management of heart failure patients: a consensus document of the Italian association of hospital cardiologists (A.N.M.C.O), the Italian society of cardiology (S.I.C.) and the Italian society for telemedicine and eHealth (Digital S.I.T.). Eur. Heart J. Suppl. **19**, D113–D129 (2017). https://doi.org/10.1093/eurheartj/sux024
8. Escobar, L.J.V., Salinas, S.A.: e-Health prototype system for cardiac telemonitoring. In: 2016 38th Annual International Conference of the IEEE Engineering in Medicine and Biology Society (EMBC), pp. 4399–4402. IEEE, Orlando, FL, USA (2016)
9. Farias, F.A.C.D., Dagostini, C.M., Bicca, Y.D.A., Falavigna, V.F., Falavigna, A.: Remote patient monitoring: a systematic review. Telemed. E-Health **26**, 576–583 (2020). https://doi.org/10.1089/tmj.2019.0066
10. Francula-Zaninovic, S., Nola, I.A.: Management of measurable variable cardiovascular disease' risk factors. Curr. Cardiol. Rev. **14**, 153–163 (2018). https://doi.org/10.2174/1573403X14666180222102312
11. Griffin, P.M., Nembhard, H.B., DeFlitch, C.J., Bastian, N.D., Kang, H., Munoz, D.A.: Healthcare Systems Engineering. John Wiley & Sons, Hoboken (2016)
12. Hermans, A.N.L., et al.: Long-term intermittent versus short continuous heart rhythm monitoring for the detection of atrial fibrillation recurrences after catheter ablation. Int. J. Cardiol. **329**, 105–112 (2021). https://doi.org/10.1016/j.ijcard.2020.12.077
13. Hickey, K.T., et al.: A single-center randomized, controlled trial investigating the efficacy of a mHealth ECG technology intervention to improve the detection of atrial fibrillation: the iHEART study protocol. BMC Cardiovasc. Disord. **16**, 152 (2016). https://doi.org/10.1186/s12872-016-0327-y
14. Iftikhar, Z., et al.: Multiclass classifier based cardiovascular condition detection using smartphone mechanocardiography. Sci. Rep. **8**, 9344 (2018). https://doi.org/10.1038/s41598-018-27683-9
15. Negarandeh, R., Zolfaghari, M., Bashi, N., Kiarsi, M.: Evaluating the effect of monitoring through telephone (Tele-Monitoring) on self-care behaviors and readmission of patients with

heart failure after discharge. Appl. Clin. Inform. **10**, 261–268 (2019). https://doi.org/10.1055/s-0039-1685167

16. Omboni, S.: Connected health in hypertension management. Front. Cardiovasc. Med. **6**, 76 (2019). https://doi.org/10.3389/fcvm.2019.00076

17. Omboni, S., Caserini, M., Coronetti, C.: Telemedicine and M-Health in hypertension management: technologies, applications and clinical evidence. High Blood Press. Cardiovasc. Prev. **23**(3), 187–196 (2016). https://doi.org/10.1007/s40292-016-0143-6

18. Omboni, S., Panzeri, E., Campolo, L.: E-Health in hypertension management: an insight into the current and future role of blood pressure telemonitoring. Curr. Hypertens. Rep. **22**(6), 1–13 (2020). https://doi.org/10.1007/s11906-020-01056-y

19. Omboni, S., et al.: Vascular health assessment of the hypertensive patients (VASOTENS) Registry: study protocol of an international, web-based telemonitoring registry for ambulatory blood pressure and arterial stiffness. JMIR Res. Protoc. **5**, e137 (2016). https://doi.org/10.2196/resprot.5619

20. Parati, G., Dolan, E., McManus, R.J., Omboni, S.: Home blood pressure telemonitoring in the 21st century. J. Clin. Hypertens **20**, 1128–1132 (2018). https://doi.org/10.1111/jch.13305

21. Piotrowicz, E.: The management of patients with chronic heart failure: the growing role of e-Health. Expert Rev. Med. Devices **14**, 271–277 (2017). https://doi.org/10.1080/17434440.2017.1314181

22. Smyth, J.M., Smyth, J.M.: Ecological momentary assessment research in behavioral medicine. J. Happiness Stud. **4**, 35–52 (2003). https://doi.org/10.1023/A:1023657221954

23. Vogt, H., Hofmann, B., Getz, L.: The new holism: P4 systems medicine and the medicalization of health and life itself. Med. Health Care Philos. **19**(2), 307–323 (2016). https://doi.org/10.1007/s11019-016-9683-8

24. WHO (2016) Cardiovascular diseases (CVDs). https://www.who.int/news-room/fact-sheets/detail/cardiovascular-diseases-(cvds). Accessed 5 April 2021

Co-design and Engineering of User Requirements for a Novel ICT Healthcare Solution in Murcia, Spain

Ramón Martínez[1](✉), Francisco J. Moreno-Muro[1], Francisco J. Melero-Muñoz[1,2], María V. Bueno-Delgado[1], Josefina Garrido-Lova[2], María Sánchez-Melero[2], and Kuldar Tuveter[3]

[1] Department of Information and Communication Technologies, Universidad Politécnica de Cartagena, 30202 Cartagena, Spain
ramon.martinez@upct.es
[2] Technical Research Centre of Furniture and Wood of the Region of Murcia (CETEM), 30510 Yecla, Spain
[3] Institute of Computer Science, University of Tartu, Tartu, Estonia

Abstract. This contribution summarizes the co-design and user requirements engineering work carried out in the framework of the Pharaon Large Scale Pilot project, in Pilot to be deployed in the Region of Murcia (Spain). During the co-design phase, authors defined the methodology for the co-design and representation of user requirements as goal models, use case scenarios, and user stories. The methodology entailed several up-to-date co-design methods for user requirements' elicitation. ISO 9241-210 standards were followed. The original plan for eliciting and representing user requirements was modified due to the Covid-19 outbreak. The methodology designed and used is explained to serve as inspiration for similar approaches for smart healthcare, Ambient Assisted Living, or smart environments.

Keywords: AAL · Healthcare · Co-design · User requirements · Goal models · Use cases

1 Introduction

The Pharaon[1] Large Scale Pilot project aims to design and implement a European health-care – ecosystem – in which people, software and hardware interact with each other in a smart, non-intrusive and dynamic way, that is, a novel Information and Communication Technology (ICT)-based healthcare solution. The Pharaon ecosystem is composed of a great variety of Ambient Assisted Living (AAL) technological solutions organized in clusters – Large Scale Pilots – to be deployed in 6 different sites: Murcia and Andalusia

---

[1] Pilots for Healthy and Active Ageing. Project ID: 857188, funded under the H2020 topic DT-TDS-01–2019 - Smart and healthy living at home. https://www.pharaon.eu.

© ICST Institute for Computer Sciences, Social Informatics and Telecommunications Engineering 2021
Published by Springer Nature Switzerland AG 2021. All Rights Reserved
I. M. Pires et al. (Eds.): GOODTECHS 2021, LNICST 401, pp. 279–292, 2021.
https://doi.org/10.1007/978-3-030-91421-9_21

(Spain), Portugal, The Netherlands, Slovenia and Italy (see Fig. 1). Each Pilot will be designed to perform a set of scenarios and use cases, while a Large-scale Pilot, under the Pharaon ecosystem umbrella, will orchestrate a subset of technologies deployed on each Pilot and data gathered, to perform novel and collaborative crossed-Pilot scenarios and services.

Pharaon project can be categorized as a human-service project, since its final goal consists of promoting and improving the healthy life of ageing people. In fact, Pharaon project follows a human-centric design (HCD) approach. In this context, co-design is seen as a critical phase to success [1]. Co-design helps people involved in the project development to articulate more precisely and realistically the needs of the service's customers or users and for the organizations involved. The benefits of co-design are related to improving the creative process, the service, project management, or longer-term effects. The phases of co-design are mainly twofold: (1) to identify the goals of the service design project and (2) to align their co-design activities and the associated benefits with these goals. The co-design output feeds the engineering user requirements, mandatory step for finding the technical requirements, and consequently, for the design, development, implementation and testing of the technical solution.

This contribution summarizes the co-design and user requirements engineering work carried out in the framework of the Pharaon project, in the Murcia Pilot (Spain), serving as inspiration for similar approaches in the field of ICT for healthcare, AAL or smart environments, among others.

The authors defined a methodology for the co-design and representation of user requirements as goal models, use case scenarios, and user stories. The methodology entailed several up-to-date co-design methods for user requirements' elicitation, such as the DO-BE-FEEL method, the HOW-NOW-WOW method and empathy maps, gathering the data from interviews and surveys, and also other trending goal-based approaches for representing user requirements. ISO 9241-210 standard [2] is followed for co-design and requirements elicitation, which provides a framework for human centred-design (HCD) activities. The original plan for eliciting and representing user requirements was modified due to the Covid-19 outbreak in March 20. This is explained in depth in Subsect. 3.1.

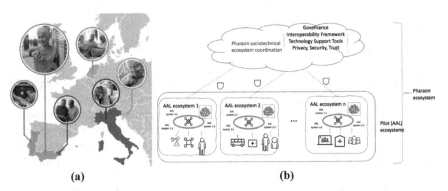

Fig. 1. Pharaon Large Scale Pilot. (a) Deployment sites. (b) Collaborative vision

The rest of the paper is organized as follows: Sect. 2 introduces the general methodology for engineering user requirements. Section 3 explains in depth the co-design engineering and user requirements performed in the Murcia Pilot. Finally, Sect. 4 summarizes the conclusions.

2   General Methodology for Engineering User Requirements

The methodology for co-design and user requirements elicitation to be applied in the Pharaon project should enable iterative co-design with the stakeholders - in particular with older adults. Iterative co-design means that the requirements are iteratively validated and elaborated through user experience design and prototyping until the stage is reached. Then, more detailed requirements for the actual implementation of the prototyped solutions can be specified. (see Fig. 2).

Fig. 2. Iterative co-design of the Pharaon ecosystem.

In the Pharaon project, user requirements were elicited by co-design workshops, managed by each pilot, with format of motivational goal modelling [3]. After that, the results of each co-design workshops must be represented in a uniform way, so that it would be possible to identify the commonalities of the co-design results by different pilots and integrate country-wide pilots into a European Large-Scale Pilot, which is a clear expectation by the European Commission (EC).

Co-design workshops involved older adults and other stakeholders in the elicitation process, such as healthcare professionals, formal and informal caregivers, and service providers. The requirements elicitation methods used by the pilot sites were interviews by phone and electronic means, in-person interviews conducted by formal caregivers trained for this purpose, web surveys, and, in some cases, virtual co-design workshops.

The useful data gathered from these workshops were basically an understanding of what activities by older adults and other stakeholders should be supported by the overall sociotechnical system to be designed, and what are the quality and emotional aspects of the activities to be supported [4]. In other words, an understanding of who should be able to perform what activities, which quality aspects should be considered in performing these activities and how should the actors feel when performing these activities. In short, workshops and other means produced the following four lists:

- **Do** (functional goals): e.g. communicate (be in touch); sustain wellbeing; call for help.
- **Be** (quality goals): e.g. easy-to-use; secure; scalable; quick response; helpful; proactive; accessible; reliable; mobile.
- **Feel** (emotional goals): e.g. helpful; purposeful; fun; engaging; positive; empowering; secure; feeling cared about; feeling independent; feeling assured; feeling in control.
- **Who** (stakeholder roles): e.g. older adults; caregivers including formal caregivers and informal caregivers; healthcare professionals including nurses and physicians.

To obtain a holistic overview of the solution to be designed, the four lists should be represented in a structured way as a single page diagram – goal model. Goal model can be considered as a container of four components (Fig. 3): functional goals, quality goals, emotional goals and stakeholder roles [5–7]. The skeleton of a goal model is a hierarchy of functional goals drawn as a tree. The hierarchical structure is to show that the subcomponent is an aspect of the top-level component. The root of the tree sits at the top of the page and represents the overall goal of the system. An example of goal model for the wellbeing support system designed for older adults is shown in Fig. 4. It reflects, the overall goal of the system is to support wellbeing, divided into "Being in touch" and "Calling for help". "Being in touch" has, in turn, been elaborated into "Communicating", "Confirming" and "Acknowledging". The roles, quality goals and emotional goals are placed at an appropriate level in the hierarchy, whereby each of them applies to the functional goal they are attached to and all the functional goals below that goal in the goal hierarchy.

Fig. 3. Notation for goal models

3   Co-design and Engineering of User Requirements in Murcia Pilot

The Region of Murcia is one of the 17 autonomous communities of Spain. It is located in the southeast of the state, on the Mediterranean coast. It has more than 1.5M inhabitants, being the 7th most populated province in Spain. One third of the population lives in the capital and its surroundings with the 16% of it is 65 years old and above. The Murcia pilot aims to deploy a new line of virtual assistance that will transform the current model of health and care service based on the patients to notice when they need help. The pilot is focused on older patients with chronic heart failure (CHF). The new telecare model would allow patients to stay in their preferred environment and provide a more intense, effective, proactive and less intrusive care and observation service. Such novel model is based on:

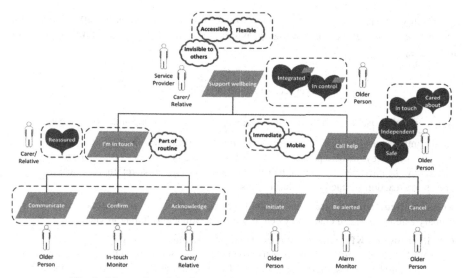

Fig. 4. The goal model of supporting wellbeing of an older adult [6].

- **Tele-assistance:** Integrating technologies like sensors, wearables, Internet of Things (IoT) or robotics.
- **Proactivity and Prevention:** Since the demographic change and the increased longevity are changing the profile of the user of the health and care services, moving from passive patient receiving treatments to active consumers of health and care that must participate in the process from the data perspective, not only in critical situations but also paying a lot of attention in prevention.
- **Users and their environment:** Because one of the main problems now is that care and health facilities are being used as care homes, being more expensive than keeping them at home as much as possible and only using institutional health facilities when intensive care is needed.

Murcia pilot defines two target scenarios for addressing two Pharaon challenges: PCH2 (Health status definition and its progress over time, focused on hearth failure) and PCH3 (Non-intrusive monitoring and alarm triggering, focused on energy consumption patterns). These scenarios are called Angel of Health and Care@Home. The definition of these scenarios includes goals, roles involved, Key Performance Indicators (KPI), quality goals, emotional goals, technologies involved and ethical concerns. Table 1 and 2 summarizes some of these features.

3.1   Planned Methodology and Contingency Plan

The methodology for engineering user and pilot requirements in the Murcia pilot was planned is depicted in Fig. 5. Three workshops were planned to be carried out during one month. The attendees of the workshops were 1–2 representatives of the target collectives: primary care doctor, cardiologist, internist, primary care/hospital nurse,

Emergency (hospital & PC), pharmacy, rehabilitation, psychologist, social workers, patient, relative/caregiver, technology provider and/or representatives of health and care authorities.

Table 1. Target scenario in Murcia Pilot: Angel of Health

Angel of health: user's information gathering, response, alarm setting and management
Goals: improve health and care services and follow up to patients with CHF; decrease older adult´s dependency; involve patients in the health and care process from the data perspective; help relieve health-care centres and their workers of workload pressure; improve health care prevention/reaction in emergency/alarm status
Roles involved: patients, caretakers, health professionals (primary care doctors, cardiologists, primary care nurses), call emergency centre staff, platform and solution providers
Quality goals and KPI: reduced number of visits of patients to health centres; reduced number of visits of health professionals to patients' homes; reduced health complications and the related number of hospitalizations; increased satisfaction of patients, caregivers and health professionals; reduced time response in emergency status (alarms); increased years of independent living; increased of the Social Return of Investment (SROI) ratio
Emotional goals: independent; empowered; safe; healthy; proactive; reactive; satisfied
Technologies: Onesait Healthcare Data Homecare (OHC)[a] platform as a communication tool, for tracking vital signs, for registering clinical information and setting alarms; other technologies, such as wearables, accelerometers, presence sensors, pill reminders, etc

[a] https://onesaitplatform.atlassian.net/

Table 2. Target scenario in Murcia Pilot: Care@Home

Care@Home
Goals: reduce the older adult's dependency; early detection of emergency situations
Roles involved: older adults; relatives/informal caregivers; neighbors; emergency services staff (nurses and medical doctors)
Quality goals and KPI: reduction of response time in an emergency situation; reduction of severity of emergency situations. reduction of complications due to emergency situations and related hospitalizations
Emotional goals: safety level perceived by older adults and relatives
Technologies: MIW+ Platform[a] as a comprehensive platform that connects individuals with their total energy consumption data at their homes; uGRID[b], energy management software; OHC platform; other technologies, such as wearables, accelerometers, and presence sensors

[a] https://www.miwenergia.com/plataforma-miw/
[b] https://ugrid.miwenergia.com

Due to the constraints imposed by Covid-19, a contingency methodology was designed (see Fig. 6), based on three main phases:

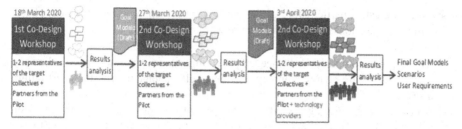

Fig. 5. The methodology planned for engineering user and pilot requirements in the Murcia pilot.

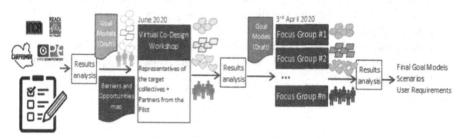

Fig. 6. The contingency methodology for engineering user and pilot requirements in the Murcia pilot.

- *Desk work phase.* Desk research on co-design workshops, data and results obtained in previous initiatives carried out by the public healthcare in Murcia framed in similar contexts than Pharaon, like ProEmpower[2], ReadiForHealth[3], INC3CA[4] and CARPRIMUR[5]. The functional, quality and emotional goals identified during this desk research phase are presented in Fig. 7. This initial phase provided a global overview of potential requirements of the stakeholders.
- *Requirement analysis phase.* The design, dissemination of a questionnaire for all the involved groups and analysis of results. The feedback received was used to further identify potential participants from the different target collectives and to complete the initial goals framework. It also helped to build a map of barriers and opportunities for the assistance of CHF in the whole region and appoint the most suitable representatives from each collective. 50 responses were gathered (56% were patients, relatives or caretakers and 44% health and care professionals). Two thirds of the respondents

---

[2] Procuring innovative ICT for patient empowerment and self-management for type 2 diabetes mellitus. Grant Agreement n° 727409. H2020 topic SC1-PM-12–2016 - PCP - eHealth innovation in empowering the patient. https://proempower-pcp.eu/.

[3] Regional Digital Agendas for Healthcare. Grant Agreement n° 320021. Funded under the FP7 topic REGIONS-2012–2013-1 - Transnational cooperation between regional research-driven clusters.

[4] INclusive INtroduction of INtegrated CAre. Grant Agreement n° 621006. Funded under the topic CIP-ICT-PSP.2013.3.1b. www.in3ca.eu.

[5] Institutional Project from the SMS aiming at transferring knowledge between cardiologists and primary health doctors for improving the attendance of patients with Chronic Heart Failure. https://carprimur.com/proyecto/.

showed interest in participating in the working groups planned for the next phase. The main conclusions of the questionnaire were:

- All focus groups agreed on the need of providing access to a personalized online and user-friendly care plan that enhances patient self-management of the heart failure disease.
- A lack of heart failure knowledge on the part of patients and caregivers has been identified that can be compensated for by mixed training (face-to-face + online).
- The disparity in heart failure-related metrics and measurements opens the door to the development of a unified monitoring plan for the disease. Need to create face-to-face communities as a link among focus groups to empower and motivate patients and families.
- It is advisable to find new flexible communication channels that adapt to the needs of the focus groups, such as WhatsApp messages, emails, Skype or notifications from mobile apps.

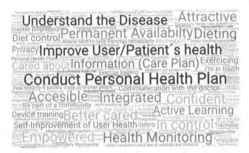

Fig. 7. Quality (blue), Functional (pink) and Emotional (green) goals and goal models (purple) identified in the desk research stage.

- *Virtual co-design phase.* To arrange a virtual co-design workshop with the selected representatives of each collective, selected in the previous step, and pilot partners for the introduction of the work framework, and create different focus groups with representatives of each collective that, through several teleconference meetings, in order to define and discuss the goals and their models. The selected participants were grouped in 6 different collectives: patients, family and caregivers, hospital physicians (cardiologists and internists), primary care physicians, nurses, and mixed practitioners (one psychologist, two social workers, one pharmacist, one rehabilitation specialist physician, one physical therapist and a nurse). Approximately fifty people involved in the six focus groups attended a webinar, organized as a workshop where partners involved in the Murcia Pilot explained the objectives and methodology of the Pharaon project, provided details about the pilot to be carried out in the region and the framework for the focus groups.

3.2 Identification and Design of Goal Models

The analysis of the results obtained from the abovementioned activities performed during the contingency methodology resulted in the identification of quality, functional and emotional goals. The main three goal models identified to be designed were: "Get involved in the health and care process", "Improve patient care" and "Detect emergency situations". The design of these goal models is represented in Fig. 8, 9 and 10, respectively.

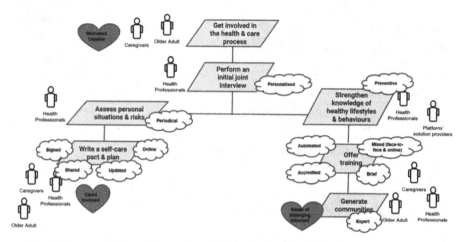

Fig. 8. Representation of the goal model "Get involved in the health and care process"

3.3 Use Case Scenarios

From the goals models and main scenarios described above, the methodology of use cases was used to identify, clarify and organize the system requirements in the Murcia Pilot. Seven use cases were defined:

- Get involved in the health & care process
- Asses personal situations and risks
- Strengthen Knowledge of Healthy Lifestyles & Behaviors
- Improve patient care
- Boost disease follow-up
- Upgrade interventions
- Detect emergency situations

The fields of the use cases descriptions have been designed to describe all requirements needed as input in the next Pilot deployment phase: to decide the technologies to be used in the use case scenarios, and how to use them as building blocks of the Pharaon ecosystem. Some of these technologies are already designed as building blocks, to be accessed by Application Programming Interfaces (API). Others need and extra software

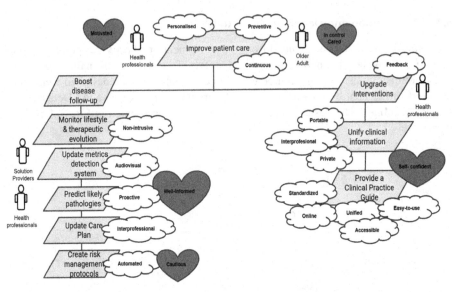

Fig. 9. Representation of the goal model "Improve patient care"

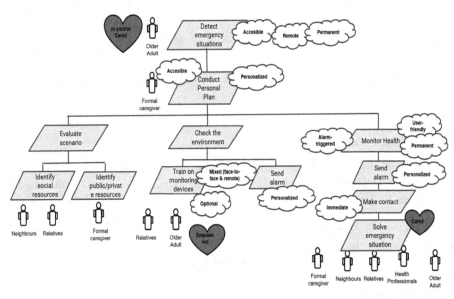

Fig. 10. Representation of the goal model "Detect emergency situations"

development for its integration as new building blocks. Then, the user requirements should be represented in even a more detailed manner as user stories.

Tables from 3, 4, 5 show a set of the use cases defined, as example of the work performed. Note that the field Potential technology enumerates those offered by the Technical and platform providers in the Pharaon consortium.

Table 3. Description/requirements of use case "Scenario for Strengthen Knowledge of Healthy Lifestyles & Behaviors"

Goal	Strengthen Knowledge of Healthy Lifestyles & Behaviors	
Initiator	Health Professionals and Platform/Solution Providers	
Trigger	Action by the Health Professional	
Description/Outline	Learning/ training process for older adults to increase their knowledge of his/her illness and have it under control	
Expected Innovation	This scenario allows the patient to participate in the health and care process from the data perspective not only when intensive care is needed with the aim of paying attention in prevention	
Condition	**Interleaved**	
Step	1	2
Activity	Training sessions and tools are made available to older adults and relatives	Generate specific communities for patients and caregivers with similar profiles and geographic proximity
Roles involved	Health professionals, platform/solution providers	Caregivers, older adults, health professionals, platform/solution providers
Quality goals	Personalised, preventive, automated, accredited, mixed, brief	Personalised, preventive, automated, accredited, mixed, brief, expert
Emotional goals	Motivated, capable	Motivated, capable, sense of belonging, informed
Potential technology	OHC platform	OHC platform, Sentab TV platform[a]; IoTool[b] and IoChat[c]; eHealth Platform[d]

[a] www.sentab.com
[b] www.iotool.io
[c] www.iochat.io
[d] http://www.rrd.nl/en/

Table 4. Description/requirements of use case "Scenario for upgrade interventions"

Goal	Upgrade Interventions	
Initiator	Health professionals	
Trigger	Action by the Health professional	
Description/ Outline	Upgrade interventions, unify clinical information, provide clinical practice guide	
Expected Innovation	It will allow to unify clinical information of the same patient to ensure their safety, continuity of care and portability in other Spanish Autonomous Communities. This will also facilitate communication among professionals (alert to Primary Care after discharge, fast communication among professionals, shared spaces among professionals), as well as the systematic use of a single Clinical Practical Regional Guide for decisions on care of patients with CHF, applied in all areas of health and care level	
Condition	Sequence	
Step	1	2
Activity	Unify Clinical Intervention	Provide a Clinical Practice Guide
Roles Involved	Health professionals, Older adults	
Quality Goals	Personalised, Preventive, Continuous, Portable, Interprofessional, Private	Personalised, Preventive, Continuous, Portable, Interprofessional, Private, Standardized, Unified, Online, Accessible, Easy-to-use
Emotional Goals	Motivated, In Control, Cared	
Potential Technology	OHC platform	

Table 5. Description/requirements of use case: "Scenario for detect emergency situations"

Goal	Detect Emergency Situations	
Initiator	Older Adult/Caregiver	
Trigger	Action by the Older Adult/Caregiver	
Description/Outline	To prevent emergency situations in older adults and improve their attendance in case they happen	
Expected innovation	It will demonstrate the feasibility of the energy domain to detect and predict emergency situations with the support of sensors and AAL devices and the definition of energy consumption patterns according to the user routines	
Condition	Sequence	Interleaved

(*continued*)

Table 5. (*continued*)

Step	1	2	3	4
Activity	A customized plan on the most relevant risks of the older adult is conducted	The scenario of each older adult is evaluated, considering those social, public and private resources available	The living environment is checked and triggers alarms in case of possible emergencies (requires caregivers/older adults to have specific skills)	The older adult's health is monitored according to his/her vital signs and emergency alarms are triggered if needed
Roles involved	Older adult, formal caregiver	Older adult, formal and informal caregivers, neighbors	Older adult, formal and informal caregivers, relatives, technology/ platform provider	Older adult, formal and informal caregivers, neighbors, health professionals
Quality goals	Accessible, remote, permanent, personalized			Accessible, remote, permanent, personalized, alarm-triggered, user-friendly, immediate
Emotional goals	In control, cared	In control, cared, empowered		In control, cared
Potential technology	OHC platform; Asistae[a]; Amicare[b] [8]; MIW+; Aladin[c]; IoTool, IoChat; Sentab TV platform; eHealth Platform, eWall Platform[d]		IoTool; MIW+; Amicare; Asistae; RB-Base2[e]; Aladin; eWall Platform; SmartHabits [9]	Discovery[f]; Sentab TV platform; MOX[g]; eHealth Platform; eWall Platform

[a] http://asistae.fama.es/
[b] http://www.cetem.es/en/projects/i/934/321/amicare-project-completed
[c] https://www.domalys.com/en/pro
[d] https://cordis.europa.eu/project/rcn/110560_it.html
[e] https://www.robotnik.eu/mobile-robots/rb-1-base/
[f] https://alfred.eu
[g] www.accelerometry.eu

4 Conclusions

This work has introduced the co-design and user requirements engineering work carried out in the Pharaon Large Scale Pilot project, focused on the Pilot in the Murcia Region (Spain). The work has been conducted by a co-design phase, where the authors had to define the methodology for the co-design and representation of user requirements as goal models, use case scenarios, and user stories. The methodology entailed several up-to-date co-design methods for user requirements' elicitation. The result of this work will feed the next step in the Pilot deployment, deciding the technologies to be used in the use case scenarios, and how to use them as building blocks of the Pharaon ecosystem. In most cases, such building blocks already exist and can be accessed by the appropriate APIs. However, whenever needed, new building blocks or wrappers to the legacy building blocks will be developed. For such cases demanding development of new software, user requirements should be represented in even a more detailed manner as user stories. This contribution can serve as inspiration for similar approaches in the field of ICT for healthcare, AAL or smart environments, among others.

Acknowledgments. We thank all participants in the Murcia Pilot co-design and workshops. Special thanks to the Murcia Health Service for its support.

This work has been partially funded by the European Union's Horizon 2020 research and innovation programme under grant agreement No 857188 – Pharaon Project, and Spanish National Project ONOFRE-2, ref. TEC2017-84423-C3-2-P (MINECO/AEI/FEDER, UE).

References

1. Steen, M., Manschot, M., De Koning, N.: Benefits of co-design in service design projects. Int. J. Des. **5**(2) (2011)
2. ISO 9241-210: Ergonomics of human-system interaction – Part 210: Human centred design for interactive systems. Geneva, Switzerland: International Standardisation Organisation (2019)
3. Lorca, A.L., Burrows, R., Sterling, L.: Teaching motivational models in agile requirements engineering. In: IEEE 8th International Workshop on Requirements Engineering Education and Training, pp. 30–39 (2018)
4. Taveter, K., Sterling, L., Pedell, S., Burrows, R., Taveter, E.M.: A method for eliciting and representing emotional requirements: two case studies in e-healthcare. In: 2019 IEEE 27th International Requirements Engineering Conference Workshops (REW), pp. 100–105 (2019). https://doi.org/10.1109/REW.2019.00021
5. Sterling, L., Taveter, K. The Art of Agent-oriented Modeling. MIT Press, Cambridge (2009)
6. Miller, T., Lu, B., Sterling, L., Beydoun, G., Taveter, K.: Requirements elicitation and specification using the agent paradigm: the case study of an aircraft turnaround simulator. IEEE Trans. Softw. Eng. **40**(10), 1007–1024 (2014)
7. Miller, T., Pedell, S., Lopez-Lorca, A.A., Mendoza, A., Sterling, L., Keirnan, A.: Emotion-led modelling for people-oriented requirements engineering: the case study of emergency systems. J. Syst. Softw. **105**, 54–71 (2015)
8. Bleda, A.L., Maestre, R., Beteta, M.A.,Vidal, J.A.: AmICare: ambient intelligent and assistive system for caregivers support. In: 2018 IEEE 16th International Conference on Embedded and Ubiquitous Computing (EUC), pp. 66–73 (2018). https://doi.org/10.1109/EUC.2018.00017
9. Grgurić, A., Mošmondor, M., Huljenić, D.: The SmartHabits: an intelligent privacy-aware home care assistance system. Sensors **19**, 907 (2019). https://doi.org/10.3390/s19040907

What Do Nurses and Careers in Portugal Wish and Need from a Digital Intelligent Assistant for Nursing Applications

Natália Machado[1] , Carina Dantas[1] , Ana Filipa Leandro[1](✉) ,
Diana Guardado[1] , Thomas Münzer[2] , Nicole Helfenberger[2] ,
Georgios Vafeiadis[3], Konstantinos Manolios[3], and Claudiu Amza[3]

[1] Innovation Department, Cáritas Diocesana de Coimbra, R. Dom Francisco de Almeida 14, 3030-382 Coimbra, Portugal
analeandro@caritascoimbra.pt
[2] Geriatrische Klinik St. Gallen, Rorschacherstr. 94, 9000 St. Gallen, Switzerland
[3] Bluepoint Consulting Srl, Barajul Arges Street, Nr. 11, 014121 Bucharest, Romania

Abstract. Cognitive disorders (CD) are challenges in healthcare and present a looming threat to the financial and social systems of most countries. There are nearly 10 million new dementia cases every year and this has a physical and psychological impact on their nurses and carers. To soften this burden, the DIANA Project (AAL Programme and FCT) is developing a solution composed of smart 3D sensors, an open management platform, and a mobile application to fulfil several functionalities such as: monitoring patient safety 24/7 (e.g., unusual behaviour, falls), support activities of daily living (e.g., toileting) and observe health trends of patients (e.g., fluid intake, changed behavioural patterns). To better understand the secondary end-users' needs and preferences regarding a solution of this kind, we applied a user-centred approach, to gather information from a questionnaire to retrieve the initial requirements of this solution. This outcome was combined with a literature review on the state-of-the-art projects in this field and the care for patients living with CD. As a result, the responses from 54 Portuguese nurses and carers were analysed regarding the establishment of a first set of functional requirements to the DIANA project, as well as the definition of use cases and personas to study. The results show that the three most important advantages of DIANA in Portugal would be assistance in nursing care, social interaction, and falls/mobility detection.

Keywords: Artificial intelligence · Cognitive disorders · Nurses · Carers

1 Introduction

In 2020, over 50 million people globally were living with cognitive disorders (CD). This number is expected to double every 20 years, reaching 75 million in 2030 and 152 million in 2050 [1]. In 2018, the combined EU28+ non-EU countries had 9,780,678

I. M. Pires et al. (Eds.): GOODTECHS 2021, LNICST 401, pp. 293–299, 2021.
https://doi.org/10.1007/978-3-030-91421-9_22

people living with CD with an estimated rise to 18,846,286 in 2050 [2]. The main cause for this increase is demographic change. As people live longer, chronic diseases become more prevalent, along with a trend of lifestyles and behaviours that favour them, since ageing is not a sine qua non condition to CD. The frequency of dementia rises exponentially with advancing age. It duplicates with every 6.3 year increment in age, from 3.9 per 1000 person-years at age 60–64 to 104.8 per 1000 person-years at age 90 and over. In Europe the peak frequency is among people aged 80–89 years [3].

In 2015, the estimated worldwide cost of CD was US\$ 818 billion [4], being one of the toughest financial challenges in healthcare. A high proportion of patients with CD eventually requires placement in a long-term care facility such as a nursing home, assisted living facility or group home. At the same time, their care is very demanding for nurses and formal carers, leading to an increase in these professionals' burnout. For this reason, it is of utmost importance to develop solutions that can support nurses and related carers in their daily working routines.

Considering this background, the digital intelligent assistant for nursing applications (DIANA), a project co-funded by the Active & Assisted Living Programme (AAL), thought of an innovative solution to assist nurses and carers in their daily lives and helping the care of persons with CD. The solution aims to alleviate medical staff of routine tasks which could be managed by an AI-powered digital assistant, e.g., monitoring the safety of patients 24/7, control walks during the night, react to alarms from existing sensors, support in activities of daily living (ADL) or observe health trends of patients and recording of such data for later assessment by clinical experts.

However, to better adapt to the medical staff routine, the integration, effectivity, and usability of these functionalities need to meet the real needs and expectations of the end-users. For this reason, nurses and formal carers were involved since the beginning of the project in the requirements collection.

This manuscript describes the methodology and the results of the users' requirements compilation.

2   Methods

DIANA builds on a user-centred approach, focussing on users and their needs in each phase of the design process [5]. This approach goes beyond consultation by building and deepening equal collaboration between citizens affected by, or attempting to, resolve a particular challenge.

Three essential phases of this study were a) a literature review, that provided a theoretical background and benchmarked some of the best practices and results of previous AAL and H2020 projects; b) a literature review about the care and special treatment of patients with cognitive disorders and c) an online questionnaire, which collected information from both nurses and carers (secondary end-users)[1] [6], including samples from Portugal and Switzerland, the other end-user organization country in the project. In this manuscript, the main objective is to present the view from the Portuguese consultation.

It is important to emphasize that, although the focus of the project is the improvement of the quality of life of patients with CD, their involvement in this phase of requirements

[1] Link to online questionnaire: https://redcap.link/51uki44z.

collection was not necessary. Nurses and carers have the main role in this project, therefore they were the first to be consulted. By collecting their opinions about the care of people with CD and the use of technology, the project collects an overview of what can be implemented through the solution.

The literature review was composed by the benchmarking of the best practices and results of previous AAL and H2020 projects in the same field of the DIANA project (intelligent digital systems in care; ambient assistance living; systems to people with mind impairment) and a review about the care and special treatment of patients with cognitive impairment, as well as statistical information about the use of technology in the daily work of nursing homes and hospitals in Portugal.

To complement these findings, an online questionnaire was used to learn more about the carers' and nurses' perception and needs to use new technologies in their work environment. The information was collected through 54 questionnaires completed by both carers and nurses.

We used a set of different approaches to achieve the targeted number of respondents. Firstly, a meeting with the Centro Region delegation of the Order of Nurses [7] was held, that engaged the organisation in the dissemination of the questionnaire, supporting Cáritas Diocesana de Coimbra (CDC) to reach potential respondents. Also, several invitations were sent to the regional delegations of the Order of Nurses all over the country. Besides this, the questionnaire was disseminated by sending it to a mailing list of stakeholders, and a broader engagement was reached through social media, local newspapers, and specific home care centres. In this last area, the direct engagement of the professionals in the units of CDC was also relevant to reach the established goal. Finally, although this consultation took place during the pandemic period, it was possible to overcome the initial goal for Portugal (n = 54).

The questionnaire was developed in REDCAP [8] and thus the answers were automatically saved and grouped, which allowed to avoid manual errors in data handling and to analyse the results in a simple and agile manner. Besides the research team, also the respondents benefited from this questionnaire, as it ensured the absolute anonymization of the answers, which was also an objective at this phase of the study.

With the results achieved, the medical, technical, and social requirements were laid down in the description of 4 personas (a fictional character in the user-centred design created to represent a user type that might use a site, brand, or product similarly).

The outcomes of these three different phases will be explored and detailed in the following sections.

3 Results

3.1 Literature Review: Benchmarking of State-of-the-Art Projects in DIANA Field

The benchmarking was designed to present true state-of-the-art of projects in the same field as DIANA. It is practically impossible to survey all the solutions that are currently on the market, given the immense number of programs and investment. Nevertheless, an overview in the AAL and H2020 programs lead the consortium to perceive some good practices that should be integrated into DIANA. With this research, it was possible to understand what should be avoided and what needs to be implemented, in terms of system design and approach.

The Roadmap project [9] observed that people are increasingly having access to technology that allows the use of app-based activity monitors. However, concerns around data security limit the use of the technology available on smartphones and tablets, as does a lack of confidence or willingness to use this technology. The project described an important factor, that people affected by CD are vulnerable and have difficulties to communicate effectively, making it increasingly difficult to know what their priorities and preferences are. Thus, nurses and carers' opinions are prioritized at this stage of development in the DIANA project.

Guidelines retrieved from ICT4Life [10] report that primary end-users are very concerned about sensors and the camera, but after testing it, generally, accept them well. During the pilot tests, the project verified that the voice commands were very well accepted by patients and that the evolution and recommendations of the system for patients were very well accepted by physicians and physiotherapists. Finally, they concluded that the communication tools between health professionals, carers, and other professionals and between patients and health professionals are the key point for integrated care platforms: this aspect has been underlined by all end-users; it has an economic impact because, according to users' opinions, it reduces personal visits to the doctors and emergency interaction.

The Toilet4me [11] started reflections both technologically and ethically for the development of smart toilets. Some guidelines have already been developed regarding data protection: Restricting access to data based on a "need to know" basis; providing users with unique login data with individual access levels; using encryption when sharing the data, developing a "clean policy," meaning not to leave personal data to unauthorized people and ensuring that all archived data is encrypted.

These conclusions will be considered during the development of the DIANA solution.

3.2 Literature Review About the Care and Special Treatment of Patients with Cognitive Disorders

Care for patients with cognitive disorders includes support in basic Activities of daily living (ADL). The health workers must do these routine tasks while encouraging the function and independence of patients for as long as possible [12], thus, promoting patient's safety, reducing their anxiety and restlessness, upgrading communication and in parallel educating the family carers. Bathing/hygiene, dressing and grooming, impaired physical mobility, wandering and risk for injury are some of the areas to which assistance from nurses and carers is needed and addressed in nursing care plans.

Risk of Falls
Inpatient fall prevention has been an individual area of concern for nursing for almost 50 years. At the international level, studies show that 30% of people over the age of 65 suffer at least one fall per year. According to the World Health Organisation (WHO), falls are the second leading cause of accidental or unintentional injury deaths worldwide and older adults suffer the greatest number of fatal falls [13].

Toileting Behaviour Analysis
Competent toileting is a critical life skill necessary for independent living, and not being able to use it adequately is a significant barrier for the quality of life of individuals with CD. Independent toileting can improve an individual's quality of life through improved hygiene and improved self-confidence, as well as reduced stigma and reduced physical discomforts. The use of technology could facilitate some tasks. For someone who regularly wets themselves, it may be helpful to develop a timetable that offers a reminder to go to the toilet. For example, real-time notifications on user's smartphone can also be useful for the person to remember to use the toilet or to check if their pad needs changing.

This information will also be considered during the development of DIANA.

3.3 Questionnaires – Requirements Collection

Demographics and Working Conditions
From the 54 respondents, most had working experience of ≤5 years or 6–10 years. The majority worked in a hospital or long-term care setting. The respondents were aged between 31 and 40 years and 78% were women. The questionnaires were broadly disseminated, so we can argue that the gender imbalance among respondents reflects the scenery in social and health care in Portugal for carers and nurses. The number of persons with CD they care for was mentioned as <25 per workspace in most of the cases and the respondents spend between less than one hour and more than 6 h together with these persons. Needs for assistive/non-acute medical devices were discovered in most cases during regular care and either the physician or family-members were informed about it. Such products arrive within less than one week.

The respondents described their residents/patients as persons who have difficulties to go to the toilet in more than 90% of the time, that also have difficulties finding the room or their way in a room. More than 83% estimate that their patients have gaps in several aspects of the correct toileting sequence [14].

The most challenging tasks when providing care for persons with dementia in Portugal was to help with mobility, eating and toilet visits.

Use of Technology - Experience and Requirements
As for new technologies, 82% of the respondents agreed or strongly agreed that they would find them simple to learn. In contrast, half of the professionals did not think their cared persons would accept DIANA or were neutral. Nevertheless, the vast majority (80%) believed that digital assistance is an important asset for the care of old persons in the future. In addition, 72% felt that their company/institution would support such technologies. The most important areas mentioned were cognitive training and security, while only 26% mentioned autonomy (e.g., using the toilet) as a goal for AAL-technology and 23% did not feel well due to data safety issues. Positive thoughts on any device were mentioned if it reminded the person to wash the hands, to detect falls and had additional intelligent features, such as light control, monitoring of unwanted movement and call for help. 65% of the participants thought that an avatar or an acoustic clue is helpful to demonstrate correct use of a toilet. Also, the use of optical guidance was deemed helpful in 76% of the health care professionals.

Use of Technology – Available Devices
As for currently available devices, the respondents had some experiences with falls sensors, intelligent toilets, and highest experience with light sensors (24%). Roughly, 30% use tablets for nursing documentation. The nurses/carers spend about 10 min per day in the management of residents/patient personal data, between 10 min and one hour per day to implement information and tasks induced by physicians, including delivery for medication, while the time spent for individual nurse care planning is largely fluctuating.

New Systems and DIANA Solution Perception
As for potential new systems, the respondents ranked patient/resident privacy protection the highest, while there were heterogeneous responses related to cables, wires, installation, mobility, and cleaning.

The three most important advantages of DIANA in Portugal would thus be assistance in nursing care, social interaction, and falls/mobility detection. Nurses and carers see the potential of DIANA in the areas of wellbeing, medication management and the monitoring of mobility. Most of the nurses/carers would also be willing to share experiences with such systems and the most frequently used resources to collect information about DIANA would be articles, conferences, and social media.

4 Discussion and Conclusion

For fall risks, the literature review revealed that it is necessary to address extrinsic and intrinsic fall risk factors to optimize patient safety. This is done mainly by the medical or nursing staff. However, the DIANA solution can support this task, by providing additional security monitoring safety of patients 24/7, e.g., bed-exits, falls, wandering, etc. If nurses and carers receive this critical information, they can be able to prevent falls in time and act accordingly. Furthermore, they can adjust the system to their patient's needs, while maintaining privacy.

Regarding toilet issues, the DIANA project has thought of an innovative solution that can foster primary end-users' autonomy all the while helping the carers and nurses' work and saving time by not having to provide toilet assistance. The use of 3D sensors in a toilet allows for private sphere protecting action by using behaviour recognition algorithms already available but trained for other application areas. The algorithms are specifically trained to recognize movement sequences during toilet visits. After training the algorithms to detect relevant actions, they are combined into a complex activity model. The solution is to have an avatar to inform the patient if he/she missed some of the steps. Through this non-intrusive way, the user can autonomously use the toilet and the carer/nurse does not need to intrude privacy.

Regarding what has been gathered from the replies to the questionnaire, the respondents believe that they can use and work with AAL solutions such as DIANA. They already know several digital technologies in their field and most of them have at least some experiences using them. The care of patients is challenging - eating and toileting - the latter being the most challenging one. Secondary end-users think DIANA should be reliable, easy to install, wireless and easy to transport. Data on patients and or nurses should be safe since this is of concern.

Based on these findings and outcomes, the first set of functional requirements that the DIANA system must provide for was developed. The DIANA solution requirements extracted from this study reinforces that the prospects and needs of secondary end-users (nurses and carers) must be considered since the beginning of the project, especially in solutions that will have a direct impact in their work routine. Further information and requirements will be developed along with the project's timeframe, especially during pilot tests.

Acknowledgements. This work is supported by the Diana project, funded by AAL (Active Assisted Living – ICT for Ageing, 2017) and in Portugal by Fundação para a Ciência e a Tecnologia.

References

1. Alzheimer's Disease International. https://www.alzint.org/about/dementia-facts-figures/dementia-statistics/. Accessed 28 Apr 2021
2. Alzheimer Europe: Dementia in Europe Yearbook 2019: Estimating the prevalence of dementia in Europe. Alzheimer Europe, Luxembourg (2019)
3. Alzheimer's Disease International, World Alzheimer Report 2015, The Global Impact of Dementia, an analysis of prevalence, incidence, cost and trends. Accessed 02 Aug 2021
4. An Alzheimer's Disease International. https://www.alzint.org/about/dementia-facts-figures/dementia-statistics/. Accessed 28 Apr 2021
5. Interaction Design Foundation Homepage. https://www.interaction-design.org/literature/topics/user-centered-design. Accessed 28 Apr 2021
6. AAL. http://www.aal-europe.eu/ageing-well-universe/i-am-a-user-2/. Accessed 28 Apr 2021
7. Ordem dos Enfermeiros da Região Centro. https://www.ordemenfermeiros.pt/centro/. Accessed 28 Apr 2021
8. REDcap. https://www.project-redcap.org/. Accessed 28 Apr 2021
9. CORDIS EU. https://cordis.europa.eu/project/id/116020. Accessed 28 Apr 2021
10. ICT4life. https://www.ict4life.com/. Accessed 28 Apr 2021
11. Toilet4me. http://www.toilet4me-project.eu/. Accessed 28 Apr 2021
12. Nurseslabs. https://nurseslabs.com/alzheimers-disease-nursing-care-plans/6/. Accessed 28 Apr 2021
13. WHO. https://www.who.int/news-room/fact-sheets/detail/falls. Accessed 28 Apr 2021
14. DIANA. http://www.aal-europe.eu/projects/diana/. Accessed 28 Apr 2021

Examining Furniture Preferences of the Elderly in Greece

Ioannis Bothos[✉] and Michael Skarvelis

Deparment of Forestry, Wood Technology and Design, University of Thessaly, Karditsa, Greece
Skarvelis@uth.gr

Abstract. The purpose of this study is to explore the characteristics of the choices of the elderly, regarding the features of furniture that people use in their daily lives. The study is limited to the age group 55–90 years old in Greece and presents chairs in their homes, which they have been used from 5 to 50 years. An early research question to be answered in this study is How the individuals behave consumeristically based on their experiences. The results at an early stage show that their choices are based on traditional-classic furniture with specific characteristics, concerning parameters such as aesthetics and functionality. Also, secondary elements in the design such as construction details (crosspieces, dimensions, spindles) play a pivotal role in their choices. Particularly important is the fact that a large percentage of the participants responded positively to the technological development of this furniture.

Keywords: Aesthetics in furniture · Chairs for elderly · Furniture for seniors in Greece

1 Introduction

The demographic group of the elderly is growing every year. In Greece (Statistics 2021), at the ages 55–85 + per gender, about 30% were men and 43.5% women in the total population. The elderly present various living problems with chronic diseases such as: dementia, visual and hearing impairment, disabilities, memory disorders, etc. (Hrovatin et al. 2012).

Until recently, the majority of products designed and produced concern other age groups, with the emphasis placed on the most productive of them and they have to cover the needs of the average user, ergonomically speaking. The elderly are a heterogenous age group (Jonsson and Sperling 2010), which according to various studies is accustomed to using products designed for healthier and younger people. In addition, in a study conducted in Slovenia, 60% of the elderly have not renovated their house for more than 20 years, while 74% seem satisfied with the existing situation, although they are not covered ergonomically (Hrovatin et al. 2012).

The literature review demonstrates that there is a big increase in studies for this age group, which focuses mainly on the following areas:

© ICST Institute for Computer Sciences, Social Informatics and Telecommunications Engineering 2021
Published by Springer Nature Switzerland AG 2021. All Rights Reserved
I. M. Pires et al. (Eds.): GOODTECHS 2021, LNICST 401, pp. 300–310, 2021.
https://doi.org/10.1007/978-3-030-91421-9_23

a) health,
b) safety,
c) creativity and technological development,
d) emotional care.

The registration of furniture, equipment and measurement systems shows a constant interest in this direction. The proposal for the development of a methodology and construction of furniture for the specific age group based on particular specifications and taking into account quantitative and qualitative parameters, is a necessity for the Greek society, as nothing similar has been developed up to now.

2 Literature Review

The main purpose of designing and manufacturing products, since the end of the 19th century (i.e. since the beginning of the industrial revolution) until today has been the mass production of objects or furniture that improve people's daily lives who constantly use them. Industrial design has contributed significantly to this. Recently, however, concepts such as Participatory Design (often called co-design) are beginning to emerge as a result of differentiation and specialization in furniture production. According to many authors (Aarhus et al. 2010; Gronvall and Kyng 2013), older people exhibit differentiated behaviors and large disparities in the access to new technologies. The above also emphasize the importance of creating an environment in relation to "participatory" design and the impact exerted through areas such as: space organization, participation and assimilation of activities, especially when applied to particularly vulnerable groups.

In the developed countries there is a demographic shift with a significant increase of the elderly. This age group also seems to suffer from chronic diseases (Population Reference Bureau 2011).

By 2060, Europe and Japan are expected to have a population of 151 million over the age of 65. This is due to the increase in life expectancy, for a better quality of life. This age group wants to spend most of their time at home, developing activities that improve health and enhance activity (State of the Art Report for Smart Habitat for Older Persons, April 2019).

The population of the European Union on January 1, 2018 was estimated at 512.4 million. Of these, 64.7% were in the age group of 15 to 67 years old, while the elderly over 65 years old were 19.7%, with an increase of 2.9% compared to the earlier decade (State of the Art Report for Smart Habitat for Older Persons, April 2019).

By 2019, the old-age dependency ratio had been 34.1%. Population projections suggest that the EU-27 old-age dependency ratio will continue to soar and will reach 56.7% by 2050, when there will be fewer than two persons of working age for each older person. In 2019, older people accounted for more than one third (36.7%) of the total population in the central Greek region of Eyrytania (Eurostat, July 2020). For these reasons, greater security is needed in homes and the creation of a more "friendly" living environment. The same is also valid for the items and furniture that make up a home. The main causes of accidents in this age group are added to this need: 31% of falls in the elderly are due to accidents in the surroundings and 17% of accidents are due to disturbances and loss of balance (State of the Art Report for Smart Habitat for Older Persons, April 2019).

As Europe's population is growing older, more patents have been filed over the last decade for "smart" and safe furniture (Wordwide.Espacenet, March 2020). A range of protection devices or health measurements are being developed, in order to meet the care needs of the elderly.

From 2009 to 2017, the number of published articles on elderly care multiplied and there is a clear growing trend for scientific research in this area (State of the Art Report for Smart Habitat for Older Persons, April 2019). Various studies refer to the lack of familiarity that older people feel with the use of computers and smart devices, in order to optimize their quality of life. There is a general finding that they are accustomed to using their existing furniture and have a reduced desire for change (Hrovatin et al. 2012).

Bumgardner and Bowe (2002) point out that wood species play a key role in furniture development and are taken into account in the preferences of designers, across the product development spectrum along with other critical choices, such as style and finish. For example, in the USA cedar wood gives the house a feeling of warmth. Pine and cedar wood used in furniture appear from previous studies to receive higher marks in aesthetics and status as opposed to plywood, fiberboard, aluminum and vinyl. Also, in relation to the better quality of furniture, light-colored wood (coniferous) seems to be considered more suitable for more everyday furniture, while darker wood (e.g. mahogany and cherry) seems more suitable for better quality furniture. Respectively, the furniture made of dark colors are considered more expensive and with a higher value. According to Nicholls and Bumgardner (2007), there is a correlation between the types of wood preferred by older and younger people, in relation to income. Younger people seem to choose lighter wood such as spruce wood and maple, while older people with lower incomes opt for oak wood. Also, beech and oak seem to be preferred more by low-income older men. Also, women with higher incomes seem to avoid wood types such as red alder, considering them to be options that give lower status. At higher incomes there is a tendency to prefer cherry wood.

In general, there is a strong scientific, technological and constructional approach and interest, mainly in relation to the specific age group, due to the demographics that are observed, but also in terms of gaining a competitive advantage from companies that will specialize in this field.

Also, various studies regarding the ergonomics of furniture (Simek 2013; Fabisiak and Klos 2012) show that the improvement and redesign of "conventional" furniture, add value to the safety and functional living of the elderly. From the above research, solutions are presented to improve the ergonomics of the furniture, to have a better quality of the upholstery (in order to have a better cleaning of the material) and to improve the access with emphasis on the safety of use.

However, it seems (as in Greece) that more information and awareness are needed in order to adopt their necessity. Also, for furniture companies, innovation and ecology in furniture is an essential competitive outlet (Papadopoulos et al. 2015).

Also, Halilovic (2017) emphasizes that consumers are interested in environmental protection and the first things they consider are comfort, material and quality of furniture.

On a second level they are interested in design and functionality, while the issue of cost is the crucial final factor for the choice.

In the above study there appears to be 9 factors that influence consumer behavior in relation to furniture, which are: gender, age, income, nationality, knowledge of materials, lifestyle, cost, behavior and needs. In relation to the construction material, in the research of Fabisiak et al. (2014), individuals are asked to compare older furniture with more modern ones and it is observed that it is desirable to have more solid wood elements. Also, the material of the upholster should be easily cleaned and should not be dominated by bright colors, but pastel shades.

Additional parameters, such as the habit of use, the emotional bond with the furniture and the nostalgia (Goulding 2002) are factors of great heterogeneity that require further approach and are an extension of the study presented here. Bumgardner and Bowe (2002) note also that furniture in a home creates associations with emotions, since it contains psychosocial meanings that must be taken into account in the construction and design of the entire product process (distribution, price, brand, etc.).

The emotional demands that furniture could provide for seniors include the emergence of intimacy, satisfaction, inspiration, dignity, reinforcement and connection to the past. The same study shows that in relation to the hierarchy of importance and time of use of the rooms of a house, the kitchen and the living room play an essential role in the time that the elderly spend with next being the bedroom (Jonsson and Sperling 2010). In addition, in the research of Fabisiak et al. (2014), it is observed that the emotions for some furniture played an essential role in the evaluation that people made of it.

A recent survey to investigate the needs of the elderly (Kamperidou 2017) conducted in Northern Greece (Thessaloniki) shows various characteristics and a necessity for furniture design at this age. Dimensions seem to play a decisive role, as it appears that there is a disproportion between the body type of the users and the furniture. In relation to the seats, taller people want deeper seats and vice versa. Hygiene and durability of materials also play a key role, especially in areas of the house such as the kitchen. Furniture should be stable, prevent injuries and be easily accessible to use. Another essential finding from this study is the fact that the 60–69 age group tends to spend more money on furniture. Finally, the lack of communication between manufacturers and this age group is pronounced.

3   Research Methodology

The research is based on the observation with an unstructured interview using photos of furniture from the homes of the respondents. A percentage of the interviews were conducted remotely, via telephone (17) and some live (8). Individuals were asked to choose a piece of furniture that they use daily (in this particular research a dining chair) and to explain the reasons why they made this choice. The sample in the first phase of the research consists of 25 people aged 56 to 87 years, with heterogeneity in educational level and income.

The tools of observation are the image of the furniture and the interview.

The main axes of the interview approach are:

- Construction material
- Construction color
- Furniture design
- Functionality-ergonomics
- Other reasons for which they are related to the specific furniture (e.g. best value for money, weight, harmony in relation to the space, etc.)
- Interest in technological or constructive development in furniture.

4   Discussion – Results

4.1   Individuals Profile

The survey was limited to Athens with a study of two more cases in the cities of Thessaloniki and Karditsa and 1 case in the area of Magnesia (Fig. 1).

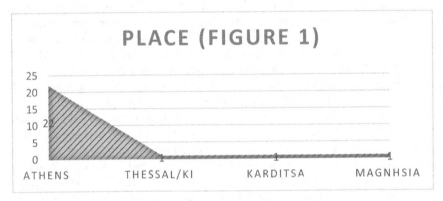

Fig. 1. The permanent residence of the individuals.

The participants in this survey consisted of 11 women and 14 men. It is worth mentioning, that in 6 cases the interviews were realized in pairs. In relation to the age groups (Fig. 2), 6 people were between 55–60 years old, 12 people between 61–70 years old, 6 people between 71–80 years old and 1 person in the age group 81–90 years old.

Based on the educational level, we have a heterogeneity with the majority of people (8) being high school graduates, 6 people primary school graduates and 10 people with higher education (Fig. 3).

As far as family income is concerned (Fig. 4), most of the people (14) are in the scale <20000€ per year and 8 people in the scale <30000€ per year.

4.2   Construction Material

The majority of the respondents (84%) prefer furniture with wooden frame. The wooden chairs chosen and presented in Chart 1 are mainly made of beech wood. The material of the seat is also interesting, as it consists of either upholstery (with modern foam

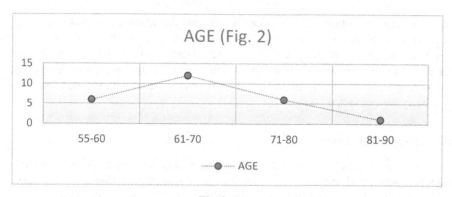

Fig. 2. Age

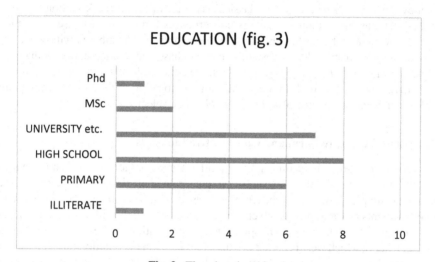

Fig. 3. The educational level.

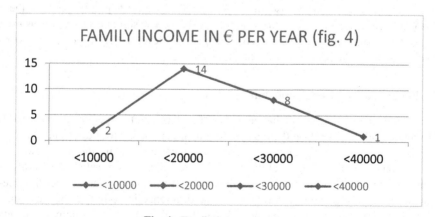

Fig. 4. Family income per year.

materials) at a percentage of 56%, or cane (36%) and the addition of a cushion, usually made by them in a big number of cases. Furthermore, it is noteworthy that in a potential new purchase (in a percentage of 80%), wood would still be chosen as construction material. Emphasis is placed on the construction material (robustness is needed) but also in some cases lighter materials. In half of the cases, chairs with wooden frame and upholstery were selected.

4.3   Construction Color

The shades of wood play an essential role in the choice made by the people, with the shades of beech with the colorless varnish finish dominating, followed by the darker shades of paints (walnut and cherry), at 70% of the cases. The rest of the options consist of beige and in one case a combination of black-white and dark brown-beige. From the above, we can deduce that the classical style prevails and the selection of more modern seats, as far as their material is concerned, is limited to two cases, in which black and white are chosen (combined with metal) and ecru (combined with wood). It is particularly interesting that in case of a new purchase and in conjunction with color, people would choose the same furniture as the one they selected and similar furniture with a darker shade of wood. In a case of a total renovation of the house, white paint would be chosen. In one case also, brighter colors are selected.

4.4   Design, Furniture Form and Constructive Elements

By means of design, simple lines prevail, without many edge profiling and carvings (although in many cases there existed more elaborate chair designs in the house, the chairs with simpler forms were chosen by the respondents). In some cases, chairs with curved elements are presented (with cross sections made in lathe either steam bent). An important element is that some chairs presented differentiations in the crossrails between legs (stretchers), which were reported as a deterrent factor in the functionality of the chair by individuals. It is also noteworthy that the chairs are used by people with an average about 22 years, with minimal structural connection problems, which are observed mainly in the detachment of tenon-mortise joints. Furthermore, it is worth pointing out that there is also damage to the material of the seats and the back. The solid beech wood was used more in the construction of the chairs and on a second level the plywood or fiberboard in the elements of the back and the seat. Also, the metal in 2 cases.

4.5   Functionality – Ergonomic Parameters

It turns out from the interviews that people are familiar with the specific characteristics of furniture and they mention them as predominant parameters in order to justify their preference. It is noteworthy that the chairs were measured during the interviews and no deviations in constructive level were found. Most people seem satisfied in terms of ergonomics in relation to their choice, and only in pair interviews there were disagreements in terms of ergonomics in relation to the difference in body type between men and women. Another important element is that the lack of some constructive elements from the furniture creates problems in their use (stretchers, rails etc.).

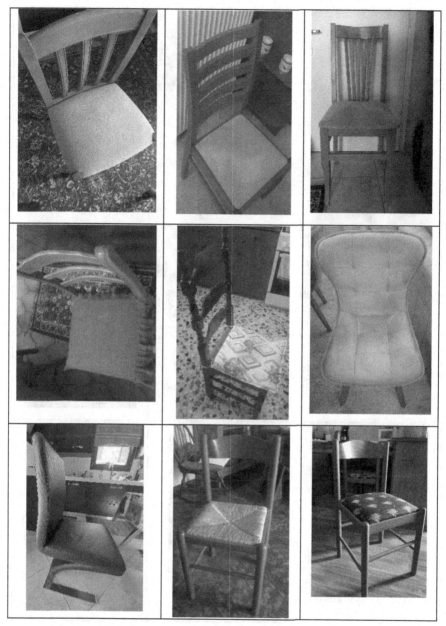

Chart 1. The furniture chosen by the participants in the sample is presented and an analysis of their preferences is following.

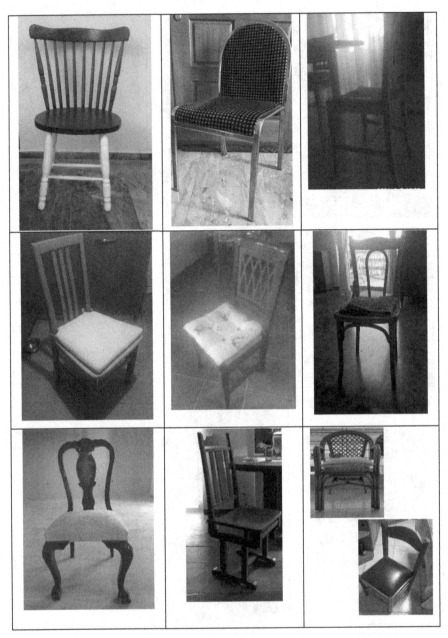

Chart 1. continued

5   Conclusions

The results illuminate that the Greeks by and large choose furniture with a good construction quality and which are expected to last for several years (in some cases the names of the manufacturers by whom they have bought them are mentioned). Furthermore, there is a tendency for minimal changes in case of buying new furniture, which suggests a sense of habit in their choices.

There is a tendency for traditional furniture, which is not designed for this age group. However, since they were informed, they deem the technological development of furniture positively, but without pronounced difference in aesthetics and style (in most cases the traditional one). We can observe a preference in wood as a material and the chairs must be perfectly constructed without lacking elements. From a color perspective, there is a tendency for a colorless finish and dark brown color. In some cases there is a disagreement in ergonomics, primarily in interviews between couples.

Finally, we should not underestimate the fact that the survey should include more geographical and social data in the future, in order to be a "tool" of social policy and business action.

References

Aarhus, R., Gronvall, E., Kyng, M.: Challenges in participation: users and their roles in the development of home-based pervasive healthcare applications. In: Gerhauser, H., Siek, K., Hornegger, J., Lueth, C. (eds.) Pervasive Health 2010, Munich, Germany. IEEE (2010). https://doi.org/10.4108/ICST.PERVASIVEHEALTH2010.8794

Eurostat. https://ec.europa.eu/eurostat/statistics-explained/index.php?title=Ageing_Europe_-_statistics_on_population_developments. Accessed 13 May 2021

Nicholls, D., Bumgardner, M.: Evaluating selected demographic factors related to consumer preferences for furniture from commercial and from underutilized species. Forest Prod. J. **57**(12), 79–82 (2007)

Halilovic, M.: Consumer behavior: a case study on consumer behavior in furniture stores in Shanghai. Linnaeus University, School of Business and Economics, Department of Organization and Entrepreneurship, p. 13 (2017)

Bumgardner, M., Bowe, S.: Species selection in secondary wood products: Implications for product design and promotion. Woodand Fiber Sci. **34**(3), 408–418 (2002)

Jonsson, O., Sperling, L.: Wishes for furniture design among persons in the third age-interviews with users in their homes. In: Judith, G., Sato, K., Desmet, P. (eds.) D&E 2010, Chicago, vol. 7. IIT Institute of Design (2010)

Kamperidou, V.: Critical points in the of aged people furniture. Pro Ligno **13**(4), 466–470 (2017)

Fabisiak, B., Klos, R.: Comparative analysis of difficulty of activities performed in kitchen by people aged 40–60 and over 60 years with visual impairment in the context of furniture design. Ann. Warsaw Univ. Life Sci. SGGW For. Wood Technol. **1**(77), 216–221 (2012)

Fabisiak, B., Klos, R., Wianderek, K., Sydor, M.: Attitudes of elderly users towards design and functionality of furniture produced in Poland in the second half of the XXth century and nowadays. Ann. Warsaw Univ. Life Sci. SGGW For. Wood Technol. **86**, 98–103 (2014)

Greek Statistics. https://www.statistics.gr/documents/20181/1515741/GreeceInFigures_2021Q1_GR.pdf/e891b0b8-82a3-30be-8f9e-1de20a6db469. Accessed 13 May 2021

Gronvall, E., Kyng, M.: On participatory design of home-based healthcare. Cogn. Technol. Work **15**(4), 389–401 (2013)

Goulding, C.: An exploratory study of age related vicarious nostalgia and aesthetic consumption. In: Broniarczyk, S., Nakamoto, K. (eds.) NA - Advances in Consumer Reaserch 2002, Valdosta, GA, vol. 29, pp. 542–546. Association for Consumer Research (2002)

Hrovatin, J., Širok, K., Jevšnik, S., Oblak, L., Berginc, J.: Adaptability of kitchen furniture for elderly people in terms of safety. Drvna Industrija **63**(2), 113–120 (2012)

Papadopoulos, I., Trigkas, M., Karagouni, G., Dedoulis, E., Papadopoulou, A., Blanas, G.: Techno-economic analysis of furniture innovation: developing a green and smart furniture for mass production. In: Andreopoulou, Z., Bochtis, D. (eds.) HAICTA 2015, Kavala, Greece, vol. 1498, pp. 393–400 (2015)

Simek, M.: Analysis of sitting furniture for elderly people. Faculty of Forestry and Wood Technology, Department of Furniture, Design and Habitation, Mendel University in Brno (2013)

PRB.   https://www.prb.org/wp-content/uploads/2011/07/2011population-data-sheet_eng.pdf. Accessed 14 May 2021

State of the Art Report for Smart Habitat for Older Persons, p. 77, 153–155, 181, 184, 185, 200, April 2019

Worldwide Espacenet. https://worldwide.espacenet.com/patent/search?q=furniture%20for%20elderly. Accessed 13 May 2021

Author Index

Printed in the United States
by Baker & Taylor Publisher Services